CHURCH HYMNARY

FOURTH EDITION

CHURCH HYMNARY

FOURTH EDITION

MELODY

CANTERBURY
PRESS

Church Hymnary – Fourth Edition is published on behalf of
The Church Hymnary Trust
by Canterbury Press Norwich.

Canterbury Press Norwich, St Mary's Works,
St Mary's Plain, Norwich NR3 3BH,
a division of SCM-Canterbury Press Ltd, a subsidiary of
Hymns Ancient & Modern Ltd, a registered charity

Church Hymnary – Fourth Edition Melody Edition
First published July 2005
Second impression October 2005

A catalogue record of this book is available from the British Library.

ISBN 1-85311-614-9

Music engraving and typesetting:
Andrew Parker, Ferndown, Dorset BH22 8BB United Kingdom
Printed in Great Britain by William Clowes Ltd, Beccles, Suffolk

CONTENTS

THE HOLY SPIRIT

INTRODUCTION

A Changed Context

When the predecessor to this book was published in 1973, the world was a very different place. The internet had yet to be developed and the Cold War had yet to be terminated. Women were still to be paid the same as men for doing the same job, and a minimum wage had yet to be agreed. No one had benefited from laser eye surgery or been brought back to life by an automatic defibrillator. Nor were there wind farms, personal computers, debit cards, junk food, speed bumps or job centres. No one and no thing was 'past its sell-by date' or the subject of scrutiny by a 'focus group'. Language and the society which articulates it have changed.

And in these three intervening decades the Church has not stood still. New translations of the scriptures, the ordination of women, increased frequency of Communion, deepening interest in the Christian Year and the Lectionary, the greater use of non-ordained leaders in worship — these and a host of other changes have increasingly featured in and enriched the corporate life of congregations.

It has not only to be expected, therefore, but it is essential, that any new hymnary should take into account the realities of faith and life today as its forerunners did in their day. This is not to suggest that all that is old has lost its value and all that is new is automatically virtuous. It is simply to attest that a book intended to be used for the worship of God in the twenty-first century should reflect the contemporary experience of humanity and the contemporary fruits of God's creative spirit, with the added engaging thought that such a book might continue to be relevant in the day and generation of the grandchildren of the compilers.

Developments in Hymnody

The first task of the committee which selected and prepared the contents of this hymnary was to produce a list of items in *The Church Hymnary,* Third Edition *(CH3)* for exclusion from the new book. This was done in consultation with the churches. The final list, which comprised almost a third of *CH3,* was approved by the General Assemblies.

The next task was to review developments in hymnody since 1973, and there was much to discover. A whole range of new genres had emerged, growing in popularity in different parts of the Church. Where repeated meditative songs were favoured by some, lively syncopated praise songs were preferred by others. Some congregations discovered their corporate identity in the Body of Christ by singing songs from non-European cultures, while others used material which expressed personal devotion or intercession for the world in contemporary language.

It was clear to the committee that this seeming new range of musical and literary styles was but an extension of the variety which already exists in any hymnary. 'Traditional' hymns are not homogeneous. Some are fast-flowing verse and chorus songs of celebration, others are profound theological musings on the purposes of God; some are personal testimonies, others communal laments; some are set to post-reformation Genevan Psalm tunes, others to folk melodies; some are rooted in the ethos and culture of the community which produced the book, some reflect international and ecumenical associations and Christian traditions from across the world; some come down from the early days of Christendom, some are contemporary.

Ordering the Material

During the rigorous and necessarily lengthy process of selection, consideration was given to the ordering of the contents of the book. Many models of ordering were considered, but the committee in the end opted to arrange the material according to aspects of faith and life which closely corresponded to the three persons of the Trinity. Of course, this scheme has its imperfections. Many items could easily fit in two or three categories. For that reason, an extensive Biblical Index and Topical Index are provided.

The Psalms precede the main three sections of the book, and a selection of shorter songs for meditative singing ends the hymnary. These songs, which in themselves are wide in variety, have also a multitude of uses — as congregational preludes to worship, as meditations during worship, as aids to devotion during Holy Communion, and as occasional choral pieces.

The Psalms

The committee, with the support of the General Assemblies, wished to encourage a wider use of the Psalms. *CH3* had interspersed the Psalms throughout the hymnary: the committee decide to revert to the earlier practice of its precursors, namely, that of providing psalms in an identifiable section at the beginning of the book. While acknowledging that at no time in the Church's history has every Psalm been equally frequently or fondly sung, it was felt desirable to represent as wide an experience of the psalter as possible, and to offer a selection of psalms which covered the full gamut of emotional expression or subject matter found in the psalter. At the same time, while the primacy of metrical psalmody in our tradition as represented by the *Scottish Psalter* of 1650 was recognised, the opportunity was taken to allow for new translations or paraphrases to articulate these ancient texts which Jesus knew by heart in the original Hebrew.

Language Issues

As noted above, language has changed in the last thirty years, and it was inevitable that issues of exclusivity and archaism had to be dealt with, as much with twentieth-century texts as with older hymns. The committee decided against adopting a blanket policy, preferring to decide on each text according to its merits.

Broadly speaking, where a text could be sensitively amended by the contemporizing of archaic language or by having an exclusive term replaced by an inclusive one, that was done. But where that was not possible, either the whole text was reworked or it was left intact.

Using the Hymnary

The aim should be to make as wide and as varied a use of the book as possible. If hymns are a record of humanity's experience of God and of God's revelation to humanity, it is important that the choice of Psalms and hymns for worship should not simply be a reflection of the minister's or the congregation's favourites. There is, of course, a place for these, clothed as they are with associations — of childhood, of important moments in personal faith, of significant events in the life of a congregation. The new material, which does not come with the inbuilt comfort of familiarity, cannot have this immediacy; but that should be seen more as a reason for welcoming it rather than for discounting it.

Singing the Hymns

The book offers opportunities to a wide range of musicians for, unlike its predecessors, it does not presume that every item will invariably be accompanied by an organ. In its provision of the music for the book, the committee sought to encourage a strong sense of musical integrity, which should ensure variety in the singing of the psalms and hymns.

If a melody, such as a traditional psalm tune, stands well on its own, let it be sung unaccompanied. If a tune comes from a folk tradition, with the harmony changing once in the bar, let it be played by traditional folk instruments — guitar, fiddle, or flute. If a tune has a strong rhythmic impulse, let it be played on the piano; if it comes from an African culture, it might best be accompanied on a drum. If the melody is a 'traditional' hymn tune which presumes a sustained or colourful keyboard accompaniment, let the organ be used to its best effect.

The committee recognises that the range of musicians required for the kind of variety of accompaniment indicated above may not be available in most churches. But whereas, in the first half of the twentieth century, the Church and its choirs benefited from people's ability to sing from sol-fa notation, it would be selling our teenagers and young adults short if we did not engage their instrumental skills as enthusiastically as our forebears would have used their vocal abilities. It is salutary, in this regard, to recount how Herrick Bunney, late Master of Music at St Giles' Cathedral, Edinburgh, responded to a particularly bad experience of music in a country church which had a 'reluctant' organist. For him the major upset was not the inadequate if earnest accompaniment, but the fact that in the congregation was an enthusiastic teenage violinist who could have led the singing far more effectively, but no one had thought to ask her.

In Conclusion

This book has been long in the making. The patience, exasperation, goodwill, and determination of many people accompanied it from its inception to its publication. None of the committee had worked on such a project before: all experienced a 'steep learning curve' (a phrase not yet known in 1973), and each made distinctive and valuable contributions to the work. But it would be inexcusable not to mention the importance to the committee's work of The Reverend Charles Robertson, the secretary, whose industriousness, gregariousness, and prodigious knowledge of the Church, its scriptures and liturgy, have been of incomparable value. Particular appreciation is also recorded to Fay Binnie, his secretary, whose skills, helpfulness, and attention to detail were always at the disposal of the committee.

This book is not the gift of the compilers to the Church. It is the gift of the Church to itself, through the guidance and grace of the Holy Spirit. Christians wrote these songs. Christians composed and arranged these tunes. And Christians will sing them. Without the tune, the text is unarticulated: without the singer, both remain silent.

John L. Bell
Convenor

USING THE BOOK

1 Printing of Full Text

As often as possible, the full text of an item is printed in poem-form, from the first verse to the last, even when the music is also underlaid with the text. In a very few cases this has not been possible.

The practice of printing out the full text allows the cohesive integrity of the verses to be seen, an integrity which may sometimes be lost if the text is set out as syllables above or beneath the musical notation. This is helpful for those who use the hymn book as a prayer book, a treasury of resources for meditation, and a means of private devotion.

There is the additional advantage that where, on occasion, it may be appropriate in public worship to read rather than sing the text, the present layout facilitates that practice.

2 Text Underlay

Some of the items are underlaid. Underlay is the name given to the printing of the syllables of the text directly below or above the musical notes to which they are to be sung.

Where a tune is completely or relatively unknown, or where it would be helpful to see how harmony parts and words relate, the music has been underlaid with the text. Where the tune is new, but short and straightforward, the metrical commas *(see below)* should be sufficient to aid sight-singing.

3 Page Turns

As long as hymn tunes were sixteen-bar melodies with simple arrangements, each tune could be printed on one page, with the text immediately below or facing. But for at least a century, it has been necessary for such tunes such as *Jerusalem* and *Praise, My Soul* to print the music on more than two pages, and they therefore require a page turn. Responsorial psalms and worship songs with extended verse and chorus structures need more than two pages, with consequent page turns. These items, however, are relatively few in *CH4*.

A problem occurs when there is a sizeable tune and a lengthy text. In order to maintain the print size, the text sometimes has to run into two pages. Where that has happened, the tune has usually been printed twice to ensure that full music is visible for every verse.

4 Harmony and Unison

Most items in *CH4* are in four-part harmony, a few are in three parts. Harmony is normally signified by a square brace at the beginning of the stave. Where items are in unison, this is indicated either by an accolade at the beginning of the stave, for those items with piano-style accompaniment, or by the word *Unison* appearing in italics.

Unison is not second best to harmony. It is often the more appropriate way for a tune to be sung, especially if the accompaniment is syncopated or harmonically complex.

5 Cantors

From before the days of the psalms, it has been common for religious songs to be shared between a soloist and the congregation. In recent years, the popularity of this practice has increased.

Where a cantor (or soloist) is designated, as in some responsorial psalms, the normal practice is for the cantor to sing the chorus or antiphon once. The congregation immediately follows, singing the same chorus or antiphon. The cantor then sings the first verse, and the congregation follows the verse, and each of the succeeding verses, with the refrain.

In some Taizé chants, the cantor is expected to sing verses over the congregation, who either hum or sing the antiphon quietly.

6 Metrical Commas

These appear not in the text, but above the top stave of the music. They are not breathing indications, but signify the end of a line of text. They are meant to aid the eye as it moves between music and verse.

7 Tempo and Dynamic Markings

Different buildings have different acoustic properties, and different instruments played with or without amplification will vary in the way they resonate in the surrounding space.

It is therefore impossible to be strict about tempo. A tune sung *allegro* with a piano accompaniment in a dry acoustic might be an impossibility in a reverberant stone building with a pipe organ. The tempo markings are therefore few and, in general, relate to recently published items.

However, the speed of a hymn is important. It should reflect the vitality, calmness, excitement, resignation or other dynamic in the text. But at the same time, it should not be so fast that it makes meaningful singing an impossibility, or so slow that it results in tedium.

As regards the dynamics, the occasion and the text should suggest which verses should be sung loudly or softly, slower or faster. Hymns such as 'Be still, my soul' and 'Be still for the presence of the Lord' may, on one occasion, be subdued in their rendition; but on another occasion, if the note of assurance needs to be emphasised, the singing might be more robust. The sensitivity of the musician must determine the appropriateness of the dynamics.

As a rule of thumb, accompanying musicians who sing the text as they play the music are more likely to play at an appropriate speed and volume. If the accompanying musician does not sing, he or she should have no reservation in asking whether the music is too fast or slow, too quiet or loud.

8   Accompanying Instruments

With the exception of texts intended for reading and a few unaccompanied songs, music in *CH4* is arranged for keyboard accompaniment — organ, piano, and electronic keyboards. This, of course, does not preclude the possibility of songs being accompanied by other instruments, or being sung unaccompanied.

Guitar chords are provided for some items. In most cases, these chords match the keyboard harmony; but, where the chords do not exactly match the harmony, an encircled cross saltire ⊗ appears at the side of the music. In such cases, there are two options: *(i)* the keyboard and guitar may accompany different verses; or *(ii)* the keyboard player may simplify the accompaniment by playing only those notes which are consonant with the guitar chords.

9   Psalms

The psalm section at the beginning of the book reflects a variety of ways of singing the psalms and using the psalter. The traditional use of metrical versions (in original and revised texts from the *Scottish Psalter*, 1650, along with modern versions) is complemented by prose psalms, responsorial psalms, antiphonal psalms, and psalms for congregational reading.

The numbering of the psalms begins the numbering of the items in the book, and the numbering continues consecutively when the psalm section ends. But each psalm also bears its own particular number. This means that the psalm chosen for worship may be announced as 'Psalm *aa* (number of psalm) at number *bb*'.

The singing of the metrical psalms, whether old or new, is straight-forward. Occasionally, as at no. 41 *(Psalm 61)*, an older harmonic version has been re-introduced, where the tune ('the people's part') is in the tenor. This 'Tune 2' is an alternative to 'Tune 1': the two arrangements are not meant to be sung at the same time.

The chants for the prose psalms have been made as accessible as possible, with the rhythm of clear natural speech being the main guide, and the melodic note changing on the syllable or word bearing the appropriate mark. In a plainsong chant (for example, *Psalm 22* at no. 12), the first two notes in brackets are sung for the first verse only.

Where no direction is given for the reading of a psalm, the psalm may be read antiphonally (verse or section about, by different individuals or sectors of the congregation).

Occasionally, there is interaction between music and the spoken text. In *Psalm 77,* at no. 49, for example, a sung antiphon responds to the spoken verse; and in *Psalm 27,* at no. 23, the words of the verse are spoken over played music, and the congregation responds in a sung antiphon.

Appropriate doxologies for the conclusion of metrical psalms in metre are provided at the end of the psalm section; doxologies for prose psalms are included with the text.

10 Paraphrases

Items from the 1781 collection of *The Scottish Paraphrases* appear in appropriate places throughout the book. They are identified in the Index of First Lines.

11 Children's Hymns

There is no separate section for items suitable for children. There is a separate First Line index of items suitable for children and young people.

12 Short Songs

A number of these appear throughout the book and several comprise the penultimate section.

A short song is not a substitute for a hymn of four or five stanzas. Rather, its purpose may be to prepare the congregation for wor-ship, to offer a congregational response to the reading of scripture or to a prayer, to meditate on words of spiritual depth, or to enable movement (as in a recessional).

In circumstances where the song needs to be sung repeatedly, the musicians should feel for how long it is appropriate for the song to continue, rather than decide in advance that it will be sung a particular number of times.

13 Longer Songs and Hymns

While there is no requirement that every verse of a longish item be sung, sometimes omitting verses can upset the flow of thought of the hymn. Rather than leaving out verses, a helpful alternative may be to invite different sectors of the congregation to sing different verses. For example, the worship leader may invite *All* to sing verses 1, 3, and 5; *Women,* verse 2; and *Men,* verse 4. Or, if the item has a clear chorus or refrain, different sectors of the congregation or soloists may sing the verses, with everyone joining in the refrain.

14 Global Church Songs

Until the 1980s, most Europeans were aware only of hymns and psalm settings which had originated in the northern hemisphere, which were generally cast in the form of strophic verse set to tunes in four-part harmony.

More recently, the marvellous textures of song from the southern hemisphere, particularly from Southern Africa and Latin America, have begun to enliven our worship. With the increasing presence among us of people from these and other countries and cultures, it is likely that we will hear more of styles of congregational song from churches round the world.

When using other people's music, it is important to respect the culture from which it comes. Most musicians would prefer to accompany an intricately harmonised Bach chorale on the organ. In the same way, a song which is meant for unaccompanied singing, or is so rhythmic that percussive sounds would best enable an effective rendition, should not be 'domesticated' by using inappropriate instrumental accompaniment.

15 Alternative Tunes

In a number of cases, two tunes are suggested to be sung to a text. This happens where both are equally well known.

Elsewhere, an alternative tune associated with another text may be suggested. Where this happens, the alternative tune should be used as a last, rather than first resort, as, for example, on occasions where it would not be possible to practise a new tune in advance.

16 Metrical Index

The metrical index is used to enable the substitution of appropriate tunes to texts, should this be required. However, as most tunes have been carefully matched to their text, such use should not be seen as an alternative to learning new music.

At its most basic, the metrical index indicates the number of syllables of each line of text. In verse 1 of *Psalm 23,* for example, the first line with its eight syllables is followed by the second line with six syllables, followed by eight, followed by six. This pattern is indicated by the formula 86 86. As this is a very common verse structure, 86 86 is called *Common Metre.* 88 88 (the metre for *Psalm 100*) is known as *Long Metre.* 66 86, the metre of *Psalm 67,* is called *Short Metre.*

All other metres are indicated by their numerals. Thus, 'Glory be to God the Father' has a metre of 87 87 87; while 'Abide with Me' is 12 12 12 10.

Occasionally, a 'D' appears either before or after the numerals. This indicates that the stated metre of the verse is doubled. *The Seven Joys of Mary* (340), for example, is described as 'DCM', meaning *Double Common Metre.* Here 'DCM' is a convenient abbreviation for 86 86 86 86.

The word *Irregular* indicates that the number of syllables in each line varies throughout the verses and, therefore, there is unlikely to be another tune which would fit the text. Where no metre is given, the likelihood is that the text and melody cannot be separated from each other.

In choosing alternative tunes, matching the syllables of the lines of a text is not, by itself, completely failsafe: it is also important to match the rhythm, the pattern of stressed syllables in the text. For example, 'The King of love my Shepherd is' and 'In the cross of Christ I glory' are both 87 87, but the tune of the first, *Dominus Regit Me,* does not fit the text of the second, and the tune of the second, *Stuttgart,* does not fit the text of the first. Similarly, 'For my sake and the Gospel's, go' and 'Lord, in love and perfect wisdom' match in metre (87 87D) but not in rhythm, and therefore their tunes, *Bishopgarth* and *Blaenwern,* are not interchangeable. However, these instances are not unduly common. But, as a safeguard, a substitute tune should always be sung through to the new text prior to any act of worship, to ensure it fits both metre and rhythm.

17 Biblical Index

A fairly extensive index of the biblical references in the hymns is provided. Many of the references amount to direct quotations, while others resonate with biblical passages.

An attempt has been made to supply individual verses of the hymns with their own references, but, occasionally, all the references apply to the whole hymn. Psalms and Paraphrases bear only the single reference of their source. Parallel passages in the Gospels are usually given.

18 Amendments to Text

The changing use of language and the changing meaning of words has led to certain texts being changed, largely to enable the language to be inclusive of male and female, and to avoid obsolete usage. Where that has happened, an asterisk * is put before the name of the text's author or source.

In other cases, where to change the text would be to interfere to the detriment of the poetry of a text, no amendment has been made.

19 Unattributed Items

There are some tunes and texts for which source and authorship has not been traced at the time of publication. Should anyone be able to supply such information, it should be sent to the publishers.

FOREWORD

In May 1994, the General Assembly of the Church of Scotland gave its Panel on Worship the remit to "Proceed with arrangements for the replacement of *The Church Hymnary,* Third Edition *(CH3)*". A Revision Committee of thirty members was appointed, drawn from Churches which were members of the Church Hymnary Trust and from the Trust itself. The Committee, comprised of representatives from the Church of Scotland, the United Free Church of Scotland, the Presbyterian Church in Ireland, and the Presbyterian Church of Wales, first met in November 1994. Both the Presbyterian Church in Ireland and the Presbyterian Church of Wales later withdrew from the joint project to produce their own hymn books, but not before giving valuable and much appreciated help towards the production of this book.

PREFACE

The committee saw its task as combining the best of new hymnody with the cherished and rich tradition that had nourished and sustained previous generations, and so sound forth the eternal gospel in a world constantly changing in customs and culture.

The committee was aware of an outpouring of hymnody in the United Kingdom and around the globe, which, in fresh and appealing ways, encapsulated and expressed the vitality and integrity of the Christian experience of God. The sheer amount of this wealth of material made an exhaustive review of it impossible: nevertheless, a wide range of publications, in books and in manuscripts from all over the world, was perused, and selections made. Annual reports were made to the General Assemblies as the book took shape; presbyteries were consulted both about the scale and shape of the book and about its texts and tunes; and workshops and consultations were held with individual congregations. At each stage of its process, the book was approved by the Church at large; and, when it was complete, it was authorised for use throughout the Church.

A project of this magnitude could not go forward without the help and good will of many people, to all of whom the committee now expresses thanks. In particular, Dr John Kitchen, of Edinburgh University, acted as music consultant, giving generously of his time and experience: this is undoubtedly a better book because of his invaluable contribution. The publisher, Gordon Knights, and his colleague, Andrew Parker, have dedicated themselves to ensuring that the printing and production of the book is of the highest standards. And, above all, the convenor of the committee, John Bell, who also acted as music editor, gave unstintingly of his unrivalled knowledge and expertise, and with his vibrant faith, scholarly gifts, pastoral concern, and warm humanity inspired the committee throughout its work. To him, and to all, the Church owes immense gratitude.

Charles Robertson
Secretary

Members of the Committee

Ian Alexander, *David Beckett, Christopher Bell, *John Bell,
*Walter Blair, *Ian Bradley, Graeme B. Bruce, *Christine Carson,
Iain Cunningham, *Marion E. Dodd, *M. Leith Fisher,
Douglas Galbraith, Iain Galbraith, Kathryn Galloway, Gwen M. Haggart,
Jared W. Hay, *Rita Jackson, T. Gwynn Jones, Finlay Macdonald,
Rory Macleod, *Gilleasbuig I. Macmillan, Glendon Macaulay,
*Moyra McCallum, *Ian McCrorie, Robert McGhee,
Michael M. Marsden, Gordon Munro, John F. Murdoch,
A. K. M. Rankin, *Colin C. Renwick, *Charles Robertson,
*Helen Scott, A. Douglas Scrimgeour, *Margaret Stein, *Robert Tait,
H. Barkley Wallace, James Weatherhead, *Malcolm J. Wood,
Alexander W. Young.

* These members served for the duration of the committee; other members came and
went by rotation; Robert McGhee died before the end of the committee's work.

COPYRIGHT

The Publishers thank the owners or controllers of copyright
for permission to use the hymns and tunes throughout this
collection. An asterisk before a name denotes that the text has
been altered with permission, where the text is in copyright. As is
customary nowadays, acknowledgements are given on-page with
the material.

Every effort have been made to trace copyright owners or
controllers, to seek permission to use text and music, and to make
alterations as necessary. The Publishers apologise to those who
have not been traced at the time of going to press, and whose rights
have inadvertently not been acknowledged. Any omissions or
inaccuracies of permissions or copyright details will be corrected
in future printings.

REPRODUCTION OF COPYRIGHT MATERIAL

For permission to reproduce copyright hymns and music from
this collection, whether in permanent or temporary form, by
whatever means, application must be made to the respective
owners or controllers at the contact addresses shown on-page.

Addresses of the principal Scottish copyright holders, whose
details are abbreviated on-page, are to be found at the back of the
book on page cxv.

PSALMS

1

PSALMS

ST BOTOLPH (Slater)   CM

PSALM 1

1   How blest are those who do not stray,
    led by the wicked's talk;
    who will not with the sinful stand,
    nor sit where scoffers mock.

2   The teaching of the Lord their God
    they follow with delight,
    and meditate upon his word
    with gladness day and night.

3   They flourish like well-watered trees
    set by a riverside,
    whose fruit matures, whose leaves remain —
    they prosper and abide.

4   The wicked, like the straw and chaff
    by wind blown far away,
    can have no place among the just
    nor stand on judgement day.

5   The Lord will guard the righteous well,
    he knows the way they take;
    but doomed to perish is the way
    the wicked undertake.

Psalm 1
Charles Robertson (*b.* 1940)

Music Gordon Archbold Slater (1896–1979)

O RIGHTEOUS GOD

LM

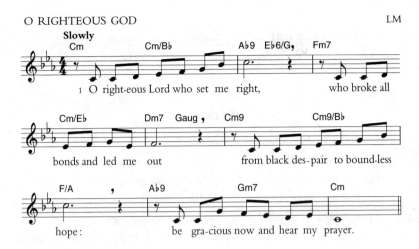

1 O right-eous Lord who set me right, who broke all bonds and led me out from black des-pair to bound-less hope: be gra-cious now and hear my prayer.

PSALM 4

1   O righteous Lord who set me right,
    who broke all bonds and led me out
    from black despair to boundless hope:
    be gracious now and hear my prayer.

2   They turn away from you, my God;
    they look for truth in clever lies,
    no honour give to your great name:
    Lord, hear me when I call to you.

3   Many demand a clear-cut sign:
    'Oh, that God's hand might bring us good!'
    Yet to my heart you bring more joy
    than they derive from all their gain.

4   Lord, teach them how you sought us out,
    and set your sign upon our hearts;
    teach them to rest in silent trust,
    shine on them with your glorious light.

5   O Lord, my Lord, who gave me joy
    surpassing all that wealth can bring:
    in peace I lie, in peace I sleep,
    safe in your care, safe in your care.

from Psalm 4
Margaret D. Wilson

Music Christopher Norton (*b.* 1953)

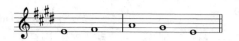

PSALM 5

1   Give ear to my words, O [|] Lord; ‖
consider my [|] medi[|]tation.

2   Hearken to my cry for help, my Sovereign and my [|] God; ‖
for I make my [|] prayer to [|] you.

3   In the morning, Lord, you hear my [|] voice; ‖
early in the morning I make my ap[|]peal and [|] watch for you.

4   For you are not a God who takes pleasure in [|] wickedness, ‖
and evil [|] cannot [|] dwell with you.

5   Braggarts cannot stand in your [|] sight; ‖
you hate all [|] those who work [|] wickedness.

6   You destroy those who speak [|] lies; ‖
the bloodthirsty and deceitful, O [|] Lord, you ab[|]hor.

7   But as for me, through the greatness of your mercy, ⌣
   I will go into your [|] house; ‖
I will bow down toward your holy [|] temple in [|] awe of you.

8   Lead me, O Lord, in your righteousness, ⌣
because of those who lie in [|] wait for me; ‖
make your way [|] straight be[|]fore me.

(Glory to the Father, and to the [|] Son, ‖
and to the [|] Holy [|] Spirit:

as it was in the beginning, is [|] now, ‖
and will be for [|] ever. A[|]men.)

Psalm 5
Book of Common Worship

Music John Martin Harper (*b.* 1947)

3 Music: © Royal School of Church Music, Cleveland Lodge, Westhumble, Dorking, Surrey. RH5 6BW

41

WINCHESTER OLD   CM

42

WINCHESTER OLD   CM

PSALM 8

1   How excellent in all the earth,
    Lord, our Lord, is thy name!
    who hast thy glory far advanced
    above the starry frame.

2   When I look up unto the heavens,
    which thine own fingers framed,
    unto the moon, and to the stars,
    which were by thee ordained;

3   Then say I, What is man, that he
    remembered is by thee?
    Or what the son of man, that thou
    so kind to him should'st be?

4   For thou a little lower hast
    him than the angels made;
    with glory and with dignity
    thou crownèd hast his head.

                    Psalm 8, verses 1, 3-5
                    The Scottish Psalter, 1929

Music Tune 1 Melody from Este's *Psalter* 1592

Music Tune 2 Melody from Este's *Psalter* 1592, as arranged in
Scottish Psalter, 1635, *edited* Gordon J. Munro (b. 1972)

TRAMPS AND HAWKERS   DCM and Coda

Music Scottish folk melody
arranged John L. Bell (*b.* 1949)

PSALM 8

1   O Lord, our Lord, throughout the earth
how glorious is your name,
and glorious too where unseen heavens
your majesty proclaim.
On infant lips, in children's song
a strong defence you raise
to counter enemy and threat,
and foil the rebel's ways.

2   When I look up and see the stars
which your own fingers made,
and wonder at the moon and stars,
each perfectly displayed;
then I must ask, 'Why do you care?
Why love humanity?
And why keep every mortal name
fixed in your memory?'

3   Yet such as us you made and meant
just less than gods to be;
with honour and with glory, Lord,
you crowned humanity.
And then dominion you bestowed
for all made by your hand,
all sheep and cattle, birds and fish
that move through sea or land.

Coda:
O Lord, our Lord, throughout the earth
how glorious is your name!

Psalm 8
John L. Bell (*b.* 1949)

STROUDWATER   CM

PSALM 9

1   God shall endure for aye; he has
     for judgement set his throne
     to rule the nations equally,
     justice to give each one.

2   God also will a refuge be
     for those who are oppressed;
     a refuge he will be in times
     of trouble to distressed.

3   And they who know your name, in you
     their confidence will place:
     for you have not forsaken them
     who truly seek your face.

4   Sing, then, sing praises to the Lord
     on Zion's sacred hill;
     let all the earth be made aware
     of God's work and God's will.

Psalm 9, verses 7–11
The Scottish Psalter, 1929

Music The Psalter in Metre 1899, from William Anchors,
A Choice Collection of Psalm-Tunes…, c. 1721

86 886

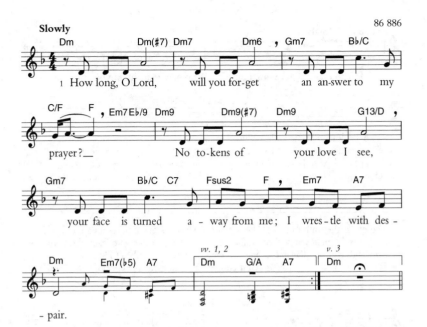

PSALM 13

1   How long, O Lord, will you forget
     an answer to my prayer?
     No tokens of your love I see,
     your face is turned away from me;
     I wrestle with despair.

2   How long, O Lord, will you forsake
     and leave me in this way?
     When will you come to my relief?
     My heart is overwhelmed with grief,
     by evil night and day.

3   How long, O Lord? But you forgive
     with mercy from above.
     I find that all your ways are just,
     I learn to praise you and to trust
     in your unfailing love.

based on Psalm 13
Barbara Woollett (*b.* 1937)

Music Christopher Norton (*b.* 1953)

7 Words: © Barbara Woollett / Jubilate Hymns, 4 Thorne Park Road, Chelston, Torquay TQ2 6RX <enquiries@jubilate.co.uk>
Used by permission.

7 Music: © 1989 HarperCollinsR.eligious. Administered by CopyCare Ltd, PO Box 77, Hailsham, East Sussex, BN27 3EF,
United Kingdom. <music@copycare.com> Used by permission.

Antiphon **Slowly**

Lord, who may en - ter your house? Who may re-main in your pre-sence?

Verse

1 Whoever leads a blame - less life, and does what is right;
2 Whoever does no wrong to friends, nor spreads false rumours a - bout neighbours;
3 Whoever keeps each so - lemn promise no matter what the cost;
4 Those who behave in this way will always remain un - shaken.

who speaks the truth from the heart, whose tongue is never used for slander.
who does not praise those God con - demns, but blesses those who fear the Lord.
who lends without demand - ing interest, and can't be bribed to hurt the innocent.
They may enter God's house and enjoy the presence of the Lord.

Final Antiphon
Unison Harmony

A – – – men. A – – men.

Music John L. Bell (*b.* 1949)

PSALM 15

Antiphon: ALL
Lord, who may enter your house?
Who may remain in your presence?

Verse: CANTOR

1 Whoever leads a blameless life,
   and does what is right;
   who speaks the truth from the heart,
   whose tongue is never used for slander.

2 Whoever does no wrong to friends,
   nor spreads false rumours about neighbours;
   who does not praise those God condemns,
   but blesses those who fear the Lord.

3 Whoever keeps each solemn promise
   no matter what the cost;
   who lends without demanding interest,
   and can't be bribed to hurt the innocent.

4 Those who behave in this way
   will always remain unshaken.
   They may enter God's house
   and enjoy the presence of the Lord.

Final antiphon:
Amen. Amen.

Psalm 15
John L. Bell (*b.* 1949)

WETHERBY

PSALM 16

1   O God, my refuge, keep me safe:
on you my good depends;
O Lord, you are my Lord alone,
your saints my choicest friends.

2   Whoever turns to other gods
will find remorse and shame;
to them I make no sacrifice,
nor will I speak their name.

3   The Lord is my inheritance,
a prize beyond compare;
his word instructs me day and night,
his own belovèd heir.

4   At all times I have set the Lord
before my face to stand;
no trial, no pain can shake my hope
with him at my right hand.

5   My heart and soul rejoice in you
and in your power to save:
you will not leave your Holy One
to perish in the grave.

6   You lead me to the path of life:
before your face I'll stand
and drink my fill of endless joys
that flow at your right hand.

from Psalm 16
David G. Preston (*b.* 1939)

Music Samuel Sebastian Wesley (1810–1876)

0

GIBSON

76 86 86

PSALM 19

1　The stars declare his glory;
　　the vault of heaven springs
　mute witness of the Master's hand
　　in all created things,
　and through the silences of space
　　their soundless music sings.

2　The dawn returns in splendour,
　　the heavens burn and blaze,
　the rising sun renews the race
　　that measures all our days,
　and writes in fire across the skies
　　God's majesty and praise.

3　So shine the Lord's commandments
　　to make the simple wise;
　more sweet than honey to the taste,
　　more rich than any prize,
　a law of love within our hearts,
　　a light before our eyes.

4　So order too this life of mine,
　　direct it all my days;
　may meditations of my heart
　　be innocence and praise,
　my rock and my redeeming Lord,
　　in all my words and ways.

　　　　　　　　　　based on Psalm 19
　　　　　　　Timothy Dudley-Smith (b. 1926)

Music Patrick Wedd (b. 1948)

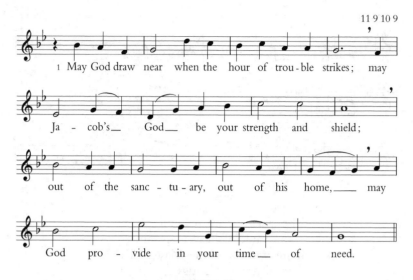

PSALM 20

1   May God draw near when the hour of trouble strikes;
may Jacob's God be your strength and shield;
out of the sanctuary, out of his home,
may God provide in your time of need.

2   May God remember the sacrifice you make
and take delight in the gifts you bring.
May God respond to your heart's deep desire
and grant fulfilment to all your plans.

3   With every blessing our mouths will shout for joy
to celebrate what the Lord has done;
and ever after, when God shows you favour,
in every triumph we'll trace his love.

4   Oh, now I know that the Lord is God indeed
and grants success to his chosen one.
From highest heaven God answers my call
and brings me victory with his right hand.

5   Some trust in weapons and some in skills of war;
but all we have is our faith in God.
They that are mighty shall stumble and fall
but we will rise and shall overcome.

Psalm 20

Music Zdenek Cep (*d.* 2004)   John L. Bell (*b.* 1949)

PSALM 22

My God, my God, why hast thou for'saken me:
why art thou so far from helping me and from the
    words of ' my roaring?

O my God, I cry in the daytime but thou ' hearest not:
and in the night season and am ' not silent.

But thou art holy, O thou that inhabitest the praises
    of Israel,
  our fathers trusted in ' thee:
they trusted and thou didst de'liver them.

They cried unto thee and were de'livered:
they trusted in thee and were not ' confounded.

But I am a worm and ' no man:
a reproach of men and despised of ' the people.

All they that see me laugh me to ' scorn:
they shoot out the lip,
  they shake the ' head saying,

He trusted on the Lord that he would de'liver him:
let him deliver him seeing he deligh'ted in him.

But thou art he that took me out of the ' womb:
thou didst make me hope when I was upon my '
    mother's breasts.

Be not far from me for trouble is ' near:
for there is ' none to help.

My strength is dried up like a potsherd,
  and my tongue cleaveth to my ' jaws:
and thou hast brought me into the ' dust of death.

For dogs have ' compassed me:
the assembly of the wicked have inclosed me,
  they pierced my ' hands and my feet.

I may tell ' all my bones:
they look and stare ' upon me.

continued overleaf

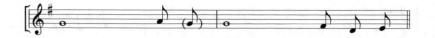

They part my garments a'mong them:
and cast lots upon ' my vesture.

But be not thou far from me, O ' Lord:
O my strength, haste thee ' to help me.

I will declare thy name unto my ' brethren:
in the midst of the congregation will ' I praise thee.

Ye that fear the Lord, ' praise him:
all ye the seed of Jacob, glorify him and fear him
    all ye the seed ' of Is rael.

For he hath not despised nor abhorred the affliction
    of the af'flicted:
neither hath he hid his face from him,
  but when he cried unto ' him he heard.

All the ends of the world shall remember and turn
    unto the ' Lord:
and all the kindreds of the nations shall worship '
    before thee.

A seed shall ' serve him:
it shall be accounted to the Lord for a ge'neration.

They shall come and shall declare his righteousness
    unto a people that shall be ' born:
that he ' hath done this.

(Glory be to the Father, and to the Son, and to the
    Holy ' Ghost.
As it was in the beginning, is now, and ever shall be,
world without ' end. Amen.)

Psalm 22, verses 1-9, 11, 15-19, 22-24, 27, 30, 31
Authorized Version

Music Tone II ending 1

PSALM 22

LEADER: My God, my God, why have you forsaken me?
I have cried desperately for help,
but still it does not come.

ALL: During the day, I call to you, O God,
but you do not answer.
I call at night, but get no rest.

LEADER: Yet you are the one enthroned as the Holy One,
you are the one whom Israel praises.

ALL: Our ancestors put their trust in you;
they trusted you and you saved them.

LEADER: They called to you and escaped from danger;
they trusted you and were not disappointed.

ALL: But I am no longer a man: I am a worm;
I am despised and scorned by everyone.

LEADER: All who see me, jeer at me;
they stick out their tongues and shake
their heads.

ALL: 'You relied on the Lord, why doesn't he
save you?
If the Lord likes you, why doesn't he help you?'

LEADER: It was you who brought me safely through birth,
and when I was a baby, you kept me safe.

ALL: I have relied on you since the day I was born,
and you have always been my God.

LEADER: Do not stay away from me!
Trouble is near and there is no one to help.

ALL: Many enemies surround me like bulls,
like fierce bulls from the land of Bashan.

LEADER: They open their mouths like lions,
roaring and tearing at me.

ALL: My strength is gone
like water spilt on the ground.
My bones are out of joint,
my heart is melted like wax.

continued overleaf

LEADER: My throat is dry as dust, my tongue sticks to
      my mouth.
      You have left me for dead in the dust.

ALL: A gang of evil men surrounds me.
      Like dogs, they close in on me,
      tearing my hands and feet.

LEADER: O Lord, don't stay away from me!
      Come quickly to my rescue.

ALL: Save me from the sword;
      save my life from these dogs.

LEADER: Rescue me from these lions,
      I am helpless before these wild bulls.

ALL: I will tell my people what you have done.
      I will praise you in the assembly.

LEADER: Praise him, you descendants of Jacob!
      Worship him, you people of Israel!

ALL: He does not neglect the poor:
      he answers when they call for help.

LEADER: Future generations will serve him;
      and will speak of the Lord to those following them.

ALL: People not yet born will be told:
      'The Lord saves his people.'

from Psalm 22, verses 1-16, 19-24, 30-31
Good News Bible

CRIMOND

CM

PSALM 23

1   The Lord's my Shepherd, I'll not want.
He makes me down to lie
in pastures green: he leadeth me
the quiet waters by.

2   My soul he doth restore again;
and me to walk doth make
within the paths of righteousness,
even for his own name's sake.

3   Yea, though I walk in death's dark vale,
yet will I fear none ill:
for thou art with me; and thy rod
and staff me comfort still.

4   My table thou hast furnishèd
in presence of my foes;
my head thou dost with oil anoint,
and my cup overflows.

5   Goodness and mercy all my life
shall surely follow me:
and in God's house for evermore
my dwelling-place shall be.

Psalm 23
The Scottish Psalter, 1929

Music Version 1 Melody possibly by Jessie Seymour Irvine
(1836–1887) or David Grant (1833–1893)
harmonised Thomas Cuthbertson Leithead Pritchard (1885–1960)

WILTSHIRE   CM

PSALM 23

1   The Lord's my Shepherd, I'll not want.
        He makes me down to lie
        in pastures green: he leadeth me
        the quiet waters by.

2   My soul he doth restore again;
        and me to walk doth make
        within the paths of righteousness,
        even for his own name's sake.

3   Yea, though I walk in death's dark vale,
        yet will I fear none ill:
        for thou art with me;   and thy rod
        and staff me comfort still.

4   My table thou hast furnishèd
        in presence of my foes;
        my head thou dost with oil anoint,
        and my cup overflows.

5   Goodness and mercy all my life
        shall surely follow me:
        and in God's house for evermore
        my dwelling-place shall be.

Psalm 23
The Scottish Psalter, 1929

Music Melody by George Thomas Smart (1776–1867)
harmonies as in *Scottish Psalter,* 1899

ORLINGTON   CM extended

PSALM 23

1   The Lord's my Shepherd, I'll not want.
        He makes me down to lie
    *   in pastures green: he leadeth me
        the quiet waters by.

2   My soul he doth restore again;
        and me to walk doth make
        within the paths of righteousness,
        even for his own name's sake.

3   Yea, though I walk in death's dark vale,
        yet will I fear none ill:
        for thou art with me; and thy rod
        and staff me comfort still.

4   My table thou hast furnishèd
        in presence of my foes;
        my head thou dost with oil anoint,
        and my cup overflows.

5   Goodness and mercy all my life
        shall surely follow me:
        and in God's house for evermore
        my dwelling-place shall be.

    *   *The third line of each verse is repeated.*

Psalm 23
The Scottish Psalter, 1929

Music John Campbell (1807–1860)

BROTHER JAMES'S AIR   CM extended

PSALM 23

1   The Lord's my Shepherd, I'll not want.
    He makes me down to lie
*   in pastures green: he leadeth me
    the quiet waters by.

2   My soul he doth restore again;
    and me to walk doth make
    within the paths of righteousness,
    ev'n for his own name's sake.

3   Yea, though I walk in death's dark vale,
    yet will I fear none ill:
    for thou art with me; and thy rod
    and staff me comfort still.

4   My table thou hast furnishèd
    in presence of my foes;
    my head thou dost with oil anoint,
    and my cup overflows.

5   Goodness and mercy all my life
    shall surely follow me:
    and in God's house for evermore
    my dwelling-place shall be.

* *The last two lines of each verse are repeated.*

Psalm 23
The Scottish Psalter, 1929

Music Melody by James Leith Macbeth Bain (1860–1925)
harmonised John L. Bell (b. 1949)

Steadily

1   The Lord   is   my shepherd;
2   He guides   me a - long   the right path;
3 You have   pre-pared   a   banquet   for   me
4   Surely   goodness   and   kindness   shall follow   me
5   To   the Father   and   Son   give glory,

there is   nothing   I   shall want.
he is   true   to his   name.   If   I should
in the   sight   of my   foes.   My
all the   days   of my   life.   In the
give glory   to the Spirit.   To God   who

Fresh   and   green   are the pastures   where he
walk   in the valley   of darkness   no
head   you have a-nointed   with oil;
Lord's   own   house   shall I   dwell
is,   who was,   and who will   be

(1) gives   me re-pose.   Near restful   waters   he
(2) evil   would I   fear.   You   are there with   your   crook   and your

leads   me,   to re - vive my drooping spi -   rit.
staff;   with these you give me com -   fort.
(3) my   cup   is   o - ver - flow -   ing.
(4) for   ev -   er and   ev -   er.
(5) for   ev -   er and   ev -   er.

Antiphon 1
(♩ = o *of Psalm*)

My shepherd   is   the   Lord, nothing indeed shall I   want.

Antiphon 2
(♩ = o *of Psalm*)

His goodness shall follow me al - ways   to the   end of my days.

full text overleaf

Music Psalm and Antiphon 1 Joseph Gelineau (*b.* 1920)
Antiphon 2 Anthony Gregory Murray (1905–1992)

PSALM 23

1   The Lord is my shepherd;
there is nothing I shall want.
Fresh and green are the pastures
where he gives me repose.
Near restful waters he leads me,
to revive my drooping spirit.

2   He guides me along the right path;
he is true to his name.
If I should walk in the valley of darkness
no evil would I fear.
You are there with your crook and your staff;
with these you give me comfort.

3   You have prepared a banquet for me
in the sight of my foes.
My head you have anointed with oil;
my cup is overflowing.

4   Surely goodness and kindness shall follow me
all the days of my life.
In the Lord's own house shall I dwell
for ever and ever.

5   To the Father and Son give glory,
give glory to the Spirit.
To God who is, who was, and who will be
for ever and ever.

Antiphons:

1   My shepherd is the Lord,
nothing indeed shall I want.

2   His goodness shall follow me always
to the end of my days.

Psalm 23
The Grail Version, 1963
Joseph Gelineau (b. 1920)

18 *Music Tune 1 A Supplement to the New Version,* 1708
probably by William Croft (1678–1727)

ST MATTHEW   DCM

PSALM 24

1   The earth belongs to God alone
and all that it contains;
the world and its inhabitants
God's steadfast love maintains.

2   The Lord who brought the world to birth
laid earth's foundations sure,
and firm within the surging seas
established them secure.

3   Who, then, are those who shall ascend
the holy hill of God?
And who is fit to stand within
the presence of the Lord?

4   All those whose hands and hearts are clean,
with no room in their mind
for worthless vanities or vows
of a deceitful kind.

5   These are the people who receive
a blessing from the Lord,
and vindication for their ways
from God, their saving God.

6   O God of Jacob, help us all
who gather in this place,
to seek your presence with us now:
we yearn to see your face.

Psalm 24, verses 1-6
*Scottish Psalter, 1929

ABBEY   CM

PSALM 24

1   The earth belongs to God alone
     and all that it contains;
     the world and its inhabitants
     God's steadfast love maintains.

2   The Lord who brought the world to birth
     laid earth's foundations sure,
     and firm within the surging seas
     established them secure.

3   Who, then, are those who shall ascend
     the holy hill of God?
     And who is fit to stand within
     the presence of the Lord?

4   All those whose hands and hearts are clean,
     with no room in their mind
     for worthless vanities or vows
     of a deceitful kind.

5   These are the people who receive
     a blessing from the Lord,
     and vindication for their ways
     from God, their saving God.

6   O God of Jacob, help us all
     who gather in this place,
     to seek your presence with us now:
     we yearn to see your face.

Psalm 24, verses 1-6
*Scottish Psalter, 1929

Music Tune 2 Melody from *Scottish Psalter,* 1615
harmonised David Evans (1874–1948)
altered Compilers of *Church Hymnary,* 3rd edition, 1973

ST GEORGE'S (EDINBURGH)   DCM Irregular

7 Ye gates, lift up your heads on high; ye
9 Ye gates, lift up your heads; ye doors, doors

doors that last for aye, be lift-ed up, that
that do last for aye, be lift-ed up, that

so the King of glo-ry en-ter may.
so the King of glo-ry en-ter may.

(Optional melody)

(8) But who of glo-ry is the King? (8) The migh-ty Lord is
(10) But who is he that (10) The King of glo-ry? who is

(8) this; even that same Lord that great in might and
(10) this? The Lord of hosts, and none but he, the

strong in bat-tle is; even that same Lord that
King of glo-ry is. The Lord of hosts, and

D.C.

great in might and strong in bat-tle is.
none but he, the King of glo-ry is.

Coda

Al-le-lu-ia! al-le-lu-ia! al-le-lu-ia! al-le-lu-ia!

al-le-lu-ia! A-men, a-men, a-men.

Music Andrew Mitchell Thomson (1778–1831)   *full text overleaf*

PSALM 24

7   Ye gates, lift up your heads on high;
ye doors that last for aye,
be lifted up, that so the King
of glory enter may.

8   But who of glory is the King?
The mighty Lord is this;
*   even that same Lord that great in might
and strong in battle is.

9   Ye gates, lift up your heads; ye doors,
doors that do last for aye,
be lifted up, that so the King
of glory enter may.

10   But who is he that is the King,
the King of glory? who is this?
The Lord of hosts, and none but he,
the King of glory is.

Coda:
Alleluia!   alleluia!
alleluia!   alleluia! alleluia!
Amen, amen, amen.

* *The last two lines of each verse are repeated.*

Psalm 24, verses 7–10, *The Scottish Psalter,* 1929

20

Refrain   6666 and refrain

Lift up the gates e - ter - nal, lift up your voic - es:

for God in glo - ry comes, the na - tion re - joic - es.

See, all the earth is God's, its peo - ple and na - tions:

God built it on the deeps and laid its foun - da - tions.

PSALM 24

Lift up the gates eternal,
lift up your voices:
for God in glory comes,
the nation rejoices.

1   See, all the earth is God's,
its people and nations:
God built it on the deeps
and laid its foundations.

2   Who can go up this mountain,
who stand in praising?
Those who are pure, who come
with clean hands upraising.

3   They shall receive forgiveness
and have God's blessing,
if they but search for God,
their Saviour confessing.

4   Come, lift your voices high,
be lifted to glory:
the Saviour God approaches,
come, shout the story.

5   Who is this glorious one,
for whom we are waiting?
We wait the mighty One,
our God celebrating.

Psalm 24
Arlo D. Duba (*d.* 1984)
and Willard F. Jabusch

Music Israeli folk melody
arranged John Ferguson (*b.* 1941)

GARELOCHSIDE   SM
Unison

21 2

SERENITY   SM

PSALM 25

1   Lord, teach me all your ways,
      reveal your paths to me;
      and lead me in your saving truth,
      show me what I should be.

2   Remember, Lord, your love,
      your care from ages past;
      and in that love remember me,
      in kindness hold me fast.

3   Forget my youthful faults,
      forgive my sinful ways;
      within the kindness of your love
      remember me always.

4   God, who is just and good,
      shows all who sin his way;
      he leads the humble in right paths,
      their teacher day by day.

5   All pathways of the Lord
      are kindly, true, and sure
      to those who keep his covenant
      and in his ways endure.

Psalm 25 (ii), verses 4, 5a, 6-10
*The Scottish Psalter, 1929

Music Tune 1 Kenneth George Finlay (1882–1974)
Music Tune 2 Cornelius Bryan (1775–1840)

21.i Music: © Broomhill Church of Scotland, Glasgow G11.

BISHOPTHORPE   CM

A higher setting is found at 424.

PSALM 27

1   The Lord's my light and saving health,
     who shall make me dismayed?
     My life's strength is the Lord, of whom
     then shall I be afraid?

2   One thing I of the Lord desired,
     and will seek to obtain,
     that all days of my life I may
     within God's house remain;

3   That I the beauty of the Lord
     behold may and admire,
     and that I in his holy place
     may reverently enquire.

4   Wait on the Lord, and be thou strong,
     and he shall strength afford
     unto thine heart;   yea, do thou wait,
     I say, upon the Lord.

Psalm 27, verses 1, 4, 14
The Scottish Psalter, 1929

Music
Melody and most of bass from *Select Portions of the Psalms,* c. 1786
Jeremiah Clarke (c. 1673–1707)

PSALM 27

Antiphon

The Lord is my light   and my sal - va - tion.

Speaker
colla voce

1 The Lord is my   light and my salvation,   Whom then shall I fear?

The Lord is my   strong refuge,   of whom then   need I be a-

A tempo   Antiphon

The Lord is my light   and my sal - va - tion.

Speaker

- fraid?

2 When the enemy came upon me to de-vour me, he   stumbled and fell to the

ground.   Though an   host of men were encamped a-gainst me, yet will I

A tempo   Antiphon

put my trust in him.   *The Lord is my*

Speaker

light   and my sal - va - tion.   3 One thing I ask of the Lord,   one

pe-tition I seek from him: to dwell in the   house of the   Lord, and serve him

A tempo   Antiphon

all my days.   *The Lord is my light   and my sal -*

Music Martin J. R. How (*b.* 1931)

- va - tion.   4 To behold the fair beauty of the Lord: and to

visit his   temple.   There will I offer him the sacrifice of thanksgiving: I will

A tempo

sing   and   speak   praises   to   my   God.

Antiphon

The Lord is   my   light   and   my   sal - va - tion.

PSALM 27

ANTIPHON
The Lord is my light and my salvation.

1   The Lord is my light and my salvation.
     Whom then shall I fear?
     The Lord is my strong refuge,
     of whom then need I be afraid?

2   When the enemy came upon me to devour me,
     he stumbled and fell to the ground.
     Though an host of men were encamped against me,
     yet will I put my trust in him.

3   One thing I ask of the Lord,
     one petition I seek from him:
     to dwell in the house of the Lord,
     and serve him all my days.

4   To behold the fair beauty of the Lord,
     and to visit his temple.
     There will I offer him the sacrifice of thanksgiving:
     I will sing and speak praise to my God.

Psalm 27, verses 1–4
Psalms for Speakers

PSALM 30

1   I will exalt you, O Lord,
     because you have ' lifted • me ' up ‖
    and have not let my enemies ' triumph ' over me.

2   O Lord my God, I ' cried out • to ' you, ‖
    and you re'stored me • to ' health.

3   You brought me up, O Lord, ' from the ' dead; ‖
    and you restored my life as I was going ' down to • the ' grave.

4   Sing to the Lord, you ' faithful ' servants; ‖
    give thanks for the remembrance ' of God's ' holiness.

5   For God's anger lasts but the twinkling ' of an ' eye, ‖
    God's favour en'dures for • a ' lifetime.

6   Weeping may linger ' for the ' night, ‖
    but joy ' comes in • the ' morning.

7   While I felt secure, I said,
     'I shall never ' be dis'turbed. ‖
    You, Lord, with your favour, made me as ' strong as • the '
     mountains.'

8   Then you ' hid your ' face, ‖
    and I was ' filled with ' fear.

9   I cried to ' you, O ' Lord; ‖
    I pleaded with the ' Lord, ' saying,

10   'What profit is there in my blood, if I go ' down to • the ' pit? ‖
    will the dust praise you or de'clare your ' faithfulness?

11   Hear, O Lord, and have ' mercy • up'on me; ‖
    O Lord, ' be my ' helper'.

12   You have turned my mourning ' into ' dancing; ‖
    you have put off my sackcloth and ' clothed me • with ' joy.

13   Therefore my heart sings to ' you with•out ' ceasing; ‖
    O Lord my God, I will give ' thanks for ' ever.

(Glory to the Father, and ' to the ' Son, ‖
and to the ' Holy ' Spirit:

as it was in the be'ginning, • is ' now, ‖
and will be for ' ever. • A'men.)

Psalm 30
Psalter for the Christian People

Music from Scottish melody *Galloway Tam*
Douglas Galbraith (*b.* 1940)

25

PSALM 31

1   In you, O Lord, have I taken refuge;
       let me never be put to shame;
    deliver me in your righteousness.

2   Incline your ear to me;
    make haste to deliver me.

3   Be my strong rock, a fortress to save me,
       for you are my rock and my stronghold;
    guide me, and lead me for your name's sake.

4   Take me out of the net that they have laid
       secretly for me,
    for you are my strength.

5   Into your hands I commend my spirit,
    for you have redeemed me, O Lord God of truth.

9   Have mercy on me, Lord, for I am in trouble;
    my eye is consumed with sorrow,
       my soul and my body also.

10   For my life is wasted with grief,
       and my years with sighing;
    my strength fails me because of my affliction,
       and my bones are consumed.

11   I have become a reproach to all my enemies
       and even to my neighbours, an object of dread
       to my acquaintances;
    when they see me in the street they flee from me.

continued overleaf

12   I am forgotten like one that is dead, out of mind;
I have become like a broken vessel.

13   For I have heard the whispering of the crowd;
    fear is on every side;
they scheme together against me, and plot to take my life.

14   But my trust is in you, O Lord.
I have said, 'You are my God.

15   My times are in your hand;
deliver me from the hand of my enemies,
    and from those who persecute me.

16   Make your face to shine upon your servant,
and save me for your mercy's sake.'

Psalm 31, verses 1–5, 9–16
Common Worship, 2000

PSALM 33

1   Rejoice in the Lord, you righteous;
    it is good for the just to sing praises.

2   Praise the Lord with the harp;
    play upon the psaltery and lyre.

3   Sing to the Lord a new song;
    sound a fanfare with all your skill upon the trumpet.

4   For your word, O Lord, is right,
    and all your works are sure.

5   You love righteousness and justice;
    your loving-kindness, O Lord, fills the whole earth.

6   By your word, O Lord, were the heavens made,
    by the breath of your mouth all the heavenly hosts.

7   You gather up the waters of the ocean as in a water-skin
    and store up the depths of the sea.

8   Let all the earth fear the Lord;
    let all who dwell in the world stand in reverence.

9   For the Lord spoke, and it came to pass;
    the Lord commanded, and it stood fast.

10 The Lord brings the will of the nations to naught
    and thwarts the designs of the peoples.

11 But the Lord's will stands fast for ever,
    and the designs of the Lord's heart from age to age.

12 Happy is the nation whose God is the Lord!
    Happy the people you have chosen to be your own!

13 O Lord, you look down from heaven
    and behold all the people in the world.

Psalm 33, verses 1–13
Psalter for the Christian People

TALADH CHRIOSTA   7776

PSALM 34

1   I will always bless the Lord,
     praise his name and love his word.
     Humble folk will fill with joy,
     as in God I glory.

2   When I prayed, God answered me,
     from my fears he set me free:
     none who trust God's faithful love
     shall be disappointed.

3   Taste and see that God is good,
     know your yearnings understood,
     find your true security,
     be God's holy people.

4   Even lions suffer need,
     hunger when they long to feed;
     yet for those who wait on God
     good will not be lacking.

Psalm 34, verses 1-5, 8-10
John L. Bell (*b.* 1949)

Music Gaelic traditional *arranged* John L. Bell (*b.* 1949)

LONDON NEW   CM

PSALM 36

1   Thy mercy, Lord, is in the heavens;
     thy truth doth reach the clouds:
     thy justice is like mountains great;
     thy judgements deep as floods:

2   Lord, all creation thou dost keep.
     How precious is thy grace!
     Therefore in shadow of thy wings
     we all our trust shall place.

3   We with the bounty of thy house
     shall be well satisfied;
     from rivers of thy pleasures thou
     wilt drink to us provide.

4   Because of life the fountain pure
     remains alone with thee;
     and in that purest light of thine
     we clearly light shall see.

                          Psalm 36, verses 5-9
                          The Scottish Psalter, 1929

Music Melody from *Scottish Psalter,* 1635,
as adapted in Playford's *Psalmes,* 1671

PSALM 37

1   Do not fret because of the wicked;
     do not envy those who do evil,
2   for they wither quickly like grass
     and fade like the green of the fields.

3   If you trust in the Lord and do good,
     then you will live in the land and be secure.
4   If you find your delight in the Lord,
     he will grant your heart's desire.

5   Commit your life to the Lord,
     be confident, and God will act,
6   so that your justice breaks forth like the light,
     your cause like the noonday sun.

7   Be still before the Lord and wait in patience;
     do not fret at those who prosper,
     those who make evil plots
     to bring down the needy and the poor.

8   Calm your anger and forget your rage;
     do not fret, it only leads to evil:
9   for those who do evil shall perish;
     those waiting for the Lord shall inherit the land.

10   A little longer — and the wicked shall have gone.
     Look at their homes, they are not there.
11   But the humble shall own the land
     and enjoy the fullness of peace.

39   The salvation of the just comes from the Lord,
     their stronghold in time of distress.
40   The Lord helps them and delivers them
     and saves them, for their refuge is in God.

Psalm 37, verses 1-11, 39-40
The Grail Version, 1963

BALLERMA CM

A lower setting is found at 668.

PSALM 40

1 I waited for the Lord my God,
  and patiently did bear;
  at length to me he did incline
  my voice and cry to hear.

2 He took me from a fearful pit,
  and from the miry clay,
  and on a rock he set my feet,
  establishing my way.

3 He put a new song in my mouth,
  our God to magnify:
  many shall see it, and shall fear,
  and on the Lord rely.

4 O blessèd are all they whose trust
  upon the Lord relies;
  respecting not the proud, nor such
  as turn aside to lies.

Psalm 40, verses 1–4
The Scottish Psalter, 1929

Music
French song by François Hyppolyte Barthélémon (1741–1808)
adapted Robert Simpson (1790–1832)

I WAITED PATIENTLY FOR GOD   CM

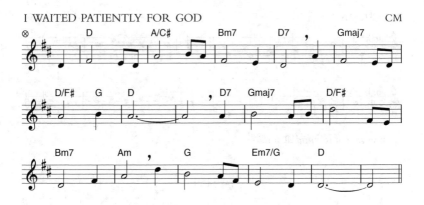

PSALM 40

1   I waited patiently for God,
      for God to hear my prayer,
      and God bent down to where I sank
      and listened to me there.

2   God raised me from a miry pit,
      from mud and sinking sand,
      and set my feet upon a rock
      where I can firmly stand.

3   And on my lips a song was put,
      a new song to the Lord.
      Many will marvel, open-eyed,
      and put their trust in God.

4   Great wonders you have done, O Lord,
      all purposed to our good:
      unable every one to name,
      I bow in gratitude.

Psalm 40, verses 1-4
John L. Bell (b. 1949)

Music Melody by Alex Muir (b. 1940)
harmonised John L. Bell (b. 1949)

MARTYRDOM (FENWICK)   CM

PSALM 42

1   As pants the hart for cooling streams
     in parched and barren ways,
     so longs my soul for you, O God,
     and your refreshing grace.

2   For you my God, the living God,
     my thirsting soul will pine:
     oh, when shall I behold your face,
     your majesty divine?

3   God of my strength, my tears have been
     by day and night my food;
     the mockers taunt continually
     and say: 'Where is your God?'

4   Why restless, why cast down, my soul?
     Hope still, and you shall sing
     the praise of him who is your God,
     your health's eternal spring.

Psalm 42
*Nahum Tate (1652–1715)
and *Nicholas Brady (1659–1726)

Music Hugh Wilson (1766–1824)
adapted Robert Archibald Smith (1780–1829)

As the deer longs for run-ning streams, so I__ long, so I__ long, __ so I__ long for you.

1 A-thirst my soul__ for you, the God who is my life! When shall I see,
(2) E-choes ...

when shall I__ see, __ see the face of God?

Music Bob Hurd (*b.* 1950) *arranged* Craig S. Kingsbury (*b.* 1952)

PSALMS 42–43

PSALMS 42–43

ANTIPHON
As the deer longs for running streams,
so I long, so I long, so I long for you.

1   Athirst my soul for you, the God who is my life!
     When shall I see, when shall I see,
     see the face of God?

2   Echoes meet as deep is calling unto deep,
     over my head, all your mighty waters
     sweeping over me.

3   Continually the foe delights in taunting me:
     'Where is God, where is your God?'
     Where, O where are you?

4   Defend me, God, send forth your light and your truth.
     They will lead me to your holy mountain,
     to your dwelling place.

5   Then shall I go unto the altar of my God.
     Praising you, O my joy and gladness:
     I shall praise your name.

Psalm 42–43, verses 1, 2, 7, 10
paraphrased Bob Hurd (*b.* 1950)

MARTYRS   CM

34 2

MARTYRS   CM

PSALM 43

1   O send thy light forth and thy truth;
let them be guides to me,
and bring me to thine holy hill,
even where thy dwellings be.

2   Then will I to God's altar go,
to God my chiefest joy:
yea, God, my God, thy name to praise
my harp I will employ.

3   Why art thou then cast down, my soul?
what should discourage thee?
And why with vexing thoughts art thou
disquieted in me?

4   Still trust in God; for him to praise,
good cause I yet shall have:
he of my countenance is the health,
my God that doth me save.

Psalm 43, verses 3–5
The Scottish Psalter, 1929

Music Tune 1 Melody from *Scottish Psalter*, 1615 (1635 rhythm)
harmonised The Scottish Psalter, 1929

Music Tune 2 Melody from *Scottish Psalter* 1615
harmonised Scottish Psalter 1625

INVOCATION   DCM extended

1 O— send thy— light forth and thy truth; let them be— guides to—
me,— and bring me to thine ho - ly— hill,— e - ven
where thy dwellings be.— Then will I to God's al - tar— go, to—
God my— chiefest joy:— yea, God, my God, thy name to praise
my— harp, my— harp, my harp I will em - ploy, I will em - ploy.

PSALM 43

1   O send thy light forth and thy truth;
let them be guides to me,
and bring me to thine holy hill,
even where thy dwellings be.
Then will I to God's altar go,
to God my chiefest joy:
yea, God, my God, thy name to praise
* my harp I will employ.

2   Why art thou then cast down, my soul?
what should discourage thee?
And why with vexing thoughts art thou
disquieted in me?
Still trust in God; for him to praise
good cause I yet shall have:
he of my countenance is the health,
my God that doth me save.

* *The last line of each verse is repeated.*

Psalm 43, verses 3-5
The Scottish Psalter, 1929

Music Robert Archibald Smith (1780–1829)

STROUDWATER

CM

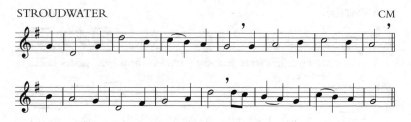

PSALM 46

1 God is our refuge and our strength,
 in straits a present aid;
 therefore, although the earth be moved
 we will not be afraid:

2 Though hills amidst the seas be cast;
 though waters roaring make,
 and troubled be; yea, though the hills
 by swelling seas do shake.

3 A river is, whose streams make glad
 the city of our God;
 the holy place, wherein the Lord
 most high hath his abode.

4 God in the midst of her doth dwell;
 nothing shall her remove;
 the Lord to her an helper will,
 and that right early, prove.

Psalm 46, verses 1–5
The Scottish Psalter, 1929

Music The Psalter in Metre 1899, from William Anchors,
A Choice Collection of Psalm-Tunes..., c. 1721

37   PSALM 46

1 God is our refuge, God our strength,
 in troubled times our aid;
 therefore, should earth itself be moved,
 we shall not be afraid.

2 Nor shall we fear if mountains fall
 beneath the roaring waves,
 or hilltops quake in surging seas:
 ours is the God who saves.

3   There is a river which delights
the city of our God;
it flows through that most hallowed place
God chose for his abode.

4   God lives for ever at her heart,
she never will be moved;
each morning at the break of day
God's saving help is proved.

Psalm 46, verses 1-5
Compilers

38

PSALM 47

2   God goes up with shouts of joy;
God goes up with trumpet blast.
Sing praise for God, sing praise, sing praises to our King,
let us all sing praise!

3   God is King of all the earth,
sing praise with all your skill.
God is King of all the earth, God reigns upon his throne,
on his holy throne.

Psalm 47

Music H. Ricardo Ramirez   H. Ricardo Ramirez

PSALM 47

God mounts his throne to shouts of joy,
a blare of trumpets for the Lord!

1. All you peoples clap your hands,
   cry to God with shouts of joy
   for the Lord, the most high, great King of all the earth,
   over all the earth!

2. God goes up with shouts of joy;
   God goes up with trumpet blast.
   Sing praise for God, sing praise, sing praises to our King,
   let us all sing praise!

3. God is King of all the earth,
   sing praise with all your skill.
   God is King of all the earth, God reigns upon his throne,
   on his holy throne.

Psalm 47
H. Ricardo Ramirez

39

HYFRYDOL   87 87 D

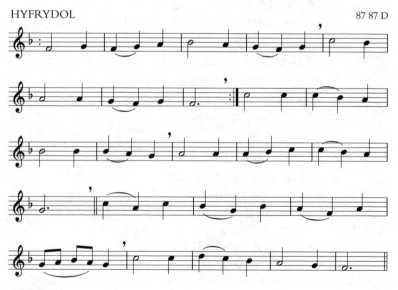

Music
Melody by Rowland Hugh Pritchard (1811–1887)
harmonised David Evans (1874–1948)

PSALM 50

1   God the Lord, the king almighty,
calls the earth from east to west;
shining out from Zion's splendour,
city loveliest and best,
comes our God! He breaks the silence,
robed in burning majesty:
'Gather all my covenant people,
bound by sacrifice to me'.

2   'Hear me testify against you;
listen, Israel, as I speak:
I do not require your offerings,
sacrifice I do not seek.
Mountain birds and meadow creatures,
cattle on a thousand hills,
all the beasts are my possession,
moving as their maker wills.'

3   God who owns the whole creation
needs no gift, no food, no house:
bring to him your heart's thanksgiving:
God most high will hear your vows.
Trust him in the day of trouble,
call to him who will redeem;
God will be your strong deliverer,
his renown your daily theme.

4   Lies increase and evil prospers;
God is silent, while men say,
'He has gone; let us forget him!'
thinking he is false as they.
But his word will judge or save us;
let us come before his throne
giving thanks, receiving mercy:
God's salvation now made known.

Psalm 50
Christopher Martin Idle (*b.* 1938)

SONG 24

10 10 10 10

PSALM 51

1   O God, be gracious to me in your love,
    and in your mercy pardon my misdeeds;
    wash me from guilt and cleanse me from my sin,
    for well I know the evil I have done.

2   Against you, Lord, you only have I sinned,
    and what to you is hateful have I done;
    I own your righteousness in charging me,
    I know you to be just should you condemn.

3   Take hyssop, sprinkle me and make me clean,
    wash me and make me whiter than the snow;
    fill me with gladness and rejoicing, Lord,
    and let my broken frame know joy once more.

4   Turn now your face, Lord God, from my misdeeds,
    and blot out all the sins that sully me;
    create a clean and contrite heart in me,
    renew my soul in faithfulness and love.

5   Drive me not from your presence, gracious Lord,
    nor keep your Holy Spirit far from me;
    restore my soul with your salvation's joy,
    and with a willing spirit strengthen me.

Psalm 51, verses 1-12
Ian Robertson Pitt-Watson (1923–1995)

Music Orlando Gibbons (1583–1625)

Psalm 61

WIGTOWN   CM

PSALM 61

1   O God, give ear unto my cry,
      and to my prayer attend;
      from distant corners of the land
      my cry to you I'll send.

2   My plea is made with fainting heart
      and great perplexity;
      lead me in safety to the rock
      that higher is than I.

3   For you have long my refuge been,
      a shelter by your power;
      a tower of strength against my foes
      in every evil hour.

4   Within your dwelling, Lord my God,
      for ever I'll abide;
      and in the shadow of your wings
      with confidence I'll hide.

Psalm 61, verses 1-4
*The Scottish Psalter, 1929

Music Melody from *Scottish Psalter* 1635
harmonised Compilers of *Church Hymnary,* 3rd edition, 1973

HOWARD (DUBLIN)   CM

PSALM 62

1   Only on God do thou, my soul,
     still patiently attend;
     my expectation and my hope
     on him alone depend.

2   He only my salvation is,
     and my strong rock is he;
     he only is my sure defence:
     I shall not movèd be.

3   In God my glory placèd is,
     and my salvation sure;
     in God I find my rock, my strength,
     my refuge most secure.

4   Ye people, place your confidence
     in him continually;
     before him pour ye out your heart;
     God is our refuge high.

Psalm 62
verses 1-2, 7-8: *The Scottish Psalter,* 1929
verse 1 Compilers of
Church Hymnary, 3rd edition, 1973

Music
Melody sometimes attributed to John Andrew Stevenson
(1762–1833) from John Wilson's *A Selection of Psalm Tunes,*
Edinburgh, 1825 as in *The Scottish Psalter,* 1929

43   RESIGNATION   DCM

Psalm 63

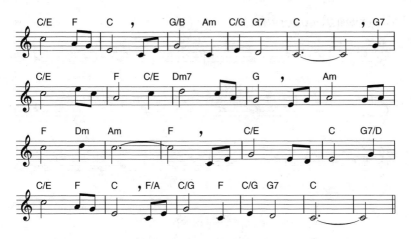

PSALM 63

1   O God, you are my God alone,
    whom eagerly I seek,
    though longing fills my soul with thirst
    and leaves my body weak.
    Just as a dry and barren land
    awaits a freshening shower,
    I long within your house to see
    your glory and your power.

2   Your faithful love surpasses life,
    evoking all my praise.
    Through every day, to bless your name,
    my hands in joy I'll raise.
    My deepest needs you satisfy
    as with a sumptuous feast.
    So, on my lips and in my heart,
    your praise has never ceased.

3   Throughout the night I lie in bed
    and call you, Lord, to mind;
    in darkest hours I meditate
    how God, my strength, is kind.
    Beneath the shadow of your wing,
    I live and feel secure;
    and daily as I follow close,
    your right hand keeps me sure.

Psalm 63, verses 1–8
John L. Bell (b. 1949)

Music American folk melody
arranged John L. Bell (b. 1949)

ST STEPHEN (ABRIDGE)   CM

PSALM 65

1   Praise waits for thee in Zion, Lord:
    to thee vows paid shall be.
    O thou that hearer art of prayer,
    all flesh shall come to thee.

2   Iniquities, I must confess,
    prevail against me do:
    but as for our transgressions all,
    them purge away shalt thou.

3   How blest are they whom thou dost choose,
    whom thou dost call to thee,
    that they within thy courts, O Lord,
    may always dwellers be:

4   We surely shall be satisfied
    with thy abundant grace,
    and with the goodness of thy house,
    even of thy holy place.

Psalm 65, verses 1-4
*The Scottish Psalter, 1929

Music Melody by Isaac Smith (1734–1805)
A Collection of Psalm Tunes c. 1780

SANDYS

SM

PSALM 67

1   Lord, bless and pity us,
shine on us with your face:
that your way may be known on earth,
all nations know your grace.

2   Let people praise you, Lord;
let all the people praise.
Oh, let the nations all be glad,
in songs their voices raise:

3   You'll justly people judge,
on earth rule nations all.
Let people praise you, Lord; let them
praise you, both great and small.

4   The earth her fruit shall yield,
our God shall blessing send.
God shall us bless; all shall him fear
unto earth's utmost end.

Psalm 67
*The Scottish Psalter, 1929

Music English traditional carol melody
from Sandys' *Christmas Carols Ancient and Modern,* 1833

SHEFFIELD   CM

PSALM 68

1   Most glorious Lord, you have gone up
to take your place on high;
as victor, you in triumph led
captive captivity.

2   Blest be the Lord who carries us
and keeps us day by day;
in God and God alone we find
salvation's surest way.

3   God is the God who freely gives
his people life and breath;
God saves and shelters, rescues us
from danger and from death.

Psalm 68, verses 18a, 19, 20
*The Scottish Psalter, 1929

Music William Mather (1756–1808)

PSALM 69

1   Save me, O God,
      for the waters have come up, even to my neck.

2   I sink in deep mire where there is no foothold;
      I have come into deep waters and the flood
            sweeps over me.

3   I have grown weary with crying;
            my throat is raw;
      my eyes have failed from looking so long
            for my God.

4   Those who hate me without any cause
      are more than the hairs of my head;

5   Those who would destroy me are mighty;
      my enemies accuse me falsely:
            must I now give back what I never stole?

6   O God, you know my foolishness,
      and my faults are not hidden from you.

7   Let not those who hope in you be put to shame
            through me, Lord God of hosts;
      let not those who seek you be disgraced
            because of me, O God of Israel.

8   For your sake have I suffered reproach;
      shame has covered my face.

9   I have become a stranger to my kindred,
      an alien to my mother's children.

10 Zeal for your house has eaten me up;
      the scorn of those who scorn you has
            fallen upon me.

11 I humbled myself with fasting,
      but that was turned to my reproach.

12 I put on sackcloth also
      and became a byword among them.

13 Those who sit at the gate murmur against me,
      and the drunkards make songs about me.

14   But as for me,
          I make my prayer to you, O Lord;
      at an acceptable time, O God.

15   Answer me, O God,
          in the abundance of your mercy
      and with your sure salvation.

16   Draw me out of the mire, that I sink not;
      let me be rescued from those who hate me
          and out of the deep waters.

17   Let not the water flood drown me,
          neither the deep swallow me up;
      let not the Pit shut its mouth upon me.

18   Answer me, Lord,
          for your loving-kindness is good;
      turn to me in the multitude of your mercies.

19   Hide not your face from your servant;
      be swift to answer me, for I am in trouble.

20   Draw near to my soul and redeem me;
      deliver me because of my enemies.

21   You know my reproach, my shame
          and my dishonour;
      my adversaries are all in your sight.

22   Reproach has broken my heart;
          I am full of heaviness.
      I looked for some to have pity,
          but there was no one,
          neither found I any to comfort me.

23   They gave me gall to eat,
      and when I was thirsty,
          they gave me vinegar to drink.

31   As for me, I am poor and in misery;
      your saving help, O God, will lift me up.

32   I will praise the name of God with a song;
      I will proclaim his greatness with thanksgiving.

33   This will please the Lord
          more than an offering of oxen,
      more than bulls with horns and hooves.

34   The humble shall see and be glad;
you who seek God, your heart shall live.

35   For the Lord listens to the needy,
and his own who are imprisoned
he does not despise.

36   Let the heavens and the earth praise him,
the seas and all that moves in them.

37   For God will save Zion
and rebuild the cities of Judah;
they shall live there and have it in possession.

38   The children of his servants shall inherit it,
and they that love his name shall dwell therein.

Psalm 69, verses 1–23, 31–38
Common Worship, 2000

EFFINGHAM   CM

PSALM 72

1   His large and great dominion shall
     from sea to sea extend:
     it from the river shall reach forth
     unto earth's utmost end.

2   The kings of Tarshish, and the isles,
     to him shall presents bring;
     and unto him shall offer gifts
     Sheba's and Seba's king.

3   Yea, all the mighty kings on earth
     before him down shall fall;
     and all the nations of the world
     do service to him shall.

4   His name for ever shall endure;
     last like the sun it shall:
     all shall be blest in him, and blest
     all nations shall him call.

5   Now blessèd be the Lord our God,
     the God of Israel,
     for he alone doth wondrous works,
     in glory that excel.

6   And blessèd be his glorious name
     to all eternity:
     the whole earth let his glory fill.
     Amen, so let it be.

Psalm 72, verses 8, 10-11, 17-19
*The Scottish Psalter, 1929

Music Adapted from a melody in
Musikalisches Hand-Buch, Hamburg, 1690

Antiphon *(optional)*

I cried a - loud,— a - loud to—— God. I cried to God and he heard me.

PSALM 77

ANTIPHON *(optional)*
I cried aloud, aloud to God. I cried to God and he heard me.

1   I cried aloud to God,
       I cried to God and he heard me.

2   In the day of my distress I sought the Lord,
       and by night I lifted my hands in prayer.
       My tears ran unceasingly,
       I refused all comfort. *(antiphon)*

11   I call to mind the deeds of the Lord;
       I recall your wonderful acts of old;

12   I reflect on all your works
       and consider what you have done.

13   Your way, God, is holy;
       what god is as great as our God?

14   You are a God who works miracles;
       you have shown the nations your power. *(antiphon)*

15   With your strong arm you rescued your people,
       the descendants of Jacob and Joseph.

16   The waters saw you, God,
       they saw you and writhed in anguish;
       the ocean was troubled to its depths.

17   The clouds poured down water, the skies thundered,
       your arrows flashed hither and thither.

18   The sound of your thunder was in the whirlwind,
       lightning-flashes lit up the world,
       the earth shook and quaked.

continued overleaf

Music Douglas Galbraith *(b.* 1940)

I cried a - loud,— a - loud to——

God. I cried to God and he heard me.

19   Your path was through the sea,
      your way through mighty waters,
      and none could mark your footsteps.

20   You guided your people like a flock
      shepherded by Moses and Aaron. *(antiphon)*

Psalm 77, verses 1-2, 11-20
The Revised English Bible

50

CAITHNESS   CM

PSALM 78

1   The praises of the Lord our God,
     and his almighty strength,
     the wondrous works that he has done,
     we will show forth at length.

2   His testimony and his law
     in Israel he did place,
     and charged our forebears it to show
     to their succeeding race;

3   So that the race which was to come
     might learn and know them well;
     and generations yet unborn
     might their own children tell:

Music Melody from *Scottish Psalter,* 1635
harmonised Compilers of *English Hymnal,* 1906

4   That they might set their hope in God,
      and not forget his ways,
      but hold in mind his mighty works
      and keep his laws always.

Psalm 78, verses 4b–7
The Scottish Psalter, 1929

1

ST BEES   77 77

PSALM 80

1   God of hosts, you chose a vine
      meant to bear the finest wine,
      set it in a promised land,
      nurtured by your careful hand.

2   Like a cedar, it grew strong,
      deep its roots, its tendrils long;
      yet, in envy, those around
      stripped its branches to the ground.

3   Desolate, to God we cry:
      'Spare us from the enemy!'
      God of hosts, turn back again,
      all such wickedness restrain.

4   Turn us too, for we have failed,
      faithfulness has not prevailed;
      visit, Lord, and heal your vine,
      on its fruit let glory shine!

from Psalm 80, verses 7–10, 14–15
David Mowbray (*b.* 1938)

Music John Bacchus Dykes (1823–1876)

HARINGTON (RETIREMENT)   CM

PSALM 84

1   How lovely is thy dwelling-place,
     O Lord of hosts, to me!
     The tabernacles of thy grace,
     how pleasant, Lord, they be!

2   My thirsty soul longs vehemently,
     yea faints, thy courts to see:
     my very heart and flesh cry out,
     O living God, for thee.

3   Behold, the sparrow findeth out
     an house wherein to rest;
     the swallow also for herself
     hath found her place to nest;

4   Even thine own altars, where she safe
     her young ones forth may bring,
     O thou almighty Lord of hosts,
     who art my God and King.

5   Blest are they in thy house who dwell,
     they ever give thee praise.
     And blest are they whose strength thou art,
     in whose heart are thy ways.

                              Psalm 84, verses 1-5
                              The Scottish Psalter, 1929

Music Melody and bass by Henry Harington (1727–1816)

ST STEPHEN (NEWINGTON)   CM

PSALM 89

1   Oh, greatly blest the people are
     the joyful sound that know;
     in brightness of thy face, O Lord,
     they ever on shall go.

2   They in thy name shall all the day
     rejoice exceedingly;
     and in thy righteousness shall they
     exalted be on high.

3   For God is our defence; and he
     to us doth safety bring:
     the Holy One of Israel
     is our almighty King.

> Psalm 89, verses 15, 16, 18
> *The Scottish Psalter,* 1929

Music
Melody and most of the harmony by William Jones (1726–1800)

ATHCHUINGE   LM

PSALM 90

1   Lord, you have always been our home
       through every generation known;
       before the hills or earth were made
       you are the eternal God alone.

2   From dust we came, to dust return,
       for in your clear eternal sight
       a thousand years pass as a day
       or as a few hours in the night.

3   Our lives like grass spring from the ground
       and flourish in the morning sun;
       then evening comes, and brightness fades
       and we and all our strength are done.

4   Teach us to value life's brief span,
       and let our minds be truly wise.
       'How long, O Lord, till you return?'
       In mercy hear your servants' cries.

5   At each day's dawning, make us glad;
       fill us with your love all our days;
       and we will sing aloud for joy
       and offer you our lifelong praise.

Psalm 90, verses 1-6, 12-14
Compilers

Music Tune 1 John MacDonald *Còisir a' Mhòid–3,* 1931

SOLDAU (PAVIA)   LM

PSALM 90

1   Lord, you have always been our home
through every generation known;
before the hills or earth were made
you are the eternal God alone.

2   From dust we came, to dust return,
for in your clear eternal sight
a thousand years pass as a day
or as a few hours in the night.

3   Our lives like grass spring from the ground
and flourish in the morning sun;
then evening comes, and brightness fades
and we and all our strength are done.

4   Teach us to value life's brief span,
and let our minds be truly wise.
'How long, O Lord, till you return?'
In mercy hear your servants' cries.

5   At each day's dawning, make us glad;
fill us with your love all our days;
and we will sing aloud for joy
and offer you our lifelong praise.

Psalm 90, verses 1-6, 12-14
Compilers

Music Tune 2 Melody from *Geystliche gesangk Buchleyn,*
Wittenberge, 1524, as in *An Laoidheadair,* 1935
arranged Compilers

CREATOR GOD

PSALM 91

1   Safe in the shadow of the Lord
    beneath his hand and power,
        I trust in him,
        I trust in him,
    my fortress and my tower.

2   My hope is set on God alone
    though Satan spreads his snare;
        I trust in him,
        I trust in him,
    to keep me in his care.

3   From fears and phantoms of the night,
    from foes about my way,
        I trust in him,
        I trust in him,
    by darkness as by day.

4   His holy angels keep my feet
    secure from every stone;
        I trust in him,
        I trust in him,
    and unafraid go on.

5   Strong in the everlasting name,
    and in my Father's care,
        I trust in him,
        I trust in him
    who hears and answers prayer.

Music Norman Warren (*b.* 1934)
harmonised Compilers of *Common Ground,* 1998

6 Safe in the shadow of the Lord,
   possessed by love divine,
       I trust in him,
       I trust in him,
   and meet his love with mine.

based on Psalm 91
Timothy Dudley-Smith (b. 1926)

6

ST FULBERT   CM

PSALM 92

1 How good it is to thank you, Lord,
   proclaim your name, most High;
   to praise your faithfulness at dawn,
   your love when night is nigh;

2 And on a ten-stringed instrument,
   and with a harp's sweet sound,
   and with the music of the lute
   to make your praise abound.

3 For all your actions make me glad,
   your works inspire my praise:
   I sing for joy with my whole heart
   today, and all my days.

Psalm 92, verses 1-4
Compilers

Music Henry John Gauntlett (1805–1876)

STROUDWATER

CM

PSALM 93

1   The Lord doth reign, and clothed is he
    with majesty most bright;
    his works do show him clothed to be,
    and girt about with might.

2   The world is also stablishèd,
    that it cannot depart,
    thy throne is fixed of old, and thou
    from everlasting art.

3   The floods, O Lord, have lifted up,
    they lifted up their voice;
    the floods have lifted up their waves,
    and made a mighty noise.

4   But yet the Lord, that is on high,
    is more of might by far
    than noise of many waters is,
    or great sea-billows are.

5   Thy testimonies every one
    in faithfulness excel;
    and holiness for ever, Lord,
    thine house becometh well.

Psalm 93, *The Scottish Psalter*, 1929

Music The Psalter in Metre 1899, from William Anchors,
A Choice Collection of Psalm-Tunes..., c. 1721

PSALM 95
Venite, exultemus

1 O come, let us ' sing unto • the' Lord: ‖
let us heartily rejoice in the ' strength of ' our sal'vation.

2 Let us come before his ' presence • with ' thanksgiving: ‖
and show ourselves ' glad in ' him with ' psalms.

3 For the Lord is a ' great ' God: ‖
and a great ' King a'bove all ' gods.

4 In his hand are all the ' corners • of the ' earth: ‖
and the strength of the ' hills is ' his ' also.

5 The sea is ' his and • he ' made it: ‖
and his hands pre'pared the ' dry ' land.

6 O come, let us ' worship and • fall ' down: ‖
and ' kneel be•fore the ' Lord our ' Maker:

7 For he is our God and ' we are • his ' people: ‖
he is our ' shepherd • and ' we are • his ' flock.

(Glory ' be • to the ' Father: ‖
and to the Son ' and to • the ' Holy ' Ghost;

as it ' was in • the be'ginning: ‖
is now and ever shall be, ' world with•out ' end. A'men.)

Psalm 95, verses 1-7, *The Book of Common Prayer*

Music George Alexander Macfarren (1813–1887)

IRISH   CM

PSALM 95

1   Oh, come, and let us to the Lord
in songs our voices raise,
with joyful noise let us the Rock
of our salvation praise.

2   Let us before his presence come
with praise and thankful voice;
let us sing psalms to him with grace,
and make a joyful noise:

3   For God, a great God, and great King,
above all gods he is.
Depths of the earth are in his hand,
the strength of hills is his.

4   To him the spacious sea belongs,
for he the same did make;
the dry land also from his hands
its form at first did take.

5   Oh, come, and let us worship him,
let us bow down withal,
and on our knees before the Lord
our Maker let us fall.

Psalm 95, verses 1-6
verse 1: *The Irish Presbyterian Psalter*
verses 2-6: *The Scottish Psalter,* 1929

Music
Melody from *A Collection of Hymns and Sacred Poems*, Dublin, 1749
harmonised Compilers of *English Hymnal,* 1906

BON ACCORD   CM extended

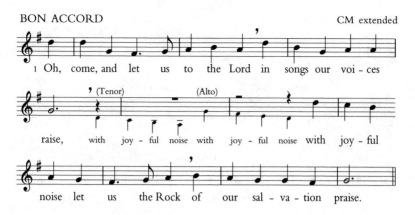

1 Oh, come, and let us to the Lord in songs our voi - ces
raise, with joy - ful noise with joy - ful noise with joy - ful
noise let us the Rock of our sal - va - tion praise.

PSALM 95

1   Oh, come, and let us to the Lord
     in songs our voices raise,
     with joyful noise let us the Rock
     of our salvation praise.

2   Let us before his presence come
     with praise and thankful voice;
     let us sing psalms to him with grace,
     and make a joyful noise:

3   For God, a great God, and great King,
     above all gods he is.
     Depths of the earth are in his hand,
     the strength of hills is his.

4   To him the spacious sea belongs,
     for he the same did make;
     the dry land also from his hands
     its form at first did take.

5   Oh, come, and let us worship him,
     let us bow down withal,
     and on our knees before the Lord
     our Maker let us fall.

Psalm 95, verses 1-6
verse 1: *The Irish Presbyterian Psalter*
verses 2-6: *The Scottish Psalter,* 1929

Music Scottish Psalter, 1625

CHILEAN VENITE

66 66 44 44

1 Come, let us praise the Lord, with joy our God ac - claim, his great-ness tell a - broad and bless his sav - ing name.

Lift high your songs be - fore his throne to whom a - lone all praise be - longs.

Music Chilean folk melody
arranged Michael Robertson Paget (1936–1994)

PSALM 95

1   Come, let us praise the Lord,
      with joy our God acclaim,
his greatness tell abroad
    and bless his saving name.
      Lift high your songs
        before his throne
        to whom alone
      all praise belongs.

2   Our God of matchless worth,
      our King beyond compare,
the deepest bounds of earth,
    the hills, are in his care.
      He all decrees,
        who by his hand
        prepared the land
      and formed the seas.

3   In worship bow the knee,
      our glorious God confess;
the great Creator, he,
    the Lord our righteousness.
      He reigns unseen:
        his flock he feeds
        and gently leads
      in pastures green.

4   Come, hear his voice today,
      receive what love imparts;
his holy will obey
    and harden not your hearts.
      His ways are best;
        and lead at last,
        all troubles past,
      to perfect rest.

based on Psalm 95
Timothy Dudley-Smith (b. 1926)

ST MAGNUS (NOTTINGHAM)

CM

PSALM 98

1   Oh, sing a new song to the Lord,
     for wonders he has done;
     with his right hand and holy arm
     the vict'ry he has won.

2   The Lord has made this triumph known,
     displayed his saving might;
     he has revealed his righteousness
     in every nation's sight.

3   He mindful of his grace and truth
     to Israel's house has been;
     the saving power of God our Lord
     earth's farthest ends have seen.

4   Earth, shout aloud to God the Lord
     and make a joyful noise;
     break into song and celebrate,
     sing praises and rejoice.

5   Sing to the Lord with sound of harp,
     let harp and voices ring;
     with blare of trumpets, blast of horn,
     acclaim the Lord, the King.

6   Let seas, and all within them, roar,
     the world, and dwellers there;
     let streams clap hands, and mountains sing —
     as one their joy declare.

7   Let these all sing before the Lord
     who comes earth's judge to be;
     he'll judge the world with righteousness,
     its folk with equity.

Psalm 98
*The Scottish Psalter, 1929

Music Melody and bass slightly altered from
Jeremiah Clarke (*c.*1673–1707)

ONSLOW SQUARE

7 7 11 8

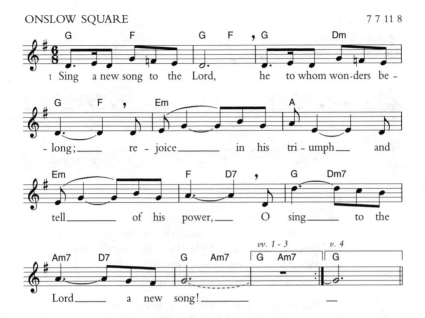

1 Sing a new song to the Lord, he to whom won-ders be-long;____ re-joice____ in his tri-umph__ and tell____ of his power,__ O sing____ to the Lord____ a new song!____

PSALM 98

1   Sing a new song to the Lord,
        he to whom wonders belong;
      rejoice in his triumph and tell of his power,
        O sing to the Lord a new song!

2   Now to the ends of the earth
        see his salvation is shown;
      and still he remembers his mercy and truth,
        unchanging in love to his own.

3   Sing a new song and rejoice,
        publish his praises abroad;
      let voices in chorus, with trumpet and horn,
        resound for the joy of the Lord!

4   Join with the hills and the sea
        thunders of praise to prolong;
      in judgement and justice he comes to the earth,
        O sing to the Lord a new song!

based on Psalm 98
Timothy Dudley-Smith (b. 1926)

Music David Gordon Wilson (b. 1940)

OLD 100TH LM

PSALM 100

1   All people that on earth do dwell,
sing to the Lord with cheerful voice.
Him serve with mirth, his praise forth tell,
come ye before him and rejoice.

2   Know that the Lord is God indeed;
without our aid he did us make;
we are his folk, he doth us feed,
and for his sheep he doth us take.

3   Oh, enter then his gates with praise,
approach with joy his courts unto:
praise, laud, and bless his name always,
for it is seemly so to do.

4   For why? the Lord our God is good,
his mercy is for ever sure;
his truth at all times firmly stood,
and shall from age to age endure.

Psalm 100
The Scottish Psalter, 1929

Music   Melody from *Genevan Psalter,* 1551

CHRISTE SANCTORUM

11 11 11 5

Unison

A higher setting is found at 135.

PSALM 100

1   Sing all creation, sing to God in gladness;
joyously serve him, singing hymns of homage,
chanting his praises, come before his presence:
praise the Almighty!

2   Know that our God is Lord of all the ages;
he is our maker: we are all his creatures,
people he fashioned, sheep he leads to pasture:
praise the Almighty!

3   Enter his temple, ringing out his praises;
sing in thanksgiving as you come before him;
blessing his bounty, glorify his greatness:
praise the Almighty!

4   Great in his goodness is the Lord we worship;
steadfast his kindness, love that knows no ending;
faithful his word is, changeless, everlasting:
praise the Almighty!

Psalm 100
James Quinn (*b.* 1919)

Music Melody from *Paris Antiphoner,* 1681
harmonised David Evans (1874–1948)

JUBILATE DEO Irregular

Ju - bi - la - te, ev - ery - bo - dy, serve the Lord in_ all your ways, and

come before his presence singing, enter now his_ courts with praise.

For the Lord our God is gra - cious, and his mer - cy ev - er - last - ing.

Ju - bi - la - te, ju - bi - la - te, ju - bi - la - te De - o!

PSALM 100

Jubilate, everybody,
serve the Lord in all your ways,
and come before his presence singing,
enter now his courts with praise.
For the Lord our God is gracious,
and his mercy everlasting.
Jubilate, jubilate,
jubilate Deo!

Psalm 100, verses 4, 5a
Fred Dunn (1907–1979)

Music Fred Dunn (1907–1979)

INTERCESSOR

11 10 11 10

PSALM 102

1   Lord, hear my prayer! My cry shall come before you:
    hide not your face when I am in distress.
    My life burns up; my days have lost their glory,
    drifting like smoke, in pain and helplessness.

2   Like some wild owl among deserted ruins,
    lonely I call while enemies curse on.
    Tears are my drink; God's wrath is my undoing;
    ashes my food till all my days are gone.

3   But you, O Lord, remain enthroned for ever;
    you will arise; in you shall kingdoms trust.
    Now is the time; your city pleads your favour,
    your servants love her stones, her very dust.

4   God will rebuild! Write this to sing tomorrow;
    lips yet unformed their hallelujahs cry!
    Glory will dawn upon our world of sorrow,
    freeing from prison those condemned to die.

5   Then shall your name on Zion's hill be spoken;
    strangers shall fill Jerusalem with praise.
    But as for me, my strength is bruised and broken;
    spare me, O God; do not cut short my days!

6   The heavens and earth you formed in the beginning;
    these soon wear out — Lord, you remain the same!
    They shall be changed; your years endure unending;
    our children's children live to praise your name.

Psalm 102, *Praise Trust* version
Christopher Martin Idle (*b.* 1938)

Music Charles Hubert Hastings Parry (1848–1918)

IN DIR IST FREUDE

10 10 10 10 and refrain

PSALM 102

Let all the peoples praise you, O Lord,
let all the peoples praise you;
let all the peoples praise you, O Lord,
let all the peoples praise you.

1   Nations and rulers shall one day revere
    God's holy name and God's marvellous glory,
    when the Lord comes to build Zion again,
    showing his majesty. Alleluia.

2   For generations as yet to be born
    write this, that they may in turn praise the Lord:
    God who surveys the earth from highest heaven
    shall set the captives free. Alleluia.

3   Zion shall hear the Lord proudly declared;
    God's praise shall sound in Jerusalem's soul;
    kingdoms and peoples shall one day unite,
    serving the Lord their God. Alleluia.

The verses may be sung by a cantor, small group or choir.

Psalm 102, verses 15-16, 18-22
Antiphon Psalm 67, verse 5
Compilers

Music Giovanni Gastoldi *A lieta vita,* 1591
adapted Johann Sebastian Bach (1685–1750)
arranged Compilers

COLESHILL   CM

PSALM 103

1   O thou my soul, bless God the Lord;
and all that in me is
be stirrèd up his holy name
to magnify and bless.

2   Bless, O my soul, the Lord thy God,
and not forgetful be
of all his gracious benefits
he hath bestowed on thee.

3   All thine iniquities who doth
most graciously forgive:
who thy diseases all and pains
doth heal, and thee relieve.

4   Who doth redeem thy life, that thou
to death mayest not go down;
who thee with loving-kindness doth
and tender mercies crown:

5   Who with abundance of good things
doth satisfy thy mouth;
so that even as the eagle's age,
renewèd is thy youth.

Psalm 103, verses 1–5
The Scottish Psalter, 1929

Music Melody and bass from William Barton's
The Psalms of David in Metre, Dublin, 1706

KILMARNOCK   CM

A higher setting is found at 482(1).

PSALM 103

1   Just as a father shows his love
to all his children dear,
so God bestows his love on those
who worship him in fear.

2   For God knows well how we were made,
remembers we're but clay;
our days, like grass, pass quickly by,
a flower that fades away.

3   A wind blows, and the flower is gone,
its place is known no more;
but all the kindness of the Lord
for ever shall endure.

4   From age to age God's love shall last
for those who do his will;
and righteousness he will extend
to children's children still.

Psalm 103, verses 13-17
Compilers

Music Melody, and most of the harmony, by Neill Dougall
(1776–1862) from Clarke's *Parochial Psalmody,* 2nd edition, 1831

DUNFERMLINE CM

PSALM 106

1   Give praise and thanks unto the Lord,
for bountiful is he;
his tender mercy doth endure
unto eternity.

2   God's mighty works who can express?
or show forth all his praise?
Blessèd are they that judgment keep,
and justly do always.

3   Remember me, Lord, with that love
which thou to thine dost bear;
with thy salvation, O my God,
to visit me draw near:

4   That I thy chosen's good may see,
and in their joy rejoice;
and may with thine inheritance
triumph with cheerful voice.

5   Blest be Jehovah, Israel's God,
to all eternity:
let all the people say, Amen.
Praise to the Lord give ye.

Psalm 106, verses 1-5, 48
The Scottish Psalter, 1929

Music Melody from *Scottish Psalter,* 1615
harmonised David Evans (1874–1948)

WATSON   DCM

Give thanks un-to the_ Lord our God. How good and kind is_

he_____ whose ten-der mer - cy shall en-dure through

all e-ter - -ni-ty. Let God's re-deemed_ re-

-peat these words   and   give him thanks and_   praise____   who

res-cued them from   hos-tile hands, pre-served them all   their   days.

PSALM 107

1   Give thanks unto the Lord our God.
How good and kind is he
whose tender mercy shall endure
through all eternity.
Let God's redeemed repeat these words
and give him thanks and praise
who rescued them from hostile hands,
preserved them all their days.

2   He gathered them from out the lands,
from north, south, east, and west.
They strayed in desert's pathless way,
no city found to rest.
Their weary soul within them faints
when thirst and hunger press;
in trouble then they cried to God;
he saved them from distress.

Music Merla Watson

71 Music: © Catacombs Productions Ltd. Administered by CopyCare Ltd, PO Box 77, Hailsham, East Sussex, BN27 3EF, United
Kingdom. <music@copycare.com> Used by permission.

3   He made the way before them straight,
    and he became their guide,
    that they might to a city go
    wherein they might abide.
    Let all the children of the Lord
    now praise him for his grace,
    and for his works of wonder done
    in every time and place!

Psalm 107, verses 1–8
*The Scottish Psalter, 1929

PSALM 111

1   Alleluia.
    I will give thanks to the Lord with my whole heart,
    in the company of the faithful and in the congregation.

2   The works of the Lord are great,
    sought out by all who delight in them.

3   His work is full of majesty and honour
    and his righteousness endures for ever.

4   He appointed a memorial for his marvellous deeds;
    the Lord is gracious and full of compassion.

5   He gave food to those who feared him;
    he is ever mindful of his covenant.

6   He showed his people the power of his works
    in giving them the heritage of the nations.

7   The works of his hands are truth and justice;
    all his commandments are sure.

8   They stand fast for ever and ever;
    they are done in truth and equity.

9   He sent redemption to his people;
    he commanded his covenant for ever;
    holy and awesome is his name.

10   The fear of the Lord is the beginning of wisdom;
    a good understanding have those who live by it;
    his praise endures for ever.

Common Worship, 2000

CHARTRES   87 87 D

PSALM 113

1   Bless the Lord, O saints and servants,
        praise the might of God's great name;
        ageless, matchless, filled with wonder,
        yesterday, today, the same.
        When the dawn receives the sunrise
        till the night returns its rays,
        shall the glory of God's goodness
        be the theme of all our praise.

2   Who in heaven can be God's equal,
        who on earth with God compare?
        Who can raise the poor from ashes,
        lift the needy from despair?
        God alone invites the helpless
        with the strong to share reward;
        barren women he makes fruitful —
        happy mothers!   Praise the Lord!

Psalm 113

Music Old French carol *arranged* John L. Bell (*b.* 1949)

74

LUX EOI   87 87 D

PSALM 115

1 Not to us be glory given
   but to him who reigns above:
Glory to the God of heaven
   for his faithfulness and love!
What though unbelieving voices
   hear no word and see no sign,
still in God my heart rejoices,
   working out his will divine.

2 Not what human fingers fashion,
   gold and silver, deaf and blind,
dead to knowledge and compassion,
   having neither heart nor mind,
lifeless gods, yet some adore them,
   nerveless hands and feet of clay;
all become, who bow before them,
   lost indeed and dead as they.

3 Not in them is hope of blessing,
   hope is in the living Lord:
high and low, his Name confessing,
   find in him their shield and sword.
Hope of all whose hearts revere him,
   God of Israel, still the same!
God of Aaron! Those who fear him,
   he remembers them by name.

4 Not the dead, but we the living
   praise the Lord with all our powers;
of his goodness freely giving,
   his is heaven; earth is ours.
Not to us be glory given
   but to him who reigns above:
Glory to the God of heaven
   for his faithfulness and love!

Psalm 115
Timothy Dudley-Smith (*b.* 1926)

Music Arthur Seymour Sullivan (1842–1900)

ST FLAVIAN (OLD 132nd)   CM

PSALM 116

1   I love the Lord, because he heard
     my voice and earnest plea;
     and while I live I'll call on him
     who turned his ear to me.

2   The snares of death encompassed me,
     hell had me in its grasp;
     by grief and sorrow I was held,
     no comfort could I clasp.

3   I called upon the name of God,
     I called, and called again,
     'Deliver now my soul, O Lord,
     deliver me from pain.'

4   The Lord is gracious. God is good
     and shows unfailing care.
     God saves the meek: I was brought low;
     he raised me from despair.

5   Be still, my soul, be calm again,
     resume your quiet rest;
     for God has kindly dealt with you,
     his generous love expressed.

Psalm 116, verses 1-7
*The Scottish Psalter, 1929

Music Adapted from first half of melody for Psalm 132
in *The English Psalter,* 1562

JACKSON (BYZANTIUM)   CM

PSALM 116

1   How can I ever thank the Lord
    for all his gifts to me?
    I'll raise salvation's cup, and call
    on God's name joyfully.

2   I'll bring you offerings of thanks,
    call on the name of God;
    fulfil my promises among
    the people of the Lord.

3   I'll pay my vows in God's own house,
    the temple of the Lord,
    there in your midst, Jerusalem.
    Praise God with one accord!

Psalm 116, verses 12, 14, 17-19
*The Scottish Psalter, 1929

Music
Melody in *Twelve Psalm Tunes,* 1780 by Thomas Jackson (1715–1781)
harmonised David Evans (1874–1948)

77

LAUDATE DOMINUM (Berthier)

Antiphon

Lau - da - te Do - mi - num, lau - da - te Do - mi - num, om - nes

gen - tes, al - le - lu - ia! al - le - lu - ia!

1 Praise the Lord, all you na - tions, praise God, all you peo - ples.

Al - le - lu - ia. Strong is God's love and mer - cy,

God is faith - ful for ev - er. Al - le - lu - ia!

2 Al - le - lu - ia, al - le - lu - ia — let ev - ery - thing

liv - ing give praise to the Lord! Al - le - praise to the Lord!

Music Jacques Berthier (1923–1994)

PSALM 117

Laudate Dominum,
laudate Dominum,
omnes gentes, alleluia!
Alleluia!

1   Praise the Lord, all you nations,
praise God, all you peoples.
Alleluia.
Strong is God's love and mercy,
God is faithful for ever.
Alleluia!

2   Alleluia, alleluia —
let everything living
give praise to the Lord!
Alleluia, alleluia —
let everything living
give praise to the Lord!

The Antiphon is repeated as an ostinato
while the verses are being sung.

Psalm 117

SOUTHWARK   CM

PSALM 118

1   Oh, set ye open unto me
the gates of righteousness;
then will I enter into them,
and I the Lord will bless.

2   This is the gate of God, by it
the just shall enter in.
Thee will I praise, who answered me
and hast my safety been.

3   That stone is made head corner-stone,
which builders did despise:
this is the doing of the Lord,
and wondrous in our eyes.

4   This is the day God made, in it
we'll joy triumphantly.
Save now, I pray thee, Lord; I pray,
send now prosperity.

5   Thou art my God, I'll thee exalt;
my God, I will thee praise.
Give thanks to God, for he is good:
his mercy lasts always.

Psalm 118, verses 19-25, 28, 29
The Scottish Psalter, 1929

Music Adapted from Chapter 8 of *The Actes of the Apostles,* 1553 by Christopher Tye (*c.*1505–?1573)

YORK (STILT)   CM

PSALM 119

1 Teach me, O Lord, the perfect way
  of thy precepts divine,
  and to observe it to the end
  I shall my heart incline.

2 Give understanding unto me,
  so keep thy law shall I;
  yea, even with my whole heart I shall
  observe it carefully.

3 In thy law's path make me to go;
  for I delight therein.
  My heart unto thy gracious word,
  and not to greed, incline.

4 Turn thou away my sight and eyes
  from viewing vanity;
  and in thy good and holy way
  be pleased to quicken me.

5 Confirm to me thy gracious word,
  which I did gladly hear,
  even to thy servant, Lord, for I
  thy holy name revere.

6 Turn thou away my feared reproach;
  for good thy judgments be.
  Lo, for thy precepts I have longed;
  in thy truth quicken me.

Psalm 119, verses 33-40
The Scottish Psalter, 1929

Music Melody from *Scottish Psalter,* 1615
arranged John Milton, *the elder* (*c.* 1563–1647)

PSALM 119

1   Blessed are those whose way is pure,
who walk in the law of the Lord.

2   Blessed are those who keep his testimonies
and seek him with their whole heart,

3   Those who do no wickedness,
but walk in his ways.

4   You, O Lord, have charged
that we should diligently keep your commandments.

5   O that my ways were made so direct
that I might keep your statutes.

6   Then should I not be put to shame,
because I have regard for all your commandments.

7   I will thank you with an unfeigned heart,
when I have learned your righteous judgements.

8   I will keep your statutes;
O forsake me not utterly.

97   Lord, how I love your law!
All the day long it is my study.

98   Your commandments have made me wiser
      than my enemies,
for they are ever with me.

99   I have more understanding than all my teachers,
for your testimonies are my meditation.

100   I am wiser than the aged,
because I keep your commandments.

101   I restrain my feet from every evil way,
that I may keep your word.

102   I have not turned aside from your judgements,
for you have been my teacher.

103   How sweet are your words on my tongue!
They are sweeter than honey to my mouth.

104   Through your commandments I get understanding;
therefore I hate all lying ways.

105 Your word is a lantern to my feet
and a light upon my path.

106 I have sworn and will fulfil it,
to keep your righteous judgements.

107 I am troubled above measure;
give me life, O Lord, according to your word.

108 Accept the freewill offering of my mouth, O Lord,
and teach me your judgements.

109 My soul is ever in my hand,
yet I do not forget your law.

110 The wicked have laid a snare for me,
but I have not strayed from your commandments.

111 Your testimonies have I claimed as my heritage
for ever;
for they are the very joy of my heart.

112 I have applied my heart to fulfil your statutes:
always, even to the end.

137 Righteous are you, O Lord,
and true are your judgements.

138 You have ordered your decrees in righteousness
and in great faithfulness.

139 My indignation destroys me,
because my adversaries forget your word.

140 Your word has been tried to the uttermost
and so your servant loves it.

141 I am small and of no reputation,
yet do I not forget your commandments.

142 Your righteousness is an everlasting righteousness
and your law is the truth.

143 Trouble and heaviness have taken hold upon me,
yet my delight is in your commandments.

144 The righteousness of your testimonies is everlasting;
O grant me understanding and I shall live.

Psalm 119, verses 1–8, 97–112, 137–144
Common Worship, 2000

FRENCH (DUNDEE)   CM

FRENCH (DUNDEE)   CM

PSALM 121

1   I to the hills will lift mine eyes.
From whence doth come mine aid?
My safety cometh from the Lord,
who heaven and earth hath made.

2   Thy foot he'll not let slide, nor will
he slumber that thee keeps.
Behold, he that keeps Israel,
he slumbers not, nor sleeps.

3   The Lord thee keeps, the Lord thy shade
on thy right hand doth stay:
the moon by night thee shall not smite,
nor yet the sun by day.

4   The Lord shall keep thy soul; he shall
preserve thee from all ill.
Henceforth thy going out and in
God keep for ever will.

Psalm 121,
The Scottish Psalter, 1929

Music Tune 1 Melody from *Scottish Psalter,* 1615

Music Tune 2 Scottish Psalter, 1625, *edited* Gordon J. Munro (b. 1972)

ST PAUL (ABERDEEN)   CM

PSALM 122

1   Pray that Jerusalem may have
     peace and felicity:
     let them that love you and your peace
     still have prosperity.

2   Therefore I wish that peace may still
     within your walls remain,
     and ever may your palaces
     prosperity retain.

3   Now, for my friends' and family's sakes,
     peace be in you, I'll say.
     And for the house of God our Lord,
     I'll seek your good alway.

Psalm 122, verses 6-9,
The Scottish Psalter, 1929

Music Collection printed by James Chalmers, Aberdeen c.1749
possibly by Andrew Tait (*fl.* 1749) *harmonised* David Evans (1874–1948)

1 I re-joiced when I heard them say: 'Let us go to the house of God.' And now our feet are standing in your gates, O Je-ru-sa-lem!

Antiphon

Sha-lom, sha-lom, the peace of God be here. Sha-lom, sha-lom,___ God's jus-tice be ev-er near. 2 Like a near.

Music Bernadette Farrell (b. 1957)

PSALM 122

1   I rejoiced when I heard them say:
'Let us go to the house of God.'
And now our feet are standing
in your gates, O Jerusalem!
    Shalom, shalom,
    the peace of God be here.
    Shalom, shalom,
    God's justice be ever near.

2   Like a temple of unity
is the city, Jerusalem.
It is there all tribes will gather,
all the tribes of the house of God.

3   It is faithful to Israel's law,
there to praise the name of God.
All the judgement seats of David
were set down in Jerusalem.

4   For the peace of all nations, pray:
for God's peace within your homes.
May God's lasting peace surround us;
may it dwell in Jerusalem.

5   For the love of my friends and kin
I will bless you with signs of peace.
For the love of God's own people
I will labour and pray for you.

Psalm 122
Bernadette Farrell (*b.*1957)

OLD 124TH   10 10 10 10 10

PSALM 124

1   Now Israel may say, and that truly,
        if that the Lord had not our cause maintained;
        if that the Lord had not our right sustained,
        when cruel men against us furiously
        rose up in wrath, to make of us their prey;

2   Then certainly they had devoured us all,
        and swallowed quick, for aught that we could deem;
        such was their rage, as we might well esteem.
        And as fierce floods before them all things drown,
        so had they brought our soul to death quite down.

3   The raging streams, with their proud swelling waves,
        had then our soul o'erwhelmèd in the deep.
        But blest be God, who doth us safely keep,
        and hath not given us for a living prey
        unto their teeth, and bloody cruelty.

4   Even as a bird out of the fowler's snare
        escapes away, so is our soul set free:
        broke are their nets, and thus escapèd we.
        Therefore our help is in the Lord's great name,
        who heaven and earth by his great power did frame.

Psalm 124 (ii)
The Scottish Psalter, 1929

Music Genevan Psalter, 1551
harmonised Compilers of *Church Hymnary,* 3rd edition, 1973

PSALM 124

1   Now let God's people, let God's Israel
witness the truth and gratefully proclaim:
when evil folk against us made their claim,
we would have drowned beneath their violent tide
if God the Lord had not been on our side.

2   If God the Lord had not been on our side,
and thus maintained the justice of our cause,
we would have died, devoured by evil jaws,
where kindled anger lusted after blood
while vicious torrents raged beneath the flood.

3   Blest be the Lord both now and evermore
who did not grieve us on the evil day,
who did not leave us as an easy prey
destined to be so mercilessly torn
by savage teeth and unrelenting scorn.

4   Just as a bird escapes the fowler's snare,
we leave our broken trap and are set free.
Now we are saved and now, as one, agree
our help is in the name of God our Lord,
maker of heaven and earth, eternal Word.

Psalm 124
John L. Bell (*b.* 1949)

EDGBASTON   86 86

PSALM 126

1   When Zion's fortunes God restored,
it was a dream come true.
Our mouths were then with laughter filled,
our tongues with songs anew.

2   Then nations said, 'The Lord has done
great things for Israel.'
The Lord did mighty things for us,
and joy our hearts knew well.

3   Restore our fortunes, gracious Lord,
like streams in desert soil.
A joyful harvest will reward
the weeping sower's toil.

4   All those who, bearing seed to sow,
go out with tears of grief,
will come again with songs of joy,
bearing their harvest sheaf.

Psalm 126, Compilers

Music John Joubert (*b.* 1927)

MARTYRDOM (FENWICK)   CM

PSALM 130

1   Lord, from the depths to thee I cried.
     My voice, Lord, do thou hear:
     unto my supplication's voice
     give an attentive ear.

2   Lord, who shall stand, if thou, O Lord,
     should'st mark iniquity?
     But yet with thee forgiveness is,
     that feared thou mayest be.

3   I wait for God, my soul doth wait,
     my hope is in his word.
     More than they that for morning watch,
     my soul waits for the Lord;

4   I say, much more than they that watch
     the morning light to see.
     Let Israel hope in God the Lord,
     for with him mercies be;

5   And plenteous redemption
     is ever found with him.
     And from all their iniquities
     he Israel shall redeem.

Psalm 130
*The Scottish Psalter, 1929

Music Hugh Wilson (1766–1824)
adapted Robert Archibald Smith (1780–1829)

MACPHERSON'S RANT   86 86 D (DCM)

1 Up from the depths I cry to God: O listen, Lord, to me; O hear my voice in this distress, this mire of misery. I wait for God with all my heart, my hope is in his word; and more than watchmen for the dawn I'm longing for the Lord.

PSALM 130

1   Up from the depths I cry to God:
     O listen, Lord, to me;
     O hear my voice in this distress,
     this mire of misery.
          I wait for God with all my heart,
          my hope is in his word;
          and more than watchmen for the dawn
          I'm longing for the Lord.

2   If you, my God, should measure guilt
     who then stands free from blame?
     But true forgiveness comes from you;
     we trust, and fear your name.

3   O Israel, set your hope on God,
     whose mercy is supreme:
     the nation mourning for its sin
     he surely will redeem.

                              from Psalm 130
                    Christopher Martin Idle (*b.* 1938)

Music Scottish traditional melody *arranged* David Iliff (*b.* 1939)

THE ISLE OF MULL 10 10 10 10

PSALM 131

1   For you, the pride from my heart is banished;
    for you, false dreams from my eyes have vanished;
    for you, vain glory I leave admiring,
    endless ambition I cease desiring.

2   Now is my soul calm from all its testing,
    like a weaned child on her mother resting.
    May all who hear join such celebrating.
    Wait for the Lord: God is worth our waiting.

Psalm 131
John L. Bell (*b.* 1949)

Music Gaelic folk melody
arranged Hugh S. Roberton (1874–1952)

MIRREN QUÉ BUENO

PSALM 133

How good it is when God's will is done;
sisters and brothers living at one.

1   Good it is and pleasant
when God's people are together,
fragrant as the precious oil
anointing Aaron's head.

2   Good it is and pleasant
when God's people are together:
just like dew on mountain-tops,
they freshen all the earth.

3   When we live in unity
as God's beloved people,
God bestows his blessing
giving life for evermore.

Psalm 133, *Thuma Mina* and Compilers

Music Pablo Sosa (b. 1933) *arranged* Darryl Nixon (b. 1952)

1

Psalm 134

PSALM 134

1   Praise the Lord, all ye servants of the Lord,
who minister by night within his house.
Lift up your hands within the sanctuary,
and praise the Lord.

2   May this Lord, the maker of heaven and earth,
may this Lord bless you from Zion.
Lift up your hands within the sanctuary,
and praise the Lord.

Psalm 134
Ian White (*b.* 1956)

Music Ian White (*b.* 1956)

CROFT'S 136TH   6666 and refrain

PSALM 136

1   Praise God, for he is kind:
     his mercy lasts for aye.
     Give thanks with heart and mind
     to God of gods alway:
         for certainly
         his mercies dure
         most firm and sure
         eternally.

2   The Lord of lords praise ye,
     whose mercies still endure.
     Great wonders only he
     doth work by his great power:

3   Give praise to his great name,
     who, by his wisdom high,
     the heaven above did frame,
     and built the lofty sky:

4   Who hath remembered us
     when in our low estate;
     and hath delivered us
     from foes who did us hate:

5   Who to all flesh gives food;
     for his grace faileth never.
     Give thanks to God most good,
     the God of heaven, for ever:

Psalm 136 (ii), verses 1-5, 23-26
The Scottish Psalter, 1929

Music Melody by William Croft (1678–1727)

3 1

MONKLAND   77 and refrain

Refrain

3 2

HARTS   77 and refrain

Refrain

PSALM 136

1   Let us with a gladsome mind
    praise the Lord, for he is kind:
        For his mercies aye endure,
        ever faithful, ever sure.

2   Let us blaze his name abroad,
    for of gods he is the God:

3   He, with all-commanding might,
    filled the new-made world with light:

4   He his chosen race did bless
    in the wasteful wilderness:

5   All things living he doth feed;
    his full hand supplies their need:

6   Let us then with gladsome mind
    praise the Lord, for he is kind:

                    from Psalm 136
                John Milton (1608–1674)

Music Melody composed or adapted by John Antes (1740–1811)
arranged John Bernard Wilkes (1785–1869)

Music Simplified form of a melody by Benjamin Milgrove
(1731–1810), *arranged* David Evans (1874–1948)

KAS DZIEDAJA 87 87

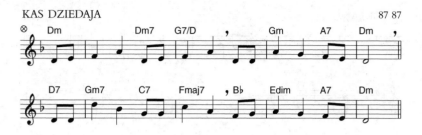

PSALM 137

1 By the Babylonian rivers
we sat down in grief and wept;
hung our harps upon a willow,
mourned for Zion while we slept.

2 There our captors, in derision,
did require of us a song;
so we sat with staring vision
and the days were hard and long.

3 Could we ever sing the Lord's song
in a strange and bitter land;
can our voices veil the sorrow?
Lord God, hear your lonely band.

Psalm 137, verses 1-4
Ewald Joseph Bash (1924–1994)

Music Latvian melody
arranged Geoff Weaver (*b.* 1943)

95

LOBERTS 99 67 9

I shall praise you, O God, from my soul, I shall

praise you, O God, from my soul; though my

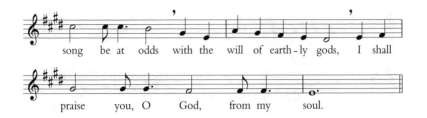

song be at odds with the will of earth-ly gods, I shall

praise you, O God, from my soul.

PSALM 138

1   I shall praise you, O God, from my soul,
I shall praise you, O God, from my soul;
though my song be at odds
with the will of earthly gods,
I shall praise you, O God, from my soul.

2   I shall bow down before heaven's throne,
I shall bow down before heaven's throne;
and with joy I'll confess
your great love and faithfulness.
I shall bow down before heaven's throne.

3   Lord, your promise is raised above heaven,
Lord, your promise is raised above heaven;
you replied to my plea,
giving hope and strength to me.
Lord, your promise is raised above heaven.

4   Let the monarchs of earth know your name,
let the monarchs of earth know your name;
let them learn of your ways
and respond in fear and praise.
Let the monarchs of earth know your name.

5   Though exalted, God cares for the poor,
though exalted, God cares for the poor;
and he notes if the proud
walk the paths he disallowed.
Though exalted, God cares for the poor.

Psalm 138, verses 1–6
John L. Bell (b. 1949)

Music John L. Bell (b. 1949)

SURSUM CORDA   10 10 10 10

PSALM 139

1   You are before me, God, you are behind,
and over me you have spread out your hand;
such knowledge is too wonderful for me,
too high to grasp, too great to understand.

2   Then from your Spirit where, God, shall I go,
and from your presence where, God, shall I fly?
If I ascend to heaven you are there,
and still are with me, if in hell I lie.

3   If I should take my flight into the dawn,
if I should dwell on ocean's farthest shore,
your mighty hand will rest upon me still,
and your right hand will guard me evermore.

4   If I should say, 'Let darkness cover me,
and I shall hide within the veil of night',
surely the darkness is not dark to you,
the night is as the day, the darkness light.

5   Search me, O God, search me and know my heart,
try me, O God, my mind and spirit try;
keep me from any path that gives you pain,
and lead me in the everlasting way.

from Psalm 139
Ian Robertson Pitt-Watson (1923–1995)

Music Alfred Morton Smith (1879–1971)

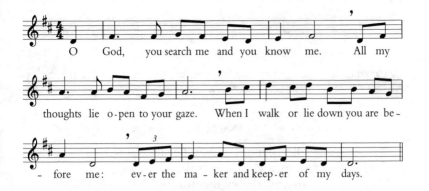

O God, you search me and you know me. All my thoughts lie o-pen to your gaze. When I walk or lie down you are be- fore me: ev-er the ma-ker and keep-er of my days.

PSALM 139

1   O God, you search me and you know me.
     All my thoughts lie open to your gaze.
     When I walk or lie down you are before me:
     ever the maker and keeper of my days.

2   You know my resting and my rising.
     You discern my purpose from afar,
     and with love everlasting you besiege me:
     in every moment of life or death, you are.

3   Before a word is on my tongue, Lord,
     you have known its meaning through and through.
     You are with me beyond my understanding:
     God of my present, my past and future, too.

4   Although your Spirit is upon me,
     still I search for shelter from your light.
     There is nowhere on earth I can escape you:
     even the darkness is radiant in your sight.

5   For you created me and shaped me,
     gave me life within my mother's womb.
     For the wonder of who I am, I praise you:
     safe in your hands, all creation is made new.

from Psalm 139
Bernadette Farrell (b. 1957)

Music Bernadette Farrell (b. 1957)

SALEN   66 66

PSALM 143

1   Oh, hear my prayer, Lord,
    unto me answer make,
    and, in thy righteousness,
    upon me pity take.

2   To thee I stretch my hands
    to thee, my help alone;
    for thou well understands
    all my complaint and moan:

3   My thirsting soul desires,
    and longeth after thee,
    as thirsty ground requires
    with rains refreshed to be.

4   Because I trust in thee,
    O Lord, cause me to hear
    thy loving-kindness free,
    when morning doth appear.

5   Cause me to know the way
    wherein my path should be;
    for why, my soul on high
    I do lift up to thee.

Psalm 143 (ii), verses 1, 6, 8
*The Scottish Psalter, 1929

Music American melody, 18th century
harmonised Compilers

LEONI   6684 D

A lower setting is found at 162.

PSALM 143

1   Oh, hear my prayer, Lord,
    be open to my plea,
    with justice and with faithfulness
    please answer me.
    My spirit shrivels up,
    my heart numbs with despair,
    in awe of your great deeds I raise
    my earnest prayer.

2   I thirst for your response,
    thirst like the desert lands;
    entreating you, my God, I lift
    my outstretched hands.
    Lord, quickly make reply
    and do not hide your face,
    or else my spirit faints from lack
    of your embrace.

3   Because I trust in you
    and offer you my prayer,
    let me, when morning comes, discern
    your loving care.
    My heart is set on you;
    this earnest plea I make,
    that you will show the road my life
    is meant to take.

Psalm 143 (ii), verses 1, 4, 6-8, 10
The Scottish Psalter, 1929

Music Hebrew melody, *arranged* Thomas Olivers (1725–1799)

DUKE STREET   LM

PSALM 145

1   O Lord, thou art my God and King;
    thee will I magnify and praise:
    I will thee bless, and gladly sing
    unto thy holy name always.

2   Each day I rise I will thee bless,
    and praise thy name time without end.
    Much to be praised, and great God is;
    his greatness none can comprehend.

3   Race shall thy works praise unto race,
    the mighty acts show done by thee.
    I will speak of the glorious grace,
    and honour of thy majesty;

4   Thy wondrous works I will record.
    By many shall the might be told
    of all thy awesome acts, O Lord:
    and I thy greatness will unfold.

Psalm 145 (ii), verses 1-6
*The Scottish Psalter, 1929

Music Melody attributed to John L. Hatton (*d.* 1793)
from Boyd's *Psalm and Hymn Tunes,* 1793
harmonised David Evans (1874–1948)

PSALM 145

8   You are kind and full of compassion,
    slow to anger, abounding in love.
9   How good you are, Lord, to all,
    compassionate to all your creatures.

10 All your creatures shall thank you, O Lord,
    and your friends shall repeat their blessing.
11 They shall speak of the glory of your reign
    and declare your might, O God,

12 to make known all your mighty deeds
    and the glorious splendour of your reign.
13 Yours is an everlasting kingdom;
    your rule lasts from age to age.

    You are faithful in all your words
    and loving in all your deeds.
14 You support all who are falling
    and raise up all who are bowed down.

15 The eyes of all creatures look to you
    and you give them their food in due season.
16 You open wide your hand,
    grant the desires of all who live.

17 You are just in all your ways
    and loving in all your deeds.
18 You are close to all who call you,
    who call on you from their hearts.

19 You grant the desires of those who fear you,
    you hear their cry and you save them.
20 Lord, you protect all who love you;
    but the wicked you will utterly destroy.

21 Let me speak your praise, O Lord,
    let people bless your holy name
    for ever, for ages unending.

Psalm 145, verses 8-21
The Grail, Inclusive Language Version, 2004

PSALM 146

1   Alleluia. Praise the Lord, O my soul:
        while I live will I praise the Lord;
    as long as I have any being,
      I will sing praises to my God.

2   Put not your trust in princes,
       nor in any human power,
    for there is no help in them.

3   When their breath goes forth,
       they return to the earth;
    on that day all their thoughts perish.

4   Happy are those who have the
       God of Jacob for their help,
    whose hope is in the Lord their God;

5   Who made heaven and earth,
       the sea and all that is in them;
    who keeps his promise for ever;

6   Who gives justice to those
       that suffer wrong
    and bread to those who hunger.

7   The Lord looses those that are bound;
    the Lord opens the eyes of the blind;

8   The Lord lifts up those
       who are bowed down;
    the Lord loves the righteous;

9   The Lord watches over the stranger
       in the land; he upholds the
       orphan and widow;
    but the way of the wicked
       he turns upside down.

10   The Lord shall reign for ever,
    your God, O Zion,
       throughout all generations. Alleluia.

Psalm 146
Common Worship, 2000

RHUDDLAN   87 87 87

PSALM 147

1   Fill your hearts with joy and gladness,
       sing and praise your God and mine!
   Great the Lord in love and wisdom,
       might and majesty divine!
   He who framed the starry heavens
       knows and names them as they shine.

2   Praise the Lord, his people, praise him!
       Wounded souls his comfort know;
   those who fear him find his mercies,
       peace for pain and joy for woe;
   humble hearts are high exalted,
       human pride and power laid low.

3   Praise the Lord for times and seasons,
       cloud and sunshine, wind and rain;
   spring to melt the snows of winter
       till the waters flow again;
   grass upon the mountain pastures,
       golden valleys thick with grain.

4   Fill your hearts with joy and gladness,
       peace and plenty crown your days;
   love his laws, declare his judgements,
       walk in all his words and ways;
   he the Lord and we his children —
       praise the Lord, all people, praise!

based on Psalm 147
Timothy Dudley-Smith (b. 1926)

Music
Welsh traditional melody in *Musical Relics of Welsh Bards* 1800
harmonised Compilers of *English Hymnal*, 1906

ST JOHN (Havergal)   6666 4444

A lower setting is found at 149.

PSALM 148

1   The Lord of heaven confess,
       on high his glory raise.
       Him let all angels bless,
       him all his armies praise.
          Him glorify
          sun, moon and stars;
          ye higher spheres,
          and cloudy sky.

2   From God your beings are,
       him therefore famous make;
       you all created were,
       when he the word but spake.
          And from that place,
          where fixed you be
          by his decree,
          you cannot pass.

Music The Parish Choir, vol. III, 1851
sometimes attributed to William Henry Havergal (1793–1870)

3   Praise God from earth below,
ye dragons, and ye deeps:
fire, hail, clouds, wind, and snow,
whom in command he keeps.
    Praise ye his name
    hills great and small,
    trees low and tall;
    beasts wild and tame;

4   All things that creep or fly.
Ye kings, ye vulgar throng,
all princes mean or high;
both men and women young,
    even young and old,
    exalt his name;
    for much his fame
    should be extolled.

5   Oh, let God's name be praised
above both earth and sky;
for he his saints hath raised,
and set their horn on high;
    even those that be
    of Israel's race,
    near to his grace.
    The Lord praise ye.

Psalm 148 (ii)
The Scottish Psalter, 1929

WELLINGTON HALL

1 Glo-ry to God___ a-bove! Heavens de-clare___ his love;

praise him, you an-gels, praise him all you high and heaven-ly host.

Wor-ship him, sun___ and moon; stars, com-ple-ment___ their tune;

ground-ed in God's good pur-pose let his grace be-come your

Refrain

boast. O___ sing hal - le - lu-jah and praise God for

vv. 1, 2   v. 3

ev - er - more!___   ev - er, ev - - er - more!

Music John L. Bell (b. 1949)

PSALM 148

1 Glory to God above!
Heavens declare his love;
praise him, you angels,
praise him all you high and heavenly host.
Worship him, sun and moon;
stars, complement their tune;
grounded in God's good purpose
let his grace become your boast.
O sing hallelujah
and praise God for evermore!

2 Glory to God below
let depths of ocean show;
lightning and hail, snow,
wind and cloud perform at his command!
Let every mountain range,
forest and grove and grange,
creatures of earth and air and sea
praise God in every land.

3 'Glory to God!' now sing
commoner, queen, and king;
women and men of every age
unite to praise the Lord.
Worship God's holy name,
and let your lives proclaim
God's saving power extends to those
who love and serve his word.
O sing hallelujah
and praise God for ever, evermore!

Psalm 148
paraphrased John L. Bell (b. 1949)

JERUSALEM

88 88 D (DLM)

1 Bring to the Lord a glad new song, children of grace ex-tol your king; worship and praise to God be-long — to in-stru-ments of mu-sic, sing! Let those be warned who spurn God's name, let ru-lers all o-bey God's word; for jus-tice shall bring ty-rants shame: let ev-ery crea-ture praise the Lord!

2 Sing praise with-in these hal-lowed walls, worship be-neath the dome of heaven; by cym-bals' sounds and trum-pets' calls let prai-ses fit for God be given: with strings and

Music Charles Hubert Hastings Parry (1848–1918)

brass and wind re-joice — then, join our song in full ac-
-cord all li-ving things with breath and voice: let ev-ery
crea-ture praise the Lord!_____

PSALMS 149, 150

1   Bring to the Lord a glad new song,
children of grace extol your king;
worship and praise to God belong —
to instruments of music, sing!
Let those be warned who spurn God's name,
let rulers all obey God's word;
for justice shall bring tyrants shame:
let every creature praise the Lord!

2   Sing praise within these hallowed walls,
worship beneath the dome of heaven;
by cymbals' sounds and trumpets' calls
let praises fit for God be given:
with strings and brass and wind rejoice —
then, join our song in full accord
all living things with breath and voice:
let every creature praise the Lord!

from Psalms 149 and 150
Michael Arnold Perry (1942–1996)

106 Words: © Mrs B. Perry / Jubilate Hymns, 4 Thorne Park Road, Chelston, Torquay TQ2 6RX <enquiries@jubilate.co.uk>
Used by permission.

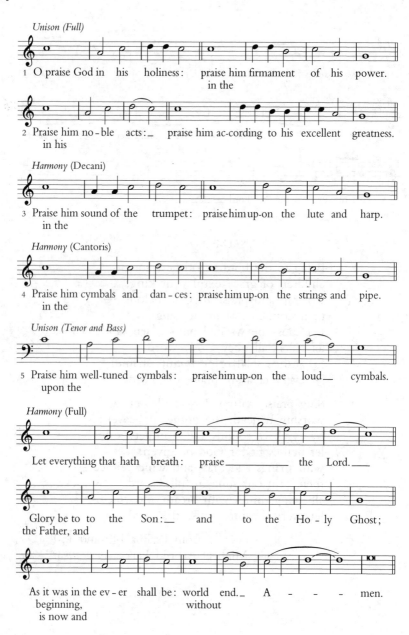

Unison (Full)

1 O praise God in his holiness : praise him firmament of his power.
in the

2 Praise him no - ble acts : _ praise him ac-cording to his excellent greatness.
in his

Harmony (Decani)

3 Praise him sound of the trumpet : praise him up-on the lute and harp.
in the

Harmony (Cantoris)

4 Praise him cymbals and dan - ces : praise him up-on the strings and pipe.
in the

Unison (Tenor and Bass)

5 Praise him well-tuned cymbals : praise him up-on the loud _ cymbals.
upon the

Harmony (Full)

Let everything that hath breath : praise_____ the Lord. _

Glory be to to the Son : _ and to the Ho - ly Ghost ;
the Father, and

As it was in the ev - er shall be : world end. _ A - - - men.
beginning, without
is now and

PSALM 150

1 O praise God in his holiness:
   praise him in the firmament of his power.

2 Praise him in his noble acts:
   praise him according to his excellent greatness.

3 Praise him in the sound of the trumpet:
   praise him upon the lute and harp.

4 Praise him in the cymbals and dances:
   praise him upon the strings and pipe.

5 Praise him upon the well-tuned cymbals:
   praise him upon the loud cymbals.

6 Let everything that hath breath:
   praise the Lord.

Psalm 150
The Book of Common Prayer

Music *Charles Villiers Stanford (1852–1924)

HERR JESU CHRIST, DICH ZU UNS WEND　　　　　　　LM

PSALM 150

1　　Praise God within his holy place,
　　　praise God within the vault of heaven,
　　　for all his deeds and matchless power
　　　let praise to God from earth be given.

2　　Praise God with glorious trumpet blast,
　　　praise God with gentle harp and lutes;
　　　praise God with timbrels and in dance,
　　　with lively strings and soaring flutes.

3　　Praise God with cymbals crashing loud,
　　　praise God with cymbals ringing high;
　　　let every thing that lives and breathes
　　　praise God. Halle, hallelujah!

　　　　　　　　　　　　　　　　Psalm 150
　　　　　　　　　　　　　　　　Compilers

Music Melody from *Gotha Cantional,* 1651
arranged Compilers

109 1

SM
To thee be glory, Lord,
whom heaven and earth adore,
to Father, Son, and Holy Ghost,
one God for evermore.

109 2

CM
To Father, Son, and Holy Ghost,
the God whom we adore,
be glory, as it was, and is,
and shall be evermore.

LM
To Father, Son and Holy Ghost,
the God whom earth and heaven adore,
be glory, as it was of old,
is now, and shall be evermore.

09 4

66 66
Now glory be to God
the Father, and the Son,
and to the Holy Ghost,
all-glorious Three in One.

09 5

66 66 44 44
To God the Father, Son,
and Spirit ever blest,
eternal Three in One,
all worship be addressed,
as heretofore
it was, is now,
and still shall be
for evermore.

09 6

87 87
Glory be to God, the Father;
glory be to God, the Son;
glory be to God, the Spirit;
while eternal ages run.

109 *continued overleaf*

10 10 10 10 10
Glory to God the Father, God the Son,
and unto God the Spirit, Three in One.
From age to age let saints his name adore,
his power and love proclaim from shore to shore,
and spread his fame, till time shall be no more.

109 8

Prose Version
Glory be to the Father:
and to the Son, and to the Holy Ghost.
As it was in the beginning:
is now, and ever shall be,
world without end. Amen.

Prose version, *Book of Common Prayer*

109 9

Prose Version
Glory to the Father, and to the Son, and to the Holy Spirit:
as it was in the beginning, is now, and will be for ever. Amen.

Prose version, ELLC

THE LIVING GOD

THE BEING OF GOD
HOLY AND ONE

REGENT SQUARE   87 87 87

1   Glory be to God the Father,
    glory be to God the Son,
    glory be to God the Spirit, —
    great Jehovah, Three in One!
    Glory, glory, glory, glory
    while eternal ages run!

2   Glory be to him who loved us,
    washed us from each spot and stain!
    Glory be to him who bought us,
    made us kings with him to reign!
    Glory, glory, glory, glory
    to the Lamb that once was slain!

3   Glory to the King of angels,
    glory to the Church's King,
    glory to the King of nations!
    Heaven and earth, your praises bring;
    glory, glory, glory, glory
    to the King of Glory bring!

4   'Glory, blessing, praise eternal!'
    Thus the choir of angels sings;
    'Honour, riches, power, dominion!'
    Thus its praise creation brings;
    glory, glory, glory, glory,
    glory to the King of kings!

                    Horatius N. Bonar (1808–1889)

Music Henry Thomas Smart (1813–1879)

NICAEA   11 12 12 10

1   Holy, holy, holy, Lord God almighty!
    early in the morning our song shall rise to thee;
    holy, holy, holy, merciful and mighty!
    God in three Persons, blessèd Trinity!

2   Holy, holy, holy! all the saints adore thee,
    casting down their golden crowns around the glassy sea;
    cherubim and seraphim falling down before thee,
    God ever living through eternity.

3   Holy, holy, holy! though the darkness hide thee,
    though the sinful human eye thy glory may not see,
    only thou art holy; there is none beside thee,
    perfect in power, in love, and purity.

4   Holy, holy, holy, Lord God almighty!
    all thy works shall praise thy name in earth and sky and sea;
    holy, holy, holy! merciful and mighty!
    God in three Persons, blessèd Trinity.

                              *Reginald Heber (1783–1826)

Music John Bacchus Dykes (1823–1876)

MOSCOW 664 6664

1 God, whose almighty word
chaos and darkness heard,
and took their flight;
hear us, we humbly pray,
and, where the gospel-day
sheds not its glorious ray,
let there be light.

2 Saviour, who came to bring,
on your redeeming wing,
healing and sight,
health to the sick in mind,
sight to the inly blind,
now to all humankind
let there be light.

3 Spirit of truth and love,
life-giving, holy dove,
speed forth your flight;
move o'er the waters' face,
bearing the lamp of grace,
and in earth's darkest place
let there be light.

4 Blessèd and holy Three,
glorious Trinity,
Wisdom, Love, Might,
boundless as ocean's tide
rolling in fullest pride,
through the world far and wide
let there be light.

*John Marriott (1780–1825)
and *Thomas Raffles (1788–1863)

Music Melody by Felice de Giardini (1716–1796)
harmonised David Evans (1874–1948)
harmony adapted Compilers

CWM RHONDDA   87 87 87 (7)

1   God the Father of Creation,
         source of life and energy,
         your creative love so shapes us
         that we share your liberty.
         Teach us how to use this freedom
    * loving children all to be.

2   Jesus Christ our Lord and brother,
         in your cross we see the way
         to be servants for each other,
         caring, suffering every day.
         Teach us patience and obedience
         never from your path to stray.

3   Holy Spirit, love that binds us
         to the Father and the Son,
         giver of the joy that fills us,
         yours the peace that makes us one,
         teach our hearts to be more open
         as we pray 'God's will be done.'

4   Members of our Saviour's body,
         here on earth his life to be,
         though we stand as different people,
         may we share the unity
         of the Father, Son and Spirit,
         perfect love in Trinity.

    * *The last line of each verse is repeated.*

Iain D. Cunningham (*b.* 1954)

Music John Hughes, *of Pontypridd* (1873–1932)

AZAIR

10 10 10 10

1 O threefold God of tender unity,
   life's great unknown that binds and sets us free:
   felt in our loving, greater than our thought,
   you are the mystery found, the mystery sought.

2 O blaze of radiance, source of light that blinds,
   fierce burning fire in clear prophetic minds,
   you live in mystery, yet in us dwell;
   life springs from you as from a living well.

3 In every making, each creative dream,
   and in the flowing of life's healing stream,
   when love is born or people reconciled,
   we share your life, O Parent, Spirit, Child.

4 O threefold God of tender unity,
   life's great unknown that binds and sets us free:
   felt in our loving, greater than our thought,
   you are the mystery found, the mystery sought.

William L. (Bill) Wallace (*b.* 1933)

Music Gaelic melody transcribed by Alasdair Codona
harmonised Compilers

AMOR DEI   10 10 10 10

1   Love is the touch of intangible joy;
        love is the force that no fear can destroy;
        love is the goodness we gladly applaud:
        God is where love is, for love is of God.

2   Love is the lilt in a lingering voice;
        love is the hope that can make us rejoice;
        love is the cure for the frightened and flawed:
        God is where love is, for love is of God.

3   Love is the light in the tunnel of pain;
        love is the will to be whole once again;
        love is the trust of a friend on the road:
        God is where love is, for love is of God.

4   Love is the Maker, and Spirit, and Son;
        love is the kingdom their will has begun;
        love is the pathway the saints all have trod:
        God is where love is, for love is of God.

Alison M. Robertson (*b.*1940)

Music John L. Bell (*b.*1949)

HALAD
55 55 55 54

1 Loving Creator,
   grant to your children
   mercy and blessing,
   songs never ceasing,
   grace to invite us,
   peace to unite us —
   Loving Creator,
   Parent and God.

2 Jesus Redeemer,
   help us remember
   your pain and passion,
   your resurrection,
   your call to follow,
   your love tomorrow —
   Jesus Redeemer,
   our Friend and Lord.

3 Spirit descending,
   your light unending
   brings hope and healing,
   is truth revealing.
   Dispel our blindness,
   inspire our kindness —
   Spirit descending,
   Spirit adored.

Daniel Thambyrajah Niles (1908–1970)

Music Philippine folk melody
arranged Lawrence Francis Bartlett (1933–2002)

117 1

MOTHER JULIAN
88 88 8

Music John L. Bell (b. 1949)

117 2

MOTHERING GOD   88 88 8

1 Mothering God, you gave me birth
   in the bright morning of this world.
   Creator, source of every breath,
   you are my rain, my wind, my sun;
   you are my rain, my wind, my sun.

2 Mothering Christ, you took my form,
   offering me your food of light,
   grain of life, and grape of love,
   your very body for my peace;
   your very body for my peace.

3 Mothering Spirit, nurturing one,
   in arms of patience hold me close,
   so that in faith I root and grow,
   until I flower, until I know;
   until I flower, until I know.

Jean Janzen (*b.* 1933)

Music Janet Peachey (*b.* 1953)

117 Words: © Jean Janzen, Fresno, California, USA. Permission applied for.
117.i Music: © WGRG, The Iona Community
117.ii Music: © Janet Peachey, Washington DC, USA. Permission applied for.

LADUE CHAPEL   87 87 D
Brightly

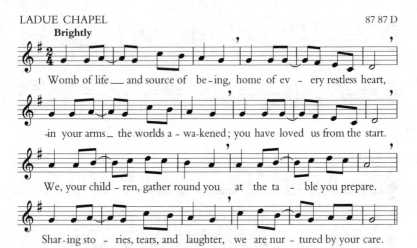

1 Womb of life ___ and source of be - ing, home of ev - ery restless heart,

in your arms_ the worlds a - wa-kened; you have loved us from the start.

We, your child - ren, gather round you   at the ta - ble you prepare.

Shar-ing sto - ries, tears, and laughter, we are nur - tured by your care.

1 Womb of life and source of being,
   home of every restless heart,
   in your arms the worlds awakened;
   you have loved us from the start.
   We, your children, gather round you
   at the table you prepare.
   Sharing stories, tears, and laughter,
   we are nurtured by your care.

2 Word in flesh, our brother Jesus,
   born to bring us second birth,
   you have come to stand beside us,
   knowing weakness, knowing earth.
   Priest who shares our human struggles,
   Life of life, and Death of death,
   risen Christ, come stand among us,
   send the Spirit by your breath.

3 Brooding Spirit, move among us;
   be our partner, be our friend.
   When our memory fails, remind us
   whose we are, what we intend.
   Labour with us, aid the birthing
   of the new world yet to be,
   free from status and division,
   free for love and unity.

Ruth C. Duck (b. 1947)

Music Ronald Kent Arnatt (b. 1930)

118 Words: © 1992, GIA Publications Inc., 7404 S. Mason Avenue, Chicago, IL 60638, USA. Used by permission.
118 Music: © 1971 Walton Music Corporation, 935 Broad Street #31, Bloomfield, New Jersey 07003, USA.

Deus Pater credentum

1   O God, thou art the Father
of all that have believed:
from whom all hosts of angels
have life and power received.
O God, thou art the maker
of all created things,
the righteous Judge of judges,
the almighty King of kings.

2   High in the heavenly Zion
thou reignest God adored;
and in the coming glory
thou shalt be sovereign Lord.
Beyond our ken thou shinest,
the everlasting light;
ineffable in loving,
unthinkable in might.

3   Thou to the meek and lowly
thy secrets dost unfold;
O God, thou doest all things,
all things both new and old.
I walk secure and blessèd
in every clime or coast,
in name of God the Father,
and Son, and Holy Ghost.

St Columba (521–597)
translated Duncan Macgregor (1854–1923)

Music Irish traditional melody, *arranged* Compilers

120 1

ODE TO JOY   87 87 D

Steadily

120 2

LUX TREMENDA   87 87 D

Unison **Steadily**

Music Tune 1
from *Symphony No. 9* Ludwig van Beethoven (1770–1827)

Music Tune 2 Alfred Victor Fedak (*b.* 1953)

1   God, we praise you. God, we bless you.
God, we name you sovereign Lord.
Mighty King whom angels worship,
Father, by your church adored:
all creation shows your glory,
heaven and earth draw near your throne
singing 'Holy, holy, holy,
Lord of hosts and God alone!'

2   True apostles, faithful prophets,
saints who set their world ablaze,
martyrs, once unknown, unheeded,
join one growing song of praise,
while your Church on earth confesses
one majestic Trinity:
Father, Son, and Holy Spirit,
God, our hope eternally.

3   Jesus Christ, the King of glory,
everlasting Son of God,
humble was your virgin mother,
hard the lonely path you trod:
by your cross is sin defeated,
hell confronted face to face,
heaven opened to believers,
sinners justified by grace.

4   Christ, at God's right hand victorious,
you will judge the world you made;
Lord, in mercy help your servants
for whose freedom you have paid:
raise us up from dust to glory,
guard us from all sin today;
King enthroned above all praises,
save your people, God, we pray.

Christopher Martin Idle (b. 1938)
from *Te Deum*

CELEBRATION

Irregular

Brightly

1   In the presence of your people
     I will praise your name,
     for alone you are holy,
     enthroned on the praises of Israel.
     Let us celebrate your goodness
     and your steadfast love;
     may your name be exalted
     here on earth and in heaven above.

2   All who love you sing your praises
     and proclaim your power,
     for alone you are holy,
     enthroned on the praises of Israel.
     You have not ignored our suffering
     but have heard our cry;
     may your power be exalted
     here on earth and in heaven above.

3   All who seek your rule will praise you
     and be satisfied;
     for alone you are holy,
     enthroned on the praises of Israel.
     All the peoples of the nations
     will bow down to you;
     may your rule be exalted
     here on earth and in heaven above.

Brent Chambers (*b.* 1948) and Bert Polman (*b.* 1945)
Music Brent Chambers (*b.* 1948)

121 Words and Music: © 1977, Scripture in Song (a division of Integrity Inc.) / Sovereign Music UK, PO Box 356, Leighton Buzzard, Bedfordshire. LU7 3WP. <www.sovereignmusic@aol.com>

LUCKINGTON   10 4 6666 10 4

1   Let all the world in every corner sing,
     'My God and King!'
     The heavens are not too high,
     his praise may thither fly;
     the earth is not too low,
     his praises there may grow.
     Let all the world in every corner sing,
     'My God and King!'

2   Let all the world in every corner sing,
     'My God and King!'
     The church with psalms must shout,
     no door can keep them out;
     but, above all, the heart
     must bear the longest part.
     Let all the world in every corner sing,
     'My God and King!'

                     George Herbert (1593–1633)

Music Basil Harwood (1859–1949)

123

THE LIVING GOD

ECCE, DEUS

87 87 D

Flowingly

1   God is love: let heaven adore him;
    God is love: let earth rejoice;
    let creation sing before him,
    and exalt him with one voice.
    He who laid the earth's foundation,
    he who spread the heavens above,
    he who breathes through all creation:
    God is love, eternal love.

2   God is love, and is enfolding
    all the world in one embrace;
    with unfailing grasp is holding
    every child of every race.
    And when human hearts are breaking
    under sorrow's iron rod,
    then they find that selfsame aching
    deep within the heart of God.

3   God is love: and though with blindness
    sin afflicts the souls of all,
    God's eternal loving-kindness
    holds and guides us when we fall.
    Sin and death and hell shall never
    o'er us final triumph gain;
    God is love, so Love for ever
    o'er the universe must reign.

Music Alfred Victor Fedak (*b.* 1953)

Timothy Rees (1874–1939)

LOBE DEN HERREN   14 14 478

An alternative harmonisation is found at 172.

Lobe den Herren

1   Praise to the Lord, the Almighty, the King of creation;
     praise God, my soul, for in him are your health and salvation;
         come all who hear,
         into his presence draw near,
     joining in glad adoration.

2   Praise to the Lord, who in all things is wondrously reigning,
     shields you from harm and is gently yet firmly sustaining.
         Have you not seen
         how your heart's wishes have been
     granted by God's wise ordaining?

3   Praise to the Lord, who with blessing and power will
             defend you;
     surely his goodness and mercy shall daily attend you;
         ponder anew
         what the Almighty can do:
     God will for ever befriend you.

4   Praise to the Lord! O let all that is in me adore him!
     All that has life and breath, come now with praises before him!
         Let the Amen
         sound from God's people again:
     gladly for ever adore him.

                              Joachim Neander (1650–1680)
                     translated *Catherine Winkworth (1827–1878)

Music Melody from *Praxis Pietatis Melica,* 1668, as set in *The Chorale Book for England,* 1863

OMBERSLEY

LM

1   Lord of all being, throned afar,
    thy glory flames from sun and star;
    centre and soul of every sphere,
    yet to each loving heart how near!

2   Sun of our life, thy quickening ray
    sheds on our path the glow of day;
    Star of our hope, thy softened light
    cheers the long watches of the night.

3   Our midnight is thy smile withdrawn,
    our noontide is thy gracious dawn,
    our rainbow arch thy mercy's sign;
    all, save the clouds of sin, are thine.

4   Lord of all life, below, above,
    whose light is truth, whose warmth is love,
    before thy ever-blazing throne
    we ask no lustre of our own.

5   Grant us thy truth to make us free,
    and kindling hearts that burn for thee,
    till all thy living altars claim
    one holy light, one heavenly flame.

                    Oliver Wendell Holmes (1809–1894)

Music William Henry Gladstone (1840–1891)

126

CANTAD AL SEÑOR

11 11 11 10

The Being of God – Holy and One

1 Let's sing to the Lord, yes, sing God a new song.
  Let's sing to the Lord, yes, sing God a new song.
  Let's sing to the Lord, yes, sing God a new song.
  Let's sing to the Lord, let's sing to the Lord.

2 For God is the Lord, and God has done wonders.
  For God is the Lord, and God has done wonders.
  For God is the Lord, and God has done wonders.
  Let's sing to the Lord, let's sing to the Lord.

3 So dance for our God and blow all the trumpets.
  So dance for our God and blow all the trumpets.
  So dance for our God and blow all the trumpets.
  Let's sing to the Lord, let's sing to the Lord.

4 Let's shout to our God, who gave us the Spirit.
  Let's shout to our God, who gave us the Spirit.
  Let's shout to our God, who gave us the Spirit.
  Let's sing to the Lord, let's sing to the Lord.

5 For Jesus is Lord!   Amen!   Alleluia!
  For Jesus is Lord!   Amen!   Alleluia!
  For Jesus is Lord!   Amen!   Alleluia!
  Let's sing to the Lord, let's sing to the Lord.

Spanish original text:

1 Cantad al Señor un cántico nuevo.
  Cantad al Señor, cantad al Señor!

2 Es él que nos da el Espíritu Santo.
  Cantad al Señor, cantad al Señor!

3 Jesús es Señor!   Amen, aleluya!
  Cantad al Señor, cantad al Señor!

Brazilian folk song
translated Gerhard M. Cartford

Music Brazilian folk melody, *arranged* Compilers

HANOVER   10 10 11 11

1   O worship the King, all glorious above;
O gratefully sing his power and his love;
our shield and defender, the Ancient of Days,
pavilioned in splendour and girded with praise.

2   O tell of his might, O sing of his grace,
whose robe is the light, whose canopy space;
his chariots of wrath the deep thunder-clouds form,
and dark is his path on the wings of the storm.

3   The earth with its store of wonders untold,
Almighty, thy power hath founded of old;
hath stablished it fast by a changeless decree,
and round it hath cast, like a mantle, the sea.

4   Thy bountiful care what tongue can recite?
It breathes in the air, it shines in the light;
it streams from the hills; it descends to the plain,
and sweetly distils in the dew and the rain.

5   Frail children of dust and feeble as frail,
in thee do we trust, nor find thee to fail;
thy mercies how tender, how firm to the end,
our maker, defender, redeemer, and friend!

6   O measureless might, ineffable love!
While angels delight to hymn thee above,
the humbler creation, in lowlier ways,
with true adoration shall sing to thy praise.

*Robert Grant (1779–1838)
from *Psalm 104*

Music Melody and most of the bass from *A Supplement to the
New Version* 1708, probably by William Croft (1678–1727)

COE FEN
Unison
DCM

1   How shall I sing that majesty
    which angels do admire?
    Let dust in dust and silence lie;
    sing, sing, ye heavenly choir.
    Thousands of thousands stand around
    thy throne, O God most high;
    ten thousand times ten thousand sound
    thy praise; but who am I?

2   Thy brightness unto them appears,
    whilst I thy footsteps trace;
    a sound of God comes to my ears,
    but they behold thy face.
    They sing because thou art their Sun;
    Lord, send a beam on me;
    for where heaven is but once begun
    there alleluias be.

3   How great a being, Lord, is thine,
    which doth all beings keep!
    Thy knowledge is the only line
    to sound so vast a deep.
    Thou art a sea without a shore,
    a sun without a sphere;
    thy time is now and evermore,
    thy place is everywhere.

John Mason (1646–1694)

Music Kenneth Nicholson Naylor (1931–1991)

CHURCH TRIUMPHANT   LM

1   The Lord is King! lift up your voice!
     Let earth and all the heavens rejoice.
     From world to world the joy shall ring,
     'The Lord omnipotent is King!'

2   The Lord is King! who then shall dare
     resist his will, distrust his care,
     or murmur at his wise decrees,
     or doubt his royal promises?

3   The Lord is King! child of the dust,
     the judge of all the earth is just;
     holy and true are all his ways:
     let every creature speak his praise.

4   Come, make your wants, your burdens known;
     Christ will present them at the throne;
     for he is at the Father's side,
     the Man of Love, the Crucified.

5   One Lord, one empire, all secures;
     he reigns, and life and death are yours:
     through earth and heaven one song shall ring,
     'The Lord omnipotent is King!'

                              Josiah Conder (1789–1855)
                                   from *Psalm 148*

Music James William Elliott (1833–1915)
rhythm slightly adapted

LAUDATE DOMINUM   10 10 11 11

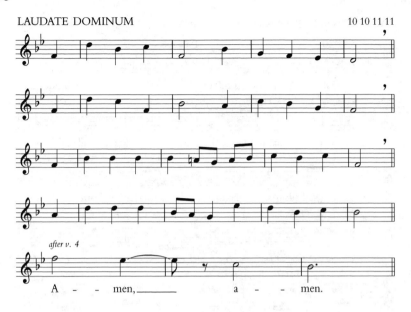

A — — men,_____ a — — men.

1   Ye servants of God, your Master proclaim,
           and publish abroad his wonderful name;
           the name all-victorious of Jesus extol;
           his kingdom is glorious, and rules over all.

2   God ruleth on high, almighty to save;
           and still he is nigh, his presence we have;
           the great congregation his triumph shall sing,
           ascribing salvation to Jesus our king.

3   'Salvation to God who sits on the throne!'
           let all cry aloud, and honour the Son:
           the praises of Jesus the angels proclaim,
           fall down on their faces, and worship the Lamb.

4   Then let us adore, and give him his right:
           all glory and power, all wisdom and might,
           all honour and blessing, with angels above,
           and thanks never-ceasing, and infinite love.
           (Amen, amen.)

                       Charles Wesley (1707–1788)

Music Charles Hubert Hastings Parry (1848–1918)

SALVATION BELONGS TO OUR GOD

1 Salvation belongs to our God,
   who sits on the throne,
   and unto the Lamb.
   Praise and glory, wisdom and thanks,
   honour and power and strength
      be to our God for ever and ever,
      be to our God for ever and ever,
      be to our God for ever and ever, amen.

2 And we, the redeemed, shall be strong
   in purpose and unity,
   declaring aloud:
   praise and glory, wisdom and thanks,
   honour and power and strength
      be to our God for ever and ever,
      be to our God for ever and ever,
      be to our God for ever and ever, amen.

                    Adrian Howard and Pat Turner

Music Adrian Howard and Pat Turner

ST DENIO (JOANNA)   11 11 11 11

1   Immortal, invisible, God only wise,
    in light inaccessible hid from our eyes,
    most blessèd, most glorious, the Ancient of Days,
    almighty, victorious, thy great name we praise.

2   Unresting, unhasting, and silent as light,
    nor wanting, nor wasting, thou rulest in might;
    thy justice like mountains, high soaring above
    thy clouds, which are fountains of goodness and love.

3   To all, life thou givest, to both great and small;
    in all life thou livest, the true life of all;
    we blossom and flourish as leaves on the tree,
    and wither and perish, but naught changeth thee.

4   Great Father of glory, pure Father of light,
    thine angels adore thee, all veiling their sight.
    All praise we would render: O help us to see
    'tis only the splendour of light hideth thee.

                                    Walter Chalmers Smith (1824–1908)

Music Welsh hymn melody, 1839, founded on a folk melody,
slightly adapted

ABERYSTWYTH 77 77 D

1   Source and Sovereign, Rock and Cloud,
     Fortress, Fountain, Shelter, Light,
     Judge, Defender, Mercy, Might,
     Life whose life all life endowed:
          May the Church at prayer recall
          that no single holy name
          but the truth that feeds them all
          is the God whom we proclaim.

2   Word and Wisdom, Root and Vine,
     Shepherd, Saviour, Servant, Lamb,
     Well and Water, Bread and Wine,
     Way who leads us to I AM:

3   Storm and Stillness, Breath and Dove,
     Thunder, Tempest, Whirlwind, Fire,
     Comfort, Counsellor, Presence, Love,
     Energies that never tire:

                              Thomas H. Troeger (*b.*1945)

Music Joseph Parry (1841–1903)

134

WESTCHASE 9 10 11 9

1   Bring many names, beautiful and good,
celebrate, in parable and story,
    holiness in glory,
    living, loving God:
Hail and Hosanna!
Bring many names!

2   Strong mother God, working night and day,
planning all the wonders of creation,
    setting each equation,
    genius at play:
Hail and Hosanna,
strong mother God!

3   Warm father God, hugging every child,
feeling all the strains of human living,
    caring and forgiving
    till we're reconciled:
Hail and Hosanna,
warm father God!

4   Old, aching God, grey with endless care,
calmly piercing evil's new disguises,
    glad of good surprises,
    wiser than despair:
Hail and Hosanna,
old, aching God!

5   Young, growing God, eager, on the move,
saying no to falsehood and unkindness,
    crying out for justice,
    giving all you have:
Hail and Hosanna,
young, growing God!

6   Great, living God, never fully known,
joyful darkness far beyond our seeing,
    closer yet than breathing,
    everlasting home:
Hail and Hosanna,
great, living God!

Brian Wren (b. 1936)

Music Carlton (Sam) Raymond Young (b. 1926)

CHRISTE SANCTORUM   11 11 11 5

Unison

A lower setting is found at 64.

1   O laughing Light, O first-born of creation,
    radiance of glory, light from light begotten,
    God self-revealing, holy, bright and blessèd:
    you shine upon us.

2   Day's light is fleeting, yours is light eternal;
    we look to you, our light within the shadow.
    We sing to you, Creator, Christ, and Spirit.
    You shine before us.

3   Light of the world, O Jesus Christ, we bless you.
    Giver of life and Child of God, we praise you.
    Hear as the universe proclaims your glory!
    You shine among us.

Sylvia G. Dunstan (1955–1993)
based on *Phos hilaron*

Music Melody from *Paris Antiphoner*, 1681
harmonised David Evans (1874–1948)

Also suitable

Father, we praise you, now the night is over   209
Father of heaven, whose love profound   483
I bind unto myself today   639
Now go in peace   789

THE ACTIVITY OF GOD
GOD IN CREATION

RODAIL

65 65 and refrain

1 God's will for creation
is Jesus' to do:
new branches to wither,
old trees to renew.
Jesus! Jesus! Jesus!
How can we help but praise him.

2 Each plant in its growing,
each shape in the strand,
is filled with God's blessing,
is stirred by God's hand.

3 All life in the river,
all fish in the sea,
earth's numberless creatures
God summoned to be.

4 Each bird in the morning,
each star in the sky,
proclaims the Lord's goodness
which never can die.

Gaelic original text:

1 Bu cho fus a dh'Iosa
an crann crion ùradh,
's an crann ùr a chrionadh,
na'm b'e rùn a dhèanamh:
Iosa! Iosa! Iosa!
Iosa bu chòir a mholadh.

2 Ni bheil lus an làr,
nach bheil làn d'a thoradh;
ni bheil cruth an tràigh,
nach bheil làn d'a shonas:

3 Ni bheil creubh am fairge,
ni bheil dearg an abhainn,
ni bheil càil an fhailbhe,
nach bheil dearbh d'a mhaitheas:

4 Ni bheil ian air sgèith,
ni bheil reul an adhar,
ni bheil sian fo'n ghrèin,
nach tog sgeul d'a mhaitheas:

Gaelic text, *Carmina Gadelica,*
English version Compilers of
Common Ground, 1998

Music Gaelic folk melody
arranged John L. Bell (*b.* 1949)

137 1

ALL THINGS BRIGHT AND BEAUTIFUL

76 76 and refrain

137 2

ROYAL OAK

76 76 and refrain

Music Tune 1 William Henry Monk (1823–1889)

Music Tune 2 English traditional melody
arranged Martin Edward Fallas Shaw (1875–1958)

All things bright and beautiful,
all creatures great and small,
all things wise and wonderful,
the Lord God made them all.

1 Each little flower that opens,
   each little bird that sings,
   he made their glowing colours,
   he made their tiny wings:

2 The purple-headed mountain,
   the river running by,
   the sunset, and the morning
   that brightens up the sky:

3 The cold wind in the winter,
   the pleasant summer sun,
   the ripe fruits in the garden,
   he made them every one:

4 He gave us eyes to see them,
   and lips that we might tell
   how great is God Almighty,
   who has made all things well.

Cecil Frances Alexander (1818–1895)

ALABANZA   Irregular

1   Nourished by the rainfall, the earth can come alive;
     woodlands swell with splendour, the moors and
             meadows thrive.
     Flowers of every colour now raise their heads in pride,
     praising God their maker throughout the countryside.
     Each flower has its purpose, and every petal its place,
     each celebrates glory, each speaks of God's good grace.
     All, all of creation delights to worship the Lord.
     Let those in God's image respond in deed and word.

2   Birds that wake the morning and fill the evening sky,
     sing not to please humans, but to praise God on high.
     Nightingale and curlew, the robin, rook, and wren,
     first rehearse their anthem, then sing it through again.
     Each bird has its purpose, and every song has its place,
     each celebrates glory, each speaks of God's good grace.
     All, all of creation delights to worship the Lord.
     Let those in God's image respond in deed and word.

Music Pablo Fernandez Badillo (*b.*1949)

3   Every land and nation, each woman, child, and man,
find their root and reason before the world began;
all by God were destined to hear the Saviour's call,
and choose to give him nothing, or gladly give him all.
Each soul has its purpose, and every child has its place,
each celebrates glory, each speaks of God's good grace.
All, all of creation delights to worship the Lord.
Let those in God's image respond in deed and word.

Pablo Fernandez Badillo (*b.* 1949)
English version John L. Bell (*b.* 1949)

39

LAUS DEO (REDHEAD No 46)   87 87

A lower setting is found at 603.

1   Praise the Lord, you heavens, adore him;
praise him, angels, in the height;
sun and moon, rejoice before him,
praise him, all you stars and light.

2   Praise the Lord! for he has spoken;
worlds his mighty voice obeyed;
laws which never shall be broken
for their guidance has he made.

3   Praise the Lord! for he is glorious;
never shall his promise fail;
God has made his saints victorious;
sin and death shall not prevail.

4   Praise the God of our salvation!
Hosts on high, his power proclaim;
heaven, and earth, and all creation,
laud and magnify his name.

Foundling Hospital Hymns c. 1796,
from *Psalm 148*

Music Richard Redhead (1820–1901)
Church Hymn Tunes, 1853

GAYON NI HIGAMI

77 77 6

1   Lord, your hands have formed this world,
     every part is shaped by you —
     water tumbling over rocks,
     air and sunlight: each day's signs
     that you make all things new.

2   Yours the soil that holds the seed,
     you give warmth and moisture too —
     sprouting blossoms, crops and buds,
     trees and plants: the season's signs
     that you make all things new.

3   Like a mat you roll out land —
     space to build, for us and you,
     earthly homes and, better still,
     homes for Christ: the truest sign
     that you make all things new.

Ramon Oliano and Sario Oliano
English version James Minchin
and Delebert Rice

Music Ikalahan traditional melody (Philippines)
arranged John L. Bell (*b.* 1949)

LIFE OF THE WORLD   13 11 12 8

1   Oh, the life of the world is a joy and a treasure,
unfolding in beauty the green-growing tree,
the changing of seasons in mountain and valley,
the stars and the bright restless sea.

2   Oh, the life of the world is a fountain of goodness
overflowing in labour and passion and pain,
in the sound of the city and the silence of wisdom,
in the birth of a child once again.

3   Oh, the life of the world is the source of our healing.
It rises in laughter and wells up in song;
it springs from the care of the poor and the broken
and refreshes where justice is strong.

4   So give thanks for the life and give love to the Maker,
and rejoice in the gift of the bright risen Son,
and walk in the peace and the power of the Spirit
till the days of our living are done.

Kathryn Galloway (b. 1952)

Music Melody by Ian Galloway (b. 1952)
arranged John L. Bell (b. 1949)

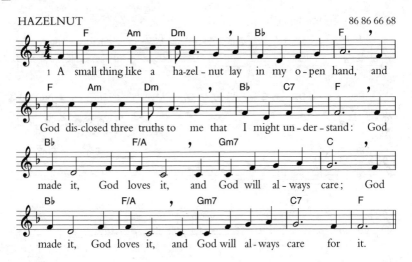

HAZELNUT   86 86 66 68

1 A small thing like a ha-zel-nut lay in my o-pen hand, and

God dis-closed three truths to me that I might un-der-stand: God

made it, God loves it, and God will al-ways care; God

made it, God loves it, and God will al-ways care for it.

1   A small thing like a hazelnut
     lay in my open hand,
     and God disclosed three truths to me
     that I might understand:
     God made it, God loves it,
     and God will always care;
     God made it, God loves it,
     and God will always care for it.

2   I marvelled that this little thing
     reveals how God can be
     our maker, lover, keeper, now
     and for eternity!
     God made you, God loves you,
     and God will always care;
     God made you, God loves you,
     and God will always care for you!

3   Until my heart is one with God,
     its aching will not cease,
     and so I rest, held close by God,
     these three truths bringing peace:

Music Iain D. Cunningham (*b.* 1954), *arranged* Compilers

The Activity of God – God in creation

God made me, God loves me,
and God will always care;
God made me, God loves me,
and God will always care for me!

Rae E. Whitney (b. 1927)

43

AUDREY-GREEN   Irregular

1 Who put the colours in the rainbow?
 Who put the salt in the sea?
 Who put the cold in the snow-flake?
 Who made you and me?
 Who put the hump upon the camel?
 Who put the neck on the giraffe?
 Who put the tail upon the monkey?
 Who made the hyena laugh?
 Who made whales and snails and quails?
 Who made hogs and dogs and frogs?
 Who made bats and rats and cats?
 Who made everything?

continued overleaf

Music Melody by Joseph Arthur Paul Booth (1931–1995)
arranged Douglas John Coombes (b. 1935)

2 Who put the gold in the sunshine?
   Who put the sparkle in the stars?
   Who put the silver in the moonlight?
   Who made Earth and Mars?
   Who put the scent into the roses?
   Who taught the honey-bee to dance?
   Who put the tree inside the acorn?
   It surely can't be chance!
   Who made seas and leaves and trees?
   Who made snow and winds that blow?
   Who made streams and rivers flow?
   God made all of these!

   Joseph Arthur Paul Booth (1931–1995)

I LOVE THE SUN   44 44

1   I love the sun,
     it shines on me;
     God made the sun,
     and God made me.

2   I love the stars,
     they twinkle on me;
     God made the stars,
     and God made me.

3   I love the rain,
     it splashes on me;
     God made the rain,
     and God made me.

4   I love the wind,
     it blows round me;
     God made the wind,
     and God made me.

5   I love the birds,
     they sing to me;
     God made the birds,
     and God made me.

Gwen F. Smith (1909–1995)

Music Gwen F. Smith (1909–1995)

GOD MADE ME 66 77

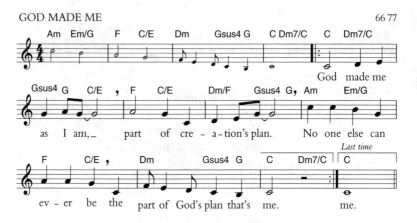

God made me as I am,_ part of cre - a - tion's plan. No one else can ev - er be the part of God's plan that's me. me.

God made me as I am,
part of creation's plan.
No one else can ever be
the part of God's plan that's me.

Bernadette Farrell (*b.* 1957)

Music Bernadette Farrell (*b.* 1957)

LASST UNS ERFREUEN   LM and Alleluias

A lower setting is found at 147.

1   From all that dwell below the skies
     let the Creator's praise arise:
          Alleluia! Alleluia!
     Let the Redeemer's name be sung
     through every land, in every tongue:
          Alleluia, Alleluia,
          Alleluia, Alleluia,
          Alleluia!

2   Eternal are your mercies, Lord;
     eternal truth attends your word:
          Alleluia! Alleluia!
     Your praise shall sound from shore to shore
     till suns shall rise and set no more:
          Alleluia, Alleluia,
          Alleluia, Alleluia,
          Alleluia!

                              Isaac Watts (1674–1748)
                                   from *Psalm 117*

Music Melody from *Geistliche Kirchengesäng*, Cologne, 1623
arranged Ralph Vaughan Williams (1872–1958)

LASST UNS ERFREUEN   88 8 88 and refrain

O___ praise him, O___ praise him, al - le -
- lu - ia, al - le - lu - ia, al - le - lu - ia!

A higher setting is found at 146.

Laudato sia Dio mio Signore

1   All creatures of our God and King,
lift up your voice and with us sing
alleluia, alleluia!
Bright brother sun with golden beam,
clear sister moon with softer gleam:
    O praise him, O praise him,
    alleluia, alleluia, alleluia!

2   Swift rushing wind, so wild and strong,
high clouds that sail in heaven along,
O praise him, alleluia!
New-breaking dawn, in praise rejoice,
and lights of evening, find a voice:

Music Melody from *Geistliche Kirchengesäng,* Cologne, 1623
arranged Ralph Vaughan Williams (1872–1958)

3   Cool flowing water, pure and clear,
make music for your Lord to hear,
alleluia, alleluia!
Fire, with your flames so fierce and bright,
giving to all both warmth and light:

4   Dear mother earth, who day by day
unfolds God's blessings on our way,
O praise him, alleluia!
All flowers and fruits that in you grow,
let them his glory also show:

5   And all who are of tender heart,
forgiving others, take your part,
O praise him, alleluia!
All who long pain and sorrow bear,
praise God and cast on him your care:

6   And you, most kind and gentle death,
waiting to hush our fading breath,
O praise him, alleluia!
You homeward lead the child of God,
and Christ our Lord the way has trod:

7   Let all things their Creator bless,
and worship God in humbleness,
O praise him, alleluia!
Praise, praise the Father, praise the Son,
and praise the Spirit, Three in One:

St Francis of Assisi (1182–1226)
translated *William Henry Draper (1855–1933)

FIRMAMENT

DLM

Music Henry Walford Davies (1869–1941)

1   The spacious firmament on high,
    with all the blue ethereal sky,
    and spangled heavens, a shining frame,
    their great Original proclaim.
    The unwearied sun, from day to day,
    does his Creator's power display,
    and publishes to every land
    the work of an almighty hand.

2   Soon as the evening shades prevail,
    the moon takes up the wondrous tale,
    and nightly to the listening earth
    repeats the story of her birth;
    while all the stars that round her burn,
    and all the planets, in their turn,
    confirm the tidings, as they roll,
    and spread the truth from pole to pole.

3   What though in solemn silence all
    move round this dark terrestrial ball;
    what though no real voice nor sound
    amid their radiant orbs be found?
    In reason's ear they all rejoice,
    and utter forth a glorious voice,
    for ever singing, as they shine,
    'The hand that made us is divine!'

                    Joseph Addison (1672–1719)

ST JOHN (Havergal)   66 66 44 44

A higher setting is found at 104.

1   Let all creation dance
in energies sublime,
as order turns with chance,
unfolding space and time;
for nature's art
in glory grows,
and newly shows
God's mind and heart.

2   Our own amazing earth,
with sunlight, cloud, and storms,
and life's abundant growth
in lovely shapes and forms
is made for praise,
a fragile whole,
and from its soul
heaven's music plays.

3   Lift heart and soul and voice:
in Christ all praises meet,
and nature shall rejoice
as all is made complete.
In hope be strong,
all life befriend,
and kindly tend
creation's song.

Brian Wren (*b.* 1936)

Music The Parish Choir, vol. III, 1851
sometimes attributed to William Henry Havergal (1793–1870)

STU MO RUN

10 9 8 11 and refrain

Unison **Brightly**

Refrain Harmony

Sing to the Lord,

sing Al - le - lu - ia, sing to the Lord, sing with joy!

1   Sing to God with gladness, all creation,
    sing to God the song of God's great love,
    sing to God who made the heavens,
    sing to God who made the loveliness of earth!
        Sing to the Lord, sing Alleluia,
        sing to the Lord, sing with joy!

2   Sing to God on high, O sun in splendour,
    sing to God on high, O silver moon,
    sing to God, O sky at dawning,
    sing to God, O starlit silence of the night!

3   Sing your song of glory, angel voices,
    sing your song of peace to all on earth,
    sing of peace, the heart's deep longing,
    sing of peace that comes from God and God alone!

4   Sing to God the Father, all creation,
    sing to God, his dear and only Son,
    sing to God the loving Spirit,
    sing with joy to God, one God, for evermore!

James Quinn (*b.* 1919)

Music Gaelic folk melody
arranged John L. Bell (*b.* 1949)

ALL YOU WORKS OF GOD   Irregular

Music Marty Haugen (*b.* 1950) .

151   Words and Music: © 1990, GIA Publications Inc., 7404 S. Mason Avenue, Chicago, IL 60638, USA. Used by permission.

All you works of God,
every mountain, star, and tree,
bless the One who shapes your beauty,
who has caused you all to be
one great song of love and grace,
ever ancient, ever new.
Raise your voices, all you works of God!

1   Sun and moon: *bless your Maker!*
    Stars of heaven: *chant your praise!*
    Showers and dew: *raise up your joyful song!*

2   Winds of God: *bless your Maker!*
    Cold and winter: *chant your praise!*
    Snowstorms and ice: *raise up your joyful song!*

3   Night and day: *bless your Maker!*
    Light and darkness: *chant your praise!*
    Lightnings and clouds: *raise up your joyful song!*

4   All the earth: *bless your Maker!*
    Hills and mountains: *chant your praise!*
    Green things that grow: *raise up your joyful song!*

5   Wells and springs: *bless your Maker!*
    Seas and rivers: *chant your praise!*
    Whales in the deep: *raise up your joyful song!*

6   Flying birds: *bless your Maker!*
    Beasts and cattle: *chant your praise!*
    Children at play: *raise up your joyful song!*

7   All who live: *bless your Maker!*
    Men and women: *chant your praise!*
    Servants of God: *raise up your joyful song!*

A Cantor may sing the first half of the verse,
and the congregation sings the second half.

Marty Haugen (*b.* 1950)

LLANFAIR   77 77 and Alleluias

1   Praise the Lord, his glories show,
         Alleluia!
     saints within his courts below,
         Alleluia!
     angels round his throne above,
         Alleluia!
     all that see and share his love,
         Alleluia!

2   Earth to heaven, and heaven to earth,
     tell his wonders, sing his worth;
     age to age and shore to shore,
     praise him, praise him evermore!

3   Praise the Lord, his mercies trace;
     praise his providence and grace,
     all that he for us has done,
     all he sends us through his Son.

4   Strings and voices, hands and hearts,
     in the concert play your parts;
     all that breathe, your Lord adore,
     praise him, praise him evermore.

                              *Henry Francis Lyte (1793–1847)

Music Melody by Robert Williams (1782–1818)
harmonised David Evans (1874–1948)

FAITHFULNESS   11 10 11 10 and refrain

Refrain

Great is thy faith-ful-ness! Great is thy faith-ful-ness!

Morn-ing by morn-ing new mer-cies I see;

all I have need-ed thy hand hath pro-vi-ded —

great is thy faith-ful-ness, Lord, un-to me.

1   Great is thy faithfulness, O God my Father,
     there is no shadow of turning with thee;
     thou changest not, thy compassions they fail not,
     as thou hast been thou for ever wilt be.
         Great is thy faithfulness! Great is thy faithfulness!
         Morning by morning new mercies I see;
         all I have needed thy hand hath provided —
         great is thy faithfulness, Lord, unto me.

2   Summer and winter, and seed-time and harvest,
     sun, moon, and stars in their courses above,
     join with all nature in manifold witness
     to thy great faithfulness, mercy, and love.

3   Pardon for sin and a peace that endureth,
     thine own dear presence to cheer and to guide;
     strength for today and bright hope for tomorrow,
     blessings all mine, with ten thousand beside.

                          Thomas O. Chisholm (1866–1960)

Music William W. Marion Runyan (1870–1957)

HOW GREAT THOU ART

11 10 11 10 and refrain

Then sings my soul, my Sa-viour God, to thee, 'How great thou

art, how great thou art!' Then sings my soul, my Sa-viour God, to

thee, 'How great thou art, how great thou art!'

1   O Lord my God! when I in awesome wonder
    consider all the works thy hand hath made,
    I see the stars, I hear the mighty thunder,
    thy power throughout the universe displayed:
        Then sings my soul, my Saviour God, to thee,
        'How great thou art, how great thou art!'
        Then sings my soul, my Saviour God, to thee,
        'How great thou art, how great thou art!'

2   When through the woods and forest glades I wander
    and hear the birds sing sweetly in the trees;
    when I look up from lofty mountain grandeur,
    and hear the brook, and feel the gentle breeze:

3   And when I think that God his Son not sparing,
    sent him to die — I scarce can take it in,
    that on the cross, my burden gladly bearing,
    he bled and died to take away my sin:

Music Swedish melody 'O store Gud'
arranged Stuart K. Hine (1899–1989)

4   When Christ shall come with shout of acclamation
and take me home — what joy shall fill my heart!
Then shall I bow in humble adoration
and there proclaim, my God, how great thou art!

Russian hymn
translated Stuart K. Hine (1899–1989)

55

GENESIS   10 9 10 9 and refrain

1   Think of a world without any flowers,
think of a wood without any trees,
think of a sky without any sunshine,
think of the air without any breeze.
We thank you, Lord, for flowers and trees and sunshine,
we thank you, Lord, and praise your holy name.

2   Think of a world without any animals,
think of a field without any herd,
think of a stream without any fishes,
think of a dawn without any bird.
We thank you, Lord, for all your living creatures,
we thank you, Lord, and praise your holy name.

3   Think of a world without any people,
think of a street with no one living there,
think of a town without any houses,
no-one to love and nobody to care.
We thank you, Lord, for families and friendships,
we thank you, Lord, and praise your holy name.

Doreen E. Newport (*b.*1927)

Music Melody by Graham Clifford Westcott (*b.*1947)

AWAKEN THE DAWN

1   Sing to the Lord with all of your heart;
     sing of the glory that's due to his name.
     Sing to the Lord with all of your soul,
     join all of heaven and earth to proclaim:
         You are the Lord, the Saviour of all,
         God of creation, we praise you.
         We sing the songs that awaken the dawn,
         God of creation, we praise you.

2   Sing to the Lord with all of your mind,
     with understanding give thanks to the King.
     Sing to the Lord with all of your strength,
     live out your lives as a praise offering.

                                          Stuart Garrard

Music Stuart Garrard

156 Words and Music: © 1994, Thankyou Music. Administered (UK and Europe) by kingswaysongs.com <tym@kingsway.co.uk>.
Remaining territories administered by worshiptogether.com songs. Used by permission.

Also suitable
Take up the song, and sing the praise of God   171
The earth is yours, O God   227
The peace of the earth be with you   798

SING OF THE LORD'S GOODNESS   12 7 12 7 and refrain

1   Sing of the Lord's goodness, Father of all wisdom,
     come to him and bless his name.
     Mercy he has shown us, his love is for ever,
     faithful to the end of days.
         Come then, all you nations,
         sing of your Lord's goodness,
         melodies of praise and thanks to God.
         Ring out the Lord's glory,
         praise him with your music,
         worship him and bless his name.

continued overleaf

Music Ernest Sands (*b.* 1949)

THE LIVING GOD

Come then, all you na-tions, sing of your Lord's good-ness, me-lo-dies of praise and thanks to God. Ring out the Lord's glo-ry, praise him with your mu-sic, wor-ship him and bless his name._____

2   Power he has wielded, honour is his garment,
    risen from the snares of death.
    His word he has spoken, one bread he has broken,
    new life he now gives to all.

3   Courage in our darkness, comfort in our sorrow,
    Spirit of our God most high;
    solace for the weary, pardon for the sinner,
    splendour of the living God.

4   Praise him with your singing, praise him with the trumpet,
    praise God with the lute and harp;
    praise him with the cymbals, praise him with your dancing,
    praise God till the end of days.

Ernest Sands (*b.* 1949)

LONDON NEW   CM

1   God moves in a mysterious way,
     his wonders to perform;
     he plants his footsteps in the sea,
     and rides upon the storm.

2   Deep in unfathomable mines
     of never-failing skill
     he treasures up his bright designs,
     and works his sovereign will.

3   You fearful saints, fresh courage take;
     the clouds you so much dread
     are big with mercy, and shall break
     in blessings on your head.

4   Judge not the Lord by feeble sense
     but trust him for his grace;
     behind a frowning providence
     he hides a smiling face.

5   Blind unbelief is sure to err,
     and scan his work in vain,
     God is his own interpreter,
     and he will make it plain.

William Cowper (1731–1800)

Music Melody from *Scottish Psalter,* 1635,
as adapted in Playford's *Psalmes,* 1671

LORD OF THE YEARS

11 10 11 10

1 Lord, for the years your love has kept and guided,
        urged and inspired us, cheered us on our way,
   sought us and saved us, pardoned and provided,
        Lord of the years, we bring our thanks today.

2 Lord, for that word, the Word of life which fires us,
        speaks to our hearts and sets our souls ablaze,
   teaches and trains, rebukes us and inspires us,
        Lord of the word, receive your people's praise.

3 Lord, for our land, in this our generation,
        spirits oppressed by pleasure, wealth and care;
   for young and old, for commonwealth and nation,
        Lord of our land, be pleased to hear our prayer.

4 Lord, for our world; when we disown and doubt him,
        loveless in strength, and comfortless in pain;
   hungry and helpless, lost indeed without him,
        Lord of the world, we pray that Christ may reign.

5 Lord, for ourselves; in living power remake us,
        self on the cross and Christ upon the throne;
   past put behind us, for the future take us,
        Lord of our lives, to live for Christ alone.

Timothy Dudley-Smith (*b.* 1926)

Music Michael Baughen (*b.* 1930)
arranged David Iliff (*b.* 1939)

PRAISE, MY SOUL   87 87 44 7

1   Praise, my soul, the King of heaven;
     to his feet thy tribute bring;
     ransomed, healed, restored, forgiven,
     who like me his praise should sing?
     Praise him! Praise him!
     Praise the everlasting King.

2   Praise him for his grace and favour
     to our fathers in distress;
     praise him, still the same for ever,
     slow to chide, and swift to bless:
     Praise him! Praise him!
     glorious in his faithfulness.

3   Father-like he tends and spares us;
     well our feeble frame he knows;
     in his hands he gently bears us,
     rescues us from all our foes:
     Praise him! Praise him!
     widely as his mercy flows.

4   Frail as summer's flower we flourish;
     blows the wind and it is gone;
     but, while mortals rise and perish,
     God endures unchanging on.
     Praise him! Praise him!
     Praise the high eternal One.

5   Angels, help us to adore him;
     ye behold him face to face;
     sun and moon, bow down before him;
     dwellers all in time and space.
     Praise him! Praise him!
     Praise with us the God of grace.

                              Henry Francis Lyte (1793–1847)
                                        from *Psalm 103*

Music John Goss (1800–1880)

ST ANNE

CM

1   O God, our help in ages past,
     our hope for years to come,
     our shelter from the stormy blast,
     and our eternal home!

2   Under the shadow of thy throne
     thy saints have dwelt secure;
     sufficient is thine arm alone,
     and our defence is sure.

3   Before the hills in order stood,
     or earth received her frame,
     from everlasting thou art God,
     to endless years the same.

4   A thousand ages in thy sight
     are like an evening gone;
     short as the watch that ends the night
     before the rising sun.

5   Time, like an ever-rolling stream,
     bears all its sons away;
     they fly forgotten, as a dream
     dies at the opening day.

6   O God, our help in ages past,
     our hope for years to come,
     be thou our guard while troubles last,
     and our eternal home.

Isaac Watts (1674–1748)

Music Variant of a melody from *A Supplement to the
New Version,* 1708 probably by William Croft (1678–1727)

LEONI   6684 D

1   The God of Abraham praise,
who reigns enthroned above,
Ancient of everlasting days,
and God of love.
Jehovah, Great I AM!
by earth and heaven confessed,
I bow, and bless the sacred name
for ever blest.

2   The God of Abraham praise,
at whose supreme command
from earth I rise, and seek the joys
at his right hand.
I all on earth forsake,
its wisdom, fame and power,
and him my only portion make,
my shield and tower.

3   He by himself has sworn,
I on his oath depend:
I shall, on eagle's wings upborne,
to heaven ascend;
I shall behold his face,
I shall his power adore
and sing the wonders of his grace
for evermore.

continued overleaf

Music Hebrew melody
arranged Thomas Olivers (1725–1799)

4   There dwells the Lord our King,
    the Lord our Righteousness,
    triumphant o'er the world and sin,
    the Prince of Peace;
    on Zion's sacred height
    his kingdom he maintains,
    and glorious with his saints in light
    for ever reigns.

5   The whole triumphant host
    give thanks to God on high;
    'Hail, Father, Son, and Holy Ghost!'
    they ever cry.
    Hail, Abraham's God, and mine! —
    I join the heavenly praise —
    all might and majesty are thine,
    through endless days.

                    *Thomas Olivers (1725–1799)
                    based on the Jewish *Yigdal*

GRACE IS   66 66 88 66

1 Grace is when God gives us
   the things we don't deserve.
   Grace is when God gives us
   the things we don't deserve.
   He does it because he loves us,
   he does it because he loves us.
   Grace is when God gives us
   the things we don't deserve.

2 Mercy is when God does not
   give us what we deserve.
   Mercy is when God does not
   give us what we deserve.
   He does it because he loves us,
   he does it because he loves us.
   Mercy is when God does not
   give us what we deserve.

Paul Crouch (b. 1963)
and David Mudie (b. 1961)

Music Paul Crouch (b. 1963) and David Mudie (b. 1961)

GOD MADE ME

86 86 86 83

1 God gave me eyes so I could see
the wonders of the world;
without my eyes I could not see
the other boys and girls.
God gave me ears so I could hear
the wind and rain and sea.
I've got to tell it to the world:
God made me.

2 God gave me lips so I could speak
and say what's in my mind;
without my lips I could not speak
a single word or line.
God made my mind so I could think,
and choose what I should be.
I've got to tell it to the world:
God made me.

3 God gave me hands so I could touch,
and hold a thousand things;
without my hands I could not write,
nor could I fetch and bring.
God gave me feet so I could run,
and meant me to be free.
I've got to tell it to the world:
God made me.

Alan Pinnock

Music Alan Pinnock

BONNIE GEORGE CAMPBELL   10 10 10 10

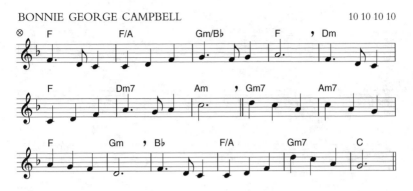

1   Praise to the Lord for the joys of the earth:
     cycles of season and reason and birth,
     contrasts in outlook and landscape and need,
     challenge of famine, pollution, and greed.

2   Praise to the Lord for the progress of life:
     cradle and grave, bond of husband and wife,
     pain of youth growing and wrinkling of age,
     questions in step with experience and stage.

3   Praise to the Lord for his care of our kind:
     faith for the faithless and sight for the blind,
     healing, acceptance, disturbance and change,
     all the emotions through which our lives range.

4   Praise to the Lord for the people we meet,
     safe in our homes or at risk in the street:
     kiss of a lover and friendship's embrace,
     smile of a stranger and words full of grace.

5   Praise to the Lord for the carpenter's son,
     dovetailing worship and work into one:
     tradesman and teacher and vagrant and friend,
     source of all life in this world without end.

        John L. Bell (*b.*1949) and Graham Maule (*b.*1958)

Music Scottish folk melody
arranged Compilers of *Church Hymnary,* 3rd edition, 1973

MINIVER   10 11 11 12

1   Lord of all hopefulness, Lord of all joy,
    whose trust, ever childlike, no cares could destroy,
    be there at our waking, and give us, we pray,
    your bliss in our hearts, Lord, at the break of the day.

2   Lord of all eagerness, Lord of all faith,
    whose strong hands were skilled at the plane and the lathe,
    be there at our labours, and give us, we pray,
    your strength in our hearts, Lord, at the noon of the day.

3   Lord of all kindliness, Lord of all grace,
    your hands swift to welcome, your arms to embrace,
    be there at our homing, and give us, we pray,
    your love in our hearts, Lord, at the eve of the day.

4   Lord of all gentleness, Lord of all calm,
    whose voice is contentment, whose presence is balm,
    be there at our sleeping, and give us, we pray,
    your peace in our hearts, Lord, at the end of the day.

                                    Jan Struther (1901–1953)

Music Cyril Vincent Taylor (1907–1991)

166   Words: From *Enlarged Songs of Praise*, 1931, Oxford University Press, Great Clarendon Street, Oxford.   OX2 6DP.
Reproduced by permission.
166   Music: © Oxford University Press, Great Clarendon Street, Oxford.   OX2 6DP.   Reproduced by permission.

CWM RHONDDA   87 87 87 (7)

Arglwydd, arwain trwy'r anialwch

1   Guide me, O thou great Jehovah,
       pilgrim through this barren land;
       I am weak, but thou art mighty;
       hold me with thy powerful hand:
       Bread of heaven, Bread of heaven,
    *   feed me till my want is o'er.

2   Open now the crystal fountain
       whence the healing stream doth flow;
       let the fire and cloudy pillar
       lead me all my journey through:
       strong Deliverer, strong Deliverer,
       be thou still my strength and shield.

3   When I tread the verge of Jordan,
       bid my anxious fears subside!
       Death of death, and hell's destruction,
       land me safe on Canaan's side!
       Songs of praises, songs of praises,
       I will ever give to thee.

    *   *The last line of each verse is repeated.*

William Williams (1717–1791)
translated Peter Williams (1727–1796)

Music John Hughes, *of Pontypridd* (1873–1932)

EMPATHY 6 4 8 10

1 God weeps
   at love withheld,
   at strength misused,
   at children's innocence abused,
and, till we change the way we love,
       God weeps.

2 God bleeds
   at anger's fist,
   at trust betrayed,
   at women battered and afraid,
and, till we change the way we win,
       God bleeds.

3 God cries
   at hungry mouths,
   at running sores,
   at creatures dying without cause,
and, till we change the way we care,
       God cries.

4 God waits
   for stones to melt,
   for peace to seed,
   for hearts to hold each other's need,
and, till we understand the Christ,
       God waits.

Shirley Erena Murray (*b.* 1931)

Music Ian P. Render (*b.* 1954)

OUR RESPONSE TO GOD
IN ADORATION AND GRATITUDE

PRAISE THE LORD   Irregular

1 Praise the Lord with the sound of trum-pet, praise the Lord with the harp and lute, praise the Lord with the gen-tle sound-ing flute. Praise the Lord in the field and fo-rest, praise the Lord in the ci-ty square, praise the Lord a-ny-time and a-ny-where. Praise the Lord in the wind and sun-shine, praise the Lord in the dark of night, praise the Lord in the rain or snow or in the morn-ing light. Praise the Lord in the deep-est val-ley, praise the Lord on the high-est hill, praise the Lord; ne-ver

Music Natalie Allyn Wakeley Sleeth (1930–1992)

let your voice be still.   way!

1   Praise the Lord with the sound of trumpet,
        praise the Lord with the harp and lute,
        praise the Lord with the gentle-sounding flute.
        Praise the Lord in the field and forest,
        praise the Lord in the city square,
        praise the Lord any time and anywhere.
        Praise the Lord in the wind and sunshine,
        praise the Lord in the dark of night,
        praise the Lord in the rain or snow
        or in the morning light.
        Praise the Lord in the deepest valley,
        praise the Lord on the highest hill,
        praise the Lord; never let your voice be still.

2   Praise the Lord with the crashing cymbal,
        praise the Lord with the pipe and string,
        praise the Lord with the joyful songs you sing.
        Praise the Lord on a weekday morning,
        praise the Lord on a Sunday noon,
        praise the Lord by the light of sun or moon.
        Praise the Lord in the time of sorrow,
        praise the Lord in the time of joy,
        praise the Lord every moment;
        nothing let your praise destroy.
        Praise the Lord in the peace and quiet,
        praise the Lord in your work or play,
        praise the Lord everywhere in every way!

*This may be sung as a two-voice canon, unaccompanied,
at a two-bar distance.*

Natalie Allyn Wakeley Sleeth (1930–1992)

169 Words and Music: From *Sunday Songbook* by Natalie Sleeth.
© 1976 Hinshaw Music (Europe), Highmead, Field Road, Stroud, Gloucestershire. GL5 2JA United Kingdom

LOBET UND PREISET

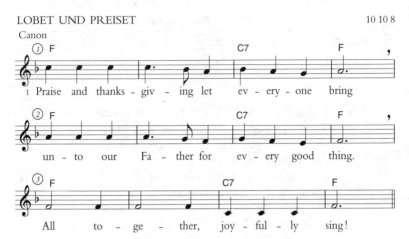

Canon

1 Praise and thanks-giv-ing let ev-ery-one bring

un - to our Fa - ther for ev-ery good thing.

All to - ge - ther, joy - ful - ly sing!

1   Praise and thanksgiving let everyone bring
    unto our Father for every good thing.
    All together, joyfully sing!

2   All people, join us and sing out God's praise.
    For all his blessings your happy songs raise.
    All together, joyfully sing!

3   God, send us out from here sharing your love.
    Help us in coming days our faith to prove.
    All together, joyfully sing!

Marie J. Post (1919–1990)

Music Traditional canon from Alsace
arranged Dale Grotenhuis (b. 1931)

TAKE UP THE SONG   10 10 10 10

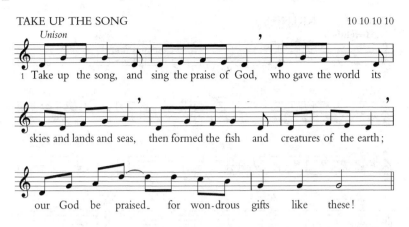

1 Take up the song, and sing the praise of God, who gave the world its skies and lands and seas, then formed the fish and creatures of the earth; our God be praised_ for won-drous gifts like these!

1   Take up the song, and sing the praise of God,
      who gave the world its skies and lands and seas,
      then formed the fish and creatures of the earth;
      our God be praised for wondrous gifts like these!

2   Take up the song, and sing the praise of God,
      who gave the power of choice to humankind,
      that we might rule the earth through servanthood,
      and so find joy in all that God designed.

3   Take up the song, and sing the praise of God;
      proclaim to all the open mystery
      that Christ, whose death destroyed the power of sin,
      was raised by God and reigns in Trinity.

4   Take up the song, and sing the praise of God;
      with music make both earth and heaven ring,
      for God is good and loves all he has made;
      so now to him all thanks and praises bring!

Rae E. Whitney (*b.* 1927)

Music Alfred Victor Fedak (*b.* 1953)

LOBE DEN HERREN   14 14 4 7 8

An alternative harmonisation is found at 124.

1   Sing for God's glory that colours the dawn of creation,
    racing across the sky, trailing bright clouds of elation;
        sun of delight
        succeeds the velvet of night,
    warming the earth's exultation.

2   Sing for God's power that shatters the chains that would
            bind us,
        searing the darkness of fear and despair that could blind us,
        touching our shame
        with love that will not lay blame,
    reaching out gently to find us.

3   Sing for God's justice disturbing each easy illusion,
    tearing down tyrants and putting our pride to confusion;
        lifeblood of right,
        resisting evil and slight,
    offering freedom's transfusion.

4   Sing for God's saints who have travelled faith's journey
            before us,
        who in our weariness give us their hope to restore us;
        in them we see
        the new creation to be,
    spirit of love made flesh for us.

                                        Kathryn Galloway (*b.* 1952)

Music Praxis Pietatis Melica 1668, *arranged* John L. Bell (*b.* 1949)

ODE TO JOY   87 87 D

1   Sing to God new songs of worship —
    all his deeds are marvellous;
    he has brought salvation to us
    with his hand and holy arm:
    he has shown to all the nations
    righteousness and saving power;
    he recalled his truth and mercy
    to his people Israel.

2   Sing to God new songs of worship —
    earth has seen his victory;
    let the lands of earth be joyful
    praising him with thankfulness:
    sound upon the harp his praises,
    play to him with melody;
    let the trumpets sound his triumph,
    show your joy to God the king!

3   Sing to God new songs of worship —
    let the sea now make a noise;
    all on earth and in the waters
    sound your praises to the Lord!
    Let the hills be joyful together
    let the rivers clap their hands,
    for with righteousness and justice
    he will come to judge the earth.

                              Michael Baughen (b. 1930)
                                       from *Psalm 98*

Music from *Symphony No. 9* Ludwig van Beethoven (1770–1827)

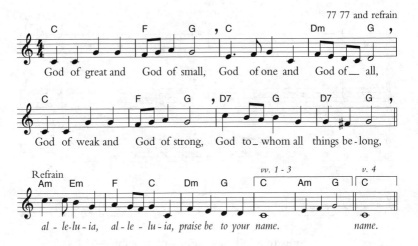

1   God of great and God of small,
     God of one and God of all,
     God of weak and God of strong,
     God to whom all things belong,
          alleluia, alleluia, praise be to your name.

2   God of land and sky and sea,
     God of life and destiny,
     God of never-ending power,
     yet beside me every hour,

3   God of silence, God of sound,
     God by whom the lost are found,
     God of day and darkest night,
     God whose love turns wrong to right,

4   God of heaven and God of earth,
     God of death and God of birth,
     God of now and days before,
     God who reigns for evermore,

                    Natalie Allyn Wakeley Sleeth (1930–1992)

Music Natalie Allyn Wakeley Sleeth (1930–1992)

JE LOUERAI L'ÉTERNEL   Irregular

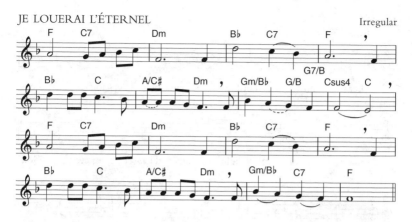

1   Praise, I will praise you, Lord, with all my heart.
     O God, I will tell the wonders of your ways,
     and glorify your name.
     Praise, I will praise you, Lord, with all my heart.
     In you I will find the source of all my joy.
     Alleluia!

2   Love, I will love you, Lord, with all my heart.
     O God, I will tell the wonders of your ways,
     and glorify your name.
     Love, I will love you, Lord, with all my heart.
     In you I will find the source of all my joy.
     Alleluia!

3   Serve, I will serve you, Lord, with all my heart.
     O God, I will tell the wonders of your ways,
     and glorify your name.
     Serve, I will serve you, Lord, with all my heart.
     In you I will find the source of all my joy.
     Alleluia!

Original French text:
Je louerai l'Éternel de tout mon cœur,
je raconterai toutes tes merveilles,
je chanterai ton nom.
Je louerai l'Éternel de tout mon cœur,
je ferai de toi le sujet de ma joie.
Alléluia!

Claude Fraysse (*b.* 1941), from Psalm 9: 1-2
translated Kenneth I. Morse (*b.* 1913)

Music Claude Fraysse (*b.* 1941), *arranged* Alain Bergèse

ROSAS

67 68 D and refrain

Let's sing un-to the Lord__ a hymn of glad re-joic-ing.__ Let's sing a hymn of love, join-ing hearts and hap-py voi-ces.__ God made the sky a-bove,__ the stars, the sun, the o-ceans;__ their voi-ces all pro-claim the__ glo-ry of the Lord.____

Refrain
Al - - le - lu-ia,__ al - le - lu-ia!__ Let's sing un - to the Lord. Al - le - lu - - ia!____

Coda after final refrain
Let's sing un - to the Lord. Al-le-lu - - ia!____

Music Melody by Carlos Rosas *(b.* 1939)
arranged Melva Treffinger Graham *(b.* 1947)

1   Let's sing unto the Lord
a hymn of glad rejoicing.
Let's sing a hymn of love,
joining hearts and happy voices.
God made the sky above,
the stars, the sun, the oceans;
their voices all proclaim
the glory of the Lord.
Alleluia, alleluia!
Let's sing unto the Lord. Alleluia!
Alleluia, alleluia!
Let's sing unto the Lord. Alleluia!

2   Let's sing unto the Lord
a hymn of adoration,
express unto the Lord
our songs of faith and hope.
Creation's broad display
proclaims the work of grandeur,
the boundless love of one
who blesses us with beauty.

Coda after refrain:
Let's sing unto the Lord. Alleluia!

Carlos Rosas *(b. 1939)*
translated Roberto Escamilla *(b. 1931)*,
Elise Eslinger *(b. 1942)*
and George Lockwood *(b. 1946)*

177 THE LIVING GOD

SOLI DEO GLORIA

99 999 and refrain

Steadily

1 O God of blessings all praise to you! Your love sur-rounds us our whole life through. You are the free-dom of those op-pressed; You are the com-fort of all dis-tressed. Come now, O ho-ly and wel-come guest: So - li___ De - o glo - ri - a!

to next verse — *Last time*

rit.

So - li___ De - o glo - ri - a! - a!

Music Marty Haugen (*b.* 1950)

1 O God of blessings, all praise to you!
   Your loves surrounds us our whole life through.
   You are the freedom of those oppressed;
   you are the comfort of all distressed.
   Come now, O holy and welcome guest:
  * *Soli Deo gloria! Soli Deo gloria!*

2 All praise for wisdom, great gift sublime,
   through words and teachers of every time;
   for stories ancient and knowledge new,
   for coaches, mentors, and counsellors true
   whose life of service brought us to you:

3 All praise for prophets, through grace inspired
   to preach and witness with hearts on fire.
   Your Spirit chooses the weak and small
   to sing the new reign where mighty fall;
   with them may we live your Gospel call:

4 All praise for music, deep gift profound,
   through hands and voices in holy sound;
   the psalms of David, and Mary's praise,
   in wordless splendour and lyric phrase,
   with all creation one song we raise:

5 All praise for Jesus, best gift divine
   through word and witness, in bread and wine;
   incarnate love song of boundless grace,
   priest, teacher, prophet in time and space,
   your steadfast kindness with human face:

6 A billion voices in one great song,
   now soft and gentle, now deep and strong,
   in every culture and style and key,
   from hill and valley, with sky and sea,
   with Christ we praise you eternally:

 * *To God alone be glory!*

Marty Haugen (*b.* 1950)

GOD IS GOOD (Kendrick)   Irregular

God is good, we sing and shout it,
God is good, we celebrate.
God is good, no more we doubt it,
God is good, we know it's true.
And when I think of his love for me,
my heart fills with praise and I feel like dancing.
For in his heart there is room for me,
and I run with arms opened wide.
    God is good, we sing and shout it,
    God is good, we celebrate.
    God is good, no more we doubt it,
    God is good, we know it's true. Hey!

Graham Kendrick (*b.* 1950)

Music Graham Kendrick (*b.* 1950)

178   Words and Music: © 1985, Thankyou Music. Administered (UK and Europe) by kingswaysongs.com <tym@kingsway.co.uk>. Remaining territories administered by worshiptogether.com songs. Used by permission.

CROFT'S 136th   6666 4444

An alternative tune DARWALL'S 148th *is found at 449.*

1 Ye holy angels bright,
   who wait at God's right hand,
   or through the realms of light
   fly at your Lord's command,
      assist our song,
      or else the theme
      too high doth seem
      for mortal tongue.

2 Ye blessèd souls at rest,
   who ran this earthly race,
   and now, from sin released,
   behold the Saviour's face,
      his praises sound,
      as in his light
      with sweet delight
      ye do abound.

3 Ye saints, who toil below,
   adore your heavenly King,
   and onward as ye go,
   some joyful anthem sing;
      take what he gives
      and praise him still
      through good and ill,
      who ever lives.

4 My soul, take now thy part,
   triumph in God above,
   and with a well-tuned heart
   sing out the songs of love.
      Let all thy days
      till life shall end,
      whate'er he send,
      be filled with praise.

                    Richard Baxter (1615–1691)
                                and others

Music Melody by William Croft (1678–1727)

GIVE THANKS

Irregular

Give thanks with a grate-ful heart, give thanks to the Ho-ly One, give thanks__ be-cause he's gi-ven__ Je-sus Christ,_____ his Son. Give Son. And now let the weak say, 'I am strong!' Let the poor say, 'I am rich be-cause of what the Lord has done for__ us!' And now let the weak say, 'I am strong!' Let the poor say, 'I am rich be-cause of what the Lord has done for__ us!' Give us!' Give thanks.

1st & 3rd times — *2nd & 4th times*

Final time to Coda

D.S. al Coda — *Coda*

Music Henry Smith (b. 1952)

Give thanks with a grateful heart,
give thanks to the Holy One,
give thanks because he's given
Jesus Christ, his Son.
Give thanks with a grateful heart,
give thanks to the Holy One,
give thanks because he's given
Jesus Christ, his Son.

And now let the weak say, 'I am strong!'
Let the poor say, 'I am rich
because of what the Lord has done for us!'
And now let the weak say, 'I am strong!'
Let the poor say, 'I am rich
because of what the Lord has done for us!'

Give thanks with a grateful heart,
give thanks to the Holy One,
give thanks because he's given
Jesus Christ, his Son.
Give thanks with a grateful heart,
give thanks to the Holy One,
give thanks because he's given
Jesus Christ, his Son.

Coda:
Give thanks.

Henry Smith (*b.* 1952)

180 Words and Music: © 1978 Scripture in Song, a division of Integrity Music / Sovereign Lifestyle Music Ltd, PO Box 356, Leighton Buzzard LU7 3WP <sovereignmusic@aol.com>

LUCERNA LAUDONIAE   7777 and refrain

God, to you we raise this our sa - cri - fice of praise.

1   For the beauty of the earth,
        for the beauty of the skies,
        for the love which from our birth
        over and around us lies:
          Christ, our God, to you we raise
          this our sacrifice of praise.

2   For the beauty of each hour
        of the day and of the night,
        hill and vale, and tree and flower,
        sun and moon and stars of light:

3   For the joy of ear and eye,
        for the heart and mind's delight,
        for the mystic harmony
        linking sense to sound and sight:

4   For the joy of human love,
        brother, sister, parent, child,
        friends on earth, and friends above,
        for all gentle thoughts and mild:

5   For each perfect gift and sign
        of your love so freely given,
        graces human and divine,
        flowers of earth and buds of heaven:

Folliott Sandford Pierpoint (1835–1917)

Music David Evans (1874–1948)

MOSELEY   7777 and refrain

Unison (vv. 1, 3, 5)

1 For the beau-ty of the earth, for the beau-ty of the skies, for the love which from our birth o-ver and a-round us lies: *Christ, our God, to you we raise this our sac-ri-fice of praise.*

Refrain

Fine

Harmony (vv. 2, 4)

2 For the beau-ty of each hour of the day and of the night, hill and vale, and tree and flower, sun and moon and stars of light: *Christ, our God, to you we raise this our sac-ri-fice of praise.*

Refrain

Music John Joubert (b. 1927)

NUN DANKET   6767 6666

1   Now thank we all our God,
        with heart and hands and voices,
        who wondrous things has done,
        in whom his world rejoices;
        who from our mothers' arms
        has blessed us on our way
        with countless gifts of love,
        and still is ours today.

2   Oh, may this bounteous God
        through all our life be near us,
        with ever-joyful hearts
        and blessèd peace to cheer us,
        and keep us in his grace,
        and guide us when perplexed,
        and free us from all ills
        in this world and the next.

3   All praise and thanks to God
        who reigns in highest heaven —
        the Father and the Son
        and Spirit — now be given:
        the one, eternal God,
        whom earth and heaven adore;
        for thus it was, is now,
        and shall be evermore.

Martin Rinkart (1586–1649)
translated *Catherine Winkworth (1827–1878)

Music Johann Crüger
Later form of a melody in Crüger's *Praxis Pietatis Melica* c. 1647
harmonised Felix Mendelssohn (1809–1847), from *Lobgesang* 1840

BILLING   CM

1   Fill now our life, O Lord our God,
in every part with praise,
that our whole being may proclaim
your being and your ways.

2   Not for the lip of praise alone,
nor even the praising heart
we ask, but for a life made up
of praise in every part:

3   Praise in the common things of life,
its goings out and in;
praise in each duty and each deed,
though humble and unseen.

4   So, gracious Lord, you shall receive
from us the glory due;
and so we shall begin on earth
the song for ever new.

Horatius N. Bonar (1808–1889)

Music Richard Runciman Terry (1865–1938)
adapted Compilers of *More Hymns for Today,* 1980

GONFALON ROYAL   LM

A — — — men.

1   Sing to the Lord a joyful song,
   lift up your hearts, your voices raise;
   to us his gracious gifts belong,
   to him our songs of love and praise.

2   For life and love, for rest and food,
   for daily help and nightly care,
   sing to the Lord, for he is good,
   and praise his name, for it is fair.

3   For strength to those who on him wait
   his truth to prove, his will to do,
   sing to our God, for he is great,
   trust in his name, for it is true.

4   For joys untold, that from above
   cheer those who love his sweet employ,
   sing to our God, for he is love;
   exalt his name, for it is joy.

5   Sing to the Lord of heaven and earth,
   whom angels serve and saints adore,
   the Father, Son, and Spirit blest,
   to whom be praise for evermore. Amen.

*John Samuel Bewley Monsell (1811–1875)

Music Percy Carter Buck (1871–1947)

MADRID   6666 666 6

1   Come, children, join and sing
alleluia! amen!
loud praise to Christ our King;
alleluia! amen!
Let all, with heart and voice,
before his throne rejoice;
praise is his gracious choice:
alleluia! amen!

2   Come, lift your hearts on high;
alleluia! amen!
let praises fill the sky;
alleluia! amen!
He is our guide and friend,
on him we can depend;
his love shall never end:
alleluia! amen!

3   Sing praises loud and long;
alleluia! amen!
life shall not end the song;
alleluia! amen!
on heaven's blissful shore
his goodness we'll adore,
singing for evermore,
alleluia! amen!

*Christian Henry Bateman (1813–1889)

Music probably based on an old Spanish melody
harmonised David Evans (1874–1948)

Father God, I wonder
how I managed to exist
without the knowledge of
your parenthood and your loving care.
But now I am your child,
I am adopted in your family,
and I can never be alone
'cause, Father God, you're there beside me.
I will sing your praises,
I will sing your praises,
I will sing your praises for evermore.

The last three lines are sung twice.

Ian Smale (*b.* 1949)

Music Ian Smale (*b.* 1949)
arranged David Christopher Peacock (*b.* 1949)

ALL FOR JESUS   87 87

1   There's a wideness in God's mercy,
        like the wideness of the sea;
        there's a kindness in his justice,
        which is more than liberty.

2   There is no place where earth's sorrows
        are more felt than in God's heaven:
        there is no place where earth's failings
        have such kindly judgment given.

3   For the love of God is broader
        than the grasp of mortal mind;
        and the heart of the Eternal
        is most wonderfully kind.

4   If our love were but more simple,
        we would take him at his word;
        and our lives be filled with glory
        from the glory of the Lord.

              *Frederick William Faber (1814–1863)

Music John Stainer (1840–1901)

ST PETERSBURG   88 88 88

Verborgne Gottesliebe du

1   Thou hidden Love of God, whose height,
    whose depth unfathomed, no one knows,
    I see from far thy beauteous light,
    inly I sigh for thy repose;
    my heart is pained, nor can it be
    at rest till it finds rest in thee.

2   Thy secret voice invites me still
    the sweetness of thy yoke to prove;
    and fain I would; but, though my will
    seem fixed, yet wide my passions rove;
    yet hindrances strew all the way;
    I aim at thee, yet from thee stray.

3   'Tis mercy all, that thou hast brought
    my mind to seek her peace in thee;
    yet, while I seek but find thee not,
    no peace my wandering soul shall see.
    Oh, when shall all my wanderings end,
    and all my steps to thee-ward tend?

4   Is there a thing beneath the sun
    that strives with thee my heart to share?
    Ah! tear it thence, and reign alone,
    the Lord of every motion there;
    then shall my heart from earth be free,
    when it has found repose in thee.

                    Gerhard Tersteegen (1697–1769)
                translated John Wesley (1703–1791)

Music Dmitry Stefanovich Bortniansky (1751–1825)

BE STILL   Irregular

1 Be still,
    for the presence of the Lord,
    the Holy One, is here;
    come bow before him now
    with reverence and fear:
    in him no sin is found —
    we stand on holy ground.
    Be still,
    for the presence of the Lord,
    the Holy One, is here.

2 Be still,
    for the glory of the Lord
    is shining all around;
    he burns with holy fire,
    with splendour he is crowned:
    how awesome is the sight —
    our radiant king of light!
    Be still,
    for the glory of the Lord
    is shining all around.

3 Be still,
    for the power of the Lord
    is moving in this place;
    he comes to cleanse and heal,
    to minister his grace:
    no work too hard for him —
    in faith receive from him.
    Be still,
    for the power of the Lord
    is moving in this place.

David J. Evans (b. 1957)

Music David J. Evans (b. 1957)

ST STEPHEN (ABRIDGE)   CM

PARAPHRASE 22, verses 3–8

1   Art thou afraid his power shall fail
when comes thy evil day?
And can an all-creating arm
grow weary or decay?

2   Supreme in wisdom as in power
the Rock of ages stands;
though him thou canst not see, nor trace
the working of his hands.

3   He gives the conquest to the weak,
supports the fainting hearts;
and courage in the evil hour
his heavenly aid imparts.

4   Mere human power shall fast decay,
and youthful vigour cease;
but they who wait upon the Lord
in strength shall still increase.

5   They with unwearied feet shall tread
the path of life divine;
with growing ardour onward move,
with growing brightness shine.

6   On eagles' wings they mount, they soar,
their wings are faith and love,
till, past the cloudy regions here,
they rise to heaven above.

Scottish Paraphrases, 1781
Isaiah 40: 28–end

Music Melody by Isaac Smith (1734–1805)
from *A Collection of Psalm Tunes* c. 1780

DO NOT BE AFRAID

Irregular

Do not be afraid, for I have redeemed you.
I have called you by your name; you are mine.

1   When you walk through the waters I'll be with you,
      you will never sink beneath the waves.

2   When the fire is burning all around you,
      you will never be consumed by the flames.

3   When the fear of loneliness is looming,
      then remember I am at your side.

4   When you dwell in the exile of the stranger,
      remember you are precious in my eyes.

5   You are mine, O my child; I am your Father,
      and I love you with a perfect love.

Gerald Markland (*b.*1953)
from *Isaiah 43: 1- 4*

Music Gerald Markland (*b.*1953)
arranged Roland T. Fudge (*b.*1947)

191 Words and Music: © 1978 Kevin Mayhew Ltd, Buxhall, Stowmarket, Suffolk. IP14 3BW,

MICHAEL   87 87 33 7

Meine Hoffnung stehet feste

1   All my hope on God is founded,
       all my trust he will renew;
       safe through change and chance he guides me,
       only good and only true.
       God unknown,
       he alone
       calls my heart to be his own.

2   Human pride and earthly glory,
       sword and crown betray God's trust;
       though with care and toil we build them,
       tower and temple fall to dust.
       But God's power,
       hour by hour,
       is my temple and my tower.

Music Herbert Norman Howells (1892–1983)

GROESWEN   87 87 33 7

3   God's great goodness lasts for ever,
deep his wisdom passing thought:
splendour, light, and life attend him,
beauty springing out of naught.
Evermore,
from his store
new-born worlds rise and adore.

4   Day by day the mighty Giver
showers gifts on us below;
his desire our souls delight in,
pleasure leads us where we go.
See love stand
at his hand,
joy awaits at his command!

5   Still from earth to God in heaven
sacrifice of praise be done,
high above all praises praising
for the gift of Christ his Son.
Hear Christ call
one and all:
those who follow shall not fall.

*Robert Bridges (1844–1930)
based on Joachim Neander (1650–1680)

Music John Ambrose Lloyd (1815–1874)

PERSONENT HODIE   666 66 and refrain

1 God is love: his the care,
   tending each, everywhere.
   God is love — all is there!
   Jesus came to show him,
   that we all might know him:
      Sing aloud, loud, loud!
      Sing aloud, loud, loud!
      God is good!
      God is truth!
      God is beauty! Praise him!

2 None can see God above;
   all must here learn to love,
   thus may we Godward move,
   finding him in others,
   sisters all, and brothers:

3 Jesus shared joy and pain,
   lived and died, rose again,
   rules our hearts, now as then;
   for he came to save us
   by the truth he gave us:

4 To our Lord praise we sing —
   light and life, friend and king,
   coming down love to bring,
   pattern for our duty,
   showing God in beauty:

   Percy Dearmer (1867–1936)

Music Piae Cantiones, 1582, *arranged* Compilers

193 Words: From *Enlarged Songs of Praise,* 1931, Oxford University Press, Great Clarendon Street, Oxford. OX2 6DP.
Reproduced by permission.

Also suitable
Praise to the Lord, the Almighty, the King of creation   124
In the Lord I'll ever be thankful   772

THE LORD'S DAY   Irregular

1 This is the day,
   this is the day that the Lord has made,
   that the Lord has made.
   We will rejoice,
   we will rejoice and be glad in it,
   and be glad in it.
   This is the day that the Lord has made,
   we will rejoice and be glad in it.
   This is the day,
   this is the day that the Lord has made.

2 This is the day ... that he rose again, *

3 This is the day ... when the Spirit came, *

   * These (last four) words in verse 2 and verse 3
      take the place of 'that the Lord has made' in verse 1.

                                    Author unknown

Music Fijian traditional melody
arranged John L. Bell (b. 1949)

KHAO I DANG

88 88 88

1 Here to the house of God we come,
home of the people of the Way,
here to give thanks for all we have,
naming our needs for every day,
we who have roof and rent and bread,
sure of a place to rest our head.

2 There is a knocking at our door,
sound of the homeless of the world,
voice of the frightened refugee,
cry of the children in the cold,
asking the least that is their right,
safety and shelter for the night.

3 God who is shelter, who is home,
in borrowed rooms you came to live,
pleaded to save the dispossessed,
crucified, lay in borrowed grave:
these are no strangers in your eyes,
this is your family which cries.

4 We are all tenants of your love;
gather us round a common fire,
warm us in company with Christ,
give us the heart to feel, to share
table and lodging with free hand,
space in our living, in our land.

Shirley Erena Murray (*b.* 1931)

Music Colin Alexander Gibson (*b.* 1933)

Come, now is the time to worship.
Come, now is the time to give your heart.
Come, just as you are to worship.
Come, just as you are before your God, come.
One day every tongue will confess Christ is Lord,
one day every knee will bow.
Still, the greatest treasure remains
for those who gladly choose him now.

The last four lines are sung twice.

Music Brian Doerksen   Brian Doerksen

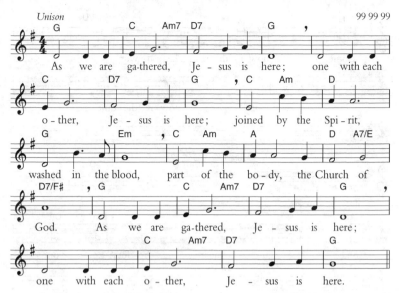

As we are gathered, Jesus is here;
one with each other, Jesus is here;
joined by the Spirit, washed in the blood,
part of the body, the Church of God.
As we are gathered, Jesus is here;
one with each other, Jesus is here.

John Daniels

Music
Melody by John Daniels *arranged* Richard Hey Lloyd (*b.*1933)

198

vi - sions, rock of faith and vault of grace; here the
love of Christ shall end di - vi - sions: All are wel - come,
all are wel - come, all are wel - come in this place.

1. Let us build a house where love can dwell
   and all can safely live,
   a place where saints and children tell
   how hearts learn to forgive;
   built of hopes and dreams and visions,
   rock of faith and vault of grace;
   here the love of Christ shall end divisions:
   All are welcome,
   all are welcome,
   all are welcome in this place.

2. Let us build a house where prophets speak,
   and words are strong and true,
   where all God's children dare to seek
   to dream God's reign anew.
   Here the cross shall stand as witness
   and as symbol of God's grace;
   here as one we claim the faith of Jesus:

3. Let us build a house where love is found
   in water, wine and wheat:
   a banquet hall on holy ground,
   where peace and justice meet.
   Here the love of God, through Jesus,
   is revealed in time and space,
   as we share in Christ the feast that frees us:

continued overleaf

Music Marty Haugen (*b.* 1950)

198 Words and Music: © 1994, GIA Publications Inc., 7404 S. Mason Avenue, Chicago, IL 60638, USA. Used by permission.

THE LIVING GOD

All are wel - come,
all are wel - come, all are wel - come in this place.

vv. 1 - 4   *v. 5*

4   Let us build a house where hands will reach
     beyond the wood and stone
     to heal and strengthen, serve and teach,
     and live the Word they've known.
     Here the outcast and the stranger
     bear the image of God's face;
     let us bring an end to fear and danger:

5   Let us build a house where all are named,
     their songs and visions heard
     and loved and treasured, taught and claimed
     as words within the Word.
     Built of tears and cries and laughter,
     prayers of faith and songs of grace,
     let this house proclaim from floor to rafter:

Marty Haugen (*b.* 1950)

1 One thing I ask,
   one thing I seek,
   that I may dwell in your
      house, O Lord,
   all of my days,
   all of my life
   that I may see you, Lord.

2 Hear me, O Lord,
   hear me when I cry;
   Lord, do not hide your
      face from me:
   you have been my strength,
   you have been my shield,
   and you will lift me up.

   One thing I ask,
   one thing I desire
   is to see you,
   is to see you.

Andy Park
from Psalm 84

Music Andy Park

199 Words and Music: © 1989, Mercy / Vineyard Publishing / Vineyard Songs Canada. Administered by CopyCare Ltd, PO Box 77, Hailsham, East Sussex, BN27 3EF, United Kingdom. <music@copycare.com>. Used by permission.

WESTMINSTER ABBEY   87 87 87

Music Henry Purcell (1659–1695)
arranged Ernest Hawkins (1802–1868), *The Psalmist,* 1842

Angularis fundamentum lapis Christus missus est

1   Christ is made the sure foundation,
     Christ the head and corner-stone,
     chosen of the Lord and precious,
     binding all the Church in one,
     holy Zion's help for ever,
     and her confidence alone.

2   To this temple, where we call you,
     come, O Lord of Hosts, today:
     with your constant loving-kindness,
     hear your servants as they pray,
     and your fullest benediction
     shed within its walls alway.

3   Here bestow on all your servants
     what they ask of you to gain,
     what they gain from you for ever
     with the blessèd to retain,
     and hereafter in your glory
     evermore with you to reign.

4   Praise and honour to the Father,
     praise and honour to the Son,
     praise and honour to the Spirit,
     ever Three and ever One,
     One in might and One in glory
     while unending ages run.

                              7th or 8th century
     translated *John Mason Neale (1818–1866)

201

MOREDUN   12 10 12 10

1   Worship the Lord in the beauty of holiness;
    bow down before him, his glory proclaim;
    gold of obedience and incense of lowliness
    bring, and adore him; the Lord is his Name!

2   Low at his feet lay thy burden of carefulness;
    high on his heart he will bear it for thee,
    comfort thy sorrows, and answer thy prayerfulness,
    guiding thy steps as may best for thee be.

3   Fear not to enter his courts, in the slenderness
    of the poor wealth thou canst reckon as thine;
    truth in its beauty and love in its tenderness,
    these are the offerings to lay on his shrine.

4   These, though we bring them in trembling and fearfulness,
    he will accept for the Name that is dear,
    mornings of joy give for evenings of tearfulness,
    trust for our trembling, and hope for our fear.

5   Worship the Lord in the beauty of holiness;
    bow down before him, his glory proclaim;
    gold of obedience and incense of lowliness
    bring, and adore him; the Lord is his Name!

John Samuel Bewley Monsell (1811–1875)

Music Henry Thomas Smart (1813–1879)

CARLISLE   SM

1   Stand up and bless the Lord;
     all people now rejoice:
     stand up and bless the Lord your God
     with heart and soul and voice.

2   Though high above all praise,
     above all blessing high,
     who would not fear his holy name,
     give thanks and glorify?

3   O for the living flame
     from his own altar brought,
     to touch our lips, our minds inspire,
     and wing to heaven our thought!

4   God is our strength and song,
     and his salvation ours;
     then be his love in Christ proclaimed
     with all our ransomed powers.

5   Stand up and bless the Lord,
     the Lord your God adore;
     stand up and bless his glorious name
     both now and evermore.

                    *James Montgomery (1771–1854)

Music Melody and most of the harmony by
Charles Lockhart (1745–1815)

ENGELBERG   10 10 10 and Alleluia

1   When, in our music, God is glorified,
       and adoration leaves no room for pride,
       it is as though the whole creation cried,
       Alleluia!

2   How often, making music, we have found
       a new dimension in the world of sound,
       as worship moved us to a more profound
       Alleluia!

3   So has the Church, in liturgy and song,
       in faith and love, through centuries of wrong,
       borne witness to the truth in every tongue:
       Alleluia!

4   And did not Jesus sing a psalm that night
       when utmost evil strove against the light?
       Then let us sing, for whom he won the fight:
       Alleluia!

5   Let every instrument be tuned for praise!
       Let all rejoice who have a voice to raise!
       And may God give us faith to sing always:
       Alleluia!

                 Frederick Pratt Green (1903–2000)

Music Charles Villiers Stanford (1852–1924)
arranged Compilers of *BBC Hymn Book,* 1951

MAYFLOWER

10 10 10 and Alleluias

With spirit

1 When, in our mu - sic, God is glo - ri - fied,
and a - do - ra - tion leaves no room for pride,
It is as though the whole cre - a - tion cried, Al - le - lu -
- ia! Al - le - lu - ia! Al - le - lu - ia!

Woodwind (recorder)

Last time

Music Marty Haugen (*b.* 1950)

203.ii Music: © 1989, GIA Publications Inc., 7404 S. Mason Avenue, Chicago, IL 60638, USA. Used by permission.

WE ARE THE CHURCH   Irregular

I am the Church! You are the Church! We are the Church to-
-ge-ther! All who fol-low Je-sus, all a-round the world,
yes, we're the Church to-ge-ther. 1 The Church is not a
build-ing, the Church is not a stee-ple. The
Church is not a resting place, the Church is a people!

Music Richard Kinsey Avery (*b.*1934)
and Donald Stuart Marsh (*b.*1923)

I am the Church! You are the Church!
We are the Church together!
All who follow Jesus, all around the world,
yes, we're the Church together.

1   The Church is not a building, the Church is not a steeple.
The Church is not a resting-place, the Church is a people!

2   We're many kinds of people with many kinds of faces:
all colours and all ages, too, from all times and places.

3   And when the people gather there's singing and
          there's praying,
there's laughing and there's crying sometimes,
          all of it saying:

4   At Pentecost some people received the Holy Spirit
and told the good news through the world to all
          who would hear it.

5   I count if I am ninety, or nine, or just a baby;
there's one thing I am sure about and I don't mean maybe:

Suggested actions during chorus:

I am the Church! — *(with your thumb, point to yourself)*
You are the Church! — *(point to your partner)*
We are the Church together! — *(shake hands with your partner)*
All who follow Jesus, — *(reach out with both hands)*
all around the world, — *(circle arms over head)*
yes, we're the Church together. — *(link arms)*

Richard Kinsey Avery (b. 1934)
and Donald Stuart Marsh (b. 1923)

RUTHERFORD   6 10 10

1 Lord, can this real - ly be?   Is this your Church, the

people that I see, who gather here and worship you with me?

Coda

Lord, could this real - ly be?   Lord, let it real - ly be.

1   Lord, can this really be?
    Is this your Church, the people that I see,
    who gather here and worship you with me?

2   And must I love them all,
    shoulder their loads, and answer when they call,
    forgive their faults and raise them when they fall?

3   Are these the ear, eye, hand,
    your body, Lord, bound firmly in one band
    and learning to obey your great command?

4   Is this the very place,
    the school of love, where we would see your face,
    and through your Spirit gain enabling grace?

5   Our faith a channel make
    to bring us grace. Our judging hearts now take,
    and lead us into oneness for your sake.

6   The true Church we'll become
    when all the world will see us live as one,
    and know you, Jesus, as the Father's Son.

    Coda:
    Lord, could this really be?
    Lord, let it really be.

*William Rutherford

Music John L. Bell (*b.* 1949)

ROBERT   10 11 10 11

1 Break not the circle of enabling love,
  where people grow, forgiven and forgiving;
  break not that circle — make it wider still,
  till it includes, embraces all the living.

2 Come, wonder at the love that comes to life,
  where words of freedom are with humour spoken
  and people keep no score of wrong and guilt,
  but will that human bonds remain unbroken.

3 Sing high! Give thanks for all who came and come
  to teach the world the craft of hopeful craving
  for peace and wholeness that will fill the earth;
  for faith that stirs us to creative living.

4 Join then the movement of the love that frees,
  till people of whatever race or nation
  will truly be themselves, stand on their feet,
  see eye to eye with laughter and elation.

Fred Kaan (b. 1929)

Music Margaret R. Tucker (b. 1936)

206 Words: © 1975, Stainer & Bell Ltd, PO Box 110, Victoria House, 23 Gruneisen Road, London N3 1DZ

206 Music: © Margaret R. Tucker, 9787 Westview Drive, Houston, TX 77055-6317, USA. From *Hymns of Truth and Light*.
Used by permission.

HALAD   10 10 10 7

Grant now your blessing upon this offering,
that we are bringing with our thanksgiving,
may you bestow, Lord, on us your children,
your grace and mercy. Amen.

Rolando S. Tinio

Music Philippine folk melody
arranged Lawrence Francis Bartlett (1933–2002)

208

Refrain

Sha - lom, __ sha - lom, __ peace to his

peo - ple. Sha - lom, sha - lom, __ the grace of

God be __ with __ you, now and for ev - er. __

1 The love __ of God be with you, __

a bound - less love with no

mea - sure, a love __ you dai - ly must trea - sure __

Music Elaine Davies

Our Response to God – in the worship of God's house

now and for ev - er.

Shalom, shalom,	1	The love of God be with you,
peace to his people.		a boundless love with no measure,
Shalom, shalom,		a love you daily must treasure
the grace of God be with you,		now and for ever.
now and for ever.		

2   The grace of God be with you,
    a loving grace with no measure,
    his grace and favour we treasure
    now and for ever.

3   The peace of God be with you,
    a quiet calm with no measure,
    God's loving peace you must treasure
    now and for ever.

The final refrain is repeated.

Elaine Davies

Also suitable

OUR RESPONSE TO GOD
IN THE MORNING AND EVENING

CHRISTE SANCTORUM · 11 11 11 5

A lower setting is found at 64.

1   Father, we praise you, now the night is over;
      active and watchful, stand we all before you;
      singing, we offer prayer and meditation;
      thus we adore you.

2   Monarch of all things, fit us for your mansions;
      banish our weakness, health and wholeness sending;
      bring us to heaven, where your saints united
      joy without ending.

3   All-holy Father, Son, and equal Spirit,
      Trinity blessèd, send us your salvation;
      yours is the glory, gleaming and resounding
      through all creation.

10th century or earlier
translated Percy Dearmer (1867–1936)

Music Melody, *Paris Antiphoner*, 1681
harmonised David Evans (1874–1948)

MORNING HYMN   LM

1   Awake, my soul, and with the sun
        your daily stage of duty run;
        shake off your sleep, and joyful rise
        to pay your morning sacrifice.

2   Wake, and lift up yourself, my heart,
        and with the angels take your part,
        who all night long unwearied sing
        high praise to the eternal King.

3   Lord, I my vows to you renew;
        disperse my sins as morning dew;
        guard my first springs of thought and will,
        and with yourself my spirit fill.

4   Direct, control, suggest, this day,
        all I design, or do, or say,
        that all my powers, with all their might
        in your sole glory may unite.

5   Praise God, from whom all blessings flow;
        praise him, all creatures here below;
        praise him above, you heavenly host;
        praise Father, Son, and Holy Ghost.

*Thomas Ken (1637–1711)

Music Melody by François Hyppolyte Barthélémon (1741–1808)
arranged Samuel Sebastian Wesley (1810–1876)

SLITHERS OF GOLD   11 10 11 10

1 To-day I a-wake___ and God is be-fore___ me. At night, as I dreamt,___ he sum-moned the day;_____ for God ne-ver sleeps___ but pat-terns the morn - - ing with sli-thers of gold_____ or glo-ry in grey._____

1 Today I awake
and God is before me.
At night, as I dreamt,
he summoned the day;
for God never sleeps
but patterns the morning
with slithers of gold
or glory in grey.

2 Today I arise
and Christ is beside me.
He walked through the dark
to scatter new light.
Yes, Christ is alive,
and beckons his people
to hope and to heal,
resist, and invite.

3 Today I affirm
the Spirit within me
at worship and work,
in struggle and rest.
The Spirit inspires
all life which is changing
from fearing to faith,
from broken to blest.

4 Today I enjoy
the Trinity round me,
above and beneath,
before and behind;
the Maker, the Son,
the Spirit together —
they called me to life
and call me their friend.

John L. Bell (b. 1949)
and Graham Maule (b. 1958)

Music John L. Bell (b. 1949)

BUNESSAN   5554 D

Another version is found at 314.

1   Morning has broken
like the first morning,
blackbird has spoken
like the first bird.
Praise for the singing,
praise for the morning,
praise for them, springing
fresh from the Word!

2   Sweet the rain's new fall
sunlit from heaven,
like the first dewfall
on the first grass.
Praise for the sweetness
of the wet garden,
sprung in completeness
where his feet pass.

3   Mine is the sunlight;
mine is the morning,
born of the one light
Eden saw play!
Praise with elation,
praise every morning,
God's re-creation
of the new day!

Eleanor Farjeon (1881–1965)

Music Gaelic folk melody
arranged Compilers of *Church Hymnary,* 3rd edition, 1973

BUNESSAN   5554 D

1 Every new morning
   God gives us freely
   hearts that are thankful,
   strength for the task,
   people who love us,
   joy in our service,
   all we have need of
   if we but ask.

2 God will be with us
   in all our thinking,
   in all our speaking,
   in all we do;
   and as we praise him
   by all our actions,
   he will be with us,
   seeing us through.

3 God in the morning,
   God in the noontide,
   God in the evening,
   all through the day;
   God is within us,
   and all around us,
   God goes before us,
   all of the way.

Carol Dixon (*b.* 1947)

This hymn was originally set to the author's own tune
EVERY NEW MORNING.

TRURO   LM

14 2

MELCOMBE   LM

1   New every morning is the love
         our wakening and uprising prove,
         through sleep and darkness safely brought,
         restored to life, and power, and thought.

2   New mercies, each returning day,
         hover around us while we pray, —
         new perils past, new sins forgiven,
         new thoughts of God, new hopes of heaven.

3   If, on our daily course, our mind
         be set to hallow all we find,
         new treasures still, of countless price,
         God will provide for sacrifice.

4   The trivial round, the common task,
         will furnish all we ought to ask, —
         room to deny ourselves, a road
         to bring us daily nearer God.

5   Prepare us, Lord, in your dear love,
         for perfect life with you above;
         and help us, this and every day,
         to live more nearly as we pray.

                       John Keble (1792–1866)

Music Tune 1 Melody in Thomas Williams's
Psalmodia Evangelica, 1789

Music Tune 2 Samuel Webbe, the elder (1740–1816)
An Essay on the Church Plain-chant, 1782

215

DUNOON

10 10 10 10

Introduction ad lib. (Verse 1 only) % Unison Verses 1 - 3

D.S.
vv. 1, 2, 3 end here

Verse 4

1 Most glorious Lord of life, that on this day
   didst make thy triumph over death and sin,
   and having harrowed hell, didst bring away
   captivity thence captive, us to win:

2 This joyous day, dear Lord, with joy begin,
   and grant that we, for whom thou diddest die,
   being with thy dear blood clean washed from sin,
   may live for ever in felicity:

3 And that thy love we, weighing worthily,
   may likewise love thee for the same again;
   and for thy sake, that all like dear didst buy,
   with love may one another entertain.

4 So let us love, dear Love, like as we ought,
   love is the lesson which the Lord us taught.

Edmund Spenser (*c.* 1552–1599)

Music Kenneth Leighton (1929–1988)

MIGHTY SAVIOUR   11 11 11 6

An alternative tune CHRISTE SANCTORUM *is found at 209.*

1   Christ, mighty Saviour, Light of all creation,
        you make the daytime radiant with the sunlight
        and to the night give glittering adornment,
        stars in the heavens.

2   Now comes the day's end as the sun is setting:
        mirror of daybreak, pledge of resurrection;
        while in the heavens choirs of stars appearing
        hallow the nightfall.

3   Therefore we come now evening rites to offer,
        joyfully chanting holy hymns to praise you,
        with all creation joining hearts and voices
        singing your glory.

4   Give heed, we pray you, to our supplication:
        that you may grant us pardon for offences,
        strength for our weak hearts, rest for aching bodies,
        soothing the weary.

5   Though bodies slumber, hearts shall keep their vigil,
        forever resting in the peace of Jesus,
        in light or darkness worshipping our Saviour
        now and for ever.

Mozarabic hymn, 10th century
translated Alan Gordon McDougall (1875–1964)
revised Anne Kingsbury LeCroy (b.1930)

Music David Hurd (b.1950)

217

JOEL

87 87 D

1   God of day and God of darkness,
     now we stand before the night;
     as the shadows stretch and deepen,
     come and make our darkness bright.
     All creation still is groaning
     for the dawning of your might,
     when the Sun of peace and justice
     fills the earth with radiant light.

2   Praise to you in day and darkness,
     you our source and you our end;
     praise to you who love and nurture us
     as a father, mother, friend.
     Grant us all a peaceful resting,
     let each mind and body mend,
     let us rise refreshed tomorrow
     for the tasks which you will send.

                              Marty Haugen (*b.* 1950)

Music Sally Ann Morris (*b.* 1952)

217   Words: © The Pilgrim Press, 700 Prospect Avenue East, Cleveland, OH 44115-1100, USA. Permission applied for.
217   Music: © GIA Publications Inc., 7404 S. Mason Avenue, Chicago, IL 60638, USA. Used by permission.

LINCOLN (Bell)   55 65

1   Now that evening falls,
    gently fades the light;
    moon replaces sun and
    day takes leave of night.

2   Gratitude we raise
    for the day that's done,
    and for what, tomorrow,
    waits to be begun.

3   Gladly we commit
    to God's gracious care
    those we love and long for,
    those whose lives we share.

4   Glory be to God,
    glory to God's Son,
    glory to the Spirit
    ever three in one.

                    John L. Bell (b. 1949)

Music John L. Bell (b. 1949)

SEBASTE   Irregular

1 Hail, gladdening Light, of his pure glo - ry poured
who is the immortal Fa - ther, heaven - ly, blest,
Ho - li - est of Ho - lies, Je - sus Christ, our Lord.
2 Now we are come to the sun's hour of rest,
the lights of eve - ning round us shine.
We hymn the Fa - ther, Son and Ho - ly Spi - rit di - vine.
3 Worthiest art thou at all times to be sung with un - de - fi - lèd
tongue, Son of our God, Gi-ver of life, a - lone:
there-fore in all the world thy glo - ries, Lord, we own.

Φῶς ἱλαρὸν ἁγίας δόξις

1   Hail gladdening Light, of his pure glory poured
    who is the immortal Father, heavenly, blest,
    Holiest of Holies, Jesus Christ, our Lord.

2   Now we are come to the sun's hour of rest,
    the lights of evening round us shine.
    We hymn the Father, Son and Holy Spirit divine.

3   Worthiest art thou at all times to be sung
    with undefilèd tongue,
    Son of our God, Giver of life, alone:
    therefore in all the world thy glories, Lord, we own.

Greek, 3rd century or earlier
translated John Keble (1792–1866)

Music John Stainer (1840–1901)

ST CLEMENT   9898

1   The day you gave us, Lord, has ended;
       the darkness falls at your behest;
       to you our morning hymns ascended,
       your praise shall sanctify our rest.

2   We thank you that your Church unsleeping,
       while earth rolls onward into light,
       through all the world her watch is keeping,
       nor rests from worship day or night.

3   As o'er each continent and island
       the dawn leads on another day,
       the voice of prayer is never silent,
       nor dies the song of praise away.

4   The sun that bids us rest is waking
       your children 'neath the western sky,
       and hour by hour fresh lips are making
       your wondrous deeds resound on high.

5   So be it, Lord! your throne shall never,
       like earth's proud empires, pass away;
       your Kingdom stands and grows for ever,
       till all your creatures own your sway.

*John Ellerton (1826–1893)

Music Clement Cotterill Scholefield (1839–1904)

ELLERS   10 10 10 10

1   Saviour, again to thy dear name we raise
with one accord our parting hymn of praise.
Guard thou the lips from sin, the hearts from shame,
that in this house have called upon thy name.

2   Grant us thy peace, Lord, through the coming night;
turn thou for us its darkness into light;
from harm and danger keep thy servants free;
for dark and light are both alike to thee.

3   Grant us thy peace throughout our earthly life;
peace to thy Church from error and from strife;
peace to our land, the fruit of truth and love;
peace in each heart, thy Spirit from above:

4   Thy peace in sorrow, balm of every pain;
thy peace in death, the hope to rise again;
then, when thy voice shall bid our conflict cease,
call us, O Lord, to thine eternal peace.

John Ellerton (1826–1893)

Music Edward John Hopkins (1818–1901)

DZUWA LAPITA (NIGHT HAS FALLEN)

Irregular

1 Night has fal - len, night has fal - len.

God our ma - ker, guard us sleep - ing.

1 Night has fallen,
  night has fallen.
  God our maker,
  guard us sleeping.

2 Darkness now has come,
  darkness now has come.

3 We are with you, Lord,
  we are with you, Lord.

4 You have kept us, Lord,
  you have kept us, Lord.

5 See your children, Lord,
  see your children, Lord.

6 Keep us in your love,
  keep us in your love.

7 Now we go to rest,
  now we go to rest.

The Cantor may begin the next verse
on the last chord of the Refrain.

Chewa (Malawian) evening hymn
adapted Tom Colvin (1925–2000)

Music Malawian traditional melody
adapted Tom Colvin (1925–2000)
arranged John L. Bell (*b.* 1949)

TALLIS'S CANON   LM

1.   All praise to thee, my God, this night,
        for all the blessings of the light!
        Keep me, O keep me, King of kings,
        beneath thine own almighty wings.

2.   Forgive me, Lord, for thy dear Son,
        the ill that I this day have done,
        that with the world, myself, and thee,
        I, ere I sleep, at peace may be.

3.   Teach me to live, that I may dread
        the grave as little as my bed;
        teach me to die, that so I may
        rise glorious at the awesome day.

4.   O may my soul on thee repose,
        and may sweet sleep mine eyelids close, —
        sleep that may me more vigorous make
        to serve my God when I awake.

5.   When in the night I sleepless lie,
        my soul with heavenly thoughts supply;
        let no ill dreams disturb my rest,
        no powers of darkness me molest.

6.   Praise God, from whom all blessings flow;
        praise him, all creatures here below;
        praise him above, ye heavenly host;
        praise Father, Son, and Holy Ghost.

Thomas Ken (1637–1711)

Music Melody and most of the harmony by
Thomas Tallis (*c.*1505–1585), Ravenscroft's *Psalmes,* 1621

VERVACITY

48 48 48 448

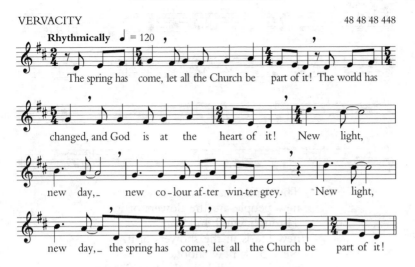

Rhythmically ♩ = 120

The spring has come, let all the Church be part of it! The world has changed, and God is at the heart of it! New light, new day,_ new co-lour af-ter win-ter grey. New light, new day,_ the spring has come, let all the Church be part of it!

1　　The spring has come,
　　　let all the Church be part of it!
　　　The world has changed,
　　　and God is at the heart of it!
　　　New light, new day,
　　　new colour after winter grey.
　　　New light, new day,
　　　the spring has come,
　　　let all the Church be part of it!

2　　The sun is warm,
　　　let all God's children play in it!
　　　The world expands,
　　　let's spread the Gospel way in it!
　　　New leaf, new thrust,
　　　new greening for the love of Christ.
　　　New leaf, new thrust,
　　　the sun is warm,
　　　let all God's children play in it!

continued overleaf

Music Colin Alexander Gibson (*b.* 1933)

3   The spring has come,
     new people are the flowers of it.
     Through wind and rain,
     new life is in the showers of it.
     New bud, new shoot,
     new hope will bear the Spirit's fruit.
     New bud, new shoot,
     the spring has come,
     new people are the flowers of it.

                                    Shirley Erena Murray (b. 1931)

225

RUTH   65 65 D

1   Summer suns are glowing
     over land and sea;
     happy light is flowing,
     bountiful and free.
     Everything rejoices
     in the mellow rays;
     all earth's thousand voices
     swell the psalm of praise.

2   See God's mercy streaming
     over all the world,
     and his banner gleaming,
     everywhere unfurled.
     Broad and deep and glorious,
     as the heaven above,
     shines in might victorious
     his eternal love.

Music Samuel Smith (1821–1917)

3 Lord, upon our blindness
  your pure radiance pour;
  for your loving-kindness
  make us love you more.
  And, when clouds are drifting
  dark across the sky,
  then, the veil uplifting,
  Father, still be nigh.

4 We will never doubt you,
  though you veil your light;
  life is dark without you;
  death with you is bright.
  Light of light, shine o'er us
  on our pilgrim way;
  still go on before us,
  to the endless day.

*William Walsham How (1823–1897)

226

SHIPSTON   87 87

1 God, whose farm is all creation,
  take the gratitude we give;
  take the finest of our harvest,
  crops we grow that all may live.

2 Take our ploughing, sowing, reaping,
  hopes and fears of sun and rain,
  all our thinking, planning, waiting,
  ripening into fruit and grain.

3 All our labour, all our watching,
  all our calendar of care,
  in these crops of your creation,
  take, O God: they are our prayer.

Leslie Thomas John Arlott (1914–1991)

Music English traditional melody
harmonised Ralph Vaughan Williams (1872–1958)

ROSSLEIGH   SM

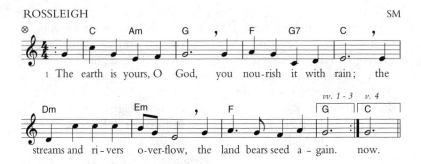

1 The earth is yours, O God, you nou-rish it with rain; the
streams and ri-vers o-ver-flow, the land bears seed a - gain. now.

1   The earth is yours, O God,
        you nourish it with rain;
        the streams and rivers overflow,
        the land bears seed again.

2   The soil is yours, O God,
        the shoots are moist with dew,
        and, ripened by the burning sun,
        the corn grows straight and true.

3   The hills are yours, O God,
        their grass is lush and green,
        providing pastures for the flocks,
        which everywhere are seen.

4   The whole rich land is yours,
        for fodder or for plough,
        and so, for rain, sun, soil, and seed,
        O God, we thank you now.

Michael Saward (*b.* 1932)
paraphrased from Psalm 65 vv. 1–13

Music Brian Dunning and Sheila Dunning

ARIRANG   Irregular

Gently

1 God,— who made the earth,— de-clared it good in— the be-
-gin - - ning, planned a time and pur-pose for all things that
were— and would be. *While earth re - mains, there— will be*
seed - time— and— har - - vest, sum - mer sun and
win - ter moon, the dead of night,— the bright day.—

1   God, who made the earth, declared it good in the
        beginning,
     planned a time and purpose for all things that were and
        would be.
     While earth remains,
     there will be seed-time and harvest,
     summer sun and winter moon,
     the dead of night, the bright day.

2   Though humanity defiled the Eden God had cherished,
     God did not despise the world; its worth he always
        could see.

3   God, in Christ, then came from paradise to imperfection,
     repossessing earth and people through a tomb and tree.

4   Wood though felled to earth produced a flower that will
        not perish,
     seed, though dead and fallen, burst to life and rose up again.

Korean text, source unknown
English version John L. Bell (*b.* 1949)

Music Korean folk melody
arranged John L. Bell (*b.* 1949)

229

WIR PFLÜGEN

76 76 D and refrain

Refrain

Music Melody by Johann Abraham Peter Schulz (1747–1800)
harmonised John Bacchus Dykes (1823–1876)

1   We plough the fields and scatter
the good seed on the land,
but it is fed and watered
by God's almighty hand;
he sends the snow in winter,
the warmth to swell the grain,
the breezes and the sunshine
and soft refreshing rain.
All good gifts around us
are sent from heaven above;
then thank the Lord, O thank the Lord,
for all his love.

2   He only is the Maker
of all things near and far;
he paints the wayside flower,
he lights the evening star;
the winds and waves obey him,
by him the birds are fed;
much more to us, his children,
he gives our daily bread.

3   We thank you then, O Father,
for all things bright and good,
the seed-time and the harvest,
our life, our health, our food.
Accept the gifts we offer
for all your love imparts,
with what we know you long for:
our humble, thankful hearts.

Matthias Claudius (1740–1815)
translated *Jane Montgomery Campbell (1817–1878)

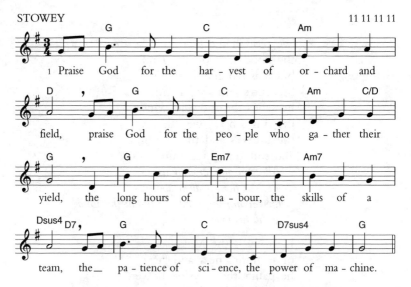

STOWEY   11 11 11 11

1 Praise God for the harvest of orchard and field, praise God for the people who gather their yield, the long hours of labour, the skills of a team, the patience of science, the power of machine.

1. Praise God for the harvest of orchard and field,
   praise God for the people who gather their yield,
   the long hours of labour, the skills of a team,
   the patience of science, the power of machine.

2. Praise God for the harvest that comes from afar,
   from market and harbour, the sea and the shore:
   foods packed and transported, and gathered and grown
   by God-given neighbours, unseen and unknown.

3. Praise God for the harvest that's quarried and mined,
   when sifted, and smelted, or shaped and refined;
   for oil and for iron, for copper and coal,
   praise God, who in love has provided them all.

4. Praise God for the harvest of science and skill,
   the urge to discover, create and fulfil:
   for dreams and inventions that promise to gain
   a future more hopeful, a world more humane.

5. Praise God for the harvest of mercy and love,
   from leaders and peoples who struggle and serve
   with patience and kindness, that all may be led
   to freedom and justice, and all may be fed.

Music English folk melody
arranged Compilers of *Common Ground,* 1998

Brian Wren (*b.* 1936)

EAST ACKLAM   84 84 888 4

1   For the fruits of all creation,
       thanks be to God;
       for these gifts to every nation,
       thanks be to God;
       for the ploughing, sowing, reaping,
       silent growth while we are sleeping,
       future needs in earth's safe-keeping,
       thanks be to God.

2   In the just reward of labour,
       God's will is done;
       in the help we give our neighbour,
       God's will is done;
       in our world-wide task of caring
       for the hungry and despairing,
       in the harvest we are sharing,
       God's will is done.

3   For the harvests of the Spirit,
       thanks be to God;
       for the good we all inherit,
       thanks be to God;
       for the wonders that astound us,
       for the truths that still confound us,
       most of all, that love has found us,
       thanks be to God.

                    Frederick Pratt Green (1903–2000)

Music Francis Jackson (*b.* 1917)

PEARS AND APPLES   7777

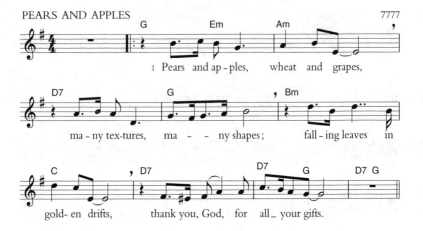

1 Pears and ap-ples, wheat and grapes, ma-ny tex-tures, ma — — ny shapes; fall-ing leaves in gold-en drifts, thank you, God, for all_ your gifts.

1   Pears and apples, wheat and grapes,
     many textures, many shapes;
     falling leaves in golden drifts,
     thank you, God, for all your gifts.

2   Flashing shoals of glistening fish,
     every colour you could wish;
     fishing boats, for you and me
     reap the harvest of the sea.

3   Deep beneath the ocean floor
     fuel and power have lain in store,
     brought to us through dangerous toil.
     Thank you, God, for gas and oil.

4   Coal and diamonds in the earth,
     minerals of priceless worth;
     skill and labour now combine,
     reaping harvests of the mine.

5   Earth and ocean, plant and beast,
     all together make the feast;
     all who long to share your grace
     at your table have their place.

Music Douglas John Coombes (*b.* 1935)

6   Loving Lord, we know you care;
let the world your goodness share;
save us from our selfish greed,
finding you in those in need.

Joseph Arthur Paul Booth (1931–1995)

33

ST GEORGE'S WINDSOR   7777 D

A higher setting is found at 411.

1   Come, you thankful people, come,
raise the song of harvest-home:
all is safely gathered in,
ere the winter storms begin;
God, our Maker, will provide
for our needs to be supplied:
come to God's own temple, come;
raise the song of harvest-home.

2   All this world is God's own field,
bearing fruit his praise to yield;
wheat and tares together sown,
are to joy or sorrow grown;
first the blade and then the ear,
then the full corn shall appear:
Lord of harvest, grant that we
wholesome grain and pure may be.

continued overleaf

Music George Job Elvey (1816–1893)

3   For the Lord our God shall come,
and shall take his harvest home;
from his field shall in that day
all offences purge away;
give his angels charge at last
in the fire the tares to cast,
but the fruitful ears to store
in his storehouse evermore.

4   Even so, Lord, quickly, come;
bring your final harvest home:
gather all your people in,
free from sorrow, free from sin;
there, for ever purified,
in your presence to abide:
come, with all your angels come,
raise the glorious harvest-home!

*Henry Alford (1810–1871)

O WALY WALY   LM

1   'Tis winter now; the fallen snow
has left the heavens all coldly clear;
through leafless boughs the sharp winds blow,
and all the earth lies dead and drear.

2   And yet God's love is not withdrawn;
his life within the keen air breathes;
his beauty paints the crimson dawn,
and clothes each branch with glittering wreaths.

3   And though abroad the sharp winds blow,
and skies are chill, and frosts are keen,
home closer draws her circle now,
and warmer glows her light within.

4   O God, you give the winter's cold,
as well as summer's joyous rays,
you warmly in your love enfold
and keep us through life's wintry days.

Samuel Longfellow (1819–1892)

Music English traditional melody
arranged Compilers of *Church Hymnary,* 3rd edition, 1973

BENSON   Irregular

1   God is working his purpose out, as year succeeds to year:
God is working his purpose out, and the time is drawing near;
nearer and nearer draws the time, the time that shall surely be,
when the earth shall be filled with the glory of God,
      as the waters cover the sea.

2   From farthest east to farthest west, where human feet have trod,
by the voice of many messengers goes forth the voice of God:
'Give ear to me, you continents, you islands give ear to me,
that the earth may be filled with the glory of God,
      as the waters cover the sea'.

3   Let us go forth in the strength of God, with the banner of
      Christ unfurled,
that the light of the glorious Gospel of truth may shine
      throughout the world:
let us all fight with sorrow and sin, to set their captives free,
that the earth may be filled with the glory of God,
      as the waters cover the sea.

4   All that we do can have no worth, unless God bless the deed;
vainly we hope for the harvest-tide, till God gives life
      to the seed;
yet nearer and nearer draws the time, the time that shall
      surely be,
when the earth shall be filled with the glory of God,
      as the waters cover the sea.

*Arthur Campbell Ainger (1841–1919)

Music Millicent Kingham (1866–1927)

CHRISTCHURCH   6666 88

1   March on, my soul, with strength,
    march forward, void of fear;
    he who has led will lead,
    through each succeeding year;
    and as you journey on your way,
    his hand shall hold you day by day.

2   March on, my soul, with strength,
    in ease you dare not dwell;
    your Master calls you forth;
    then up, and serve him well!
    Take up your cross, take up your sword,
    and fight the battles of your Lord.

3   March on, my soul, with strength,
    with strength, but not your own;
    the conquest you shall gain,
    through Christ your Lord alone;
    his grace shall power your feeble arm,
    his love preserve you safe from harm.

4   March on, my soul, with strength,
    from strength to strength march on;
    warfare shall end at length,
    all foes be overthrown.
    And then, my soul, if faithful now,
    the crown of life awaits your brow.

                    William Wright (1859–1924)

Music Charles Steggall (1826–1905)

CARDROSS   11 11 11 11

1   Look forward in faith,
all time is in God's hand.
Walk humbly with him
and trust his future plan.
God has wisely led
his people by his power.
Look forward in hope,
he gives us each new hour.

2   Look forward in faith,
the world is in God's care.
His purpose of love
he calls on us to share.
In our neighbour's need
the Lord is present still.
He blesses the meek!
The earth will know God's will.

3   Look forward in faith,
God gives us life each day.
Go onward with Christ,
his Spirit guides our way.
Now God lets us live
within the sphere of grace.
Trust ever in him,
he rules o'er earth and space!

Andrew J. Scobie (*b.* 1935)

Music Andrew A. Steele (*b.* 1945)

Also suitable

Lord, your hands have formed this world	140
Great is thy faithfulness, O God my Father	153
Put all your trust in God	270
This is a day of new beginnings	526
One more step along the world I go	530
Lord, in love and perfect wisdom	702

OUR RESPONSE TO GOD
IN THE STEWARDSHIP OF THE EARTH

LOVE UNKNOWN   66 12 88

1   Lord, bring the day to pass
      when forest, rock, and hill,
      the beasts, the birds, the grass,
      will know your finished will:
      when we attain our destiny
      and nature lives in harmony.

2   Forgive our careless use
      of water, ore, and soil —
      the plenty we abuse
      supplied by others' toil:
      save us from making self our creed,
      turn us towards each other's need.

3   Help us, when we release
      creation's secret powers,
      to harness them for peace,
      our children's peace and ours:
      teach us the art of mastering
      in servant form, like Christ our King.

4   Creation groans, travails,
      futile its present plight,
      bound — till the hour it hails
      God's children born of light:
      that we may gain our true estate,
      come, Lord, new heavens and earth create.

Ian Masson Fraser (b. 1917)

Music John Nicholson Ireland (1879–1962)

SAMOS   Irregular

1 When your Fa - ther made the world, be - fore that world was old, to his eye what he had made was love - ly to be - hold. Help your peo - ple to care for your world.

Refrain

The world is a gar - den you made, and you are the one who plant - ed the seed, the world is a gar - den you made, a life for our food, life for our joy, life we could kill with our self - ish greed.

1   When your Father made the world, before that world was old,
to his eye what he had made was lovely to behold.
Help your people to care for your world.

> *The world is a garden you made,*
> *and you are the one who planted the seed,*
> *the world is a garden you made,*
> *a life for our food, life for our joy,*
> *life we could kill with our selfish greed.*

Music Peter Rose

2   And the world that he had made, the seas, the rocks, the air,
     all the creatures and the plants he gave into our care.
     Help your people to care for your world.

3   When you walked in Galilee, you said your Father knows
     when each tiny sparrow dies, each fragile lily grows.
     Help your people to care for your world.

4   And the children of the earth, like sheep within your fold,
     should have food enough to eat, and shelter from the cold.
     Help your people to care for your world.

Ann Conlon

40

EPIPHANY   11 10 11 10

A version in a lower key is found at 638.

1   God in such love for us lent us this planet,
     gave it a purpose in time and in space:
     small as a spark from the fire of creation,
     cradle of life and the home of our race.

2   Thanks be to God for its bounty and beauty,
     life that sustains us in body and mind:
     plenty for all, if we learn how to share it,
     riches undreamed-of to fathom and find.

3   Long have our human wars ruined its harvest;
     long has earth bowed to the terror of force;
     long have we wasted what others have need of,
     poisoned the fountain of life at its source.

4   Earth is the Lord's: it is ours to enjoy it,
     ours, as God's stewards, to farm and defend.
     From its pollution, misuse, and destruction,
     good Lord, deliver us, world without end!

Frederick Pratt Green (1903–2000)

Music Joseph Francis Thrupp (1827–1867)

241

JUDAS AND MARY

Irregular

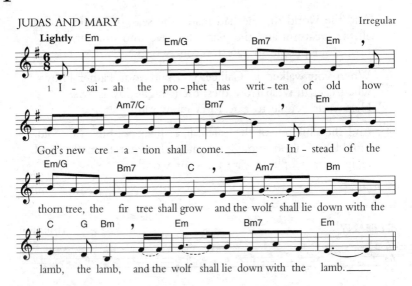

1 Isaiah the prophet has written of old how God's new creation shall come. Instead of the thorn tree, the fir tree shall grow and the wolf shall lie down with the lamb, the lamb, and the wolf shall lie down with the lamb.

1   Isaiah the prophet has written of old
     how God's new creation shall come.
     Instead of the thorn tree, the fir tree shall grow
     and the wolf shall lie down with the lamb, the lamb,
     the wolf shall lie down with the lamb.

2   The mountains and hills shall break forth into song,
     the peoples be led forth in peace;
     the earth shall be filled with the knowledge of God
     as the waters cover the sea, the sea,
     as the waters cover the sea.

3   Yet nations still prey on the meek of the world,
     and conflict turns parent from child.
     Your people despoil all the sweetness of earth;
     and the brier and the thorn tree grow wild, grow wild,
     the brier and the thorn tree grow wild.

4   God, bring to fruition your will for the earth,
     that no one shall hurt or destroy,
     that wisdom and justice shall reign in the land
     and your people shall go forth in joy, in joy,
     your people shall go forth in joy.

Joy F. Patterson (*b.* 1931)

Music Sydney Bertram Carter (1915–2004)

FIELDS OF LIGHT   LM and coda

1 Is this the way you made the world, from burned out stars and fields of light?

Is this the way you lit the fuse when *vv. 1 - 4* death ex-plo-ded in - to

v. 5 life? I will make my home in it, and praise the Ma - ker.

1   Is this the way you made the world,
       from burned out stars and fields of light?
       Is this the way you lit the fuse
       when death exploded into life?

2   Is this the way you spoke the word,
       that called the darkness to be light;
       is this the way you wrote the code,
       which shaped the fragile chain of life?

3   Are these the notes that you composed,
       are these the colours you designed,
       are these the stars that sang for joy,
       are these the patterns of your mind?

4   Are these the lives that you inspired,
       are these the faces that you love;
       is this the earth you will redeem,
       is this the world you came to save?

5   Then I will love the world you made,
       and I will love the gift you gave,
       and I will drink its beauty in,
       and I will make my home in it,
       and praise the Maker.

                                             Author unknown

Music Douglas Galbraith (*b.*1940)

TENDERNESS   10 10 10 10

Verse 2 only

1   Touch the earth lightly,
     use the earth gently,
     nourish the life of the world in our care:
     gift of great wonder,
     ours to surrender,
     trust for the children tomorrow will bear.

2   We who endanger,
     who create hunger,
     agents of death for all creatures that live,
     we who would foster
     clouds of disaster,
     God of our planet, forestall and forgive!

3   Let there be greening,
     birth from the burning,
     water that blesses and air that is sweet,
     health in God's garden,
     hope in God's children,
     regeneration that peace will complete.

4   God of all living,
     God of all loving,
     God of the seedling, the snow, and the sun,
     teach us, deflect us,
     Christ re-connect us,
     using us gently and making us one.

Shirley Erena Murray (*b.* 1931)

Music Colin Alexander Gibson (*b.* 1933)

PORTENT   LM

1   Where are the voices for the earth?
     Where are the eyes to see her pain,
     wasted by our consuming path,
     weeping the tears of poisoned rain?

2   Sacred the soil that hugs the seed,
     sacred the silent fall of snow,
     sacred the world that God decreed,
     water and sun and river flow.

3   Where shall we run who break this code,
     where shall tomorrow's children be,
     left with the ruined gifts of God,
     death for the creatures, land, and sea?

4   We are the voices for the earth,
     we who will care enough to cry,
     cherish her beauty, clear her breath,
     live that our planet may not die.

                    Shirley Erena Murray (*b.* 1931)

Music Jillian Bray

WORLD OF SUNSHINE   Irregular

It's a world of sunshine, a world of rain; it's a world of laughter, a
world of pain; it's a world we must share, where we must learn to
care, for the world be-longs to God. __ *This is God's world*
af - ter all, __ this is God's world af - ter all, __
this is God's world af - ter all. Yes, it's God's good world.

1   It's a world of sunshine, a world of rain;
       it's a world of laughter, a world of pain;
       it's a world we must share, where we must learn to care,
       for the world belongs to God.
           This is God's world after all,
           this is God's world after all,
           this is God's world after all.
           Yes, it's God's good world.

2   It's a world of plenty, a world of need;
       it's a world of love, and a world of greed;
       it's a world we must share, where we must learn to care,
       for the world belongs to God.

3   It's a world of water, a world of drought;
       it's a world of faith, and a world of doubt;
       it's a world we must share, where we must learn to care,
       for the world belongs to God.

                                    Iain D. Cunningham (b. 1954)

Music Iain D. Cunningham (b. 1954)

HIGHWOOD   11 10 11 10

1   Great God of every shining constellation
    that wheels in splendour through the midnight sky;
    grant us your Spirit's true illumination
    to read the secrets of your work on high.

2   You, Lord, have made the atom's hidden forces;
    your laws its mighty energies fulfil:
    teach us, to whom you give such rich resources,
    in all we use, to serve your holy will.

3   True Life, awaking life in cell and tissue,
    from flower to bird, from beast to humankind;
    help us to trace, from birth to final issue,
    the sure unfolding purpose of your mind.

4   You, Lord, have stamped your image on your creatures,
    and, though we mar that image, love us still;
    lift up our eyes to Christ, that in his features
    we may discern the beauty of your will.

5   Lord of creation, shaping and renewing,
    at work in nature and humanity;
    help us to tread, with grace our souls enduing,
    the road to life and immortality.

                    Albert Frederick Bayly (1901–1984)

Music Richard Runciman Terry (1865–1938)

Also suitable
Beauty for brokenness   259

OUR RESPONSE TO GOD
IN MISSION AND SERVICE

ELLACOMBE

DCM

A higher setting is found at 413.

1   Moved by the Gospel, let us move
    with every gift and art.
    The image of creative love
    indwells each human heart.
    The Maker calls creation good,
    so let us now express
    with sound and colour, stone and wood,
    the shape of holiness.

2   Let weavers form from broken strands
    a tapestry of prayer.
    Let artists paint with skilful hands
    their joy, lament, and care.
    Then mime the story: Christ has come.
    With reverence dance the word.
    With flute and organ, gong and drum
    God's praise be ever heard.

Music German melody, 18th century. as adapted in Mainz
Gesangbuch, 1833, *harmonised* St Gall *Gesangbuch,* 1863

3 O Spirit, breathe among us here;
    inspire the work we do.
    May hands and voices, eye and ear
    attest to life made new.
    In worship and in daily strife
    create among us still.
    Great Artist, form our common life
    according to your will.

          Ruth C. Duck (*b.* 1947)

48

BISHOPGARTH   87 87 D

1 'For my sake and the gospel's, go
    and tell redemption's story';
    his heralds answer, 'Be it so,
    and thine, Lord, all the glory!'
    They preach his birth, his life, his cross,
    the love of his atonement,
    for whom they count the world but loss,
    his Easter, his enthronement.

2 Hark! hark! the trump of jubilee
    proclaims to every nation,
    from pole to pole, by land and sea,
    glad tidings of salvation.
    Still on and on the anthems spread
    of alleluia voices;
    in concert with the holy dead,
    the warrior Church rejoices.

continued overleaf

Music Arthur Seymour Sullivan (1842–1900)

3   He comes, whose advent trumpet drowns
the last of time's evangels,
Immanuel, crowned with many crowns,
the Lord of saints and angels.
O Life, Light, Love, the great I AM,
Triune, who changest never,
the throne of God and of the Lamb
is thine, and thine for ever.

Edward Henry Bickersteth (1825–1906)

249

LIMPSFIELD   73 73 77 73

Music Josiah Booth (1852–1929)

1   We have heard a joyful sound,
    'Jesus saves!'
    Spread the gladness all around,
    'Jesus saves!'
    Bear the news to every land,
    climb the steeps and cross the waves.
    Onward! — 'tis our Lord's command.
    Jesus saves!

2   Waft it on the rolling tide,
    'Jesus saves!'
    Tell to sinners far and wide,
    'Jesus saves!'
    Sing, ye islands of the sea;
    echo back, ye ocean caves;
    earth shall keep her jubilee:
    Jesus saves!

3   Sing above the battle's strife,
    'Jesus saves!
    By his death and endless life
    Jesus saves!'
    Sing it softly through the gloom,
    when the heart for mercy craves;
    sing in triumph o'er the tomb,
    'Jesus saves!'

4   Give the winds a mighty voice,
    'Jesus saves!'
    Let the nations now rejoice,
    'Jesus saves!'
    Shout salvation full and free
    to every strand that ocean laves —
    this our song of victory,
    'Jesus saves!'

                    Priscilla Jane Owens (1829–1907)

250

THE LIVING GOD

SENT BY THE LORD

66 66 D

Music Central American folk melody
arranged John L. Bell (b. 1949)

1   Sent by the Lord am I;
my hands are ready now
to make the earth the place
in which the kingdom comes.
Sent by the Lord am I;
my hands are ready now
to make the earth the place
in which the kingdom comes.

2   The angels cannot change
a world of hurt and pain
into a world of love,
of justice and of peace.
The task is mine to do,
to set it really free.
Oh, help me to obey;
help me to do your will.

Jorge Maldonado

251

THE LIVING GOD

HERE I AM, LORD

7774 D and refrain

Music Daniel L. Schutte (b.1947)

1   I, the Lord of sea and sky,
I have heard my people cry.
All who dwell in dark and sin
my hand will save.
I, who made the stars of night,
I will make their darkness bright.
Who will bear my light to them?
Whom shall I send?
   Here I am, Lord.
   Is it I, Lord?
   I have heard you calling in the night.
   I will go, Lord,
   if you lead me.
   I will hold your people in my heart.

2   I, the Lord of snow and rain,
I have borne my people's pain.
I have wept for love of them.
They turn away.
I will break their hearts of stone,
give them hearts for love alone.
I will speak my Word to them.
Whom shall I send?

3   I, the Lord of wind and flame,
I will tend the poor and lame.
I will set a feast for them.
My hand will save.
Finest bread I will provide
till their hearts be satisfied.
I will give my life to them.
Whom shall I send?

Daniel L. Schutte (b. 1947)

BEACH SPRING   87 87 D

1   As a fire is meant for burning
with a bright and warming flame,
so the Church is meant for mission,
giving glory to God's name.
Preaching Christ, and not our customs,
let us build a bridge of care,
joining hands across the nations,
finding neighbours everywhere.

2   We are learners; we are teachers;
we are pilgrims on the way.
We are seekers; we are givers;
we are vessels made of clay.
By our gentle, loving actions,
we will show that Christ is light.
In a humble, listening Spirit,
we will live to God's delight.

3   As a green bud in the springtime
is a sign of life renewed,
so may we be signs of oneness
'mid earth's peoples, many-hued.
As a rainbow lights the heavens
when a storm is past and gone,
so may we reflect the radiance
of God's new and glorious dawn.

Ruth C. Duck (*b.* 1947)

Music American traditional melody
arranged Compilers of *Common Ground,* 1998

SALLEY GARDENS　　　　　　　　　　　　　　　76 76 D

1　　Inspired by love and anger,
　　　disturbed by need and pain,
　　　informed of God's own bias,
　　　we ponder once again:
　　　'How long must some folk suffer?
　　　How long can few folk mind?
　　　How long dare vain self-interest
　　　turn prayer and pity blind?'

2　　From those for ever victims
　　　of heartless human greed,
　　　their cruel plight composes
　　　a litany of need:
　　　'Where are the fruits of justice?
　　　Where are the signs of peace?
　　　When is the day when prisoners
　　　and dreams find their release?'

*3　　From those for ever shackled
　　　to what their wealth can buy,
　　　the fear of lost advantage
　　　provokes the bitter cry,
　　　'Don't query our position!
　　　Don't criticise our wealth!
　　　Don't mention those exploited
　　　by politics and stealth!'

continued overleaf

Music Irish folk melody *arranged* John L. Bell (b. 1949)

253　Words and Music: © WGRG, The Iona Community

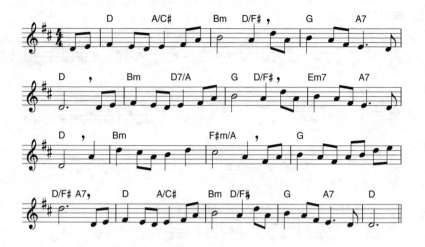

*4   To God, who through the prophets
proclaimed a different age,
we offer earth's indifference,
its agony and rage:
'When will the wrongs be righted?
When will the kingdom come?
When will the world be generous
to all instead of some?'

5   God asks, 'Who will go for me?
Who will extend my reach?
And who, when few will listen,
will prophesy and preach?
And who, when few bid welcome,
will offer all they know?
And who, when few dare follow,
will walk the road I show?'

6   Amused in someone's kitchen,
asleep in someone's boat,
attuned to what the ancients
exposed, proclaimed, and wrote,
a saviour without safety,
a tradesman without tools
has come to tip the balance
with fishermen and fools.

* *These verses may be omitted.*

John L. Bell (b. 1949)
and Graham Maule (b. 1958)

SONG 1   10 10 10 10 10 10

1   O God, we bear the imprint of your face:
the colours of our skin are your design,
and what we have of beauty in our race
as man or woman, you alone define,
who stretched a living fabric on our frame
and gave to each a language and a name.

2   Where we are torn and pulled apart by hate
because our race, our skin is not the same;
where we are judged unequal by the state
and victims made because we own our name —
humanity reduced to little worth
dishonoured is your living face on earth.

3   O God, we share the image of your Son
whose flesh and blood are ours, whatever skin,
in his humanity we find our own,
and in his family our proper kin:
Christ is the brother we still crucify,
his love the language we must learn, or die.

Shirley Erena Murray (*b.*1931)

Music Melody and most of the bass by
Orlando Gibbons (1583–1625)

GOTT WILL 'S MACHEN 87 87

1   Father, hear the prayer we offer:
    not for ease that prayer shall be,
    but for strength that we may ever
    live our lives courageously.

2   Not for ever in green pastures
    do we ask our way to be;
    but the steep and rugged pathway
    may we tread rejoicingly.

3   Not for ever by still waters
    would we idly rest and stay;
    but would smite the living fountains
    from the rocks along our way.

4   Be our strength in hours of weakness,
    in our wanderings be our guide;
    through endeavour, failure, danger,
    Father, be thou at our side.

                        Love Maria Willis (1824–1908)

Music Johann Ludwig Steiner (1688–1761)
harmonised Compilers of *English Hymnal,* 1906

ARGENTINA   11 11 11 11 and refrain

1   May the God of hope go with us every day,
       filling all our lives with love and joy and peace.
       May the God of justice speed us on our way,
       bringing light and hope to every land and race.
         Praying, let us work for peace;
         singing, share our joy with all;
         working for a world that's new,
         faithful when we hear Christ's call.

2   God will be our Shepherd as we go our way
       and will not forsake us when we go astray.
       Even though the load of life is hard to bear,
       we must not forget that God is always there.

Music Argentinian folk melody   *verse 1* Spanish traditional
arranged Emily Brink   *translated* Alvin Schutmaat
                                     verse 2 Ann Mitchell

VIENEN CON ALEGRIA   Irregular

Refrain **Brightly**

Sing-ing, we glad-ly worship the Lord to-ge-ther. Sing-ing, we glad-ly
wor-ship the Lord. Those who are tra-vel-ling the road of life
sow seeds of peace and love. Sing-ing, we glad-ly
wor-ship the Lord to-ge-ther. Sing-ing, we glad-ly wor-ship the Lord.
Those who are tra-vel-ling the road of life____ sow seeds of peace and
love. 1 Come, bring-ing hope in-to a world of fear, a
world which is burdened down with dread, a world which is yearning for a
great – er love but needs to be shown the true way.
3 When-ev – er hate-ful-ness and vi – o-lence are ban-ished for
ev – er from our hearts, then will the world be-lieve the
day is near when sad-ness and pain shall find their end.

Refrain [sung twice]:
Singing, we gladly worship the Lord together.
Singing, we gladly worship the Lord.
Those who are travelling the road of life
sow seeds of peace and love.

1   Come, bringing hope into a world of fear,
    a world which is burdened down with dread,
    a world which is yearning for a greater love
    but needs to be shown the true way.

2   Come, bringing joyfully in both your hands
    some kindling to light the path of peace,
    some hope that there is a more human world
    where justice and truth will be born.

3   Whenever hatefulness and violence
    are banished for ever from our hearts,
    then will the world believe the day is near
    when sadness and pain shall find their end.

Guatemalan traditional
English version by Christine Carson (*b.* 1965)
and John L. Bell (*b.* 1949)

Music Guatemalan folk melody
arranged John L. Bell (*b.* 1949)

258

1 When the hun-gry — who have noth-ing — share with stran-gers; —
— when the thirs-ty — give such wa - ter as they have;
when in weak-ness, — we lend strength to — one an - oth-er: —
— God goes with us — on the path - ways — of our lives.
God goes with us — on the path-ways of our lives. —

Music Jose Antonio Olivar and Miguel Manzano
arranged Alvin Schutmaat

258 Words and Music: 1971, Jose Antionio Olivar and Miguel Manzano. Published by, OCP Publications, 5536 NE Hassalo, Portland, OR 97213, USA. All rights reserved. Used with permission.

1   When the hungry who have nothing share with strangers;
     when the thirsty give such water as they have;
     when in weakness, we lend strength to one another:
     God goes with us on the pathways of our lives.
     God goes with us on the pathways of our lives.

2   When the suffering find their comfort in our blessing,
     when despair is turned to hope, radiant and bright;
     when all hating melts in embers of our loving:
     God goes with us on the pathways of our lives.
     God goes with us on the pathways of our lives.

3   When rejoicing overtakes our hearts with gladness;
     when the truth is in our lives and on our lips;
     when our love for simple things helps conquer sadness;
     God goes with us on the pathways of our lives.
     God goes with us on the pathways of our lives.

4   When true goodness makes each home a hallowed shelter;
     when our warfare yields to peace, and earth is blest;
     when we find Christ's human face in every neighbour;
     God goes with us on the pathways of our lives.
     God goes with us on the pathways of our lives.

Spanish-language hymn *Cuando el Pobre,*
Jose Antonio Olivar and Miguel Manzano
translated Mary Louise Bringle (*b.* 1953)

Also suitable

OUR RESPONSE TO GOD
IN INTERCESSION AND PETITION

259

GOD OF THE POOR

Irregular

1 Beau-ty for bro-ken-ness, hope for des-
-pair, Lord, in the suf-fer-ing this is our prayer.
Bread for the child-ren, jus-tice, joy, peace, sun-rise to sun-set your
king-dom in - crease. ___ speak.

Refrain
God of the poor, ___ friend of the ___ weak, give us com-pas-
- sion, we pray, melt our cold hearts, let tears fall like ___
rain. Come, change our love ___ from a spark.
___ to a ___ flame. ___

Music Graham Kendrick (*b.* 1950)

1 Beauty for brokenness,
   hope for despair,
   Lord, in the suffering
   this is our prayer.
   Bread for the children,
   justice, joy, peace,
   sunrise to sunset
   your kingdom increase.

2 Shelter for fragile lives,
   cures for their ills,
   work for the craftsmen,
   trade for their skills.
   Land for the dispossessed,
   rights for the weak,
   voices to plead the cause
   of those who can't speak.

   God of the poor,
   friend of the weak,
   give us compassion, we pray,
   melt our cold hearts,
   let tears fall like rain.
   Come, change our love
   from a spark to a flame.

3 Refuge from cruel wars,
   havens from fear,
   cities for sanctuary,
   freedoms to share.
   Peace to the killing fields,
   scorched earth to green,
   Christ for the bitterness,
   his cross for the pain.

4 Rest for the ravaged earth,
   oceans and streams,
   plundered and poisoned,
   our future, our dreams.
   Lord, end our madness,
   carelessness, greed;
   make us content with
   the things that we need.

   God of the poor,
   friend of the weak,
   give us compassion, we pray,
   melt our cold hearts,
   let tears fall like rain.
   Come, change our love
   from a spark to a flame.

5 Lighten our darkness,
   breathe on this flame,
   until your justice
   burns brightly again;
   until the nations
   learn of your ways,
   seek your salvation
   and bring you their praise.

   God of the poor,
   friend of the weak,
   give us compassion, we pray,
   melt our cold hearts,
   let tears fall like rain.
   Come, change our love
   from a spark to a flame.

Graham Kendrick (*b.* 1950)

MELITA   8888 88

1   Eternal Father, strong to save,
whose arm hath bound the restless wave,
who bade the mighty ocean deep
its own appointed limits keep:
    Oh, hear us when we cry to thee
    for those in peril on the sea.

2   O Christ, whose voice the waters heard
and hushed their raging at thy word,
who walked upon the foaming deep,
and calm amid the storm didst sleep:
    Oh, hear us when we cry to thee
    for those in peril on the sea.

3   O Holy Spirit, who didst brood
upon the waters dark and rude,
and bid their angry tumult cease,
and give, for wild confusion, peace:
    Oh, hear us when we cry to thee
    for those in peril on the sea.

4   O Trinity of love and power,
shield all of them in danger's hour;
from rock and tempest, fire and foe,
protect them whereso'er they go:
    thus evermore shall rise to thee
    glad hymns of praise from land and sea.

William Whiting (1825–1878)

Music John Bacchus Dykes (1823–1876)

Alternative version

1   Eternal Father, strong to save,
     whose arm restrains the restless wave,
     who told the mighty ocean deep
     its own appointed bounds to keep:
     we cry, O God of majesty,
     for those in peril on the sea.

2   O Christ, whose voice the waters heard
     and hushed their raging at your word,
     who walked across the surging deep,
     and in the storm lay calm in sleep:
     we pray, O Lord of Galilee,
     for those in peril on the sea.

3   Creator Spirit, by whose breath
     were fashioned sea and sky and earth;
     who made the stormy chaos cease,
     and give us life and light and peace:
     we pray, O Spirit, strong and free,
     for those in peril on the sea.

4   O Trinity of love and power,
     preserve their lives in danger's hour;
     from rock and tempest, flood and flame,
     protect them by your holy name:
     and to your glory let there be
     glad hymns of praise from land and sea.

William Whiting (1825–1878)
adapted Jubilate Hymns

260   Adaptation: © in this version, Jubilate Hymns, 4 Thorne Park Road, Chelston, Torquay   TQ2 6RX
<enquiries@jubilate.co.uk>   Used by permission.

OLD 124th   11 10 11 10 and refrain

Refrain

1   Father Eternal, Ruler of Creation,
    Spirit of Life, by whom all things are made,
    through the thick darkness covering every nation,
    light to our blindness, come now to our aid!
    Your kingdom come, O Lord, your will be done.

2   Races and peoples, still we stand divided,
    and, sharing not our griefs, no joy can share;
    by wars and tumults Love is mocked, derided,
    his conquering cross no kingdom wills to bear;

3   Envious of heart, blind-eyed, with tongues confounded,
    nation by nation still goes unforgiven;
    in wrath and fear, by jealousies surrounded,
    building proud towers which shall not reach to heaven.

4   Lust of possession causes desolations;
    meekness is honoured nowhere on the earth.
    Led by no star, the rulers of the nations
    still fail to bring us to the blissful birth.

5   How shall we love you, holy, hidden Being,
    if we love not the world which you have made?
    Oh, give us purer love, for better seeing
    your Word made flesh and in a manger laid.

                              *Laurence Housman (1865–1959)

Music Genevan Psalter, 1551, rhythm adapted
harmonised Compilers of *Church Hymnary,* 3rd edition, 1973

SOMOS PUEBLO   87 87

1 For the world and all its peo - ple,

we ad - dress our prayers to God.   *Con - fi - dent - ly, all can*

wor - ship in the pre - sence of the Lord.

SOMOS PUEBLO   87 87

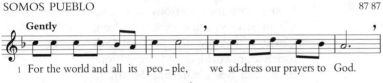

1 For the world and all its peo - ple,   we ad-dress our prayers to God.

Con - fi - dent - ly, all can wor - ship in the pre - sence of the Lord.

1   For the world and all its people,
    we address our prayers to God.
    Confidently, all can worship
    in the presence of the Lord.

2   All the powerless, all the hungry
    are most precious to their God.

3   For the poor, God has a purpose,
    for the desperate, a word.

4   Christ is here, and Christ is stronger
    than the strength of sin or sword.

5   God will fill the earth with justice
    when our will and his accord.

Spanish, from *Misa Popular Nicaraguense*,
English version John L. Bell (*b.* 1949)

Only one arrangement of the tune should be sung.

Music Spanish, from *Misa Popular Nicaraguense*,
arranged John L. Bell (*b.* 1949)

262

PICARDY

Unison

87 87 87

1. God of freedom, God of justice,
God whose love is strong as death,
Christ who saw the dark of prison,
Christ who knew the price of faith:
touch our world of sad oppression
with your Spirit's healing breath.

2. Rid the earth of torture's terror,
you whose hands were nailed to wood;
hear the cries of pain and protest,
you who shed both tears and blood;
move in us the power of pity
to pursue the common good.

3. Make in us a captive conscience
quick to hear, to act, to plead;
make us truly sisters, brothers
of whatever race or creed —
teach us to be fully human,
open to each other's need.

Shirley Erena Murray (*b.* 1931)

Music French carol melody
harmonised Ralph Vaughan Williams (1872–1958)

RHUDDLAN   87 87 87

1   Judge Eternal, throned in splendour,
       Lord of lords and King of kings,
       with your living fire of judgement
       purge this land of bitter things;
       solace all its wide dominion
       with the healing of your wings.

2   Still the weary folk are pining
       for the hour that brings release;
       and the city's crowded clangour
       cries aloud for sin to cease;
       and the homesteads and the woodlands
       plead in silence for their peace.

3   Crown, O God, your own endeavour;
       cleave our darkness with your sword;
       feed the faithless and the hungry
       with the richness of your word;
       cleanse the body of this nation
       through the glory of the Lord.

                 Henry Scott Holland (1847–1918)

Music Welsh traditional melody in *Musical Relics of Welsh Bards,* 1800
harmonised Compilers of *English Hymnal,* 1906

APANÁS   LM

1   Pray for a world where every child
         finds welcome in a sheltered place,
         where love is tender, undefiled,
         and firmness intertwines with grace.

2   Pray for a world where passion's fire
         burns not in force or careless lust,
         where God's good gift of deep desire
         is safe in arms of faith and trust.

3   Pray for a nation just and fair
         that seeks the welfare of us all,
         where leaders guide with prudent care
         and nurture life for great and small.

4   Pray for a world where all have voice
         and none will batter, rape, abuse.
         Till then, may all have rightful choice
         and pray for wisdom as they choose.

                                   Ruth C. Duck (*b.* 1947)

Music Jim Strathdee (*b.* 1941)

RUSSIA   11 10 11 9

1   God the Omnipotent! King, who ordainest
       great winds thy clarions, lightnings thy sword:
       show forth thy pity on high where thou reignest;
       give to us peace in our time, O Lord.

2   God the All-merciful! earth hath forsaken
       meekness and mercy, and slighted thy word;
       bid not thy wrath in its terrors awaken;
       give to us peace in our time, O Lord.

3   God the All-righteous One! we have defied thee;
       yet to eternity standeth thy word;
       falsehood and wrong shall not tarry beside thee;
       give to us peace in our time, O Lord.

4   God the All-wise! by the fire of thy chastening,
       earth shall to freedom and truth be restored;
       through the thick darkness thy Kingdom is hastening;
       thou wilt give peace in thy time, O Lord.

5   So shall thy children, with thankful devotion,
       praise him who saved them from peril and sword,
       singing in chorus, from ocean to ocean,
       peace to the nations, and praise to the Lord.

Henry Fothergill Chorley (1808–1872)
and John Ellerton (1826–1893)

Music Alexei Fyodorovich Lvov (1799–1871)

DANDASOY   10 9 10 9

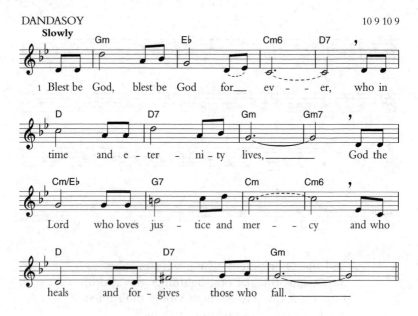

1. Blest be God, blest be God for ever,
   who in time and eternity lives,
   God the Lord who loves justice and mercy
   and who heals and forgives those who fall.

2. God will bandage the wounds of the broken,
   and pay heed to each body and soul;
   God has asked humankind not to fear
   but believe that the kingdom's at hand.

3. Come, O Lord, come and save the oppressed,
   lift the poor from the doors of despair;
   put a song in the hearts of your people,
   those whose hope and whose trust is in you.

Salvador T. Martinez (b. 1939)
adapted John L. Bell (b. 1949)

Music Phillipine melody from island of Negros
arranged John L. Bell (b. 1949)

SALZBURG (HAYDN)   CM

PARAPHRASE 2

1   O God of Bethel! by whose hand
     thy people still are fed,
     who through this earthly pilgrimage
     hast all our fathers led:

2   Our vows, our prayers, we now present
     before thy throne of grace:
     God of our fathers! be the God
     of their succeeding race.

3   Through each perplexing path of life
     our wandering footsteps guide;
     give us each day our daily bread,
     and raiment fit provide.

4   O spread thy covering wings around,
     till all our wanderings cease,
     and at our Father's loved abode
     our souls arrive in peace.

5   Such blessings from thy gracious hand
     our humble prayers implore;
     and thou shalt be our chosen God,
     and portion evermore.

                         Scottish Paraphrases 1781
                         from *Genesis 28: 20-22*

Music Johann Michael Haydn (1737–1806)
adapted Compilers of *Revised Church Hymnary* 1927

SONG 1   10 10 10 10 10 10

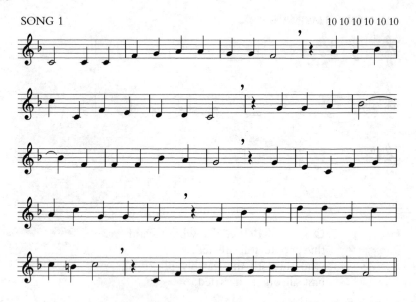

1   Eternal ruler of the ceaseless round
       of circling planets singing on their way,
       guide of the nations from the night profound
       into the glory of the perfect day:
       rule in our hearts, and keep us ever true,
       directed, strengthened, and upheld by you.

2   We are your own, the children of your love,
       your family, with your belovèd Son;
       come to us, Holy Spirit, like a dove,
       and fill our hearts that we may be as one;
       as one with you, our comforter and friend;
       as one with him, our way, our life, our end.

3   We would be one in hatred of all wrong,
       one in our love of all things kind and fair,
       one with the joy that finds a voice in song,
       one with the grief that trembles into prayer,
       one in the power that sets us free from fear
       to follow truth, and so to find you near.

                             John White Chadwick (1840–1904)

Music Melody and most of the bass by
Orlando Gibbons (1583–1625)

ICH HALTE TREULICH STILL   DSM

Befiehl du deine Wege

1   Put all your trust in God,
    in duty's path go on;
    walk in his strength with faith and hope,
    so shall your work be done.
    Give to the winds your fears;
    hope, and be undismayed;
    God hears your sighs and counts your tears,
    God shall lift up your head.

2   Through waves, and clouds, and storms
    he gently clears your way;
    await his time; so shall this night
    soon end in joyful day.
    Leave to his sovereign sway
    to choose and to command;
    then you shall marvel at his way
    how wise, how strong his hand!

3   You see our weakness, Lord;
    our hearts are known to you:
    give strength to every failing hand
    and keep our footsteps true.
    Let us, in life, in death,
    your steadfast truth declare,
    confessing, with our final breath,
    your love and guardian care.

                    Paul Gerhardt (1607–1676)
                 adapted *John Wesley (1703–1791)

Music Johann Sebastian Bach (1685–1750)

271

KÄRE GUD   77 76

1 Loving God, you see us here, know our names and who we are.
Though we never have seen you, we believe you are here.

1   Loving God, you see us here,
    know our names and who we are.
    Though we never have seen you,
    we believe you are here.

2   Loving God, you hear our prayer
    for all those in need today.
    Show us how we can help you,
    help us do what we can.

3   Loving God, you stay with us,
    wide awake and when we sleep.
    Thank you for every moment,
    thank you for your great care.

L. Å Person and G. Strandsjö
translated Leif Nahnfeldt

Music Leif Nahnfeldt

ST PAUL (ABERDEEN)   CM

PARAPHRASE 60

1   Father of peace, and God of love!
     we own your power to save,
     that power by which our Shepherd rose
     victorious o'er the grave.

2   Him from the dead you brought again,
     when, by his sacred blood,
     confirmed and sealed for evermore
     the eternal covenant stood.

3   O may your Spirit seal our souls,
     and mould them to your will,
     that our weak hearts no more may stray,
     but keep your precepts still;

4   That to perfection's sacred height
     we nearer still may rise,
     and all we think, and all we do,
     be pleasing in your eyes.

                              Scottish Paraphrases, 1781
                              Hebrews 13: 20, 21

Music Collection printed by James Chalmers, Aberdeen c.1749,
possibly by Andrew Tait *(fl.* 1749)
harmonised Compilers of *Church Hymnary,* 3rd edition, 1973

Also suitable
Where high the heavenly temple stands   451
Your will be done on earth, O God   805

LIFE IN CHRIST

CHRIST INCARNATE
PROMISE OF THE MESSIAH

VENI EMMANUEL

LM and refrain

Veni, Emmanuel

1 O come, O come, Emmanuel,
   and ransom captive Israel,
   that mourns in lonely exile here
   until the Son of God appear.
   Rejoice! Rejoice! Emmanuel
   shall come to thee, O Israel.

2 O come, O come, thou Lord of might,
   who to thy tribes, on Sinai's height,
   in ancient times didst give the law
   in cloud and majesty and awe:

3 O come, thou Rod of Jesse, free
   thine own from Satan's tyranny;
   from depths of hell thy people save,
   and give them victory o'er the grave:

4 O come, thou Key of David, come,
   and open wide our heavenly home;
   make safe the way that leads on high,
   and close the path to misery:

5 O come, thou Dayspring, come and cheer
   our spirits by thine advent here;
   disperse the gloomy clouds of night,
   and death's dark shadows put to flight:

18th century, based on the
ancient *Advent Antiphons*
translated John Mason Neale (1818–1866)

Music Plainsong melody, 15th-century France

GENEVAN 42   87 87 77 88

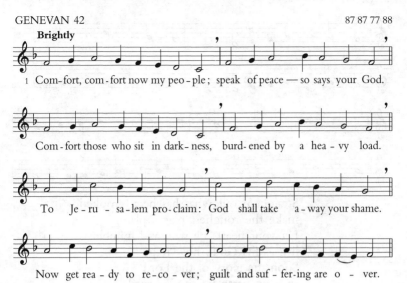

1 Com-fort, com-fort now my peo-ple; speak of peace — so says your God.

Com-fort those who sit in dark-ness, burd-ened by a hea-vy load.

To Je-ru-sa-lem pro-claim: God shall take a-way your shame.

Now get rea-dy to re-co-ver; guilt and suf-fer-ing are o-ver.

1   Comfort, comfort now my people;
        speak of peace — so says your God.
        Comfort those who sit in darkness,
        burdened by a heavy load.
        To Jerusalem proclaim:
        God shall take away your shame.
        Now get ready to recover;
        guilt and suffering are over.

2   Hear the herald's proclamation
        in the desert far and near,
        calling all to true repentance,
        telling that the Lord is near.
        Oh, that warning cry obey!
        For your God prepare a way.
        Let the valleys rise to greet him
        and the hills bow down to meet him.

continued overleaf

Music Melody by Louis Bourgeois (*c.* 1510–1561)
in *34 Pseaulmes de David,* Geneva 1551
harmonised John L. Bell (*b.* 1949)

3   Straighten out what has been crooked,
     make the roughest places plain.
     Let your hearts be true and humble,
     live as fits God's holy reign.
     Soon the glory of the Lord
     shall on earth be shed abroad.
     All the world shall surely see it,
     God is ready to decree it.

Isaiah 40: 1-5
adapted Johannes Olearius (1611–1684)
translated Catherine Winkworth (1827–1878)
revised John L. Bell (b. 1949)

O SO SO   65 56

Gently

1   Come now, O Prince of peace,
       make us one body;
       come, O Lord Jesus,
       reconcile your people.

2   Come now, O God of love,
       make us one body;
       come, O Lord Jesus,
       reconcile your people.

3   Come now and set us free,
       O God, our Saviour;
       come, O Lord Jesus,
       reconcile all nations.

4   Come, Hope of unity,
       make us one body;
       come, O Lord Jesus,
       reconcile all nations.

Geonyong Lee
revised Marion Pope

Music Geonyong Lee

WAIT FOR THE LORD   44 44

Ostinato

Wait for the Lord, his day is near.

Wait for the Lord: keep watch, take heart. *Fine*

Cantor (or group)

1 Pre-pare a way for the Lord. Make a straight path for him.

Pre-pare a way for the Lord. 2 Re-joice in the Lord al-ways:

God is at hand. Joy and glad-ness for all who seek the Lord.

3 The glo-ry of the Lord shall be re-vealed. All the

earth will see the Lord. 4 I wait-ed for the

Lord. God heard my cry. 5 Our

eyes are fixed on the Lord our God. 6 Seek

first the king-dom of God. Seek and you shall find.

7 O Lord, show us your way. Guide us in your truth.

Music Jacques Berthier (1923–1994)

Wait for the Lord, his day is near.
Wait for the Lord: keep watch, take heart.

1   Prepare a way for the Lord. Make a straight path for him. Prepare a way for the Lord.

2   Rejoice in the Lord always: God is at hand. Joy and gladness for all who seek the Lord.

3   The glory of the Lord shall be revealed. All the earth will see the Lord.

4   I waited for the Lord. God heard my cry.

5   Our eyes are fixed on the Lord our God.

6   Seek first the kingdom of God. Seek and you shall find.

7   O Lord, show us your way. Guide us in your truth.

The Ostinato, 'Wait for the Lord', and the verses are used simultaneously. The congregation sings the Ostinato at least once before a cantor or small group begins to sing the verses, and continues to sing (or, instruments to play) to the end of the verses, and beyond, if desired.

The Ostinato may also be used by itself as a sung response in a prayer.

Taizé Community 1984

CREDITON   CM

v. 1 only

PARAPHRASE 39

1   Hark the glad sound! the Saviour comes,
     the Saviour promised long;
     let every heart exult with joy,
     and every voice with song!

2   He comes, the prisoners to relieve,
     in Satan's bondage held;
     the gates of brass before him burst,
     the iron fetters yield.

3   He comes the broken hearts to bind,
     the bleeding souls to cure;
     and with the treasures of his grace
     to enrich the humble poor.

4   The sacred year has now revolved,
     accepted of the Lord,
     when heaven's high promise is fulfilled,
     and Israel is restored.

5   Our glad hosannas, Prince of Peace,
     thy welcome shall proclaim;
     and heaven's exalted arches ring
     with thy most honoured name.

Scottish Paraphrases, 1781
St Luke 4: 18, 19

Music Melody by Thomas Clark (1775–1859)
in *A Second Set of Psalm Tunes,* c. 1807

WACHET AUF   898 D 66 4 88

Wachet auf! ruft uns die Stimme

1   'Wake, awake! for night is flying',
     the watchmen on the heights are crying.
     'Awake, Jerusalem, at last!'
     Midnight hears the welcome voices,
     and at the thrilling cry rejoices:
     'Come forth, you virgins, night is past!
     The Bridegroom comes; awake,
     your lamps with gladness take,
     Alleluia!
     and for his marriage feast prepare,
     for you must go to meet him there.'

2   Zion hears the watchmen singing,
     and all her heart with joy is springing;
     she wakes, she rises from her gloom;
     for the Lord comes down all-glorious,
     the strong in grace, in truth victorious;
     her Star is risen, her Light is come!
     Now come, O blessèd One,
     God's own belovèd Son,
     Alleluia!
     We follow to the festal hall
     to sup with you, the Lord of all.

continued overleaf

Music Melody by Philipp Nicolai (1556–1608)
arranged Felix Mendelssohn (1809–1847)
from *St Paul*, 1836, adapted

3   All the heavens and earth adore you,
     and saints and angels sing before you,
     with harp and cymbal's clearest tone;
     Zion's gates of pearl before us
     resound as angels sing in chorus
     and lead us to your dazzling throne.
     No mortal eye nor ear
     can comprehend or bear
     such great glory;
     but we rejoice and sing the song,
     Alleluia! through ages long.

Philipp Nicolai (1556–1608)
translated *Catherine Winkworth (1827–1878)

279

MAKE WAY   Irregular

1 Make way, make way, for Christ the — King in splen - dour ar -
- rives; fling wide the gates and wel - come — him in -
- to your lives. (Men) *Make way,* (Women) *make — way, make —*

Christ Incarnate – Promise of the Messiah

1. Make way, make way, for Christ the King
   in splendour arrives;
   fling wide the gates and welcome him
   into your lives.
   Make way, make way, for the King of kings;
   make way, make way, and let his kingdom in.

2. He comes the broken hearts to heal,
   the prisoners to free;
   the deaf shall hear, the lame shall dance,
   the blind shall see.

3. And those who mourn with heavy hearts,
   who weep and sigh,
   with laughter, joy, and royal crown
   he'll beautify.

4. We call you now to worship him
   as Lord of all,
   to have no gods before him,
   their thrones must fall!

Graham Kendrick (*b.* 1950)

Music Graham Kendrick (*b.* 1950)

279 Words and Music: © 1986, Thankyou Music. Administered (UK and Europe) by kingswaysongs.com <tym@kingsway.co.uk>.
Remaining territories administered by worshiptogether.com songs. Used by permission.

HURRY, THE LORD IS NEAR   Irregular

Alleluia! Hurry, the Lord is near.
Alleluia, alleluia! Hurry, the Lord is near.

1 Sound the trumpet, the Lord is near,
   hurry, the Lord is near;
   see, he comes to save us all,
   hurry, the Lord is near!

2 Earth has longed for his approach;
   hurry, the Lord is near;
   straighten the road, smooth the path,
   hurry, the Lord is near!

3 Go out to meet him, shout his name:
   hurry, the Lord is near;
   his mighty kingdom shall never end,
   hurry, the Lord is near!

4 He is the mighty One, he is the Word;
   hurry, the Lord is near;
   God everlasting, Prince of Peace,
   hurry, the Lord is near!

Patrick Lee (1930–2004)

Music Ernest Sands (b. 1949)

BESANÇON   87 98 87

1   People, look East. The time is near
     of the crowning of the year.
     Make your house fair as you are able,
     trim the hearth and set the table.
     People, look East, and sing today:
     Love, the Guest, is on the way.

2   Furrows, be glad. Though earth is bare,
     one more seed is planted there:
     give up your strength the seed to nourish,
     that in course the flower may flourish.
     People, look East, and sing today:
     Love, the Rose, is on the way.

3   Stars, keep the watch. When night is dim
     one more light the bowl shall brim,
     shining beyond the frosty weather,
     bright as sun and moon together.
     People, look East, and sing today:
     Love, the Star, is on the way.

4   Angels, announce with shouts of mirth
     Christ who brings new life to earth.
     Set every peak and valley humming
     with the word, the Lord is coming.
     People, look East, and sing today:
     Love, the Lord, is on the way.

                              Eleanor Farjeon (1881–1965)

Music French traditional carol
harmonised Martin Edward Fallas Shaw (1875–1958), altered

ADVENT RING   Irregular

'Christ - mas is com - ing!', the Church is glad to sing, and

let the Ad - vent can - dles bright - ly burn in a ring. 1 The

first is for God's pro - mise to put the wrong things right, and

bring to earth's dark - ness the hope of love and light.

'Christmas is coming!',
the Church is glad to sing,
and let the advent candles
brightly burn in a ring.

1 The first is for God's promise
   to put the wrong things right,
   and bring to earth's darkness
   the hope of love and light.

2 The second for the prophets,
   who said that Christ
        would come
   with good news for many
   and angry words for some.

3 The third is for the Baptist,
   who cried, 'Prepare the way.
   Be ready for Jesus,
   today and every day.'

4 The fourth is for the Virgin,
   who mothered God's own Son
   and sang how God's justice
   was meant for everyone.

*5 At last we light the candle
   kept new for Christmas day.
   This shines bright for Jesus,
   new-born, and here to stay.

Christ is among us.
The candles in the ring
remind us that our Saviour
will light up everything.

*   *The verses may be sung progressively*
    through Advent until verse 5 on Christmas Day.

John L. Bell (*b.* 1949)

Music John L. Bell (*b.* 1949)

MORESTEAD   10 10 10 10
Unison

1   The voice of God goes out to all the world;
     his glory speaks across the universe.
     The great King's herald cries from star to star:
     with power, with justice, he will walk his way.

2   The Lord has said: 'Receive my messenger,
     my promise to the world, my pledge made flesh,
     a lamp to every nation, light from light':
     with power, with justice, he will walk his way.

3   The broken reed he will not trample down,
     nor set his heel upon the dying flame.
     He binds the wounds, and heals with his strong hand:
     with power, with justice, he will walk his way.

4   Anointed with the Spirit and with power,
     he comes to crown with comfort all the weak,
     to show the face of justice to the poor:
     with power, with justice, he will walk his way.

5   His touch will open eyes that darkness held;
     the lame shall run, the halting tongue shall sing,
     and prisoners laugh in light and liberty:
     with power, with justice, he will walk his way.

                              Luke Connaughton (1917–1979)

Music Sydney Watson (1903–1991)

GALLOWAY TAM　　　　　　　　　　　　　　　　11 10 11 8

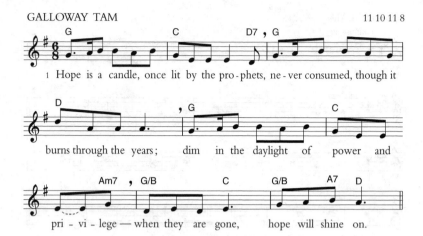

1　Hope is a candle, once lit by the pro-phets, ne-ver consumed, though it burns through the years; dim in the daylight of power and pri-vi-lege — when they are gone, hope will shine on.

1　　Hope is a candle, once lit by the prophets,
　　　never consumed, though it burns through the years;
　　　dim in the daylight of power and privilege —
　　　when they are gone, hope will shine on.

2　　Peace is a candle to show us a pathway,
　　　threatened by gusts from our rage and our greed.
　　　Friend, feel no envy for those in the shadows —
　　　violence and force their dead-end course.

3　　Love is a candle whose light makes a circle,
　　　where every face is the face of a friend.
　　　Widen the circle by sharing and giving —
　　　God's holy dare:　love everywhere.

4　　Joy is a candle of mystery and laughter,
　　　mystery of light that is born in the dark;
　　　laughter at hearing the voice of an angel,
　　　ever so near, casting out fear.

5　　Christ is the light that the prophets awaited,
　　　Christ is the lion, the lamb, and the child.
　　　Christ is the love and the mystery and laughter —
　　　candles, make way!　Christ is the day.

　　　　　　　　　　　　　　　　　　　Richard Leach

Music Scottish folk melody
arranged Douglas Galbraith (*b.* 1940)

GABRIEL'S MESSAGE   10 10 11 10

Glo - - - - ri - a!_____

1   The Angel Gabriel from heaven came,
    his wings as drifted snow, his eyes as flame;
    'All hail,' said he, 'thou lowly maiden Mary,
    most highly favoured lady.'
    Gloria!

2   'For known a blessèd Mother thou shalt be,
    all generations laud and honour thee,
    thy son shall be Emmanuel, by seers foretold;
    most highly favoured lady.'
    Gloria!

3   Then gentle Mary meekly bowed her head,
    'To me be as it pleaseth God,' she said.
    'My soul shall laud and magnify his holy name':
    most highly favoured lady.
    Gloria!

4   Of her, Emmanuel, the Christ was born
    in Bethlehem, all on a Christmas morn,
    and Christian folk throughout the world will ever say,
    'Most highly favoured lady.'
    Gloria!

Basque carol
adapted Sabine Baring-Gould (1834–1924)

Music Basque carol
arranged Charles Edgar Pettman (1866–1943)

WOODLANDS   10 10 10 10

Unison

The original version is found at 518.

1   Tell out, my soul, the greatness of the Lord!
        Unnumbered blessings, give my spirit voice;
    tender to me the promise of his word;
        in God my Saviour shall my heart rejoice.

2   Tell out, my soul, the greatness of his name!
        Make known his might, the deeds his arm has done;
    his mercy sure, from age to age the same;
        his holy Name, the Lord, the Mighty One.

2   Tell out, my soul, the greatness of his might!
        Powers and dominions lay their glory by.
    Proud hearts and stubborn wills are put to flight,
        the hungry fed, the humble lifted high.

4   Tell out, my soul, the glories of his word!
        Firm is his promise, and his mercy sure.
    Tell out, my soul, the greatness of the Lord
        to children's children and for evermore!

Timothy Dudley-Smith (*b.* 1926)
based on the *Magnificat* from *The New English Bible*

Music Walter Greatorex (1877–1949)

COLUMCILLE   11 11 11 11

1 No wind at the window,
   no knock on the door;
   no light from the lampstand,
   no foot on the floor;
   no dream born of tiredness,
   no ghost raised by fear:
   just an angel and a woman
   and a voice in her ear.

2 'O Mary, O Mary,
   don't hide from my face.
   Be glad that you're favoured
   and filled with God's grace.
   The time for redeeming
   the world has begun;
   and you are requested
   to mother God's Son.'

3 'This child must be born
   that the kingdom might come:
   salvation for many,
   destruction for some;
   both end and beginning,
   both message and sign;
   both victor and victim,
   both yours and divine.'

4 No payment was promised,
   no promises made;
   no wedding was dated,
   no blueprint displayed.
   Yet Mary, consenting
   to what none could guess,
   replied with conviction,
   'Tell God I say, "Yes"'.

John L. Bell (*b.*1949)

Music Irish traditional
arranged John L. Bell (*b.*1949)

CONDITOR ALME   LM

A - men.

1   Creator of the stars of night,
     your people's everlasting light,
     O Christ, redeemer of us all,
     we pray you, hear us when we call.

2   When earth drew on to darkest night,
     you came, but not in splendour bright,
     not as a king, but as the child
     of Mary, Virgin mother mild.

3   At your great name, majestic now,
     all knees must bend, all hearts must bow:
     all things on earth with one accord
     join those in heaven to call you Lord.

4   To God the Father, God the Son,
     and God the Spirit, Three in One,
     praise, honour, might, and glory be
     from age to age eternally. Amen.

                    Latin hymn, 9th century
       translated John Mason Neale (1818–1866)

Music Mode iv
harmonised Compilers

289

C.H. THREE   84 84 88 444

Al - le - lu - ia!   Al - le - lu - ia!   Al - le - lu - ia!

1   Lift up your heads, eternal gates,
    Alleluia!
    see how the King of glory waits,
    Alleluia!
    The Lord of Hosts is drawing near,
    the Saviour of the world is here.
    Alleluia! Alleluia! Alleluia!

2   But not in arms or battle dress,
    Alleluia!
    god comes, a child amidst distress,
    Alleluia!
    No mighty armies shield the way,
    only coarse linen, wool, and hay.
    Alleluia! Alleluia! Alleluia!

3   God brings a new face to the brave,
    Alleluia!
    God redefines who best can save:
    Alleluia!
    not those whose power relies on threat,
    terror or torture, destruction or debt.
    Alleluia! Alleluia! Alleluia!

4   God's matchless and majestic strength,
    Alleluia!
    in all its height, depth, breadth, and length,
    Alleluia!
    now is revealed, its power to prove,
    by Christ protesting 'God is love!'
    Alleluia! Alleluia! Alleluia!

George Weissel (1590–1635)
translated Catherine Winkworth (1827–1878)
vv. 2 - 4 adapted John L. Bell (b. 1949)

Music John L. Bell (b. 1949)

289 Adaptation: © WGRG, The Iona Community
289 Music: © WGRG, The Iona Community

ST MAGNUS (NOTTINGHAM)   CM

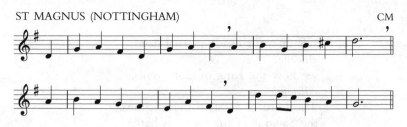

290 2

TIVERTON   CM

PARAPHRASE 19

1   The race that long in darkness pined
       has seen a glorious light;
       the people dwell in day, who dwelt
       in death's surrounding night.

2   To us a Child of hope is born;
       to us a Son is given;
       him shall the tribes of earth obey,
       him all the hosts of heaven.

3   His name shall be the Prince of Peace,
       for evermore adored;
       the Wonderful, the Counsellor,
       the great and mighty Lord.

4   His power increasing still shall spread,
       his reign no end shall know:
       justice shall guard his throne above,
       and peace abound below.

Scottish Paraphrases, 1781
Isaiah 9: 2-7

Music Tune 1 Jeremiah Clarke (*c.*1673–1707)

Music Tune 2 Jacob Grigg
from John Rippon's *Selection of Psalms and Hymn Tunes,* 1796

KINGSFOLD   DCM

1. When out of poverty is born
   a dream that will not die,
   and landless, weary folk find strength
   to stand with heads held high,
   it's then we learn from those who wait
   to greet the promised day,
   'The Lord is coming; don't lose heart.
   Be blest; prepare the way!'

2. When people wander far from God,
   forget to share their bread,
   they find their wealth an empty thing,
   their spirits are not fed.
   For only just and tender love
   the hungry soul will stay.
   And so God's prophets echo still
   'Be blest; prepare the way!'

3. When God took flesh and came to earth,
   the world turned upside down,
   and in the strength of woman's faith
   the Word of Life was born.
   She knew that God would raise the low,
   it pleased her to obey.
   Rejoice with Mary in the call,
   'Be blest; prepare the way!'

Kathryn Galloway (*b.* 1952)

Music Melody from *English Country Songs* 1893
harmonised Ralph Vaughan Williams (1872–1958)

KINGSFOLD   DCM

1   When out of poverty is born
    a dream that will not die,
    and landless, weary folk find strength
    to stand with heads held high,
    it's then we learn from those who wait
    to greet the promised day,
    'The Lord is coming; don't lose heart.
    Be blest; prepare the way!'

2   When people wander far from God,
    forget to share their bread,
    they find their wealth an empty thing,
    their spirits are not fed.
    For only just and tender love
    the hungry soul will stay.
    And so God's prophets echo still
    'Be blest; prepare the way!'

3   When God took flesh and came to earth,
    the world turned upside down,
    and in the strength of woman's faith
    the Word of Life was born.
    She knew that God would raise the low,
    it pleased her to obey.
    Rejoice with Mary in the call,
    'Be blest; prepare the way!'

Kathryn Galloway (b. 1952)

Music Melody from *English Country Songs* 1893
harmonised Compilers

Christ Incarnate – Promise of the Messiah

THE HOLLY AND THE IVY

76 87 and refrain

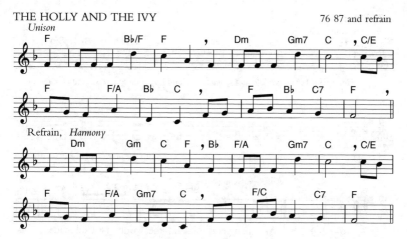

1   It's rounded like an orange
this earth on which we stand;
and we praise the God who holds it
in the hollow of his hand.
So Father, we would thank you
for all that you have done,
and for all that you have given us
through the coming of your Son.

2   A candle, burning brightly,
can cheer the darkest night,
and these candles tell how Jesus
came to bring a dark world light.

3   The ribbon round the orange
reminds us of the cost;
how the Shepherd, strong and gentle,
gave his life to save the lost.

4   Four seasons with their harvest
supply the food we need,
and the Spirit gives a harvest
that can make us rich indeed.

5   We come with our Christingles
to tell of Jesus' birth,
and we praise the God who blessed us
by his coming to this earth.

Basil Ernest Bridge (b. 1927)

This song is part of the Christingle service.

Music Old English carol, *harmonised* Compilers

292   Words: © 1990 Oxford University Press, Great Clarendon Street, Oxford. OX2 6DP. From *New Songs of Praise 5*, 1991.
Reproduced by permission.

CANDLE   Irregular

Bring your Christingle with gladness and joy!
Sing praise to God who gave us his Son;
so give him, give him your love.

LEADER

1   Here is an orange —

         ALL

An orange as round as the world that God made.

Music Valerie Anne Ruddle (*b.* 1932)

LEADER
2 Here is a candle —
ALL
A candle for Jesus, the Light of the world;
an orange as round as the world that God made;

LEADER
3 Here is red ribbon —
ALL
Red ribbon reminds us Christ died for us all;
a candle for Jesus, the Light of the world;
an orange as round as the world that God made;

LEADER
4 Here are the fruits —
ALL
The fruits of the earth God has given us to share;
red ribbon reminds us Christ died for us all;
a candle for Jesus, the Light of the world;
an orange as round as the world that God made;

Valerie Anne Ruddle (*b.* 1932)
and William Horton

This song is part of the Christingle service.

Also suitable

Come, thou long-expected Jesus 472
Hail, to the Lord's Anointed 474
Christ is coming! let creation 475
Lo, he comes with clouds descending 477

CHRIST INCARNATE
CHRISTMAS AND EPIPHANY

SUSSEX CAROL   LM Irregular

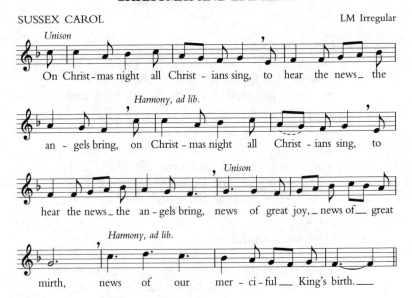

Unison
On Christ-mas night all Christ - ians sing, to hear the news the

Harmony, ad lib.
an - gels bring, on Christ - mas night all Christ - ians sing, to

Unison
hear the news the an - gels bring, news of great joy, news of great

Harmony, ad lib.
mirth, news of our mer - ci - ful King's birth.

Music English traditional melody
arranged Ralph Vaughan Williams (1872–1958)

294 Music: © 1919, Stainer & Bell Ltd, PO Box 110, Victoria House, 23 Gruneisen Road, London N3 1DZ

1   On Christmas night all Christians sing,
to hear the news the angels bring,
on Christmas night all Christians sing,
to hear the news the angels bring,
news of great joy, news of great mirth,
news of our merciful King's birth.

2   Then why should we on earth be so sad,
since our Redeemer made us glad,
then why should we on earth be so sad,
since our Redeemer made us glad,
when from our sin he set us free,
all for to gain our liberty?

3   When sin departs before his grace,
then life and health come in its place;
when sin departs before his grace,
then life and health come in its place;
heaven and earth with joy may sing,
all for to see the new-born King.

4   All out of darkness we have light,
which made the angels sing this night:
all out of darkness we have light,
which made the angels sing this night;
'Glory to God, on earth be peace,
goodwill to all shall never cease.'

English traditional after
Luke Wadding (*d.* 1686)

WHITE ROSETTES 87 87 D

1 Who would think that what was needed
to transform and save the earth
might not be a plan or army,
proud in purpose, proved in worth?
Who would think, despite derision,
that a child should lead the way?
God surprises earth with heaven,
coming here on Christmas Day.

2 Shepherds watch and wise men wonder,
monarchs scorn and angels sing;
such a place as none would reckon
hosts a holy helpless thing.
Stable beasts and by-passed strangers
watch a baby laid in hay:
God surprises earth with heaven,
coming here on Christmas Day.

3 Centuries of skill and science
span the past from which we move,
yet experience questions whether,
with such progress, we improve.
While the human lot we ponder,
lest our hopes and humour fray,
God surprises earth with heaven,
coming here on Christmas Day.

John L. Bell (*b.* 1949)
and Graham Maule (*b.* 1958)

Music John L. Bell (*b.* 1949)

WINCHESTER OLD   CM

PARAPHRASE 37

1   While humble shepherds watched their flocks
     in Bethlehem's plains by night,
     an angel sent from heaven appeared,
     and filled the plains with light.

2   'Fear not' he said, for sudden dread
     had seized their troubled mind;
     'Glad tidings of great joy I bring
     to you and all mankind.

3   'To you in David's town, this day,
     is born, of David's line,
     the Saviour, who is Christ the Lord;
     and this shall be the sign:

4   'The heavenly Babe you there shall find
     to human view displayed,
     all meanly wrapped in swaddling-bands,
     and in a manger laid.'

5   Thus spake the seraph; and forthwith
     appeared a shining throng
     of angels praising God; and thus
     addressed their joyful song:

6   'All glory be to God on high,
     and to the earth be peace;
     good will is shown from heaven above
     and never more shall cease.'

Scottish Paraphrases, 1781
St Luke 2: 8-14

Music Melody from Este's *Psalter,* 1592

BALULALOW   DLM

1 I come from hevin [heich] to tell   the best no-wells that e'er be - fell.
To you thir tythings trew I bring and I will of them say and sing.

2 This day to you   is — born ane Child   of Ma-rie meik and Vir - gin

mild.   That bliss — — it bairn_____   be - ning   and
                                                    (4) gude   and
                                                    (6) were   to
                                                    (8) sall   I

kind, be - ning and_ kind,   sall you re-joyce baith hart and mind.
fair, sa gude and_ fair?
thee, it were to _ thee
bow,_ sall_ I__ bow

1   I come from hevin [heich] to tell
     the best nowells that e'er befell.
     To you thir tythings trew I bring
     and I will of them say and sing.

2   This day to you is born ane Child
     of Marie meik and Virgin mild.
*   That blissit bairn bening and kind,
     sall you rejoyce baith hart and mind.

Music Melody and bass from John Gamble's *Commonplace-Book,*
c. 1660, *edited* Kenneth Elliott (*b.* 1929)

3   Lat us rejoyis and be blyth
and with the Hyrdis go full swyth
and see what Godis grace hes done
throu Christ to bring us to his throne.

4   My saull and life stand up and see
wha lyis in ane cribbe of tree.

*   What Babe is that, sa gude and fair?
It is Christ, Godis Son and Air.

5   The silk and sandell thee to eis
ar hay and sempill sweilling clais
wharin thou gloris greitest King
as thou in hev'n war in thy ring.

6   And war the warld ten times sa wide
cled ouer with gold and stanes of pride

*   unworthie yit it were to thee
under they feet ane stule to be.

7   O my deir hart, yung Jesus sweit
prepair thy creddill in my spreit!
And I sall rock thee in my hart
and never mair fra thee depart.

8   Bot I sall praise thee evermoir
with sangis sweit unto thy gloir.

*   The kneis of my hart sall I bow
and sing that rycht Balulalow.

*   *'bening and kind' is repeated,
as are the equivalent words in subsequent verses.*

Martin Luther (1483–1546)
translated John or Robert Wedderburn (*fl.* 1540)
The Gude and Godlie Ballatis, 1578
edited Kenneth Elliott (*b.* 1929)

BALULALOW

DLM

1   I come from heaven high to tell
     the best nowells that e'er befell.
     To you these tidings true I bring
     and I will of them say and sing.

2   This day to you is born a Child
     of Mary meek and Virgin mild.
*   That blessed bairn benign and kind,
     shall you rejoice baith heart and mind.

3   Let us rejoice now and be blithe
     and with the shepherds go full lithe
     and see what God's good grace has done
     through Christ to bring us to his throne.

4   My soul and life stand up and see
     who lies there in a cribbe of tree.
*   What Babe is that, so good and fair?
     It is Christ, God's own Son and Heir.

5   The silk and satin thee to ease
     are hay and simple swaddling clothes
     wherein thou gloriest greatest King
     as thou in heaven were in thy ring.

6   And were the world ten times as wide
     clad o'er with gold and stones of pride
*   unworthy yet it were to thee
     under thy feet a stool to be.

Music Melody and bass from John Gamble's *Commonplace-Book,*
c. 1660, *edited* Kenneth Elliott (*b.* 1929)

7   O my dear heart, young Jesus sweet
    prepare thy cradle in my spirit!
    And I shall rock thee in my heart
    and never more from thee depart.

8   But I shall praise thee evermore
    with songs so sweet unto thy gloir.
    The knees of my heart shall I bow
    and sing that bright Balulalow.

*   'benign and kind' is repeated,
    as are the equivalent words in subsequent verses.

Martin Luther (1483–1546)
translated John or Robert Wedderburn (*fl.* 1540)
The Gude and Godlie Ballatis, 1578
edited Compilers

99

STEP-WISE   99 99

1   One day an angel here on this earth
    spoke of God's presence coming to birth.
    Mary was listening; humbly her heart
    sang at the Word God chose to impart.

2   Mary gave birth in Bethlehem's cave,
    blessed by the child God chose her to have.
    Love was the reason God had become
    close to his mother, far from her home.

3   Out in the fields a heavenly throng
    broke through the dark with resonant song.
    Shepherds, who saw God's glory by night,
    sped on their way to worship the Light.

4   Jesus, your Spirit, shining with care,
    speaks to the world you treasure and share.
    Come with the human touch of your birth;
    find in our hearts your home on this earth.

Alison M. Robertson (*b.* 1940)

Music Alison M. Robertson (*b.* 1940)

300   LIFE IN CHRIST

THE VIRGIN MARY   Irregular

1 The Vir - gin Ma - ry had a ba - by boy,_ the Vir - gin Ma - ry had a ba - by boy,_ the Vir - gin Ma - ry had a ba - by boy_ and they say that his name is Je - sus._

He come from the glo - ry, he come from the glorious kingdom; he come from the glo - ry, he come from the glorious kingdom. O__ yes, be - lie - ver! O__ yes, be - lie - ver! He come from the glo - ry, he come from the glorious kingdom.

vv. 1, 2   *v. 3*

glorious kingdom.   2 The glo - rious king - dom.__

Music West Indian traditional as in *The Popular Carol Book*, n.d., Mowbray

1   The Virgin Mary had a baby boy,
    the Virgin Mary had a baby boy,
    the Virgin Mary had a baby boy
    and they say that his name is Jesus.
        He come from the glory,
        he come from the glorious kingdom;
        he come from the glory,
        he come from the glorious kingdom.
        O yes, believer!
        O yes, believer!
        He come from the glory,
        he come from the glorious kingdom.

2   The angels sang when the baby was born,
    the angels sang when the baby was born,
    the angels sang when the baby was born
    and they sang that his name is Jesus.

3   The shepherds came where the baby was born,
    the shepherds came where the baby was born,
    the shepherds came where the baby was born
    and they say that his name is Jesus.

                              West Indian carol

MENDELSSOHN (BETHLEHEM)   7777 D and refrain

1   Hark! the herald angels sing,
     'Glory to the new-born King,
     peace on earth, and mercy mild,
     God and sinners reconciled!'
     Joyful, all ye nations, rise,
     join the triumph of the skies,
     with the angelic hosts proclaim,
     'Christ is born in Bethlehem'.
           Hark! the herald angels sing,
           'Glory to the new-born King'.

2   Christ, by highest heaven adored,
     Christ, the everlasting Lord,
     late in time behold him come,
     offspring of a virgin's womb.
     Veiled in flesh the Godhead see;
     hail, the Incarnate Deity,
     pleased as Man with man to dwell,
     Jesus, our Immanuel!

3   Hail, the heaven-born Prince of Peace!
     Hail, the Sun of Righteousness!
     Light and life to all he brings,
     risen with healing in his wings.
     Mild he lays his glory by,
     born that man no more may die,
     born to raise the sons of earth,
     born to give them second birth:

                              Charles Wesley (1707–1788)
                                      and others

Music Felix Mendelssohn (1809–1847)
adapted William Hayman Cummings (1831–1915)

A STARRY NIGHT   Irregular

1   It was on a starry night when the hills were bright,
earth lay sleeping, sleeping calm and still;
then in a cattle shed, in a manger bed,
a boy was born, King of all the world.
And all the angels sang for him,
the bells of heaven rang for him;
for a boy was born, King of all the world.
And all the angels sang for him,
the bells of heaven rang for him;
for a boy was born, King of all the world.

2   Soon the shepherds came that way, where the baby lay,
and were kneeling, kneeling by his side,
to celebrate his birth bringing peace on earth;
a boy was born, King of all the world.

Music Joy Webb (*b.*1932)   Joy Webb (*b.*1932)

NOEL   DCM

1   It came upon the midnight clear,
     that glorious song of old,
     from angels bending near the earth
     to touch their harps of gold:
     'Peace on the earth, good will to you
     from heaven's all-gracious King!'
     The world in solemn stillness lay
     to hear the angels sing.

2   Still through the cloven skies they come,
     with peaceful wings unfurled;
     and still their heavenly music floats
     o'er all the weary world;
     above its sad and lowly plains
     they bend on hovering wing,
     and ever o'er its Babel-sounds
     the blessèd angels sing.

3   But with the woes of sin and strife
     the world has suffered long;
     beneath the angels' hymn have rolled
     two thousand years of wrong;
     and warring humankind hears not
     the love-song which they bring;
     oh, hush the noise and still the strife
     to hear the angels sing.

Music Traditional melody
adapted Arthur Seymour Sullivan (1842–1900)

4   And you, beneath life's crushing load
whose forms are bending low,
who toil along the climbing way
with painful steps and slow,
look now! for glad and golden hours
come swiftly on the wing;
oh, rest beside the weary road,
and hear the angels sing.

5   For lo! the days are hastening on,
by prophet bards foretold,
when, with the ever-rolling years,
still dawns the Age of Gold,
when peace shall over all the earth
its ancient splendours fling,
and all the world give back the song
which now the angels sing.

*Edmund Hamilton Sears (1810–1876)

)4

FOREST GREEN   DCM Irregular

1   O little town of Bethlehem,
how still we see you lie!
Above your deep and dreamless sleep
the silent stars go by;
yet in your streets is shining
the everlasting Light;
the hopes and fears of all the years
are met in you tonight.

continued overleaf

Music English traditional melody
harmonised Ralph Vaughan Williams (1872–1958)

2   O morning stars, together
    proclaim the holy birth,
    and praises sing to God the King,
    and peace to all on earth.
    For Christ is born of Mary;
    and, gathered all above,
    while mortals sleep, the angels keep
    their watch of wondering love.

3   How silently, how silently,
    the wondrous gift is given!
    So God imparts to human hearts
    the blessings of his heaven.
    No ear may hear his coming;
    but in this world of sin,
    where meek souls will receive him, still
    the dear Christ enters in.

4   O holy Child of Bethlehem,
    descend to us, we pray;
    cast out our sin, and enter in;
    be born in us today.
    We hear the Christmas angels
    the great glad tidings tell;
    O come to us, abide with us,
    our Lord Emmanuel.

*Phillips Brooks (1835–1893)

CRANHAM   Irregular

1 In the bleak mid - win - - ter
2 Our God, heaven can - not hold him,
3 E - nough for him whom che - ru - bim
4 An - gels and arch - an - - gels
5 What can I give him,

fros - ty wind made moan, earth stood hard as
nor earth sus - tain; heaven and earth shall
wor - ship night and day, a breast - - ful of
may have ga - thered there, che - ru - bim and
poor as I am? If I were a

i - - ron, wa - ter like a stone;
flee a - way when he comes to reign:
milk and a man - ger - ful of hay; e -
se - ra - phim thronged the air, but
shep - - herd I would bring a lamb,

snow had fal - len, snow on snow,
in the bleak mid - win - - ter a
- nough for him whom an - - gels
on - - ly his mo - - ther,
if I were a wise man

snow on snow, in the bleak mid -
sta - ble - place suf - ficed the Lord God Al -
fall down be - fore, the ox and ass and
in her mai - den bliss, wor - shipped the Be -
I would do my part, — yet what I can I

- win - ter, long a - go.
- migh - ty, Je - - - sus Christ.
ca - - mel which a - dore.
- lov - - ed with a kiss.
give him, give my heart.

Christina Georgina Rossetti (1830–1894)

full text overleaf

Music Gustav Theodore von Holst (1874–1934)

1   In the bleak midwinter
    frosty wind made moan,
    earth stood hard as iron,
    water like a stone;
    snow had fallen, snow on snow,
    snow on snow,
    in the bleak midwinter,
    long ago.

2   Our God, heaven cannot hold him,
    nor earth sustain;
    heaven and earth shall flee away
    when he comes to reign:
    in the bleak midwinter
    a stable-place sufficed
    the Lord God Almighty,
    Jesus Christ.

3   Enough for him whom cherubim
    worship night and day,
    a breastful of milk,
    and a mangerful of hay;
    enough for him whom angels
    fall down before,
    the ox and ass and camel
    which adore.

4   Angels and archangels
    may have gathered there,
    cherubim and seraphim
    thronged the air;
    but only his mother,
    in her maiden bliss,
    worshipped the Beloved
    with a kiss.

5   What can I give him,
    poor as I am?
    If I were a shepherd
    I would bring a lamb;
    if I were a wise man,
    I would do my part, —
    yet what I can I give him,
    give my heart.

                    Christina Georgina Rossetti (1830–1894)

ADESTE FIDELES   Irregular

Adeste, fideles

1   O come, all ye faithful,
     joyful and triumphant,
     O come ye, O come ye to Bethlehem;
     come and behold him,
     born the King of angels;
          O come, let us adore him,
          O come, let us adore him,
          O come, let us adore him, Christ the Lord.

2   God of God,
     Light of light,
     Lo! he abhors not the Virgin's womb;
     very God,
     begotten, not created;

3   Sing, choirs of angels,
     sing in exultation,
     sing, all ye citizens of heaven above,
     'Glory to God
     in the highest':

4   Yea, Lord, we greet thee,
  * born this happy morning;
     Jesus, to thee be glory given:
     Word of the Father,
     now in flesh appearing:

  * *or, when not on Christmas Day,* born for our salvation

                    Latin, 18th century, possibly by
                    John Francis Wade (*c.* 1711–1786)
                                        and others

Music Melody probably by
John Francis Wade (*c.* 1711–1786)

ADESTE FIDELES   Irregular

Adeste, fideles

1   Adeste, fideles,
     laeti, triumphantes,
     venite, venite in Bethlehem;
     natum videte
     regem angelorum:
         venite, adoremus,
         venite, adoremus,
         venite, adoremus Dominum.

2   Deum de Deo,
     Lumen de Lumine,
     gestant puellae viscera,
     Deum verum,
     genitum, non factum:

3   Cantet nunc hymnos
     chorus angelorum;
     cantet nunc aula caelestium:
     gloria
     in excelsis Deo!

4   Ergo qui natus
     die hodierna,
     Jesu, tibi sit gloria:
     Patris aeterni
     verbum caro factum:

         Latin, 18th century, possibly by
         John Francis Wade (*c.* 1711–1786)

Music Melody probably by
John Francis Wade (*c.* 1711–1786)

DUNLAP'S CREEK   CM

1   Behold the great Creator makes
      himself a house of clay,
      in human flesh, our form he takes
      which he will bear alway.

2   Hark, how the wise eternal Word
      as a weak infant cries!
      In form of servant is the Lord,
      and God in cradle lies.

3   This wonder all the world amazed,
      it shook the starry frame;
      the hosts of heaven stood to gaze,
      and bless the Saviour's name.

4   Glad shepherds ran to view this sight;
      a choir of angels sings,
      and eastern sages with delight
      adore this King of kings.

5   Join then, all hearts that are not stone,
      to sing with choirs above
      and celebrate this holy One,
      the God of peace and love.

Thomas Pestel (1585–1659)

Music Samuel McFarland
harmonised Richard Proulx (*b.*1937)

308 Harmonisation: © 1986, GIA Publications Inc., 7404 S. Mason Avenue, Chicago, IL 60638, USA. Used by permission.

STILLE NACHT   Irregular

Stille Nacht, heilige Nacht

1   Still the night, holy the night!
     Sleeps the world; hid from sight,
     Mary and Joseph in stable bare
     watch o'er the Child belovèd and fair,
     sleeping in heavenly rest,
     sleeping in heavenly rest.

2   Still the night, holy the night!
     Shepherds first saw the light,
     heard resounding clear and long,
     far and near, the angel-song,
     'Christ the Redeemer is here!'
     'Christ the Redeemer is here!'

3   Still the night, holy the night!
     Son of God, O how bright
     love is smiling from thy face!
     Strikes for us now the hour of grace,
     Saviour, since thou art born!
     Saviour, since thou art born!

Music Melody by Franz Xaver Grüber (1787–1863)
harmonised David Evans (1874–1948)

Original German text:

1 Stille Nacht, heilige Nacht!
Alles schläft, einsam wacht
nur das traute hochheilige Paar.
Holder Knabe im lockigen Haar,
Schlaf in himmlischer Ruh!
Schlaf in himmlischer Ruh!

2 Stille Nacht, heilige Nacht,
Hirten erst kund gemacht!
Durch der Engel Halleluja
tönet es laut von fern und nah:
Christ der Retter ist da!
Christ der Retter ist da!

3 Stille Nacht, heilige Nacht,
Gottes Sohn, o wie lacht
Lieb' aus deinem göttlichen Mund,
da uns schlägt die rettende Stund,
Christ, in deiner Geburt!
Christ, in deiner Geburt!

Joseph Mohr (1792–1848)
translated Stopford Augustus Brooke (1832–1916)
and Compilers of *Revised Church Hymnary,* 1927

CALYPSO CAROL   Irregular

1 See him ly - ing on a bed of straw: a draugh-ty sta - ble with an o - pen door; Ma - ry cra - dl-ing the babe she bore — the Prince of glo - ry is his name. Oh, now car - ry me to Beth - le - hem_ to see the Lord_ of love a - gain:_ just as poor_ as was the sta - ble then,_ the Prince of glo - ry when he came.___ Prince of glo - ry when he came.___

Music Michael Arnold Perry (1942–1996)
arranged Stephen Coates (b. 1952)

1   See him lying on a bed of straw:
a draughty stable with an open door;
Mary cradling the babe she bore —
the Prince of glory is his name.
Oh, now carry me to Bethlehem
to see the Lord of love again:
just as poor as was the stable then,
the Prince of glory when he came.

2   Star of silver, sweep across the skies,
show where Jesus in the manger lies;
shepherds, swiftly from your stupor rise
to see the Saviour of the world!

3   Angels, sing again the song you sang,
sing the glory of God's gracious plan;
sing that Bethl'em's little baby can
be the saviour of us all.

4   Mine are riches, from your poverty,
from your innocence, eternity;
mine, forgiveness by your death for me,
child of sorrow for my joy.

Michael Arnold Perry (1942–1996)

SING LULLABY (OI BETLEEM)   Irregular

1 Je-sus is born, formed in a womb and now a ba-by. Je-sus is born: swad-dled and small he sleeps in hay. Set-ting a-side his power and glo-ry, home-less he en-ters hu-man sto-ry: Christ comes to earth.

1   Jesus is born:
formed in a womb and now a baby,
Jesus is born.
Swaddled and small he sleeps in hay.
Setting aside his power and glory,
homeless he enters human story:
Christ comes to earth.

2   Jesus is born:
angels announce a joyful message,
Jesus is born.
Peace on the earth, goodwill to all.
This is the hour God shows his favour,
sending his Son, creation's Saviour:
Hope comes to earth.

3   Jesus is born:
high overhead a star is shining,
Jesus is born.
Earth houses uncreated light.
Now is the hold of darkness broken
as hearts and minds to God are opened:
Light comes to earth.

Music Basque traditional, Bordes, 1895
arranged Charles Edgar Pettman (1866–1943)

4   Jesus is born:
this night the world is changed for ever.
Jesus is born,
and in this babe, for all to see,
Love is revealed; God's heart lies open
as the incarnate Word is spoken:
God comes to earth.

Pat Bennett (b. 1957)

12

CRADLE SONG   11 11 11 11

1   Away in a manger, no crib for a bed,
the little Lord Jesus laid down his sweet head;
the stars in the bright sky looked down where he lay,
the little Lord Jesus asleep on the hay.

2   The cattle are lowing, the Baby awakes,
but little Lord Jesus no crying he makes.
I love you, Lord Jesus! look down from the sky,
and stay by my side until morning is nigh.

3   Be near me, Lord Jesus; I ask you to stay
close by me for ever, and love me, I pray.
Bless all the dear children in your tender care,
and fit us for heaven, to live with you there.

Little children's book, Philadelphia, 1885
Author unknown

Music Melody by William James Kirkpatrick (1838–1921)
Around the World with Christmas, 1895
harmonised Compilers

HUMILITY (OXFORD)

7777 and refrain

1. See! in yonder manger low,
   born for us on earth below,
   see! the tender Lamb appears
   promised from eternal years.
   Hail, thou ever-blessèd morn!
   Hail, redemption's happy dawn!
   Sing through all Jerusalem,
   'Christ is born in Bethlehem!'

2. Lo! within a manger lies
   he who built the starry skies,
   he who, throned in height sublime,
   sits amid the cherubim.

3. Say, ye holy shepherds, say,
   what your joyful news today;
   wherefore have ye left your sheep
   on the lonely mountain steep?

4. 'As we watched at dead of night,
   lo! we saw a wondrous light:
   angels, singing peace on earth,
   told us of the Saviour's birth.'

5. Sacred Infant, all Divine,
   what a tender love was thine,
   thus to come from highest bliss
   down to such a world as this!

Edward Caswall (1814–1878)

Music John Goss (1800–1880)

BUNESSAN   55 53 D

1 Child in the man - ger, in - fant of Ma - ry; out - cast and stran - ger, Lord of all! Child who in - her - its all our trans - gres - sions, all our de - mer - its on him fall.

An alternative arrangement is found at 212.

Leanabh an àigh

1   Child in the manger,
    infant of Mary;
    outcast and stranger,
      Lord of all!
    Child who inherits
    all our transgressions,
    all our demerits
      on him fall.

2   Once the most holy
    child of salvation
    gently and lowly
      lived below;
    now, as our glorious
    mighty Redeemer,
    see him victorious
      o'er each foe.

3   Prophets foretold him,
    infant of wonder;
    angels behold him
      on his throne;
    worthy our Saviour
    of all their praises;
    happy for ever
      are his own.

Mary Macdonald (1789–1872)
translated Lachlan Macbean (1853–1931)

Gaelic text version overleaf

Music Gaelic traditional melody
arranged David Evans (1874–1948)

Original Gaelic text:

1 Leanabh an àigh,
an leanabh bh'aig Màiri;
rugadh an stàbull
  Rìgh nan dùl:
thànig don fhàsach,
dh'fhuling nar na-àite —
son' iad an àireamh
  bhitheas dha dlùth!

2 Ged a bhios leanaban
aig rìghrean na talmhainn,
'n greadnachas garbh
  's anabarr mùirn,
's geàrr gus am falbh iad
's fàsaidh iad anfhann,
an àilleachd 's an dealbh
  a' searg 'san ùir.

3 Cha b'ionnan 's an t-Uan
a tháinig gar fuasgladh,
iriosal stuama
  ghluais e 'n tùs;
e naomha gun truailleachd,
Cruithear an t-sluaigh,
dh' èirich e suas
  le buaidh on ùir.

4 Leanabh an àigh
mar dh'aithris na fàidhean,
's na h-ainglean àrd'
  b'e miann an sùl:
's e 's airidh ar gràdh
's ar n-urram thoirt dha:
is sona an àireamh
  bhitheas dha dlùth.

Mary Macdonald (1789–1872)

IRBY   87 87 77

1   Once in royal David's city
     stood a lowly cattle shed,
     where a mother laid her Baby
     in a manger for his bed.
     Mary was that mother mild,
     Jesus Christ her little Child.

2   He came down to earth from heaven
     who is God and Lord of all,
     and his shelter was a stable,
     and his cradle was a stall.
     With the poor and meek and lowly
     lived on earth our Saviour holy.

3   And our eyes at last shall see him,
     through his own redeeming love;
     for that Child so dear and helpless
     is our Lord in heaven above;
     and he leads his children on
     to the place where he is gone.

4   Not in that poor lowly stable,
     with the oxen standing by,
     we shall see him; but in heaven,
     set at God's right hand on high,
     where his children gather round,
     bright like stars, with glory crowned.

               *Cecil Frances Alexander (1818–1895)

Music Henry John Gauntlett (1805–1876)
harmony, as in Appendix to *Hymns Ancient & Modern,* 1868

GARTAN　　　　　　　　　　　　　　　　　　　　　6767

1　　Love came down at Christmas,
　　　Love all lovely, Love Divine;
　　　Love was born at Christmas,
　　　star and angels gave the sign.

2　　Worship we the Godhead,
　　　Love Incarnate, Love Divine;
　　　worship we our Jesus:
　　　but wherewith for sacred sign?

3　　Love shall be our token,
　　　love be yours and love be mine,
　　　love to God and all men,
　　　love for plea and gift and sign.

　　　　　Christina Georgina Rossetti (1830–1894)

Music Irish traditional melody
harmonised David Evans (1874–1948)

INCARNATION   64 64 66 64

1 Before the world began
   one Word was there;
   grounded in God he was,
   rooted in care;
   by him all things were made,
   in him was love displayed,
   through him God spoke
        and said
   'I am for you'.

2 Life found in him its source,
   death found its end;
   light found in him its course,
   darkness its friend;
   for neither death nor doubt
   nor darkness can put out
   the glow of God, the shout
   'I am for you'.

3 The Word was in the world
   which from him came;
   unrecognised he was,
   unknown by name;
   one with all humankind,
   with the unloved aligned,
   convincing sight and mind
   'I am for you'.

4 All who received the Word,
   by God were blessed,
   sisters and brothers they
   of earth's fond guest.
   So did the Word of grace
   proclaim in time and space,
   and with a human face,
   'I am for you'.

John L. Bell (*b.*1949)
and Graham Maule (*b.*1958)
based on *John 1: 1-13*

Music John L. Bell (*b.*1949)

QUELLE EST CETTE ODEUR AGRÉABLE   98 98 98

1   Lord, you were rich beyond all splendour,
      yet, for love's sake, became so poor;
      leaving your throne in glad surrender,
      sapphire-paved courts for stable floor:
      Lord, you were rich beyond all splendour,
      yet, for love's sake, became so poor.

2   You are our God beyond all praising,
      yet, for love's sake, became a man;
      stooping so low, but sinners raising
      heavenwards, by your eternal plan:
      you are our God, beyond all praising,
      yet for love's sake, became a man.

3   Lord, you are love beyond all telling,
      Saviour and King, we worship you;
      Emmanuel, within us dwelling,
      make us and keep us pure and true:
      Lord, you are love beyond all telling,
      Saviour and King, we worship you.

Frank Houghton (1894–1972)
from *2 Corinthians 8: 9*

Music French traditional melody
arranged Charles Herbert Kitson (1874–1944)

CORDE NATUS (DIVINUM MYSTERIUM)   87 87 87 7

Corde natus ex Parentis

1   Of the Father's love begotten
      ere the worlds began to be,
      he is Alpha and Omega,
      he the source, the ending he,
      of the things that are, that have been,
      and that future years shall see,
      evermore and evermore.

2   By his word was all created;
      he commanded; it was done:
      heaven and earth and depths of ocean,
      universe of three in one;
      all that sees the moon's soft shining,
      all that breathes beneath the sun,
      evermore and evermore.

3   O that birth for ever blessèd,
      when the Virgin, full of grace,
      by the Spirit's power conceiving,
      bore the Saviour of our race,
      and the Babe, the world's Redeemer,
      first revealed his sacred face,
      evermore and evermore.

continued overleaf

Music Late form of plainsong trope in *Piae Cantiones*, 1582
harmonised Compilers of *Hymns for Church and School*, 1964

4   This is he whom seers and sages
sang of old with one accord,
whom the voices of the prophets
promised in their faithful word;
now he shines, the long-expected;
let creation praise its Lord,
evermore and evermore.

5   All the heights of heaven, adore him;
angel hosts, his praises sing;
powers, dominions bow before him,
and extol our God and King;
let no tongue on earth be silent,
every voice in concert ring,
evermore and evermore.

6   Christ, to thee, with God the Father,
and, O Holy Ghost, to thee,
hymn and chant and high thanksgiving,
and unwearied praises be,
honour, glory, and dominion,
and eternal victory,
evermore and evermore.

Prudentius (348–c. 413)
translated John Mason Neale (1818–1866) and
Henry Williams Baker (1821–1877)

ANTIOCH (COMFORT (Mason))   86 86 extended

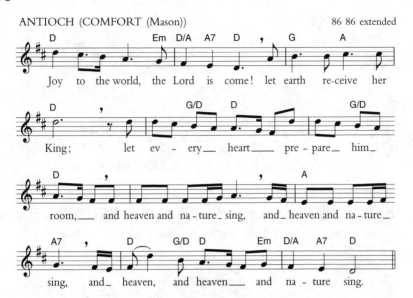

Joy to the world, the Lord is come! let earth re-ceive her King; let ev - ery heart pre - pare him room, and heaven and na - ture sing, and heaven and na - ture sing, and heaven, and heaven and na - ture sing.

1 Joy to the world, the Lord is come!
 let earth receive her King;
 let every heart prepare him room,
 and heaven and nature sing,
 and heaven and nature sing,
 and heaven, and heaven and nature sing.

2 Joy to the world, the Saviour reigns!
 let all their songs employ;
 while fields and floods, rocks, hills and plains
 repeat the sounding joy,
 repeat the sounding joy,
 repeat, repeat the sounding joy.

3 He rules the world with truth and grace,
 and makes the nations prove
 the glories of his righteousness
 and wonders of his love,
 and wonders of his love,
 and wonders, wonders of his love.

Isaac Watts (1674–1748)

Music W. Holford's *Voce di Melodia,* (c.1834)
arranged Lowell Mason (1792–1872)

CELEBRATIONS   11 14 and refrain

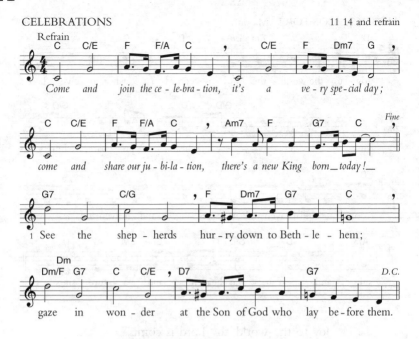

Come and join the celebration, it's a very special day; come and share our jubilation, there's a new King born today!

1 See the shepherds hurry down to Bethlehem; gaze in wonder at the Son of God who lay before them.

Come and join the celebration,
it's a very special day;
come and share our jubilation,
there's a new King born today!

1   See the shepherds
      hurry down to Bethlehem;
      gaze in wonder
      at the Son of God who lay before them.

2   'God is with us',
      round the world the message sing;
      he is with us,
      'Welcome!' all the bells on earth are pealing.

Valerie Collison (*b.* 1933)

Music Valerie Collison (*b.* 1933)

IN DULCI JUBILO   66 7778 55

1   Good Christians, all rejoice
with heart and soul and voice;
now give heed to what we say,
Jesus Christ is born today:
ox and ass before him bow,
and he is in the manger now.
Christ is born today!
Christ is born today!

2   Good Christians, all rejoice
with heart and soul and voice;
now you hear of endless bliss,
Jesus Christ was born for this:
he has opened heaven's door,
and all are blessed for evermore
Christ was born for this!
Christ was born for this!

3   Good Christians, all rejoice
with heart and soul and voice;
now you need not fear the grave,
Jesus Christ was born to save,
calls you one, and calls you all,
to gain his everlasting hall.
Christ was born to save!
Christ was born to save!

*John Mason Neale (1818–1866)

Music German, 14th century, source of harmonisation untraced

THE FIRST NOWELL   Irregular

, Refrain

1   The first Nowell the angel did say
     was to certain poor shepherds in fields as they lay:
     in fields where they lay a-keeping their sheep
     on a cold winter's night that was so deep:
         Nowell, Nowell, Nowell, Nowell,
         born is the King of Israel.

2   They lookèd up and saw a star,
     shining in the east, beyond them far;
     and to the earth it gave great light,
     and so it continued both day and night.

3   And by the light of that same star
     three wise men came from country far;
     to seek for a king was their intent,
     and to follow the star wherever it went.

4   This star drew nigh to the north-west,
     o'er Bethlehem it took its rest,
     and there it did both stop and stay
     right over the place where Jesus lay.

5   Then entered in those wise men three,
     full reverently upon their knee,
     and offered there in his presence
     their gold and myrrh and frankincense.

6   Then let us all with one accord
     sing praises to our heavenly Lord,
     that hath made heaven and earth of naught,
     and with his blood mankind hath bought.

                                   English traditional carol

Music English traditional melody
harmonised David Evans (1874–1948)

IRIS   87 87 and refrain

Come and wor - ship Christ, the new-born King; __ wor-ship Christ, the new - born King.

1   Angels from the realms of glory,
    wing your flight o'er all the earth;
    ye who sang creation's story
    now proclaim Messiah's birth:
        Come and worship
        Christ, the new-born King.
        Come and worship,
        worship Christ, the new-born King.

2   Shepherds in the fields abiding,
    watching o'er your flocks by night,
    God with us is now residing,
    yonder shines the infant Light:

3   Wise men, leave your contemplations;
    brighter visions beam afar;
    seek the great Desire of nations;
    ye have seen his natal star:

4   Though an infant now we view him,
    he will share his Father's throne,
    gather all the nations to him;
    every knee shall then bow down:

5   All creation, join in praising
    God the Father, Spirit, Son,
    evermore your voices raising
    to the eternal Three in One:

verses 1, 2, 3 & 5, James Montgomery (1771–1854)
verse 4, unascribed text in *The Christmas Box,* 1825

Music French carol melody
harmonised Martin Edward Fallas Shaw (1875–1958)

STUTTGART　　　　　　　　　　　　　　　　　　87 87

A lower setting is found at 397.

O sola magnarum urbium

1　Bethlehem, a noble city,
　has been blessed beyond compare,
　for the gracious God of heaven
　once became incarnate there.

2　Fairer than the sun at morning
　was the star that told his birth,
　to the world its God announcing,
　seen in human form on earth.

3　From the east came men of wisdom
　bringing treasures prized of old,
　tributes to a greater wisdom,
　gifts of incense, myrrh, and gold.

4　Sacred gifts of mystic meaning:
　incense shows that God has come,
　gold proclaims him king of nations,
　myrrh foretells his saving tomb.

5　Holy Jesus, in your brightness
　to the Gentile world displayed,
　with the Father and the Spirit
　endless praise to you be paid.

　　　　　　　　Prudentius (348–*c.* 413)
　　　translated *Edward Caswall (1814–1878)

Music adapted from a melody in Christian Friedrich Witt's
Psalmodia Sacra, Gotha, 1715
harmonised Compilers of *Church Hymnary,* 1898

DIX   7777 77

1   As with gladness men of old
did the guiding star behold,
as with joy they hailed its light,
leading onwards, beaming bright;
so, most gracious Lord, may we
evermore be led to thee.

2   As with joyful steps they sped,
Saviour, to thy lowly bed,
there to bend the knee before
thee, whom heaven and earth adore;
so may we with willing feet
ever seek thy mercy-seat.

3   As they offered gifts most rare
at thy homely cradle bare;
so may we with holy joy,
pure, and free from sin's alloy,
all our costliest treasures bring,
Christ, to thee, our heavenly King.

continued overleaf

Music from a chorale by Conrad Kocher (1786–1872)
arranged William Henry Monk (1823–1889)

4 Holy Jesus, every day
   keep us in the narrow way;
   and, when earthly things are past,
   bring our ransomed souls at last
   where they need no star to guide,
   where no clouds thy glory hide.

5 In the heavenly country bright,
   need they no created light;
   thou its light, its joy, its crown,
   thou its sun which goes not down;
   there for ever may we sing
   alleluias to our King.

        *William Chatterton Dix (1837–1898)

WAS LEBET, WAS SCHWEBET   11 10 11 10

An Alternative tune EPIPHANY *is found at 240.*

1   Brightest and best of the sons of the morning,
      dawn on our darkness, and lend us thine aid;
      star of the east, the horizon adorning,
      guide where our infant Redeemer is laid.

2   Cold on his cradle the dew-drops are shining;
      low lies his head with the beasts of the stall;
      angels adore him in slumber reclining,
      Maker and Monarch and Saviour of all.

3   Say, shall we yield him, in costly devotion,
      odours of Edom, and offerings divine,
      gems of the mountains and pearls of the ocean,
      myrrh from the forest or gold from the mine?

4   Vainly we offer each ample oblation,
      vainly with gifts would his favour secure;
      richer by far is the heart's adoration;
      dearer to God are the prayers of the poor.

5   Brightest and best of the sons of the morning,
      dawn on our darkness, and lend us thine aid;
      star of the east, the horizon adorning,
      guide where our infant Redeemer is laid.

Reginald Heber (1783–1826)

Music Melody from Rheinhardt MS, Üttingen, 1754
harmonised Ralph Vaughan Williams (1872–1958)

NEUMARK   98 98 88

1   Wise men, they came to look for wisdom,
     finding one wiser than they knew;
     rich men, they met with one yet richer —
     King of the kings, they knelt to you:
       Jesus, our wisdom from above,
       wealth and redemption, life and love.

2   Pilgrims they were, from unknown countries,
     searching for one who knows the world;
     lost are their names, and strange their journeys,
     famed is their zeal to find the child:
       Jesus, in you the lost are claimed,
       strangers are found, and known, and named.

3   Magi, they stooped to see your splendour;
     led by a star to light supreme;
     promised Messiah, Lord eternal,
     glory and peace are in your name.
       Joy of each day, our song by night,
       shine on our path your holy light.

4   Guests of their God, they opened treasures,
     incense and gold and solemn myrrh,
     welcoming one too young to question
     how came these gifts, and what they were.
       Gift beyond price of gold or gem,
       make among us your Bethlehem.

Christopher Martin Idle (*b.* 1938)

Music Melody by Georg Neumark (1621–1681)
harmonised John L. Bell (*b.* 1949)

PEACE CAROL

LM

1   O little Love, who comes again,
the Word made flesh to make God plain,
O Child who shines, the Jesus light,
disarm the world,
this Christmas night!

2   No heart so hard it may not move,
no hate resist your open love;
defenceless in our hands you come
to Herod's power,
to Mary's home.

3   As all the wise look for your star,
so I must follow where you are:
as you are light so must I be,
as you are peace,
be peace in me.

Shirley Erena Murray (*b.* 1931)

Music Nigel Eastgate (*b.* 1930)

329 Words and Music: © 1992, Hope Publishing Company. Administered by CopyCare Ltd,
PO Box 77, Hailsham, East Sussex, BN27 3EF, United Kingdom. <music@copycare.com> Used by permission.

AGINCOURT
Unison
LM

1   The tyrant issues his decree,
       and only those forewarned can flee;
       while children, true to prophecy,
       are culled because of jealousy.

2   Bewildered parents claw the air
       with shrieks of horror and despair,
       and all of Bethlehem laments
       the slaughter of the innocents.

3   Only a tyrant could impose
       this murder of imagined foes;
       yet still the power of love defies
       the love of power and all its lies.

4   A Saviour, saved by sacrifice
       of those who died there in his place,
       shall live to die another day,
       and, dying, show another way.

Iain D. Cunningham (*b.* 1954)

Music English melody, 15th century, adapted
arranged John Hind (1916–1984)

PUER NOBIS   76 777 Irregular

1   Unto us a boy is born!
     King of all creation,
     came he to a world forlorn,
     the Lord of every nation,
     the Lord of every nation.

2   Cradled in a stall was he
     with sleepy cows and asses;
     and the very beasts could see
     that he all folk surpasses,
     that he all folk surpasses.

3   Herod then with fear was filled:
     'A prince', he said, 'in Jewry!'
     All the little boys he killed
     at Bethl'em in his fury,
     at Bethl'em in his fury.

4   Now may Mary's son, who came
     so long ago to love us,
     lead us all with hearts aflame
     unto the joys above us,
     unto the joys above us.

5   Omega and Alpha he!
     Let the organ thunder,
     while we sing our songs with glee
     and rend the air asunder,
     and rend the air asunder.

                              Latin, 15th century
              translated Percy Dearmer (1867–1936)

Music Melody *Piae Cantiones,* 1582
harmonised George Herbert Palmer (1846–1926)

AVE MARIA KLARE

76 76 67 6

1. When Mary brought her
    treasure
   unto the holy place,
   no human eye could measure
   the joy upon her face.
   He was but six weeks old,
   her dearest joy and pleasure,
   her silver and her gold.

2. Then Simeon, on him gazing
   with wonder and with love,
   his agèd voice up-raising,
   gave thanks to God above:
   'Now welcome sweet release!
   For I, my Saviour praising,
   may die at last in peace'.

3. And she, all sorrow scorning,
   rejoiced in Jesus' fame.
   The child her arms adorning
   shone softly like a flame
   that burns the long night
    through,
   and keeps from dusk till
    morning
   its vigil clear and true.

4. As by the sun in splendour
   the flags of night are furled,
   so darkness shall surrender
   to Christ who lights the world:
   to Christ the Star of day,
   who once was small and tender,
    a candle's gentle ray.

Jan Struther (1901–1953)

Music Psalteriolum Harmonicum, 1642
arranged Compilers

LAND OF REST   CM

PARAPHRASE 38, selected verses

Nunc dimittis

1   Now, Lord! according to thy word,
      let me in peace depart;
      mine eyes have thy salvation seen,
      and gladness fills my heart.

2   That Sun I now behold, whose light
      shall heathen darkness chase,
      and rays of brightest glory pour
      around thy chosen race.

3   This great salvation, long prepared,
      and now disclosed to view,
      hath proved thy love was constant still,
      and promises were true.

Scottish Paraphrases, 1781
St Luke 2: 29-32

Music American traditional melody
collected by Annabel Morris Buchanan (1899–1983)
harmonised Charles Haizlip Webb (*b.* 1933)

Also suitable
He came down that we may have love   359

CHRIST INCARNATE – PUBLIC MINISTRY

WINCHESTER NEW (CRASSELIUS)   LM

Iordanis oras praevia

1   On Jordan's bank the Baptist's cry
announces that the Lord is nigh;
awake and hearken for he brings
glad tidings of the King of kings.

2   Then cleansed be every heart from sin;
make straight the way for God within;
prepare we in our hearts a home,
where such a mighty Guest may come.

3   For you are our salvation, Lord,
our refuge and our great reward;
without your grace we waste away,
like flowers that wither and decay.

4   Stretch out your hand, to heal our sore,
and make us rise to fall no more;
once more upon your people shine,
and fill the world with love divine.

5   All praise to you, eternal Son,
whose advent has our freedom won,
whom with the Father we adore,
and Holy Spirit, evermore.

Charles Coffin (1676–1749)
translated John Chandler (1806–1876)
and others

Music adapted from a chorale in Georg Wittwe's
Musikalisches Hand-Buch, Hamburg, 1690
arranged William Henry Havergal (1793–1870)

OAKFIELD   64 44

1 Out of the flow-ing ri - ver Je-sus a - scends

bap-tized by John wait - - ing the sign.____

1   Out of the flowing river
       Jesus ascends
       baptized by John
       waiting the sign.

2   Out of the open heavens
       God's Spirit comes
       down like a dove
       in peace and power.

3   Out speaks the voice from heaven:
       'You are my Son,
       chosen and loved,
       my own delight'.

4   Out through the life of Jesus
       God's word of love,
       calling in grace,
       comes to our lives.

5   Out in the world we live in
       we will make known
       the love revealed
       through God in Christ.

Leith Fisher (*b.* 1941)

Music Timothy Redman (1943–2005)

HIGHLAND CATHEDRAL   10 10 10 10

1   Christ is our light! the bright and morning star
      covering with radiance all from near and far.
      Christ be our light, shine on, shine on we pray
      into our hearts, into our world today.

2   Christ is our love! baptized that we may know
      the love of God among us, swooping low.
      Christ be our love, bring us to turn our face
      and see in you the light of heaven's embrace.

3   Christ is our joy! transforming wedding guest!
      Through water turned to wine the feast was blessed.
      Christ be our joy; your glory let us see,
      as your disciples did in Galilee.

                        Leith Fisher (b. 1941)

Music Uli Roever and Michael Korb
arranged Compilers

AUS DER TIEFE (HEINLEIN) 77 77

1   Forty days and forty nights
thou wast fasting in the wild;
forty days and forty nights
tempted, and yet undefiled.

2   Sunbeams scorching day by day;
chilly dewdrops nightly shed;
prowling beasts about thy way;
stones thy pillow; earth thy bed.

3   Shall not we thy sorrows share,
learn thy discipline of will,
and, like thee, by fast and prayer
wrestle with the powers of ill?

4   And if Satan, vexing sore,
flesh and spirit should assail,
thou, his vanquisher before,
wilt not suffer us to fail.

5   Watching, praying, struggling thus,
victory ours at last shall be;
angels minister to us
as they ministered to thee.

*George Smyttan (1822–1870)
and *Francis Pott (1832–1909)

Music 'M. H.' in *Nürnbergisches Gesangbuch,* 1677, altered
Martin Herbst (1654–1681)
harmonised Compilers of *Revised Church Hymnary,* 1927

EBENEZER (TON-Y-BOTEL)

87 87 D

Music Thomas John Williams (1869–1944)
adapted from an anthem

1   Jesus, tempted in the desert,
lonely, hungry, filled with dread:
'Use your power,' the tempter tells him;
'turn these barren rocks to bread!'
'Not alone by bread,' he answers,
'can the human heart be filled.
Only by the Word that calls us
is our deepest hunger stilled!'

2   Jesus, tempted at the temple,
high above its ancient wall:
'Throw yourself from lofty turret;
angels wait to break your fall!'
Jesus shuns such empty marvels,
feats that fickle crowds request:
'God, whose grace protects, preserves us,
we must never vainly test.'

3   Jesus, tempted on the mountain
by the lure of vast domain:
'Fall before me! Be my servant!
Glory, fame, you're sure to gain!'
Jesus sees the dazzling vision,
turns his eyes another way:
'God alone deserves our homage!
God alone will I obey.'

4   When we face temptation's power,
lonely, struggling, filled with dread,
Christ, who knew the tempter's hour,
come and be our living bread.
By your grace, protect, preserve us
lest we fall, your trust betray.
Yours, above all other voices,
be the Word we hear, obey.

Herman G. Stuempfle, Jr *(b. 1923)*

NETTLETON

87 87 D

1   Sing of Andrew, John's disciple,
led by faith through ways untrod,
till the Baptist cried at Jordan,
'There behold the Lamb of God.'
Stirred by hearing this new teacher,
Andrew, freed from doubt and fear,
ran to tell his brother Simon,
'God's Anointed One is here!'

2   Sing of Andrew, called by Jesus
from the shores of Galilee,
leaving boats and nets and kindred,
trusting in that 'Follow me.'
When a boy's small meal fed thousands,
when inquiring Greeks found care,
when the Spirit came in blessing —
Andrew faithfully was there.

3   Sing of Andrew, bold apostle,
sent to make the gospel known,
faithful to his Lord's example,
called to make a cross his own.
So may we who prize his memory
honour Christ in our own day,
bearing witness to our neighbours,
living what we sing and pray.

Carl P. Daw, Jr (*b.* 1944)

Music American melody in Wyeth's
Repository of Sacred Music, Part II, 1813

THE SEVEN JOYS OF MARY   DCM

1   When Jesus saw the fishermen
in boats upon the sea,
he called to them, 'Come, leave your nets
and follow, follow me'.
They followed where he healed the sick
and gave the hungry bread,
and others joined them as they went
wherever Jesus led.

2   And now his friends are everywhere;
the circle once so small
extends around the whole wide world,
for Jesus calls us all.
In this great circle we belong,
wherever we may be,
if we will answer when he calls,
'Come, follow, follow me'.

Edith Agnew *(b. 1897)*

Music English carol melody
arranged John L. Bell *(b. 1949)*

1 Blest are they, the poor in spi-rit, theirs is the king-dom of God._____ Blest are they, full of sor-row, they shall be con-soled._____

Refrain
Re-joice_____ and be glad!_____ Bless-ed are you, ho-ly are you! Re-joice_____ and be glad!_____ Yours is the king-dom of God._____

2 Blest are they, the low-ly ones, they shall in-he-rit the earth._____ Blest are they who hun-ger and thirst, they shall have their fill._____ 3 Blest are they who show mer-cy; mer-cy shall be theirs._____ Blest are they, the pure of heart; they_____ shall see God._____

341 Words and Music: © 1986, GIA Publications Inc., 7404 S. Mason Avenue, Chicago, IL 60638, USA. Used by permission.

Christ Incarnate – Public Ministry

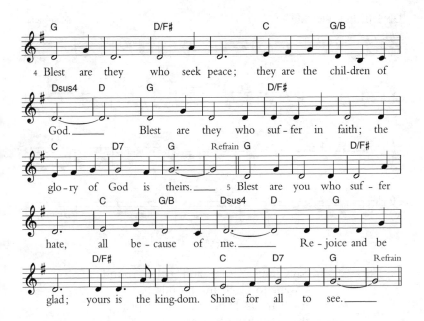

4 Blest are they who seek peace; they are the chil-dren of God._____ Blest are they who suf-fer in faith; the glo-ry of God is theirs.____ **5** Blest are you who suf-fer hate, all be-cause of me._____ Re - joice and be glad; yours is the king-dom. Shine for all to see._____

Blest are they, the poor in spirit,
theirs is the kingdom of God.
Blest are they, full of sorrow;
they shall be consoled.
  Rejoice and be glad!
  Blessèd are you,
  holy are you!
  Rejoice and be glad!
  Yours is the kingdom of God!

2 Blest are they, the lowly ones;
they shall inherit the earth.
Blest are they who hunger
      and thirst;
they shall have their fill.

3 Blest are they who show mercy;
mercy shall be theirs.
Blest are they, the pure of heart;
they shall see God.

4 Blest are they who seek peace;
they are the children of God.
Blest are they who suffer in faith;
the glory of God is theirs.

5 Blest are you who suffer hate,
all because of me.
Rejoice and be glad; yours is
      the kingdom.
Shine for all to see.

David Haas (*b.*1957)
based on *Matthew 5: 3-12*

Music Melody by David Haas (*b.*1957)
arranged David Haas (*b.*1957) and Michael Joncas (*b.*1951)

UNE JEUNE PUCELLE   86 86 88 86

1   Says Jesus, 'Come and gather round.
I want to teach my friends
some truths about the love I bring,
the love that never ends.
Look to the child, here in your midst,
who has so much and more to say
of what it means to follow me,
to come and walk my way.'

Music French carol melody, adapted
arranged Douglas Galbraith (*b.* 1940)

2   Christ speaks to us who, growing old,
get burdened down with care;
while caution reigns, we seldom see
God's presence everywhere.
He points to gifts that children bring —
the will to risk, the trust to dare,
through which, no matter where we are,
we'll find God always there.

3   When was it that we first forgot
that questions helped us grow,
or lost the openness to ask
and learn what we don't know?
Christ points to gifts that children bring,
the searching heart and lively mind
which let God's kingdom grow in those
who seek until they find.

4   Lord Jesus, we have gathered round
to hear you teach your friends
the truths about the love you bring,
the love that never ends.
We look to children in our midst,
for they have much and more to say,
and join with them to follow you,
to live and walk your way.

Leith Fisher (*b.* 1941)

LAND OF REST   CM

1   The reign of God, like farmer's field,
          bears weeds along with wheat;
          the good and bad are intertwined
          till harvest is complete.

2   Like mustard tree, the reign of God
          from tiny seed will spread,
          till birds of every feather come
          to nest, and there be fed.

3   Though hidden now, the reign of God
          may, yet unnoticed, grow;
          from deep within it rises up,
          like yeast in swelling dough.

4   The reign of God is come in Christ;
          the reign of God is near.
          Ablaze among us, kindling hearts,
          the reign of God is here!

Delores Dufner, OSB

Music American traditional melody
collected by Annabel Morris Buchanan (1899–1983)
harmonised Charles Haizlip Webb (*b.* 1933)

LACE   888 44 8

1 And Je-sus said: Don't be a-fraid — I've come to turn your fear to hope, I've come to take you through the deep, to be your friend until the end, to let your troubled heart find sleep.

1   And Jesus said: Don't be afraid -
     I've come to turn your fear to hope,
     I've come to take you through the deep,
     to be your friend
     until the end,
     to let your troubled heart find sleep.

2   And Jesus said: Don't be afraid -
     I know your emptiness and grief,
     I hear your words of unbelief,
     but if you will,
     I'll heal your soul
     and give your doubting heart relief.

3   And Jesus said: Don't be afraid —
     I am the Way, I am the Light,
     I am the Truth that holds you tight,
     and in God's home
     you have a room,
     a place of welcome and delight.

                       Shirley Erena Murray (*b.* 1931)

Music Jillian Bray

344   Words: © 1999, Hope Publishing Company. Administered by CopyCare Ltd,
PO Box 77, Hailsham, East Sussex, BN27 3EF, United Kingdom. <music@copycare.com> Used by permission.
344   Music: © composer <braydon@xtra.co.nz>

HALLE

Irregular

Refrain

Hal - le, hal - le, hal - le - - lu - - - jah!

Hal - le, hal - le, hal - le - - lu - - - jah!

Hal - le, hal - le, hal - le - - lu - - - jah! Hal - le -

- lu - jah! Hal - le - - lu - - jah!_____

Solo (sung over sotto voce refrain)

1 O God,___ to whom shall we go? You a - lone have the
2 My sheep hear my voice, says the Lord. When I call them they

words of life. Let your words be our prayer and the song we
fol - low me. I will lead them to rest by the peace - ful

sing: hal - le - lu - jah, hal - le - lu - jah._____
streams :

3 I am the light of the world, says the Lord. Walk in the light of

life. All who fol - low my words shall have life in - deed; hal - le -

- lu - jah, hal - le - lu - jah._____ 4 Now Christ is raised up from

Music Caribbean traditional
with verses by Marty Haugen (b. 1950)
arranged John L. Bell (b. 1949)

death.___ He will ne - ver die a - gain. All who fol - low his

way shall have life in him: hal-le - lu-jah, hal - le - lu - jah.___

Halle, halle, hallelujah!
Halle, halle, hallelujah!
Halle, halle, hallelujah!
Hallelujah! Hallelujah!

1   O God, to whom shall we go?
    You alone have the words of life.
    Let your words be our prayer
    and the song we sing:
    hallelujah, hallelujah!

2   My sheep hear my voice, says the Lord.
    When I call them, they follow me.
    I will lead them to rest
    by the peaceful streams:
    hallelujah, hallelujah!

3   I am the light of the world, says the Lord.
    Walk in the light of life.
    All who follow my words
    shall have life indeed:
    hallelujah, hallelujah!

4   Now Christ is raised up from death.
    He will never die again.
    All who follow his way
    shall have life in him:
    hallelujah, hallelujah!

Marty Haugen (*b.*1950)

346

CELTIC ALLELUIA   Irregular

Al - le - lu - ia, al - le - - lu - - ia! Al - le - lu - ia, al - - le - lu - ia!____ 1 The word of the Lord lasts for ev - er. What is the word that is liv-ing? It is brought to us___ through his Son___ Je - sus Christ.___

Music Fintan O'Carroll (*d.* 1977)
and Christopher Walker (*b.* 1947)

Alleluia, alleluia!
Alleluia, alleluia!

1   The word of the Lord lasts for ever.
    What is the word that is living?
    It is brought to us through his Son: Jesus Christ.

2   God brings the world to himself
    now through his Christ reconciling;
    he has trusted us with the news of redeeming love.

3   The word of the Lord is alive,
    the word of the Lord is active.
    It can judge our thoughts, bring us closer to the Father.

4   Father of all you are blessed,
    creator of earth and heaven,
    for the mysteries of the Kingdom shown to children.

5   'I call you friends,' says the Lord,
    'you who are my disciples.
    I make known to you all I've learned from my Father.'

6   'The sheep of my flock,' says the Lord,
    'hearing my voice, will listen.
    They will follow me, for I know them; they are mine.'

7   'Even if you have to die,
    close to my Word keep faithful:
    for your faithfulness I will give you the crown of life.'

8   Stay awake, pray at all times,
    praying that you may be strengthened,
    that with confidence you can meet the Son of Man.

Verses may be selected to accord with Scripture readings.

Fintan O'Carroll (*d.* 1977)
and Christopher Walker (*b.* 1947)

Unless a single grain of wheat fall on the ground and die,
it remains but a single grain, nothing more.

1　　If we have died with him, then we shall live with him;
　　if we hold firm, we shall reign with him.

2　　If any would serve me, then they must follow me;
　　wherever I am, my servants will be.

3　　Make your home in me as I make mine in you;
　　those who remain in me bear much fruit.

4　　If you remain in me and my word lives in you,
　　then you will be my disciples.

5　　Those who love me are loved by my Father;
　　we shall be with them and dwell in them.

6　　Peace I leave with you, my peace I give to you;
　　peace which the world cannot give is my gift.

Bernadette Farrell (*b.* 1957)

Music Bernadette Farrell (*b.* 1957)

JOEL   87 87 D

1   Praise the One who breaks the darkness
with a liberating light.
Praise the One who frees the prisoners
turning blindness into sight.
Praise the One who preached the Gospel,
curing every dread disease,
calming storms, and feeding thousands
with the very bread of peace.

2   Praise the One who blessed the children
with a strong yet gentle word.
Praise the One who drove out demons
with a piercing, two-edged sword.
Praise the One who brings cool water
to the desert's burning sand;
from this well comes living water,
quenching thirst in every land.

3   Praise the one true love incarnate,
Christ, who suffered in our place.
Jesus died and rose for many
that we may know God by grace.
Let us sing for joy and gladness,
seeing what our God has done.
Praise the one redeeming glory.
Praise the One who makes us one.

Rusty Edwards (*b.* 1955)

Music Sally Ann Morris (*b.* 1952)

GOOD GROUND (Dixon)   77 76 and refrain

In our lives plant seeds of hope,
in our homes plant seeds of love,
in our church plant seeds of joy.
Tell the world about God's love,
tell the world about God's love.

1   Jesus said, 'If you have faith
     small as a mustard seed,
     in my name you'll do great things,
     you'll do great things indeed.'

2   'If a seed falls to the ground,
     lies buried like the grain',
     Jesus said, 'until it dies
     it cannot grow again.'

3   Jesus told the story of
     the seed the sower sows,
     'Listen to my Father's words
     and then your faith will grow.'

4   'Some words fall among the thorns
     and some on stony ground;
     some are carried off and lost,
     but others find good ground.'

Carol Dixon (*b.* 1947)

Music Carol Dixon (*b.* 1947)
arranged I. Morrison

HEALER   11 6 11 5

1   When Jesus the healer passed through Galilee,
    Heal us, heal us today.
    the deaf came to hear and the blind came to see.
    Heal us, Lord Jesus.

2   A paralysed man was let down through a roof.
    Heal us, heal us today.
    His sins were forgiven, his walking the proof.
    Heal us, Lord Jesus.

3   The death of his daughter caused Jairus to weep.
    Heal us, heal us today.
    The Lord took her hand, and he raised her from sleep.
    Heal us, Lord Jesus.

4   When blind Bartimaeus cried out to the Lord,
    Heal us, heal us today.
    his faith made him whole and his sight was restored.
    Heal us, Lord Jesus.

5   The twelve were commissioned and sent out in twos,
    Heal us, heal us today.
    to make the sick whole and to spread the good news.
    Heal us, Lord Jesus.

6   The lepers were healed and the demons cast out.
    Heal us, heal us today.
    A bent woman straightened to laugh and to shout.
    Heal us, Lord Jesus.

7   There's still so much sickness and suffering today.
    Heal us, heal us today.
    We gather together for healing, and pray,
    Heal us, Lord Jesus.

Peter David Smith (*b.* 1938)

Music Peter David Smith (*b.* 1938)

AU CLAIR DE LA LUNE   11 11 11 11

1   Jesus' hands were kind hands, doing good to all,
     healing pain and sickness, blessing children small;
     washing tired feet, and saving those who fall;
     Jesus' hands were kind hands, doing good to all.

2   Take my hands, Lord Jesus, let them work for you,
     make them strong and gentle, kind in all I do;
     let me watch you, Jesus, till I'm gentle too,
     till my hands are kind hands, quick to work for you.

                    Margaret Beatrice Cropper (1886–1980)

Music Old French melody
arranged Compilers of *Church Hymnary,* 3rd edition, 1973

352 1

RICHMOND   CM

1   O for a thousand tongues, to sing
     my great Redeemer's praise,
     the glories of my God and King,
     the triumphs of his grace!

Music Melody by Thomas Haweis (1734–1820)
harmonised Samuel Webbe, *the younger* (c. 1770–1843)

DESERT (LYNGHAM)   CM extended

1 O for a thou – – sand tongues, to___ sing my great Re-deem-er's praise, my great___ Re-deem-er's praise, the glo-ries of___ my God___ and King, the triumphs of the triumphs of his grace, the triumphs of _ his _ grace, the tri – – umphs of his grace!

2   Jesus! the name that charms our fears,
        that bids our sorrows cease;
        'tis music in the sinner's ears,
        'tis life, and health, and peace.

3   He breaks the power of cancelled sin,
        he sets the prisoner free;
        his blood can make the foulest clean,
        his blood availed for me.

4   He speaks, and, listening to his voice,
        new life the dead receive,
        the mournful, broken hearts rejoice,
        the humble poor believe.

5   Hear him, ye deaf; his praise, ye dumb,
        your loosened tongues employ;
        ye blind, behold your Saviour come;
        and leap, ye lame, for joy!

6   My gracious Master and my God,
        assist me to proclaim,
        to spread through all the earth abroad
        the honours of thy name.

                            Charles Wesley (1707–1788)

Music Thomas Jarman (1782–1862), rhythm slightly adapted

LUX TREMENDA

87 87 87 and refrain

Unison

1 Bright the cloud and bright the glory,
brighter far than mere sun's rays,
opening up a glimpse of heaven
to disciples' awestruck gaze:
power past their comprehension,
splendour too profound for praise.
All was changed, all was changed;
they would never be the same.

2 Bright the cloud but dark the glory
wrought by human enterprise,
opening wide with awful terror
stark new worlds before our eyes:
power grasped but far from mastered,
knowledge keen but not yet wise.
All has changed, all has changed;
we shall never be the same.

3 From the cloud and from the glory
human need brought Jesus down:
down to death, then from death rising
to receive a victor's crown.
Lead us, Christ, to prize compassion
more than riches or renown.
Help us change, help us change,
may we never be the same.

Carl P. Daw, Jr (*b.* 1944)

Music Alfred Victor Fedak (*b.* 1953)

EISENACH (LEIPZIG)   LM

O amor quam ecstaticus

1   O Love, how deep, how broad, how high!
       Surpassing thought and fantasy
       that God, the Son of God, should take
       our mortal form for mortals' sake.

2   For us baptized, for us he bore
       his holy fast, and hungered sore;
       for us temptations sharp he knew;
       for us the tempter overthrew.

3   For us he prayed, for us he taught,
       for us the lost with love he sought,
       by words, and signs, and actions, he
       brought health and hope to set us free.

4   For us to wicked men betrayed,
       scourged, mocked, in crown of thorns arrayed,
       he bore the shameful cross and death;
       for us at length gave up his breath.

5   For us he rose from death again,
       for us he went on high to reign,
       for us he sent his Spirit here
       to guide, to strengthen, and to cheer.

6   To him whose boundless love has won
       salvation for us through his Son,
       to God the Father, glory be
       both now and through eternity.

Latin, 15th century
translated Benjamin Webb (1819–1885)

Music Johann Hermann Schein (1586–1630)
adapted from tune in revised *Cantional*, 1645
from harmonisations by Johann Sebastian Bach (1685–1750)

TRIUMPH   87 87 87

An alternative tune REGENT SQUARE *is found at 439.*

1   You, Lord, are both Lamb and Shepherd.
    You, Lord, are both prince and slave.
    You, peacemaker and sword-bringer
    in the way you took and gave.
    You, the everlasting instant;
    you, whom we both scorn and crave.

2   Clothed in light upon the mountain,
    stripped of might upon the cross,
    shining in eternal glory,
    harrowing hell to save the lost,
    you, the everlasting instant;
    you, who are our gift and cost.

3   You, who walk each day beside us,
    sit in power at God's side.
    You, who preach a way that's narrow,
    have a love that reaches wide.
    You, the everlasting instant;
    you, who are our pilgrim guide.

4   Worthy is our earthly Jesus!
    Worthy is our cosmic Christ!
    Worthy your defeat and vict'ry.
    Worthy still your peace and strife.
    You, the everlasting instant;
    you, who are our death and life.

Sylvia G. Dunstan (1955–1993)

Music *Henry John Gauntlett (1805–1876)

THIS IS YOUR GOD   Irregular

1   Meekness and majesty, manhood and deity,
    in perfect harmony — the man who is God:
    Lord of eternity, dwells in humanity,
    kneels in humility and washes our feet.
        Oh, what a mystery — meekness and majesty:
        bow down and worship, for this is your God,
        this is your God!

2   Father's pure radiance, perfect in innocence,
    yet learns obedience to death on a cross:
    suffering to give us life, conquering through sacrifice —
    and, as they crucify, prays, 'Father forgive'.

3   Wisdom unsearchable, God the invisible,
    love indestructible in frailty appears:
    Lord of infinity, stooping so tenderly,
    lifts our humanity to the heights of his throne.

Music Graham Kendrick (*b.* 1950)   Graham Kendrick (*b.* 1950)
arranged Christopher Norton (*b.* 1953)

SUANTRAI   LM

1   'This is my will, my new command,
that love should dwell among you all.
This is my will, that you should love
as I have shown that I love you.

2   There is no greater love than this:
to lay your life down for your friends.
You are my friends if you obey
what I've commanded you to do.

3   I call you servants now no more;
no servant knows his lord's full mind.
I call you friends, for I've told you
all I have heard my Father say.

4   You did not choose me: I chose you,
appointed you, and chose you all,
each one to go and bear much fruit,
fruit that will last beyond all time.

5   All that you ask the Father now
for my name's sake you shall receive.
This is my will, my one command,
that love should dwell in each, in all.'

James Quinn (*b.* 1919)

Music Irish traditional melody
arranged Thomas Henry Weaving (1881–1966)

NORMANDY   11 11 11 11

A unison version is found at 383.

1   The great love of God is revealed in the Son,
     who came to this earth to redeem every one.
     That love, like a stream flowing clear to the sea,
     makes clean every heart that from sin would be free.

2   It binds the whole world, every barrier it breaks,
     the hills it lays low, and the mountains it shakes.
     It's yours, it is ours, see how lavishly given —
     the pearl of great price, and the treasure of heaven!

                    Daniel Thambyrajah Niles (1908–1970)

Music Basque carol
arranged Charles Edgar Pettman (1866–1943)

HE CAME DOWN   LM

1   He came down that we may have love;
he came down that we may have love;
he came down that we may have love,
hallelujah for evermore.
CANTOR: (Why did he come?)
(repeat verse)

2   He came down that we may have peace;
he came down that we may have peace;
he came down that we may have peace,
hallelujah for evermore.

3   He came down that we may have joy;
he came down that we may have joy;
he came down that we may have joy;
hallelujah for evermore.

*This song is sung at a moderate speed and, at the end
of the first singing of each verse, the cantor calls,
'Why did he come?' to encourage the company to repeat
what they have sung.*

Traditional, from Cameroon

Music Melody from Cameroon
transcribed and arranged John L. Bell (b. 1949)

NOEL NOUVELET   11 11 10 11

An alternative harmonisation is found at 417.

1   Jesus Christ is waiting,
     waiting in the streets;
     no one is his neighbour,
     all alone he eats.
     Listen, Lord Jesus,
     I am lonely too:
     make me, friend or stranger,
     fit to wait on you.

2   Jesus Christ is raging,
     raging in the streets,
     where injustice spirals
     and real hope retreats.
     Listen, Lord Jesus,
     I am angry too:
     in the Kingdom's causes
     let me rage with you.

3   Jesus Christ is healing,
     healing in the streets,
     curing those who suffer,
     touching those he greets.
     Listen, Lord Jesus,
     I have pity too:
     let my care be active,
     healing, just like you.

continued overleaf

Music French carol
harmonised John L. Bell (*b.* 1949)

4   Jesus Christ is dancing,
     dancing in the streets,
     where each sign of hatred
     he, with love, defeats.
     Listen, Lord Jesus,
     I should triumph too:
     where good conquers evil
     let me dance with you.

5   Jesus Christ is calling,
     calling in the streets,
     'Who will join my journey?
     I will guide their feet.'
     Listen, Lord Jesus,
     let my fears be few:
     walk one step before me,
     I will follow you.

                    John L. Bell (b.1949)
               and Graham Maule (b.1958)

SOLAS AN T'SAOGHAIL   67 67 D

1 For - giveness is __ your gift, __ both cleansing and _ re - new - ing, __

to catch us when we drift, __ our base de - sires pur - su - ing; __

and hug us back to life __ and bring us to a feast __

where all will ce - le - brate __ the life __ your love re - leased. __

1   Forgiveness is your gift,
       both cleansing and renewing,
       to catch us when we drift,
       our base desires pursuing;
       and hug us back to life
       and bring us to a feast
       where all will celebrate
       the life your love released.

2   Your grace goes out to meet
       the sinful and the doubting,
       your arms and dancing feet
       speak louder than all shouting:
       O God, how great your love
       which takes us empty in,
       and, with our worth unproved,
       lets better life begin.

                 Ian Masson Fraser (*b.* 1917)

Music Skye folk melody
arranged Alasdair A. Codona

361   Words: © 1994, Stainer & Bell Ltd, PO Box 110, Victoria House, 23 Gruneisen Road, London N3 1DZ
361   Music: © Composer, via Church of Scotland Panel on Worship

HEAVEN SHALL NOT WAIT   12 11 12 11

Unison

1 Heaven shall not wait for the poor to lose their pa - tience, the scorned to smile, the des - pised to find a __ friend: Je - sus is Lord; he has cham - pioned the un - want - ed; in him in - jus - tice con - fronts its time - ly __ end.

vv. 1 - 3   *v. 4*

2 Heaven shall not ev - - er more.

Music John L. Bell (*b.* 1949)

1 Heaven shall not wait
for the poor to lose their patience,
the scorned to smile, the despised to find a friend:
Jesus is Lord;
he has championed the unwanted;
in him injustice confronts its timely end.

2 Heaven shall not wait
for the rich to share their fortunes,
the proud to fall, the élite to tend the least:
Jesus is Lord;
he has shown the master's privilege —
to kneel and wash servants' feet before they feast.

3 Heaven shall not wait
for the dawn of great ideas,
thoughts of compassion divorced from cries of pain:
Jesus is Lord;
he has married word and action;
his cross and company make his purpose plain.

4 Heaven shall not wait
for triumphant Hallelujahs,
when earth has passed and we reach another shore:
Jesus is Lord
in our present imperfection;
his power and love are for now; and then for evermore.

John L. Bell (*b.* 1949)
and Graham Maule (*b.* 1958)

Also suitable for this section

WALTON (FULDA) LM

1 We have a gospel to proclaim,
   good news for all throughout the earth;
   the gospel of a Saviour's name:
   we sing his glory, tell his worth.

2 Tell of his birth at Bethlehem
   not in a royal house or hall
   but in a stable dark and dim,
   the Word made flesh, a light for all.

3 Tell of his death at Calvary,
   hated by those he came to save,
   in lonely suff'ring on the cross;
   for all he loved his life he gave.

4 Tell of that glorious Easter morn —
   empty the tomb, for he was free.
   He broke the power of death and hell
   that we might share his victory.

5 Tell of his reign at God's right hand,
   by all creation glorified.
   He sends his Spirit on his Church
   to live for him, the Lamb who died.

6 Now we rejoice to name him King:
   Jesus is Lord of all the earth.
   This gospel-message we proclaim:
   we sing his glory, tell his worth.

Edward Joseph Burns (*b.* 1938)

Music Sacred Melodies, 1815, William Gardiner (1770–1853)

A list of hymns also suitable for this section is on the previous page.

ST THEODULPH   76 76 and refrain

A higher setting is found at 446.

Gloria, laus et honor

*All glory, laud, and honour,
to you, Redeemer, King,
to whom the lips of children
made sweet hosannas ring!*

1   You are the King of Israel,
    great David's royal Son,
    now in the Lord's name coming,
    the King and Blessèd One.

2   The company of angels
    is praising you on high,
    while we and all creation
    together make reply.

3   The people of the Hebrews
    with palms before you went;
    our praise and prayer and anthems
    before you we present.

4   To you before your Passion
    they sang their hymns of praise;
    to you, now high exalted,
    our melody we raise.

5   Their praises you accepted;
    accept the prayers we bring,
    in every good delighting,
    our great and gracious King:

St Theodulph of Orleans (*d.* 821)
translated *John Mason Neale (1818–1866)

Music Melody by Melchior Teschner (1584–1635)
later form, c. 1613, *harmonised* David Evans (1874–1948)

WINCHESTER NEW (CRASSELIUS)   LM

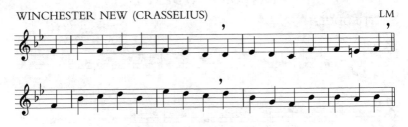

1   Ride on! ride on in majesty!
Hark! all the tribes 'Hosanna!' cry;
O Saviour meek, pursue thy road
with palms and scattered garments strowed.

2   Ride on! ride on in majesty!
In lowly pomp ride on to die;
O Christ, thy triumphs now begin
o'er captive death and conquered sin.

3   Ride on! ride on in majesty!
The wingèd squadrons of the sky
look down with sad and wondering eyes
to see the approaching sacrifice.

4   Ride on! ride on in majesty!
Thy last and fiercest strife is nigh;
the Father on his sapphire throne
awaits his own anointed Son.

5   Ride on! ride on in majesty!
In lowly pomp ride on to die;
bow thy meek head to mortal pain,
then take, O God, thy power, and reign.

Henry Hart Milman (1791–1868)

Music Adapted from a chorale in
Musikalisches Hand-Buch, Hamburg, 1690
arranged William Henry Havergal (1793–1870)

SEE SAW SACCARA DOWN   77 77 and refrain

Come and fol-low my lea - der, come and fol-low my lea - der,

Je - sus Christ is ri - ding by, come and fol-low my lea - der!

1   Come into the streets with me!
         Come to where the crowds will be,
         see a strange and gentle king
         on a donkey travelling.
         Come and follow my leader,
         come and follow my leader,
         Jesus Christ is riding by,
         come and follow my leader!

2   All the people shout his name,
         wave their branches, sing his fame,
         throw their coats upon his road,
         glad to praise the Son of God.

3   If the soldiers draw their swords,
         will we dare to sing these words,
         be his friends for just a day,
         cheer him on, then run away?

4   Jesus goes where things are rough,
         Jesus knows when life is tough,
         always comes to us, his friends,
         so his story never ends …

                   Shirley Erena Murray (*b.*1931)

Music English folk melody
arranged Charles Edward Strange (1902–1984)

ELLACOMBE   76 76 D

A higher setting is found at 413.

1   Hosanna, loud hosanna,
the little children sang;
through city street and temple
their joyful welcome rang.
They shouted out their praises
to Christ, the children's friend,
who welcomes all with blessing,
whose love will never end.

2   From Olivet they followed,
a large exultant crowd,
the victor palm branch waving,
and chanting clear and loud;
bright angels joined the chorus,
beyond the cloudless sky,
'Hosanna in the highest!
Glory to God on high!'

3   'Hosanna in the highest!'
That ancient song we sing,
for Christ is our Redeemer,
the Lord of heaven our King.
Oh, may we ever praise him
with heart and life and voice,
and in his living presence
eternally rejoice.

*Jennette Threlfall (1821–1880)

Music German melody, 18th century, as adapted in Mainz
Gesangbuch, 1833, *harmonised* St Gall *Gesangbuch,* 1863

Christ Incarnate – Passion and Death

SHOUT HOSANNA   Irregular

1   Shout, 'Hosanna, welcome to Jesus the King!
     Welcome to Jerusalem!
*   God bless him who comes in the name of the Lord.'
     Wave palm branches and be a disciple.
     He is coming to save his people.
     Shout, 'Hosanna, welcome to Jesus our King!'

2   Line the roadside, welcome the Son of our God!
     Welcome to Jerusalem!
*   Make a pathway, welcome him into your heart!
     Wave palm branches and be a disciple.
     He is coming to save his people.
     Sing his praises, welcome the Son of our God!

*   *The last four syllables of these lines in each verse are repeated.*

                                        Iain D. Cunningham (b. 1954)

Music Iain D. Cunningham (b. 1954)

1. Here comes Jesus on a donkey
   riding, oh, so slow!
   All the children run before him,
   singing as they go.
   Hosanna, hosanna, singing all along.
   Hosanna, hosanna, Jesus loves their song.

2. People lay their coats before him
   as they ride along,
   waving branches, loudly singing,
   hear their happy song.

3. In God's house their voices ringing,
   praising loud and long;
   though men try to stop their singing,
   Jesus wants their song.

The song starts slowly, the tempo increasing with each verse.

Lillian Waldecker

Music Lillian Waldecker

370 RIDE ON   LM

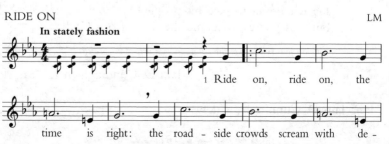

- light; palm branch – es mark the pil – grim way where

beg – gars squat and chil – dren play. 2 Ride

Fine

1 Ride on, ride on, the time is right:
the roadside crowds scream with delight;
palm branches mark the pilgrim way
where beggars squat and children play.

2 Ride on, ride on, your critics wait,
intrigue and rumour circulate;
new lies abound in word and jest,
and truth becomes a suspect guest.

3 Ride on, ride on, while well aware
that those who shout and wave and stare
are mortals who, with common breath,
can crave for life and lust for death.

4 Ride on, ride on, though blind with tears,
though dumb to speak and deaf to jeers.
Your path is clear, though few can tell
their garments pave the road to hell.

5 Ride on, ride on, the room is let,
the wine matured, the saw is whet;
and dice your death-throes shall attend,
though faith, not fate, dictates your end.

6 Ride on, ride on, God's love demands;
justice and peace lie in your hands.
Evil and angel voices rhyme:
this is the man and this the time.

John L. Bell (*b.* 1949)
and Graham Maule (*b.* 1958)

Music John L. Bell (*b.* 1949)

370 Words and Music: © WGRG, The Iona Community

RESTING   84 84 84 84

1   Lay down your head, Lord Jesus Christ,
    fast falls the night.
    Close follow those who crave your end,
    blinded by sight.
    God give you rest, strength for your task,
    light for our way.
    Lay down your head and, by your side,
    we'll sleep and stay.

2   All that you've done and all you've said,
    suffered, and shared,
    proves you're the one for whom the world
    waits unprepared.
    Had you conformed, had you condoned,
    had you complied,
    none would be heard pricing your head,
    nursing their pride.

3   What lies ahead we fear to guess,
    you fail to fear;
    hopes seem to fade, heaven seems far,
    hell seems so near.
    Here, with our faith stretched to the full,
    put to the test,
    you calmly talk, then kneel to pray,
    then take your rest.

Music John L. Bell (*b.* 1949)

4   Lay down your head, Lord Jesus Christ,
     fast falls the night.
     Close follow those who crave your end,
     blinded by sight.
     God give you rest, strength for your task,
     light for our way.
     Lay down your head and, by your side,
     we'll sleep and stay.

John L. Bell (*b.* 1949)
and Graham Maule (*b.* 1958)

72

HERZLIEBSTER JESU   11 11 11 5

1   Lord Jesus, as the shadows long are stealing
     across your path, we turn and see you kneeling
     with towel in hand, the servant way revealing,
     all for our healing.

2   Strange majesty we find at work before us
     as we, unnerved, take up the ready chorus,
     'Keep back, great Lord, we rather would revere you
     than be so near you.'

3   Yet still you come, on God's low road persisting,
     from force and power so quietly desisting,
     your every act upon love's way insisting.
     Quell our resisting!

Leith Fisher (*b.* 1941)

Music Johann Crüger *Neues vollkömliches Gesangbuch,* Berlin, 1640
harmonised Johann Sebastian Bach (1685–1750)

HEILIGER GEIST 777

1   All is ready for the Feast!
      Every Jew is wondering how
      God will liberate them now.

2   Pilate, fearful of revolt
      he, at all costs, must avert,
      puts the legion on alert.

3   Listen! Galilean crowds
      hail the Man from Nazareth,
      Jesus, riding to his death.

4   What authority he wields!
      With a whip of cords he clears
      temple courts of profiteers!

5   Watched by priests and pharisees,
      all he says and all he does
      fans the hatred of his foes.

6   Now he gathers those he loves
      in a room where bread and wine
      turn to sacrament and sign.

7   In that dark betrayal night,
      moved by hope, or fear, or greed,
      Judas sets about his deed.

8   Jesus in the olive grove,
      waiting for a traitor's kiss,
      rises free from bitterness.

Music Vollständige Psalmen, Bremen, 1639
adapted Johann Crüger *Neues vollkömliches Gesangbuch,*
Berlin, 1640, first half of melody
harmonised John Whitridge Wilson (1905–1992)

9   As he wakes his comrades up
    torches flicker in the glen,
    shadows turn to marching men.

10 In that dawn of blows and lies
    Church and State conspire to kill,
    hang three rebels on a hill.

11 Innocent and guilty drown
    in a flood of blood and sweat,
    how much darker can it get?

12 How much darker must it be
    for a God to see and care
    that men perish in despair?

13 It is God himself who dies!
    God in man shall set us free,
    God as Man — and only he.

14 Let him claim us as his own.
    We will serve as best we can
    such a God and such a Man!

*Additional verse, for conclusion when a
limited number of verses is sung.*

15 What does our salvation cost?
    Jesus, we shall never know
    all you gave and all we owe.

*The text may be interspersed with verses of
scripture and / or meditations.*

Frederick Pratt Green (1903–2000)

373   Words: © 1969, 1979, Stainer & Bell Ltd, PO Box 110, Victoria House, 23 Gruneisen Road, London N3 1DZ

THE SERVANT KING   Irregular

1. From heaven you came, helpless babe,
   entered our world, your glory veiled;
   not to be served but to serve,
   and give your life that we might live.
   This is our God, the Servant King,
   he calls us now to follow him,
   to bring our lives as a daily offering
   of worship to the Servant King.

2. There in the garden of tears,
   my heavy load he chose to bear;
   his heart with sorrow was torn,
   'Yet not my will but yours,' he said.

3. Come see his hands and his feet,
   the scars that speak of sacrifice,
   hands that flung stars into space
   to cruel nails surrendered.

Music Graham Kendrick (*b.* 1950)

374   Words and Music: © 1983, Thankyou Music. Administered (UK and Europe) by kingswaysongs.com <tym@kingsway.co.uk>.
Remaining territories administered by worshiptogether.com songs. Used by permission.

4   So let us learn how to serve,
and in our lives enthrone him;
each other's needs to prefer,
for it is Christ we're serving.

Graham Kendrick (b. 1950)

375

INTERCESSOR   11 10 11 10

1   This is the night, dear friends, the night for weeping,
when powers of darkness overcome the day,
the night the faithful mourn the weight of evil
whereby our sins the Son of Man betray.

2   This night the traitor, wolf within the sheepfold,
betrays himself into his victim's will;
the Lamb of God for sacrifice preparing,
sin brings about the cure for sin's own ill.

3   This night Christ institutes his holy supper,
blest food and drink for heart and soul and mind;
this night injustice joins its hand to treason's,
and buys the ransom-price of humankind.

4   This night the Lord by slaves shall be arrested,
he who destroys our slavery to sin;
accused of crime, to criminals be given,
that judgement on the righteous Judge begin.

5   O make us sharers, Saviour, of your Passion,
that we may share your glory that shall be;
let us pass through these three dark nights of sorrow
to Easter's laughter and its liberty.

Latin text by Peter Abélard (1079–1142)
translated Richard Lyman Sturch (b. 1936)

Music Charles Hubert Hastings Parry (1848–1918)

375 Words: © 1990, Stainer & Bell Ltd, PO Box 110, Victoria House, 23 Gruneisen Road, London N3 1DZ

ROCKINGHAM (COMMUNION)   LM

PARAPHRASE 35

1   'Twas on that night when doomed to know
     the eager rage of every foe,
     that night in which he was betrayed,
     the Saviour of the world took bread;

2   And, after thanks and glory given
     to him that rules in earth and heaven,
     that symbol of his flesh he broke,
     and thus to all his followers spoke:

3   'My broken body thus I give
     for you, for all; take, eat, and live:
     and oft the sacred rite renew
     that brings my wondrous love to view.'

4   Then in his hands the cup he raised,
     and God anew he thanked and praised,
     while kindness in his bosom glowed,
     and from his lips salvation flowed.

5   'My blood I thus pour forth,' he cries,
     'to cleanse the soul in sin that lies;
     in this the covenant is sealed,
     and heaven's eternal grace revealed.

6   'With love to all this cup is fraught,
     let each partake the sacred draught;
     through latest ages let it pour
     in memory of my dying hour.'

Scottish Paraphrases, 1781
Matthew 26: 26-29

Music Melody *Tunbridge* from *A Second Supplement to Psalmody in
Miniature,* c. 1780, *arranged* Edward Miller (1731–1807)
harmonised David Evans (1874–1948)

PETRA (REDHEAD 76)   77 77 77

1   Go to dark Gethsemane,
    you that feel the tempter's power;
    your Redeemer's conflict see,
    watch with him one bitter hour.
    From his grief turn not away;
    learn of Jesus Christ to pray.

2   Follow to the judgement hall;
    see him beaten, bound, arraigned;
    patiently he bears it all,
    all our pain his soul sustained.
    Shun not suffering, shame, or loss;
    learn from Christ to bear the cross.

3   Climb to Calvary's mournful site:
    there the Lord of glory reigns;
    there, through weakness, wins the fight,
    over sin our victory gains.
    'It is finished!' hear him cry;
    there, in Christ, we dare to die.

                    James Montgomery (1771–1854)
                revised Andrew Donaldson (*b.* 1951)

Music Richard Redhead (1820–1901)

GERONTIUS   CM

378 2

CHORUS ANGELORUM (SOMERVELL)   CM

Music Tune 1 John Bacchus Dykes (1823–1876)
Music Tune 2 Arthur Seymour Somervell (1863–1937)

1   Praise to the Holiest in the height,
    and in the depth be praise, —
    in all his words most wonderful,
    most sure in all his ways.

2   O loving wisdom of our God!
    when all was sin and shame,
    a second Adam to the fight
    and to the rescue came.

3   O wisest love! that flesh and blood,
    which did in Adam fail,
    should strive afresh against the foe,
    should strive and should prevail.

4   O generous love! that he who smote
    in Man, for man, the foe,
    the double agony in Man
    for man should undergo;

5   And in the garden secretly,
    and on the Cross on high,
    should teach his brethren, and inspire
    to suffer and to die.

6   Praise to the Holiest in the height,
    and in the depth be praise, —
    in all his words most wonderful,
    most sure in all his ways.

John Henry Newman (1801–1890)

TRISAGION AND REPROACHES   Irregular

Trisagion and The Reproaches

CHOIR OR CANTOR:
Holy God, holy and mighty, holy and immortal,
have mercy upon us.

CONGREGATION:
Holy God, holy and mighty, holy and immortal,
have mercy upon us.

CHOIR OR CANTOR:
O my people, what ' have I done to thee? or wherein
have I wea'ried thee?   Answer me.
I brought thee forth out of the land of Egypt,
and led thee to a land ex'ceeding good: and thou hast
prepared a cross ' for thy Saviour.

Music Anthony Gregory Murray (1905–1992)

CONGREGATION:
Holy God, holy and mighty, holy and immortal,
have mercy upon us.

CHOIR OR CANTOR:
Before thee I o'pened the sea:
and with a spear thou hast o'pened my side.
I went before thee in a pil'lar of cloud:
and thou hast brought me to the judgment ' hall of Pi late.

CONGREGATION:
Holy God, holy and mighty, holy and immortal,
have mercy upon us.

CHOIR OR CANTOR:
I fed thee with manna ' in the de sert:
and thou hast beaten me with ' blows and stripes.
I made thee to drink the water of salvation ' from the rock:
and thou hast made me to drink ' gall and vi ne gar.

CONGREGATION:
Holy God, holy and mighty, holy and immortal,
have mercy upon us.

CHOIR OR CANTOR:
I gave thee a ' royal scep tre:
and thou hast given my head a ' crown of thorns.
I lifted thee up ' with great power:
and thou hast hung me upon the gibbet ' of the cross.

CONGREGATION:
Holy God, holy and mighty, holy and immortal,
have mercy upon us.

Trisagion (Early Church)
The Reproaches (Gallican Church)

HORSLEY   CM

1   There is a green hill far away,
outside a city wall,
where the dear Lord was crucified,
who died to save us all.

2   We may not know, we cannot tell
what pains he had to bear;
but we believe it was for us
he hung and suffered there.

3   He died that we might be forgiven,
he died to make us good,
that we might go at last to heaven,
saved by his precious blood.

4   There was no other good enough
to pay the price of sin;
he only could unlock the gate
of heaven, and let us in.

5   Oh, dearly, dearly has he loved,
and we must love him too,
and trust in his redeeming blood,
and try his works to do.

*Cecil Frances Alexander (1818–1895)

Music William Horsley (1774–1858)

HERZLIEBSTER JESU   11 11 11 5

Herzliebster Jesu

1   Ah, holy Jesus, how hast thou offended,
that man to judge thee hath in hate pretended?
By foes derided, by thine own rejected,
O most afflicted.

2   Who was the guilty? Who brought this upon thee?
Alas, my treason, Jesus, hath undone thee.
'Twas I, Lord Jesus, I it was denied thee:
I crucified thee.

3   Lo, the good Shepherd for the sheep is offered;
the slave hath sinnèd, and the Son hath suffered;
for man's atonement, while he nothing heedeth,
God intercedeth.

4   For me, kind Jesus, was thy incarnation,
thy mortal sorrow, and thy life's oblation;
thy death of anguish and thy bitter passion,
for my salvation.

5   Therefore, kind Jesus, since I cannot pay thee,
I do adore thee, and will ever pray thee,
think on thy mercy and thy love unswerving,
not my deserving.

Johann Heermann (1585–1647)
based on Latin meditation, 11th century
paraphrased Robert Bridges (1844–1930)

Music Johann Crüger *Neues vollkömliches Gesangbuch,* Berlin, 1640
harmonised Johann Sebastian Bach (1685–1750)

PASSION CHORALE

76 76 D

An alternative harmonisation is found at 391.

Music Traditional secular melody in Hans Leo Hassler's
Lustgarten neuer teutscher Gesäng, 1601
harmonised Johann Sebastian Bach (1685–1750)

O Haupt voll Blut und Wunden

1   O Sacred Head! sore wounded,
with grief and shame bowed down!
O Kingly Head, surrounded
with thorns, thine only crown!
How pale art thou with anguish,
with sore abuse and scorn!
How does that face now languish,
which once was bright as morn!

2   O Lord of life and glory,
what bliss till now was thine!
I read the wondrous story;
I joy to call thee mine.
Thy grief and bitter Passion
were all for sinners' gain;
mine, mine was the transgression,
but thine the deadly pain.

3   What language shall I borrow
to praise thee, heavenly Friend,
for this, thy dying sorrow,
thy pity without end?
O make me thine for ever,
and, should I fainting be,
Lord, let me never, never
outlive my love to thee.

4   Be near me, Lord, when dying;
O show thy cross to me;
and, my last need supplying,
come, Lord, and set me free;
these eyes, new faith receiving,
from thee shall never move;
for they who die believing
die safely through thy love.

Paul Gerhardt (1607–1676)
translated *James Waddell Alexander (1804–1859)

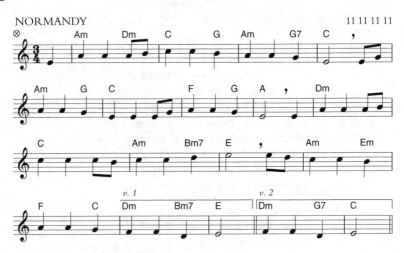

NORMANDY   11 11 11 11

A harmony version is found at 358.

1   While Mary was watching, they hung Jesus high.
     His feet hung beyond her; his hands reached the sky.
     His blood and his sweat soaked and matted his hair.
     She wished she could touch him, and show him her care.

2   She wished he could hear her: not even her shout
     would carry; the hubbub was shutting her out.
     His friends kept safe distance, away from the scorn;
     but she stood there rueing the day he was born.

3   She thought of the angel, before he began.
     She thought of the song of the faithful old man.
     She thought of the day she delighted to find
     her boy in the temple, with God in his mind.

4   She gazed at the Son, whom the Father had sent;
     and looking, and thinking, she saw what he meant.
     Lord Jesus, our Saviour, with Mary we bow
     to honour the death which gives life to us now.

                         Alison M. Robertson *(b.1940)*

Music Basque carol
arranged Charles Edgar Pettman (1866–1943)
harmonised Guthrie Foote (1897–1972)

APANÁS   LM
Gently

1   The Love that clothes itself in light
     stands naked now, despised, betrayed,
     receiving blows to face and head
     from hands that Love itself has made.

2   The Love that lifts the stars and sun
     collapses, spent, beneath the cross;
     the Love that fills the universe,
     goes on to death and total loss.

3   Love, helpless, comes to Calvary,
     rejected, scorned, and crucified;
     Love hangs in shame, and dies alone,
     but Love, abased, is glorified.

4   Extinguished with the sun at noon,
     Love's light transcends all history;
     Love wrapped in linen, Love entombed,
     still wraps all heaven in mystery.

5   Though Love is lost, Love finds us here;
     though Love is absent, Love remains;
     where Love is finished, Love begins;
     where Love is dead, Love lives and reigns!

Alan Gaunt (*b.* 1935)

Music Jim Strathdee (*b.* 1941)
slightly altered

384 Words: © 1991, Stainer & Bell Ltd, PO Box 110, Victoria House, 23 Gruneisen Road, London N3 1DZ
384 Music: © 1983 Desert Flower Music, Carmichael, CA 95609, USA.

SHRUB END   76 76

1   Here hangs a man discarded,
    a scarecrow hoisted high,
    a nonsense pointing nowhere
    to all who hurry by.

2   Can such a clown of sorrows
    still bring a useful word
    when faith and love seem phantoms
    and every hope absurd?

3   Yet here is help and comfort
    for lives by comfort bound,
    when drums of dazzling progress
    give strangely hollow sound:

4   Life, emptied of all meaning,
    drained out in bleak distress,
    can share in broken silence
    our deepest emptiness;

5   And love that freely entered
    the pit of life's despair,
    can name our hidden darkness
    and suffer with us there.

6   Christ, in our darkness risen,
    help all who long for light
    to hold the hand of promise,
    till faith receives its sight.

Brian Wren (b. 1936)

Music Peter Warwick Cutts (b. 1937)

PULLING BRACKEN

Lifted high on your cross,
drawing all folk,
drawing all folk;
lifted high on your cross,
drawing all folk to you.

1   Down you come to live among us
    part of your creation,
    knowing poverty and sorrow,
    sharing each temptation.

2   On the gallows there they nail you
    God despised, rejected;
    deep within your earth they hide you
    till you're resurrected.

3   Light and love pour down upon us,
    healing, recreating;
    you relive your life within us,
    all life consecrating.

Ian Cowie (1923–2005)
from John 12: 24

Music Scottish folk melody
arranged John L. Bell (*b.* 1949)

STABAT MATER   887 D

Stabat mater dolorosa

1   At the cross, her vigil keeping,
      stood the mournful mother weeping,
      where he hung, the dying Lord;
      for her soul, of joy bereavèd,
      bowed with sorrow, deeply grievèd,
      felt the sharp and piercing sword.

2   Who, on Christ's dear mother gazing,
      pierced with anguish so amazing,
      born of woman, would not weep?
      Who, on Christ's dear mother thinking,
      such a cup of sorrow drinking,
      would not share her sorrows deep?

3   For his people's sins chastisèd,
      she beheld her Son despisèd,
      scourged, and crowned with thorns entwined;
      saw him then from judgment taken,
      and in death by all forsaken,
      till his spirit he resigned.

4   Jesus, may her deep devotion
      stir in me the same emotion,
      fount of love, Redeemer kind,
      that my heart, fresh ardour gaining,
      and a purer love attaining,
      may with thee acceptance find.

13th century
translated Edward Caswall (1814–1878), and others

Music Mainzisch Gesangbuch, 1661, *adapted* Samuel Webbe, *the elder*
(1740–1816), in *An Essay on the Church Plain Chant,* 1782

SHIMPI   77 77

1   'Why has God forsaken me?'
     cried out Jesus from the cross,
     as he shared the loneliness
     of our deepest grief and loss.

2   Jesus, as his life expired,
     placed himself within God's care:
     at our dying, Lord, may we
     trust the love which conquers fear.

3   Myst'ry shrouds our life and death
     but we need not be afraid,
     for the mystery's heart is love,
     God's great love which Christ displayed.

                    William L. (Bill) Wallace (*b.* 1933)

Music Taihei Sato (*b.* 1936)

389

HOLY LAMB (MWANA MWERERE)

8 12 and refrain

Be-hold the ho-ly Lamb of God!

All: Be-hold the man who

Ho-ly Lamb of God,

bears for us a hea-vy load.

raised high on the cross to bear for us the pain and loss.

Music Tumbuka (Malawian) melody
arranged John L. Bell (b. 1949)

1   CANTOR: Behold the holy Lamb of God!
       ALL: Behold the man who bears for us a heavy load.
       CANTOR: *Holy Lamb of God,*
       ALL: *raised high on the cross*
                  to bear for us the pain and loss.

2   CANTOR: In humble silence forth goes he,
       ALL: in grief and pain, to bear our sins upon the tree.

3   CANTOR: And there, outside the city wall,
       ALL: high on the cross they nail the one who saves
                  us all.

4   CANTOR: O, listen to his anguished cry,
       ALL: 'My God, my God, why have you left me here
                  to die?'

5   CANTOR: But, dying on that awful tree,
       ALL: he pardons all our sinfulness and sets us free.

Tumbuka (Malawian) hymn
Charles G. Chinula (1885–1970)
translated Helen M. Taylor (1902–1993)
adapted Tom Colvin (1925–2000)

SONG 13   7777

1   Open are the gifts of God,
     gifts of love to mind and sense;
     hidden is love's agony,
     love's endeavour, love's expense.

2   Love that gives, gives evermore,
     gives with zeal, with eager hands,
     spares not, keeps not, all outpours,
     ventures all, its all expands.

3   Drained is love in making full,
     bound in setting others free,
     poor in making many rich,
     weak in giving power to be.

4   Therefore he who shows us God
     helpless hangs upon the tree;
     and the nails and crown of thorns
     tell of what God's love must be.

5   Here is God: no monarch he,
     throned in easy state to reign;
     here is God, whose arms of love,
     aching, spent, the world sustain.

            William Hubert Vanstone (1923–1999)

Music Melody and bass by Orlando Gibbons (1583–1625)
harmonised Compilers of *Church Hymnary,* 3rd edition, 1973
based on *Revised Church Hymnary,* 1927

PASSION CHORALE   76 76 D

An alternative harmonisation is found at 382.

1   This is your coronation —
      thorns pressed upon your head;
      no bright angelic heralds,
      but angry crowds instead;
      beneath your throne of timber,
      and struggling with the load,
      you go in cruel procession
      on sorrow's royal road;

2   Eternal judge on trial,
      God's law, by law denied;
      love's justice is rejected
      and truth is falsified.
      We who have charged, condemned you
      are sentenced by your love;
      your blood pronounces pardon
      as you are stretched above.

3   High Priest, you are anointed
      with blood upon your face,
      and in this hour appointed
      the offering for our race.
      For weakness interceding;
      for sin, you are the price;
      for us your prayer unceasing,
      O living sacrifice.

                         Sylvia G. Dunstan (1955–1993)

Music Traditional secular melody in Hans Leo Hassler's
Lustgarten neuer teutscher Gesäng, 1601
harmonised Johann Sebastian Bach (1685–1750)

ROCKINGHAM (COMMUNION) LM

1 When I survey the wondrous cross
   on which the Prince of Glory died,
   my richest gain I count but loss,
   and pour contempt on all my pride.

2 Forbid it, Lord, that I should boast,
   save in the death of Christ, my God;
   all the vain things that charm me most,
   I sacrifice them to his blood.

3 See! from his head, his hands, his feet,
   sorrow and love flow mingled down;
   did e'er such love and sorrow meet,
   or thorns compose so rich a crown?

4 Were the whole realm of nature mine,
   that were an offering far too small;
   love so amazing, so divine,
   demands my soul, my life, my all.

                              Isaac Watts (1674–1748)

Music Melody *Tunbridge* from *A Second Supplement to Psalmody in Miniature,* c. 1780, *arranged* Edward Miller (1731–1807) *harmonised* David Evans (1874–1948)

EVENTIDE   10 10 10 10

Menschen gehen zu Gott in ihrer Not

1   We turn to God when we are sorely pressed;
     we pray for help, and ask for peace and bread;
     we seek release from illness, guilt, and death:
     all people do, in faith or unbelief.

2   We turn to God when he is sorely pressed,
     and find him poor, scorned, without roof and bread,
     bowed under weight of weakness, sin, and death:
     faith stands by God in his dark hour of grief.

3   God turns to us when we are sorely pressed,
     and feeds our souls and bodies with his bread;
     for one and all Christ gives himself in death:
     through his forgiveness sin will find relief.

                    Dietrich Bonhoeffer (1906–1945)
          Letters and Papers in Prison, 1953, SCM Press
                              translated Compilers

Music William Henry Monk (1823–1889)

394

Music John Pantry (*b.*1946)

1 He came to earth, not to be served
   but gave his life to be a ransom for many.
   The Son of God, the Son of Man —
   he shared our pain and bore our sins in his body.
   King of kings and Lord of lords,
   I lift my voice in praise: such amazing love!
   But I do believe this King has died for me.

2 And so I stand, a broken soul,
   to see the pain that I have brought to Jesus;
   a yielding heart will be consoled,
   and be made new, the joy of all believers.

3 And from now on, through all my days,
   I vow to live each moment here for Jesus;
   not looking back, but giving praise
   for all my Lord has done for this believer.

John Pantry (*b.* 1946)

WONDROUS LOVE

12 9 12 12 9

1 What wondrous love is this, O my soul, O my soul;
   what wondrous love is this, O my soul;
   what wondrous love is this that caused the Lord of bliss
   to bear the dreadful curse for my soul, for my soul,
   to bear the dreadful curse for my soul?

2 When I was sinking down, sinking down, sinking down,
   when I was sinking down, sinking down;
   when I was sinking down beneath God's righteous frown,
   Christ laid aside his crown for my soul, for my soul,
   Christ laid aside his crown for my soul.

3 To God and to the Lamb I will sing, I will sing;
   to God and to the Lamb I will sing;
   to God and to the Lamb, who is the great I AM,
   while millions join the theme, I will sing, I will sing,
   while millions join the theme, I will sing.

4 And when from death I'm free, I'll sing on, I'll sing on;
   and when from death I'm free, I'll sing on;
   and when from death I'm free I'll sing and joyful be,
   and through eternity I'll sing on, I'll sing on;
   and through eternity I'll sing on.

Appalachian Hymn, 1867

Music Melody by William Walker (1809–1875)
arranger unknown

SURREY (CAREY'S)   88 88 88

1   And can it be, that I should gain
        an interest in the Saviour's blood?
        Died he for me, who caused his pain —
        for me, who him to death pursued?
        Amazing love! how can it be
        that thou, my God, shouldst die for me?

2   'Tis mystery all: the Immortal dies!
        Who can explore his strange design?
        In vain the first born seraph tries
        to sound the depths of love divine.
        'Tis mercy all! Let earth adore,
        let angel minds inquire no more.

3   He left his Father's throne above, —
        so free, so infinite his grace —
        emptied himself of all but love,
        and bled for Adam's helpless race:
        'tis mercy all, immense and free;
        for, O my God, it found out me!

4   Long my imprisoned spirit lay
        fast bound in sin and nature's night;
        thine eye diffused a quickening ray;
        I woke, the dungeon flamed with light;
        my chains fell off, my heart was free,
        I rose, went forth, and followed thee.

5   No condemnation now I dread;
        Jesus, and all in him, is mine!
        Alive in him, my living Head,
        and clothed in righteousness divine,
        bold I approach the eternal throne,
        and claim the crown, through Christ, my own.

                       Charles Wesley (1707–1788)

Music Melody by Henry Carey (1687–1743)
harmonised David Evans (1874–1948)

SAGINA   88 88 88 extended

Repeat words of lines 5 and 6

A - maz - ing love! how can it be that thou, my God, shouldst die for me?

Music Thomas Campbell *The Bouquet,* 1825
harmonised in *Primitive Methodist Hymnal,* 1889

1   And can it be, that I should gain
an interest in the Saviour's blood?
Died he for me, who caused his pain —
for me, who him to death pursued?
* Amazing love! how can it be
that thou, my God, shouldst die for me?

2   'Tis mystery all: the Immortal dies!
Who can explore his strange design?
In vain the first born seraph tries
to sound the depths of love divine.
'Tis mercy all! Let earth adore,
let angel minds inquire no more.

3   He left his Father's throne above, —
so free, so infinite his grace —
emptied himself of all but love,
and bled for Adam's helpless race:
'tis mercy all, immense and free;
for, O my God, it found out me!

4   Long my imprisoned spirit lay
fast bound in sin and nature's night;
thine eye diffused a quickening ray;
I woke, the dungeon flamed with light;
my chains fell off, my heart was free,
I rose, went forth, and followed thee.

5   No condemnation now I dread;
Jesus, and all in him, is mine!
Alive in him, my living Head,
and clothed in righteousness divine,
bold I approach the eternal throne,
and claim the crown, through Christ, my own.

* *When the tune* SAGINA *is being used,*
lines 5 and 6 of each verse are repeated.

Charles Wesley (1707–1788)

STUTTGART   87 87

A higher setting is found at 325.

1   In the cross of Christ I glory,
    towering o'er the wrecks of time;
    all the light of sacred story
    gathers round its head sublime.

2   When the woes of life o'ertake me,
    hopes deceive and fears annoy,
    never shall the cross forsake me;
    lo! it glows with peace and joy.

3   When the sun of bliss is beaming
    light and love upon my way,
    from the cross the radiance streaming
    adds more lustre to the day.

4   Bane and blessing, pain and pleasure,
    by the cross are sanctified;
    peace is there that knows no measure,
    joys that through all time abide.

5   In the cross of Christ I glory,
    towering o'er the wrecks of time;
    all the light of sacred story
    gathers round its head sublime.

                              John Bowring (1792–1872)

Music adapted from a melody in Christian Friedrich Witt's
Psalmodia Sacra, Gotha, 1715
harmonised Compilers of *Church Hymnary,* 1898

398

PANGE LINGUA   87 87 87
Unison

                                              A - - men.

Pange, lingua, gloriosi proelium certaminis

1 Sing, my tongue, how glorious battle
glorious victory became;
and above the cross, his trophy,
tell the triumph and the fame:
tell how he, the earth's Redeemer,
by his death for all o'ercame.

2 When the thirty years were ended,
humbly lived for all to see,
willingly he met his passion,
born to set his people free:
on the cross the Lamb is lifted,
there the sacrifice to be.

3 His the nails, the spear, the spitting,
reed and vinegar and gall;
from his patient body piercèd
blood and water streaming fall:
earth and sea and stars and mankind
by that stream are cleansèd all.

4 Faithful cross, above all other,
one and only noble tree,
none in foliage, none in blossom,
none in fruit your match can be:
focus of the world's redemption,
your dear burden makes us free.

5 Praise and honour to the Father,
praise and honour to the Son,
praise and honour to the Spirit,
ever Three and ever One,
One in might, and One in glory,
while eternal ages run.

Venantius Honorius Clementianus
Fortunatus (*c.* 535–609)
translated *William Mair (1830–1920),
*Arthur Wellesley Wotherspoon (1853–1936)
and *John Mason Neale (1818–1866)

Music Plainsong, Mode iii (Sarum form)
harmonised Compilers of *Church Hymnary,* 3rd edition, 1973

LOVE UNKNOWN   66 12 88

1. My song is love unknown,
my Saviour's love to me,
love to the loveless shown, that they might lovely be.
Oh, who am I, that for my sake
my Lord should take frail flesh and die?

2. He came from his blest throne,
salvation to bestow:
but people scorned, and none the longed-for Christ
would know.
But O my Friend, my Friend indeed,
who at my need his life did spend!

3. Sometimes they strew his way,
and his sweet praises sing;
resounding all the day hosannas to their King.
Then 'Crucify!' is all their breath,
and for his death they thirst and cry.

4. Why, what hath my Lord done?
What makes this rage and spite?
He made the lame to run, he gave the blind their sight.
Sweet injuries! yet they at these
themselves displease, and 'gainst him rise.

5. They rise, and needs will have
my dear Lord done away;
a murderer they save, the Prince of Life they slay.
Yet cheerful he to suffering goes,
that he his foes from thence might free.

6. In life, no house, no home
my Lord on earth might have;
in death, no friendly tomb but what a stranger gave.
What may I say? Heaven was his home:
but mine the tomb wherein he lay.

Music John Nicholson Ireland (1879–1962)

7 Here might I stay and sing:
   no story so divine;
   never was love, dear King, never was grief like thine!
   This is my Friend, in whose sweet praise
   I all my days could gladly spend.

*Samuel Crossman (c. 1624–1683)

00

FAITH   10 10 10 6

1   When we are tempted to deny your Son,
     because we fear the anger of the world,
     and we are few who bear the insults hurled:
     your will, O God, be done.

2   When we are tempted to betray your Son,
     because he leads us in a harder way,
     and makes demands we do not want to pay:
     your will, O God, be done.

3   When we forget the cross that held your Son,
     and would avoid the burden of this life,
     the cry for justice, and an end to strife:
     your will, O God, be done.

4   When doubt obscures the victory of your Son,
     and faith is weak and all resolve has fled,
     help us to know him risen from the dead:
     your will, O God, be done.

David W. Romig (b. 1965)

Music J. Harold Moyer (b. 1927)

THOMAS

87 87 7

1   Tree of Life and awesome mystery,
        in your death we are reborn;
        though you die in all of history,
    * still you rise with every morn.

2   Seed that dies to rise in glory,
        may we see ourselves in you;
        if we learn to live your story
        we may die to rise anew.

3   We remember truth once spoken,
        love passed on through act and word;
        every person lost and broken
        wears the body of our Lord.

4   Gentle Jesus, mighty Spirit,
        come inflame our hearts anew;
        we may all your joy inherit
        if we bear the cross with you.

5   Christ, you lead and we shall follow,
        stumbling though our steps may be;
        one with you in joy and sorrow,
        we the river, you the sea.

    * *The last line of each verse is repeated.*

Marty Haugen (b. 1950)

Music Marty Haugen (b. 1950)
harmonised Compilers

401 Words and Music: © 1986, GIA Publications Inc., 7404 S. Mason Avenue, Chicago, IL 60638, USA. Used by permission.

BRESLAU   LM

1   'Take up your cross,' the Saviour said,
       'if you would my disciple be;
       take up your cross, with willing heart,
       and humbly follow after me.'

2   Take up your cross; let not its weight
       fill your weak soul with vain alarm:
       his strength shall bear your spirit up,
       and brace your heart, and nerve your arm.

3   Take up your cross, nor heed the shame,
       and let your foolish pride be still:
       the Lord refused not even to die
       upon a cross, on Calvary's hill.

4   Take up your cross, then, in his strength,
       and calmly every danger brave;
       it guides you to a better home,
       and leads to victory o'er the grave.

5   Take up your cross, and follow Christ,
       nor think till death to lay it down;
       for only those who bear the cross
       may hope to wear the glorious crown.

*Charles William Everest (1814–1877)

Music German, 15th century, as adapted in
As hymnodus sacer, Leipzig, 1625
adapted Compilers of *Church Hymnary,* 3rd edition, 1973

HESPERUS   LM

1   'Take up your cross,' the Saviour said,
      'if you would my disciple be;
      take up your cross, with willing heart,
      and humbly follow after me.'

2   Take up your cross; let not its weight
      fill your weak soul with vain alarm:
      his strength shall bear your spirit up,
      and brace your heart, and nerve your arm.

3   Take up your cross, nor heed the shame,
      and let your foolish pride be still:
      the Lord refused not even to die
      upon a cross, on Calvary's hill.

4   Take up your cross, then, in his strength,
      and calmly every danger brave;
      it guides you to a better home,
      and leads to victory o'er the grave.

5   Take up your cross, and follow Christ,
      nor think till death to lay it down;
      for only those who bear the cross
      may hope to wear the glorious crown.

*Charles William Everest (1814–1877)

Music Henry Baker (1835–1910)

WERE YOU THERE

Irregular

1 Were you there when they cru-ci-fied my Lord?___ Were you

there when they cru-ci-fied my Lord? Oh!___

Some-times it cau-ses me to trem-ble, trem-ble, trem-ble.___

— Were you there when they cru-ci-fied my Lord?___

1   Were you there when they crucified my Lord?
       Were you there when they crucified my Lord?
       Oh! Sometimes it causes me to tremble,
           tremble, tremble.
       Were you there when they crucified my Lord?

2   Were you there when they nailed him to the tree?
       Were you there when they nailed him to the tree?
       Oh! Sometimes it causes me to tremble,
           tremble, tremble.
       Were you there when they nailed him to the tree?

3   Were you there when they laid him in the tomb?
       Were you there when they laid him in the tomb?
       Oh! Sometimes it causes me to tremble,
           tremble, tremble.
       Were you there when they laid him in the tomb?

4   Were you there when God raised him from the dead?
       Were you there when God raised him from the dead?
       Oh! Sometimes it causes me to tremble,
           tremble, tremble.
       Were you there when God raised him from the dead?

African–American spiritual

Music African–American spiritual
arranged Charles Winfred Douglas (1867–1944)

LORD OF THE DANCE   Irregular and refrain

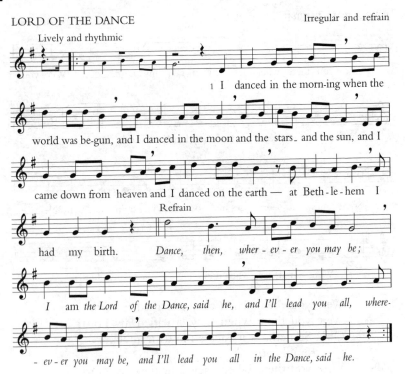

1   I danced in the morning
      when the world was begun,
      and I danced in the moon
      and the stars and the sun,
      and I came down from heaven
      and I danced on the earth —
      at Bethlehem
      I had my birth.

          Dance then, wherever you may be,
          I am the Lord of the Dance, said he,
          and I'll lead you all, wherever you may be,
          and I'll lead you all in the Dance, said he.

Music Shaker melody
adapted Sydney Bertram Carter (1915–2004)

2   I danced for the scribe
      and the pharisee,
      but they would not dance
      and they wouldn't follow me.
      I danced for the fishermen,
      for James and John —
      they came with me
      and the Dance went on.

3   I danced on the Sabbath
      and I cured the lame,
      the holy people
      said it was a shame.
      They whipped and they stripped
      and they hung me on high,
      and they left me there
      on a Cross to die.

4   I danced on a Friday
      when the sky turned black —
      it's hard to dance
      with the devil on your back.
      They buried my body
      and they thought I'd gone —
      but I am the Dance
      and I still go on.

5   They cut me down
      and I leapt up high —
      I am the life
      that'll never, never die.
      I'll live in you
      if you'll live in me,
      I am the Lord
      of the Dance, said he.

Sydney Bertram Carter (1915–2004)

Also suitable for Good Friday

We do not hope to ease our minds	537
How deep the Father's love for us	549
So much wrong and so much injustice	572
Jesus, remember me	775

*A list of hymns also suitable for Lent
and the Passion is found after 378.*

WALTON (FULDA)   LM

1   We sing the praise of him who died,
of him who died upon the cross;
the sinner's hope though all deride —
for this we count the world but loss.

2   Inscribed upon the cross we see
in shining letters, 'God is love';
he bears our sins upon the tree;
he brings us mercy from above.

3   The cross! it takes our guilt away;
it holds the fainting spirit up;
it cheers with hope the gloomy day,
and sweetens every bitter cup;

4   It makes the coward spirit brave,
and nerves the feeble arm for fight;
it takes its terror from the grave,
and gilds the bed of death with light;

5   The balm of life, the cure of woe,
the measure and the pledge of love,
the sinner's refuge here below,
the angels' theme in heaven above.

Thomas Kelly (1769–1855)

Music Sacred Melodies, 1815, William Gardiner (1770–1853)

CHRIST RISEN
RESURRECTION AND EXALTATION

ASCENSIUS

13 13 13 9 and refrain

Brightly

1 They cru-ci-fied my Sav-iour and nailed him to the tree, they

cru-ci-fied my Sav-iour and nailed him to the tree, they

cru-ci-fied my Sav-iour and nailed him to the tree,— and the

Lord will bear my spi – rit home.

Refrain

He rose, he rose, he rose— from the dead! He

rose, he rose, he rose— from the dead! He

rose, he rose, he rose— from the dead,— and the

Lord will bear my spi – rit home.

1   They crucified my Saviour and nailed him to the tree,
       they crucified my Saviour and nailed him to the tree,
       they crucified my Saviour and nailed him to the tree,
       and the Lord will bear my spirit home.
            He rose, he rose, he rose from the dead!
            He rose, he rose, he rose from the dead!
            He rose, he rose, he rose from the dead,
            and the Lord will bear my spirit home.

2   Then Joseph begged his body and laid it in the tomb,
       then Joseph begged his body and laid it in the tomb,
       then Joseph begged his body and laid it in the tomb,
       and the Lord will bear my spirit home.

continued overleaf

He rose, he rose, he rose___ from the dead! He
rose, he rose, he rose___ from the dead! He
rose, he rose, he rose___ from the dead,___ and the
Lord will bear my spi - rit home.

3 Sister Mary she came running a-looking for my Lord,
 Sister Mary she came running a-looking for my Lord,
 Sister Mary she came running a-looking for my Lord,
 and the Lord will bear my spirit home.

4 An angel came from heaven and rolled the stone away,
 an angel came from heaven and rolled the stone away,
 an angel came from heaven and rolled the stone away,
 and the Lord will bear my spirit home.

African-American spiritual
adapted William Farley Smith (1941–1997)

Music African-American spiritual
arranged William Farley Smith (1941–1997)

CHURCH CLOSE   6 7 7 11

1   Comes Mary to the grave;
        no singing bird has spoken,
        nor has the world awoken,
        and in her grief all love lies lost and broken.

2   Says Jesus at her side,
        no longer Jesus dying,
        'Why, Mary, are you crying?'
        She turns, with joy, 'My Lord! My love!' replying.

3   With Mary on this day
        we join our voices, praising
        the God of Jesus' raising,
        and sing the triumph of his love amazing.

Michael Arnold Perry (1942–1996)

Music David Iliff (*b.* 1939)

VOX DILECTI   86 86 D

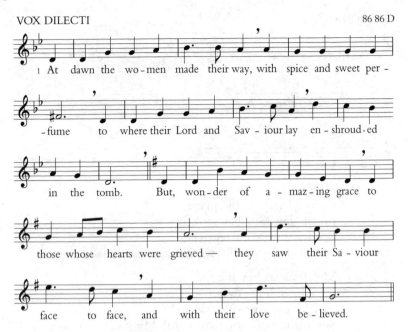

1 At dawn the wo-men made their way, with spice and sweet per-

-fume to where their Lord and Sav-iour lay en-shroud-ed

in the tomb. But, won-der of a - maz-ing grace to

those whose hearts were grieved — they saw their Sa-viour

face to face, and with their love be-lieved.

Music John Bacchus Dykes (1823–1876)

1   At dawn the women made their way,
    with spice and sweet perfume,
    to where their Lord and Saviour lay
    enshrouded in the tomb.
    But, wonder of amazing grace
    to those whose hearts were grieved —
    they saw their Saviour face to face,
    and with their love believed.

2   The mystery of this risen Lord
    a matchless peace bestows:
    a table set, a cup outpoured,
    whose goodness overflows.
    Our ointments, too, we gladly bring
    as each new dawn arrives —
    the sweetness of the songs we sing,
    the spice of faithful lives.

                    Mary Louise Bringle (b. 1953)

MFURAHINI HALELUYA   9999 and refrain

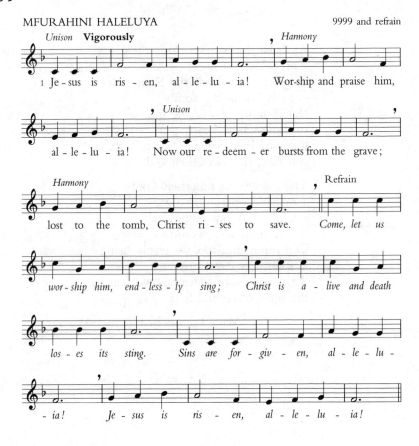

1 Jesus is risen, alleluia! Worship and praise him, alleluia! Now our redeemer bursts from the grave; lost to the tomb, Christ rises to save. Come, let us worship him, endlessly sing; Christ is alive and death loses its sting. Sins are forgiven, alleluia! Jesus is risen, alleluia!

Music Haya (Tanzanian) traditional melody
arranged John L. Bell (b. 1949)

1   Jesus is risen, alleluia!
Worship and praise him, alleluia!
Now our redeemer bursts from the grave;
lost to the tomb, Christ rises to save.
     Come, let us worship him, endlessly sing;
     Christ is alive and death loses its sting.
     Sins are forgiven, alleluia!
     Jesus is risen, alleluia!

2   Buried for three days, destined for death,
now he returns to breathe with our breath.
Blest are the ears alert to his voice,
blest are the hearts which for him rejoice.

3   'Don't be afraid!' the angel had said,
'Why seek the living here with the dead?
Look, where he lay, his body is gone,
risen and vibrant, warm with the sun.'

4   'Go and tell others, Christ is alive.'
Love is eternal, faith and hope thrive.
What God intended, Jesus fulfilled;
what God conceives can never be killed.

5   Let heaven echo, let the earth sing:
Jesus is saviour of everything.
All those who trust him, Christ will receive;
therefore rejoice, obey and believe!

Bernard Kyamanywa
English version John L. Bell (b. 1949)

EASTER HYMN   7777 and Alleluias

1   Jesus Christ is risen today, *Alleluia!*
     our triumphant holy day, *Alleluia!*
     who did once, upon the cross, *Alleluia!*
     suffer to redeem our loss. *Alleluia!*

2   Hymns of praise then let us sing
     unto Christ, our heavenly King,
     who endured the cross and grave,
     sinners to redeem and save.

3   But the anguish he endured
     our salvation has procured;
     now in heavèn Christ is King,
     where the angels ever sing.

4   Sing we to our God above
     praise eternal as his love;
     praise him, all you heavenly host,
     Father, Son, and Holy Ghost.

                              Lyra Davidica, 1708

Music Melody and bass from *Lyra Davidica,* 1708
altered later in 18th century
harmonised William Henry Monk (1823–1889)
altered Compilers of *Church Hymnary,* 3rd edition, 1973

ST GEORGE'S WINDSOR   7777 D

A lower setting is found at 233.

1   'Christ the Lord is risen today',
all on earth and angels say;
raise your joys and triumphs high;
sing, ye heavens, and earth reply.
Love's redeeming work is done,
fought the fight, the battle won;
lo! our Sun's eclipse is o'er;
lo! he sets in blood no more.

2   Vain the stone, the watch, the seal;
Christ has burst the gates of hell:
death in vain forbids his rise;
Christ has opened Paradise.
Lives again our glorious King;
where, O Death, is now thy sting?
Once he died, our souls to save;
where thy victory, O grave?

3   Soar we now where Christ has led,
following our exalted Head;
made like him, like him we rise;
ours the cross, the grave, the skies.
Hail, the Lord of earth and heaven!
Praise to thee by both be given;
thee we greet triumphant now;
hail, the Resurrection thou!

*Charles Wesley (1707–1788)

Music George Job Elvey (1816–1893)

VULPIUS (GELOBT SEI GOTT) 888 and Alleluias

Al - le - lu - ia! Al - le - lu - ia! Al - le - lu - ia!

Finita iam sunt prœlia

1   The strife is o'er, the battle done;
    now is the Victor's triumph won;
    now be the song of praise begun,
        Alleluia! Alleluia! Alleluia!

2   The powers of death have done their worst,
    but Christ their legions has dispersed;
    let shouts of holy joy outburst,

3   The three sad days have quickly sped;
    he rises glorious from the dead;
    all glory to our risen Head!

4   He broke the bonds of death and hell;
    the bars from heaven's gateway fell;
    let hymns of praise his triumph tell.

5   Lord, by the painful wounds you bore,
    death lost its sting for evermore;
    living in you, our praises soar.

                        Latin, 17th century
                translated *Francis Pott (1832–1909)

Music melody from Melchior Vulpius's *Gesangbuch*, 1609
harmonised Henry George Ley (1887–1962)

ELLACOMBE   76 76 D

A lower setting is found at 367.

Ἀναστάσεως ἡμέρα

1 The day of resurrection!
Earth, tell it out abroad;
the passover of gladness,
the passover of God!
From death to life eternal,
from sin's dominion free,
our Christ has brought us over
with hymns of victory.

2 Our hearts be pure from evil,
that we may see aright
the Lord in rays eternal
of resurrection light;
and, listening to his accents,
may hear, so calm and plain,
his own 'All hail!' and, hearing,
may raise the victor strain.

3 Now let the heavens be joyful
and earth her song begin,
the round world keep high triumph
and all that is therein;
let all things seen and unseen
their notes of gladness blend,
for Christ the Lord has risen,
our Joy that has no end.

St John of Damascus (*c.* 675–*c.* 750)
translated *John Mason Neale (1818–1866)

Music German melody, 18th century
as adapted in Mainz *Gesangbuch,* 1833
harmonised St Gall *Gesangbuch,* 1863

AVE VIRGO VIRGINUM   76 76 D

Brightly

Αἴσωμεν πάντες λαοί

1 Come, you faithful, raise the
      strain
of triumphant gladness;
God has brought his Israel
into joy from sadness;
loosed from Pharaoh's bitter
      yoke
Jacob's sons and daughters;
led them with unmoistened
      foot
through the Red Sea waters.

2 'Tis the spring of souls today;
Christ has burst his prison,
and from three days' sleep
      in death
as a sun has risen;
all the winter of our sins,
long and dark, is flying
from his light, to whom we
      give
love and praise undying.

3 Now the queen of seasons,
      bright
with the day of splendour,
with the royal feast of feasts
comes its joy to render;
comes to gladden Christian
      hearts,
which, with true affection,
welcome in unwearied strains
Jesus' resurrection.

4 Neither could the gates of
      death,
nor the grave's dark portal,
nor the watchers, nor the seal,
hold you as a mortal.
Here today amid your own
now you stand, bestowing
your own peace, which
      evermore
passes human knowing.

St John of Damascus (*c.*675–*c.*750)
translated John Mason Neale (1818–1866)

Music Melody from Johann Horn's *Gesangbuch,* 1544
harmonised Compilers

VRUECHTEN   6767 and refrain

Had Christ, who once was slain, not burst his three-day pri - - son, our faith had been in vain: but Christ has now a - ri - sen, a - ri - sen, a - ri - sen, a - ri - - - - - - sen!

1   This joyful Eastertide,
         away with sin and sorrow.
         My Love, the Crucified,
         has sprung to life this morrow:
            Had Christ, who once was slain,
            not burst his three-day prison,
            our faith had been in vain:
    *   *but Christ has now arisen!*

2   My flesh in hope shall rest,
         and for a season slumber:
         till trump from east to west
         shall wake the dead in number:

3   Death's flood has lost its chill,
         since Jesus crossed the river:
         Lover of souls, from ill
         my passing soul deliver:

    *   *The word 'arisen' is sung three more times.*

George Ratcliffe Woodward (1848–1934)

Music Melody from *David's Psalmen*, Amsterdam, 1685
harmonised Charles Wood (1866–1926)

OLD CLARENDONIAN   LM

A higher setting is found at 681.

1   Christ is alive! Let Christians sing.
     The cross stands empty to the sky.
     Let streets and homes with praises ring.
     Love, drowned in death, shall never die.

2   Christ is alive! No longer bound
     to distant years in Palestine,
     but saving, healing, here and now,
     and touching every place and time.

3   In every insult, rift, and war,
     where colour, scorn, or wealth divide,
     Christ suffers still, yet loves the more,
     and lives, where even hope has died.

4   Women and men, in age and youth,
     can feel the Spirit, hear the call,
     and find the way, the life, the truth,
     revealed in Jesus, freed for all.

5   Christ is alive, and comes to bring
     good news to this and every age,
     till earth and sky and ocean ring
     with joy, with justice, love, and praise.

Brian Wren (*b.* 1936)

Music Olwen Wonnacott (*b.* 1930)

416 Words: © 1969, 1995, Stainer & Bell Ltd, PO Box 110, Victoria House, 23 Gruneisen Road, London N3 1DZ
416 Music: © Olwen E. Wonnacott.

NOËL NOUVELET   11 10 10 and refrain

An alternative harmonisation is at 360.

1   Now the green blade riseth from the buried grain,
     wheat that in dark earth many days has lain;
     love lives again, that with the dead has been:
         Love is come again,
         like wheat that springeth green.

2   In the grave they laid him, Love whom men had slain,
     thinking that never he would wake again,
     laid in the earth like grain that sleeps unseen:

3   Forth he came at Easter, like the risen grain,
     he that for three days in the grave had lain,
     quick from the dead my risen Lord is seen:

4   When our hearts are wintry, grieving, or in pain,
     thy touch can call us back to life again,
     fields of our hearts that dead and bare have been:

                John Macleod Campbell Crum (1872–1958)

Music French carol melody
harmonised Martin Edward Fallas Shaw (1875–1958)

MORNING STAR 8886 86

1 A - way with gloom, a - way with doubt! With all the morn - ing
stars we sing; with all the hosts of heaven we shout the
prai - ses of a King, al - le - lu - ia! al - le -
- lu - ia! of our re - turn - ing King, al - le -
- lu - ia! al - le - lu - ia! of our re - turn - ing

vv. 1, 2 | *last time*

King. 2 A -

1   Away with gloom, away with doubt!
      With all the morning stars we sing;
      with all the hosts of heaven we shout
      the praises of a King,
  * alleluia! alleluia!
      of our returning King.

2   Away with death, and welcome life;
      in him we died and live again;
      and welcome peace, away with strife!
      for he returns to reign,
      alleluia! alleluia!
      the Crucified shall reign.

3   Then welcome beauty, he is fair;
      and welcome youth, for he is young;
      and welcome spring; and everywhere
      let merry songs be sung,
      alleluia! alleluia!
      for such a King be sung!

     * *The last two lines in each verse are repeated.*

Edward Shillito (1872–1948)

Music John L. Bell (*b.* 1949)

MACCABAEUS

10 11 11 11 and refrain

A toi la gloire, O Ressuscité

1   Thine be the glory, risen, conquering Son,
     endless is the victory thou o'er death hast won;
     angels in bright raiment rolled the stone away,
     kept the folded grave-clothes, where thy body lay.
      Thine be the glory, risen, conquering Son,
      endless is the victory thou o'er death hast won.

2   Lo! Jesus meets us, risen from the tomb;
     lovingly he greets us, scatters fear and gloom;
     let the Church with gladness hymns of triumph sing,
     for her Lord now liveth; death hath lost its sting.

3   No more we doubt thee, glorious Prince of Life;
     life is naught without thee: aid us in our strife;
     make us more than conquerors, through thy
         deathless love:
     bring us safe through Jordan to thy home above.

Edmond Budry (1854–1932)
translated Richard Birch Hoyle (1875–1939)

Music George Frederick Handel (1685–1759)
from *Judas Maccabaeus,* 1746

STUEMPFLE

LM and Alleluias

1 Earth, earth, a-wake; your prai-ses sing: *Al - le - lu - ia!*

Greet with the dawn your ri-sen King: *Al - le - lu - ia!*

Bright suns and stars, your ho-mage pay: *Al - le - lu - ia!*___

Life reigns a-gain this Eas-ter day: *Al - le - lu - ia!*

1   Earth, earth, awake; your praises sing: *Alleluia!*
     Greet with the dawn your risen King: *Alleluia!*
     Bright suns and stars, your homage pay: *Alleluia!*
     Life reigns again this Easter day: *Alleluia!*

2   All nature sings of hope reborn:
     Christ lives to comfort those who mourn:
     First fruit of all the dead who sleep:
     Promise of joy for all who weep:

3   Winter is past, the night is gone:
     Christ's light, triumphant, pales the dawn:
     Creation spreads its springtime bloom:
     Life bursts like flame from death's cold tomb:

4   Praise we the Father, Spirit, Son:
     Praise we the victory God has won:
     Praise we the Lamb who reigns above:
     Praise we the King whose rule is love:

Herman G. Stuempfle, Jr *(b.1923)*

Music Sally Ann Morris *(b.1952)*

KIRN   11 11 12 11 11

Harmony

Unison

Oh, sing hal - le - lu - jah, oh, sing hal - le - lu - jah,

Harmony

oh, sing hal - le - lu - - jah! Be joy - ful and sing,

(1) our great_ foe is baf - fled — Christ Je - sus is King!

1   Our Lord Christ hath risen!   The tempter is foiled;
    his legions are scattered, his strongholds are spoiled.
    Oh, sing hallelujah, oh, sing hallelujah,
    oh, sing hallelujah!   Be joyful and sing,
    our great foe is baffled — Christ Jesus is King!

2   O death, we defy thee!   A stronger than thou
    hath entered thy palace; we fear thee not now!
    Oh, sing hallelujah, oh, sing hallelujah,
    oh, sing hallelujah!   Be joyful and sing,
    death cannot affright us — Christ Jesus is King!

3   O sin, thou art vanquished, thy long reign is o'er;
    though still thou dost vex us, we dread thee no more.
    Oh, sing hallelujah, oh, sing hallelujah,
    oh, sing hallelujah!   Be joyful and sing,
    who now can condemn us? — Christ Jesus is King!

4   Our Lord Christ hath risen!   Day breaketh at last;
    the long night of weeping is now well-nigh past.
    Oh, sing hallelujah, oh, sing hallelujah,
    oh, sing hallelujah!   Be joyful and sing,
    our foes are all conquered — Christ Jesus is King!

William Conyngham Plunket (1828–1897)

Music John Prentice Taylor (1871–1936)

HEARTBEAT   13 12 13 13 11

1 Christ is alive, and the universe must celebrate
   and the stars and the suns shout on this joyful Day!
   Christ is alive, and his family must celebrate
        in a great alleluia,
        a great alleluia
   to praise the power that made the stone roll away.

2 Here is our hope: in mystery of suffering
   is the heartbeat of Love, Love that will not let go;
   here is our hope, that in God we are not separate,
        and we sing alleluia,
        we sing alleluia
   to praise the power that made the stone roll away.

3 Christ Spirit, dance through the dullness of humanity
   to the music of God, God who has set us free!
   You are the pulse of the new creation's energy;
        with a great alleluia,
        a great alleluia
   we praise the power that made the stone roll away.

Shirley Erena Murray (b. 1931)

Music Jillian Bray

SHOUT ON   LM and Alleluias

1 I know that my Re-deem-er lives, glo-ry, hal-le-lu-jah! What joy and peace this sen-tence gives, glo-ry, hal-le-lu-jah! Shout on, pray on, we're gain-ing ground, glo-ry, hal-le-lu-jah! The dead's a-live and the lost is found, glo-ry, hal-le-lu-jah!

1   I know that my
     Redeemer lives,
     glory, hallelujah!
What joy and peace
     this sentence gives,
     glory, hallelujah!
Shout on, pray on,
     we're gaining ground,
     glory, hallelujah!
The dead's alive
     and the lost is found,
     glory, hallelujah!

2   He lives, to bless me
     with his love,
     glory, hallelujah!
He lives, to plead
     for me above,
     glory, hallelujah!
He lives, my hungry
     soul to feed,
     glory, hallelujah!
He lives, to help
     in time of need,
     glory, hallelujah!

3   He lives, all glory to his name,
         glory, hallelujah!
     He lives, my Saviour, still the same,
         glory, hallelujah!
     What joy the blest assurance gives,
         glory, hallelujah!
     I know that my Redeemer lives,
         glory, hallelujah!

                 Samuel Medley (1738–1799)

Music Melody attributed to F. C. Wood
from *The Sacred Harp*, 1850, *arranged* Alice Parker (*b.* 1925)

BISHOPTHORPE   CM

A lower setting is found at 22.

PARAPHRASE 61

1   Blest be the everlasting God,
       the Father of our Lord!
       Be his abounding mercy praised,
       his majesty adored!

2   When from the dead he raised his Son,
       and called him to the sky,
       he gave our souls a lively hope
       that they should never die.

3   To an inheritance divine
       he taught our hearts to rise;
       'tis uncorrupted, undefiled,
       unfading in the skies.

4   Saints by the power of God are kept,
       till the salvation come:
       we walk by faith as strangers here;
       but Christ shall call us home.

Scottish Paraphrases, 1781,   *1 Peter 1: 3-5*

Music Melody and most of bass from
Select Portions of the Psalms, c. 1786
Jeremiah Clarke (c. 1673–1707)

ST ANDREW (TANS'UR)   CM

PARAPHRASE 48, verses 5–9

1   The Saviour died, but rose again
       triumphant from the grave;
       and pleads our cause at God's right hand,
       omnipotent to save.

2   Who then can e'er divide us more
       from Jesus and his love,
       or break the sacred chain that binds
       the earth to heaven above?

3   Let troubles rise, and terrors frown,
       and days of darkness fall;
       through him all dangers we'll defy,
       and more than conquer all.

4   Nor death nor life, nor earth nor hell,
       nor time's destroying sway,
       can e'er efface us from his heart,
       or make his love decay.

5   Each future period that will bless,
       as it has blessed the past:
       he loved us from the first of time,
       he loves us to the last.

Scottish Paraphrases, 1781
Romans 8: 34–end

Music Melody in Tans'ur's *New Harmony of Zion,* 1764
harmonised Thomas Cuthbertson Leithead Pritchard (1885–1960)
in *Scottish Psalter,* 1929

1 All heaven de-clares the glo-ry of the ris-en Lord; who can com-pare with the beau-ty of the Lord? For ev-er he will be the Lamb up-on the throne; I glad-ly bow the knee, and wor-ship him a-lone.

1   All heaven declares
the glory of the risen Lord;
who can compare
with the beauty of the Lord?
For ever he will be
the Lamb upon the throne;
I gladly bow the knee,
and worship him alone.

2   I will proclaim
the glory of the risen Lord,
who once was slain
to reconcile the world to God.
For ever you will be
the Lamb upon the throne;
I gladly bow the knee,
and worship you alone.

Noel Richards (*b.* 1955)
and Tricia Richards

Music Noel Richards (*b.* 1955)
and Tricia Richards

LUX EOI   87 87 D

1   Alleluia! Alleluia!
     hearts to heaven and voices raise;
     sing to God a hymn of gladness,
     sing to God a hymn of praise:
     he who on the Cross a victim
     for the world's salvation bled,
     Jesus Christ, the King of glory,
     now is risen from the dead.

2   Christ is risen, Christ the firstfruits
     of the holy harvest field,
     which will all its full abundance
     at his second coming yield;
     then the golden ears of harvest
     will their heads before him wave,
     ripened by his glorious sunshine,
     from the furrows of the grave.

3   Christ is risen, we are risen;
     shed upon us heavenly grace,
     rain, and dew, and gleams of glory
     from the brightness of thy face;
     so that we, with hearts in heaven,
     here on earth may fruitful be,
     and by angel hands be gathered,
     and be ever, Lord, with thee.

continued overleaf

Music Arthur Seymour Sullivan (1842–1900)

4   Alleluia! Alleluia!
        Glory be to God on high;
        Alleluia to the Saviour,
        who has gained the victory;
        Alleluia to the Spirit,
        fount of love and sanctity:
        Alleluia! Alleluia!
        to the blessèd Trinity.

            Christopher Wordsworth (1807–1885)

EASTERTIDE ACCLAMATION

Irregular

Al - le-lu - ia, al - le - lu - ia, Je - sus, ri - sen Lord of life!

Al - le-lu - ia, al - le - lu - ia, al - le - lu - ia! - ia!

Cantor All Cantor All

1 Word of the Fa - ther: *Je - sus Christ!* Hope of the world: *Je - sus Christ!*

Cantor All Cantor All D.C.

Bro - ken and bur - ied: *Je - sus Christ!* Ris - en to life: *Je - sus Christ!*

Alleluia, alleluia,
Jesus, risen Lord of life!
Alleluia, alleluia, alleluia!

1   Word of the Father: *Jesus Christ!*
     Hope of the world: *Jesus Christ!*
     Broken and buried: *Jesus Christ!*
     Risen to life: *Jesus Christ!*

2   Light of the nations: *Jesus Christ!*
     Way, Truth, and Life: *Jesus Christ!*
     Bearing our sorrow: *Jesus Christ!*
     With us through time: *Jesus Christ!*

3   Living among us: *Jesus Christ!*
     Word in our flesh: *Jesus Christ!*
     Servant of others: *Jesus Christ!*
     Friend of the poor: *Jesus Christ!*

Bernadette Farrell (b. 1957)

Music Bernadette Farrell (b. 1957)

EARTH AND ALL STARS   9 10 9 10 and refrain

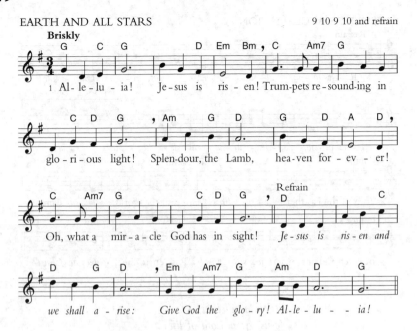

1   Alleluia! Jesus is risen!
Trumpets resounding in glorious light!
Splendour, the Lamb, heaven forever!
Oh, what a miracle God has in sight!
    Jesus is risen and we shall arise:
    Give God the glory! Alleluia!

2   Weeping, be gone; sorrow, be silent:
death is defeated, and Easter is bright.
Angels announce, 'Jesus is risen!'
Clothe us in wonder, adorn us in light.

3   Walking the way, Christ walking with us,
telling the story to open our eyes;
breaking the bread, showing his glory;
Jesus our blessing, our constant surprise.

Herbert F. Brokering (*b.* 1926)

Music David N. Johnson (1922–1987)

429 Words: 1995 Augsburg Fortress, PO Box 1209, Minneapolis, MN 55440-1209, USA.
429 Music: 1969 Augsburg Fortress, PO Box 1209, Minneapolis, MN 55440-1209, USA.

TRANSFORMATION   87 87 D

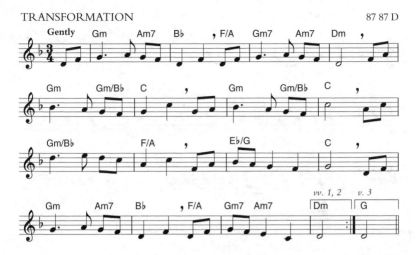

1   Christ has risen while earth slumbers,
    Christ has risen where hope died,
    as he said and as he promised,
    as we doubted and denied.
    Let the moon embrace the blessing;
    let the sun sustain the cheer;
    let the world confirm the rumour.
    Christ is risen, God is here!

2   Christ has risen for the people
    whom he loved and died to save;
    Christ has risen for the women
    bringing flowers to grace his grave.
    Christ has risen for disciples
    huddled in an upstairs room.
    He whose word inspired creation
    is not silenced by the tomb.

3   Christ has risen, and for ever
    lives to challenge, and to change
    all whose lives are messed or mangled,
    all who find religion strange.
    Christ is risen. Christ is present,
    making us what he has been —
    evidence of transformation
    in which God is known and seen.

                        John L. Bell (*b.* 1949)
                    and Graham Maule (*b.* 1958)

Music John L. Bell (*b.* 1949)

O FILII ET FILIAE

888 and Alleluias

431 2

O filii et filiæ

* *Alleluia! Alleluia! Alleluia!*

1   O sons and daughters, let us sing!
     The King of heaven, the glorious King,
     o'er death today rose triumphing.
         Alleluia!

Music Tune 1 Airs sur les hymnes sacrez, **Paris,** 1623
harmonised Compilers

Music Tune 2 Alison M. Robertson (*b.* 1940)

2   That Easter morn, at break of day,
the faithful women went their way
to seek the tomb where Jesus lay:

3   An angel robed in white they see,
who sat, and spoke unto the three,
'Your Lord goes on to Galilee.'

4   That night the apostles met in fear;
among them came their Lord most dear,
and said, 'My peace be on all here.'

5   When Thomas first the tidings heard,
he doubted if it were their Lord;
until he came and spoke the word:

6   'My piercèd side, O Thomas, see;
behold my hands, my feet,' said he;
'not faithless, but believing be.'

7   No longer Thomas then denied;
he saw the feet, the hands, the side;
'You are my Lord and God,' he cried:

8   How blest are they who have not seen,
and yet whose faith has constant been,
for they eternal life shall win:

9   On this most holy day of days,
our hearts and voices, Lord, we raise
in this triumphant hymn of praise:

*   *These Alleluias are sung before the first verse only when the
tune* O FILII ET FILIAE *is being used.*

*On Easter Sunday, verses 1-4, 9 may be sung; on the
Sunday following (Low Sunday), verses 1, 5-8.*

Jean Tisserand (*d.* 1494)
translated John Mason Neale (1818–1866)

RERES HILL   76 76 D

1 How often we, like Thomas,
   need proof before we trust.
   Lord Jesus, friend of doubters,
   come, speak your truth to us.
   We long to feel your presence,
   and gain new faith from you,
   to find, without our seeing,
   the blessing Thomas knew.

2 You always stand among us,
   no doors can lock you out.
   Your presence reassures us
   though we still live with doubt.
   As present-day disciples,
   whose lives by sin are flawed,
   we want to come believing,
   and cry: 'My Lord, my God!'

Edith Sinclair Downing (b. 1922)

Music Scottish folk melody
arranged John L. Bell (b. 1949)

HAVEN'T YOU HEARD   10 9 10 10 and refrain

1   Haven't you heard that Jesus is risen?
    Mary was there at crack of the dawn;
    weeping, she found him down in the garden:
    laughter is living and grieving is gone.
        Our hearts are glowing,
        our eyes are showing
        that Jesus lives.

2   Haven't you heard that Jesus is risen?
    Cleopas told us. Evening drew on;
    walking and talking, travelling with them
    Jesus was present: now grieving is gone.

3   Haven't you heard that Jesus is risen?
    Peter was fishing. Out of the dawn
    Jesus called, 'Shoot your net to the starboard' —
    fishing is thriving and grieving is gone.

4   Haven't you heard that Jesus is risen?
    Haven't you heard that Jesus goes on?
    Haven't you heard that Jesus is with us?
    Laughter is living and grieving is gone.

    Verses may be sung solo.

                                    Alison M. Robertson (*b.*1940)

Music Alison M. Robertson (*b.*1940)

CHILDER

888 and Alleluia

1   Jesus is risen from the grave;
     Jesus is risen from the grave;
     Jesus is risen from the grave.
      Alleluia!

2   Jesus was seen by Mary ...

3   Peter will soon be smiling ...

4   Thomas will stop his doubting ...

5   Jesus will meet his people ...

6   Jesus is here in bread and wine ...

7   Jesus will live for ever ...

John L. Bell *(b.1949)*
and Graham Maule *(b.1958)*

Music John L. Bell *(b.1949)*

435

YOU HEAR THE LAMBS

irregular

Refrain **Tenderly**

You hear the lambs a-cry-in', hear the lambs a-cry-in',

hear the lambs a-cry-in', O Shep-herd, feed my sheep.

Cantor
1 My Saviour spoke these words so sweet,   Saying,

All: O Shepherd, feed my sheep.

'Peter, if you love me, feed my sheep'.   *D.C.*

O Shepherd, feed my sheep.

You hear the lambs a-cryin',
hear the lambs a-cryin',
hear the lambs a-cryin',
O Shepherd, feed my sheep.

1 CANTOR: My Saviour spoke these words so sweet,
   ALL: O Shepherd, feed my sheep.
   CANTOR: Saying, 'Peter, if you love me, feed my sheep'.
   ALL: O Shepherd, feed my sheep.

2 O Lord, my love you see and know;
      O Shepherd, feed my sheep.
   Then give me grace to love you more;
      O Shepherd, feed my sheep.

3 O wasn't it an awful shame?
      O Shepherd, feed my sheep.
   He hung three hours in mortal pain.
      O Shepherd, feed my sheep.

Traditional spiritual

Music Traditional spiritual
arranged John L. Bell (*b.* 1949)

GUITING POWER   85 85 and refrain

1   Christ triumphant, ever reigning,
    Saviour, Master, King!
    Lord of heaven, our lives sustaining,
    hear us as we sing:
        Yours the glory and the crown,
        the high renown, the eternal name!

2   Word incarnate, truth revealing,
    Son of Man on earth!
    Power and majesty concealing
    by your humble birth:

3   Suffering servant, scorned, ill-treated,
    victim crucified!
    Death is through the cross defeated,
    sinners justified:

4   Priestly king, enthroned for ever
    high in heaven above!
    Sin and death and hell shall never
    stifle hymns of love:

5   So, our hearts and voices raising
    through the ages long,
    ceaselessly upon you gazing,
    this shall be our song:

                            Michael Saward (*b.* 1932)

Music John Barnard (*b.* 1948)

1   He is exalted,
        the King is exalted on high;
        I will praise him.
        He is exalted,
        for ever exalted
        and I will praise his name!

2   He is the Lord;
        for ever his truth shall reign.
        Heaven and earth
        rejoice in his holy name.
        He is exalted,
        the King is exalted on high.

Twila Paris (*b.* 1958)

Music Twila Paris (*b.* 1958)

437   Words and Music: © 1985, Straightway / Mountain Spring / EMI Christian Music Publishing. BMG Music Publishing Ltd, Bedford House, 69-79 Fulham High Street, London   SW6 3JW.

ST MAGNUS (NOTTINGHAM)   CM

1   The Head that once was crowned with thorns
       is crowned with glory now;
       a royal diadem adorns
       the mighty Victor's brow.

2   The highest place that heaven affords
       is his, is his by right,
       the King of kings, and Lord of lords,
       and heaven's eternal Light;

3   The joy of all who dwell above,
       the joy of all below
       to whom he manifests his love,
       and grants his name to know:

4   To them the cross, with all its shame,
       with all its grace, is given;
       their name an everlasting name,
       their joy the joy of heaven.

5   They suffer with their Lord below,
       they reign with him above,
       their profit and their joy to know
       the mystery of his love.

6   The cross he bore is life and health,
       though shame and death to him,
       his people's hope, his people's wealth,
       their everlasting theme.

               Thomas Kelly (1769–1855)

Music Jeremiah Clarke (*c.* 1673–1707)

REGENT SQUARE   87 87 87

1   Look, ye saints, the sight is glorious!
        See the Man of Sorrows now,
        from the fight returned victorious —
        every knee to him shall bow.
        Crown him! crown him! crown him! crown him!
        crowns become the Victor's brow.

2   Crown the Saviour, angels, crown him!
        Rich the trophies Jesus brings;
        in the seat of power enthrone him,
        while the vault of heaven rings.
        Crown him! crown him! crown him! crown him!
        crown the Saviour King of kings!

3   Sinners in derision crowned him,
        mocked the dying Saviour's claim;
        saints and angels crowd around him,
        own his title, praise his name.
        Crown him! crown him! crown him! crown him!
        spread abroad the Victor's fame.

4   Hark, those bursts of acclamation!
        hark, those loud triumphant chords!
        Jesus takes the highest station —
        Oh, what joy the sight affords!
        Crown him! crown him! crown him! crown him!
        King of kings, and Lord of lords!

                          Thomas Kelly (1769–1855)

Music Henry Thomas Smart (1813–1879)

ASCENDIT DEUS   887 D

1   The Lord ascendeth up on high,
the Lord hath triumphed gloriously,
in power and might excelling;
the grave and hell are captive led,
see him return, our glorious Head,
to his eternal dwelling.

2   The heavens with joy receive their Lord,
by saints, by angel hosts adored;
O day of exultation!
Come earth, adore thy glorious King!
His rising, his ascension sing
with grateful adoration!

3   Our great High Priest hath gone before,
now on his Church his grace to pour,
and still his love he giveth:
oh, may our hearts to him ascend;
may all within us upward tend
to him who ever liveth!

Arthur Tozer Russell (1806–1874)

Music Johann Gottfried Schicht (1753–1823)
Allgemeines Choral-Buch, Leipzig, 1819

BONNIE GEORGE CAMPBELL   10 10 10 10

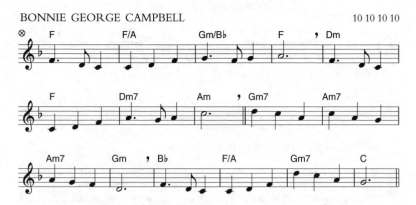

1   Blessing and honour and glory and power,
     wisdom and riches and strength evermore
     give to the Lord who our battle hath won,
     whose are the Kingdom, the crown, and the throne.

2   Into the heaven of the heavens hath he gone;
     sitteth he now in the joy of the throne;
     weareth he now of the Kingdom the crown;
     singeth he now the new song with his own.

3   Soundeth the heaven of the heavens with his name;
     ringeth the earth with his glory and fame;
     ocean and mountain, stream, forest, and flower
     echo his praises and tell of his power.

4   Ever ascendeth the song and the joy;
     ever descendeth the love from on high;
     blessing and honour and glory and praise, —
     this is the theme of the hymns that we raise.

5   Give we the glory and praise to the Lamb;
     take we the robe and the harp and the palm;
     sing we the song of the Lamb that was slain,
     dying in weakness, but rising to reign.

                              Horatius N. Bonar (1808–1889)

Music Scottish folk melody
arranged Compilers of *Church Hymnary,* 3rd edition, 1973

ANCIENT OF DAYS

Irregular

1 Bless - ing_ and hon - our, glo - ry_ and pow - er
be un - to_ the An - cient of days; _
from ev - 'ry na - tion, all of_ cre - a - tion
bow be - fore_ the An - cient of Days. _

Refrain

Ev - ery tongue in hea - ven and earth_ shall de - clare_ your glo - ry,
ev - ery knee_ shall bow at your throne_ in wor - ship;
you will be_ ex - alt - ed, O God, _ and your
king - dom_ shall not pass a - way, _ O An - cient of Days. _

2 Your king - dom shall reign ov - er

Music Garry Sadler (b. 1954)
and Jamie Harvill (b. 1960)

Christ Risen – Ascension

all the earth: sing un-to__ the An - cient of__
Days. For none shall com-pare to__ your match-less
worth: sing un-to__ the An - cient of__ Days.

1   Blessing and honour, glory and power
     be unto the Ancient of Days;
     from every nation, all of creation
     bow before the Ancient of Days.
          Every tongue in heaven and earth shall declare your glory,
          every knee shall bow at your throne in worship;
          you will be exalted, O God,
          and your kingdom shall not pass away,
          O Ancient of Days.

2   Your kingdom shall reign over all the earth:
     sing unto the Ancient of Days.
     For none shall compare to your matchless worth:
     sing unto the Ancient of Days.

Garry Sadler (*b.* 1954)
and Jamie Harvill (*b.* 1960)

442 Words and Music: © Praise Music / Hosanna Music / Sovereign Music Ltd, PO Box 356, Leighton Buzzard LU7 3WP
<sovereignmusic@aol.com>

HE IS LORD

6 11 10 6

1   He is Lord, he is Lord;
    he is risen from the dead, and he is Lord;
    every knee shall bow, every tongue confess
    that Jesus Christ is Lord.

2   He is love, he is love;
    he has shown us by his cross that he is love;
    all his people sing with one voice of joy
    that Jesus Christ is love.

3   He is life, he is life;
    he has died to set us free and he is life;
    and he calls us all to live evermore
    for Jesus Christ is life.

4   He is King, he is King;
    he will draw all nations to him, he is King;
    and the time shall be when the world shall sing
    that Jesus Christ is King.

                                Author unknown

Music Source unknown
arranged Norman Warren (*b.* 1934)

444

GENTLE JESUS

77 77

Christ Risen – Ascension

1   Out of sight, the Lord has gone
into heaven, now his home;
told his friends, before he left,
that they'd never be alone.

2   Jesus Christ we call him still,
and we love him as our friend;
close to God, he prays for us,
so we trust him to the end.

3   Work for Jesus, wait for him,
all his wisdom learn to know;
walk his ways and love his friends,
help his kingdom here to grow.

Jock Stein (*b.* 1941)

Music Martin Edward Fallas Shaw (1875–1958)

45

HYFRYDOL   87 87 D

1   Alleluia, sing to Jesus!
his the sceptre, his the throne;
alleluia, his the triumph,
his the victory alone.
Hark! the songs of peaceful Zion
thunder like a mighty flood:
'Jesus, out of every nation,
hath redeemed us by his blood.'

continued overleaf

2 Alleluia, not as orphans
   are we left in sorrow now;
   alleluia, he is near us,
   faith believes, nor questions
      how.
   Though the cloud from sight
      received him
   when the forty days were o'er,
   shall our hearts forget his
      promise,
   'I am with you evermore'?

3 Alleluia, bread of angels,
   here on earth our food,
      our stay;
   alleluia, here the sinful
   flee to you from day to day.
   Intercessor, friend of sinners,
   earth's redeemer, plead
      for me,
   where the songs of all the
      sinless
   sweep across the crystal sea.

4 Alleluia, King eternal,
   Lord omnipotent we own;
   alleluia, born of Mary,
   earth your footstool, heaven
      your throne.
   As within the veil you entered,
   robed in flesh, our great high
      priest,
   here on earth both priest and
      victim
   in the eucharistic feast.

5 Alleluia, sing to Jesus!
   his the sceptre, his the throne;
   alleluia, his the triumph,
   his the victory alone.
   Hark! the songs of peaceful
      Zion
   thunder like a mighty flood:
   'Jesus, out of every nation,
   hath redeemed us by his
      .blood.'

*Verse 4 may be omitted when
Holy Communion is not celebrated.*

William Chatterton Dix (1837–1898)

Music Melody by Rowland Hugh Pritchard (1811–1887)
harmonised David Evans (1874–1948)

ST THEODULPH 76 76 D

A lower setting is found at 364.

1 Lift up your hearts, believers!
This is the holy day
when Jesus, our Redeemer,
completes salvation's way.
The forty days are over,
and clouds shine high and bright
as Christ, the overcomer,
is lifted from our sight.

2 Lift up your hearts, believers!
Ye gates, lift up your heads!
though minds be full of wonder,
though souls be filled with dread.
The Spirit has been promised,
and, though we are alone,
we wait until the moment
when fire and wind are known.

3 Lift up your hearts, believers!
And do not be downcast,
for Jesus, our Redeemer,
receives the crown at last.
The thorns of crucifixion
are changed to stars of light,
and Christ, the Lord of glory,
is named as God's delight.

4 Lift up your hearts, believers!
This is the holy day
when Jesus, our Redeemer,
completes salvation's way.

Author unknown

Music Melody by Melchior Teschner (1584–1635)
later form, c. 1613, *harmonised* David Evans (1874–1948)

SING TO THE WORLD (UNIVERSA LAUS)   10 10 10 10 10

1 Sing to the world of Christ our sov-ereign Lord,
tell of his birth that brought new life _ to all.
Speak of his life, his love, his ho-ly word: let ev-ery na - tion
hear and know his call. Sing to the world of Christ our sove- reign

vv. 1 - 4   *v. 5*

Lord.   hand.

Music Ernest Sands (*b.* 1949)
arranged Paul Inwood (*b.* 1947)

1   Sing to the world of Christ our sovereign Lord,
    tell of his birth which brought new life to all.
    Speak of his life, his love, his holy word:
    let every nation hear and know his call.
    Sing to the world of Christ our sovereign Lord.

2   Sing to the world of Christ the Prince of Peace,
    showing to us the Father's loving care,
    pleading that love should reign and wars might cease,
    teaching us all the love of God to share.
    Sing to the world of Christ the Prince of Peace.

3   Sing to the world of Christ our steadfast friend,
    offering himself to live the constant sign,
    food for our souls until we meet life's end,
    gives us his flesh for bread, his blood for wine.
    Sing to the world of Christ our steadfast friend.

4   Sing to the world of Christ our Saviour King,
    born that his death the world's release should win.
    Hung on a cross, forgiveness he could bring;
    buried, he rose to conquer death and sin.
    Sing to the world of Christ our Saviour King.

5   Sing to the world of Christ at God's right hand;
    praise to the Spirit both have sent from heaven,
    living in us till earth shall reach its span,
    time be no more, and Christ shall come again.
    Sing to the world of Christ at God's right hand.

                                    Patrick Lee (1930–2004)

SHINE, JESUS, SHINE   Irregular

1 Lord, the light of your love is shin - ing in the midst of the dark - ness, shin - ing; Je - sus, light of the world, shine up-on us, set us free by the truth you now bring us.

Shine on me, shine on me:

Refrain
Shine, Je - sus, shine, fill this land with the Fa - ther's glo - ry;
blaze, Spi - rit blaze, set our hearts on fire.
Flow, ri - ver, flow, flood the na - tions with grace and mer - cy;
send forth your word, Lord, and let there be

vv. 1, 2   *v. 3*

light!

Music Graham Kendrick *(b.*1950)

1   Lord, the light of your love is shining
    in the midst of the darkness, shining;
    Jesus, Light of the world, shine upon us,
    set us free by the truth you now bring us.
    Shine on me, shine on me.
        Shine, Jesus, shine,
        fill this land with the Father's glory;
        blaze, Spirit, blaze,
        set our hearts on fire.
        Flow, river, flow,
        flood the nations with grace and mercy;
        send forth your word, Lord,
        and let there be light!

2   Lord, I come to your awesome presence,
    from the shadows into your radiance;
    by your blood I may enter your brightness,
    search me, try me, consume all my darkness.
    Shine on me, shine on me.

3   As we gaze on your kingly brightness,
    so our faces display your likeness,
    ever changing from glory to glory,
    mirrored here may our lives tell your story.
    Shine on me, shine on me.

                    Graham Kendrick (*b.* 1950)

Also suitable
One is the body and one is the Head   679
Hark how the adoring hosts above   744

CHRIST RISEN
REIGN AND PRIESTHOOD

DARWALL'S 148th   6666 88

1.   Rejoice! the Lord is King,
       your Lord and King adore.
       Mortals, give thanks and sing,
       and triumph evermore:
          Lift up your heart, lift up your voice;
          rejoice; again I say: Rejoice!

2.   Jesus the Saviour reigns,
       the God of truth and love;
       when he had purged our stains,
       he took his seat above:

3.   His kingdom cannot fail;
       he rules both earth and heaven;
       the keys of death and hell
       are to our Jesus given:

4.   He sits at God's right hand
       till all his foes submit,
       and bow to his command,
       and fall before his feet:

5.   Rejoice in glorious hope,
       for Christ, the Judge, shall come,
       and take his servants up
       to their eternal home:
          We then shall hear the archangel's voice;
          the trump of God shall sound: Rejoice!

Charles Wesley (1707–1788)

Music John Darwall (1731–1789)

MOVILLE   76 76 D

Christus Redemptor gentium

1   Christ is the world's Redeemer,
the lover of the pure,
the fount of heavenly wisdom,
our trust and hope secure;
the armour of his soldiers,
the Lord of earth and sky;
our health while we are living,
our life when we shall die.

2   Christ has our host surrounded
with clouds of martyrs bright,
who wave their palms in triumph
and fire us for the fight.
For Christ the cross ascended
to save a world undone,
and, suffering for the sinful,
our full redemption won.

continued overleaf

Music Irish traditional melody
arranged John L. Bell (*b.* 1949)

3   Down in the realm of darkness
    he lay a captive bound,
    but at the hour appointed
    he rose, a victor crowned;
    and now, to heaven ascended,
    he sits upon the throne
    in glorious dominion,
    his Father's and his own.

4   Glory to God the Father,
    the unbegotten One;
    all honour be to Jesus,
    his sole-begotten Son;
    and to the Holy Spirit —
    the perfect Trinity.
    Let all the worlds give answer,
    'Amen, so let it be'.

St Columba (521–597)
translated Duncan Macgregor (1854–1923)

PUER NOBIS NASCITUR   LM

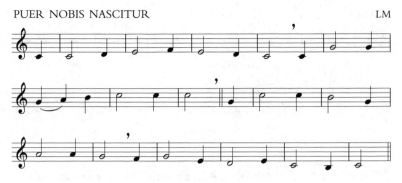

PARAPHRASE 58

1   Where high the heavenly temple stands,
the house of God not made with hands,
a great High Priest our nature wears,
Jesus, the Son of God, appears.

2   He who for us our surety stood,
and poured on earth his precious blood,
pursues in heaven his mighty plan,
eternal God and Son of Man.

3   Though now ascended up on high,
he bends on earth a brother's eye;
partaker of the human name,
he knows the frailty of our frame.

4   Our fellow-sufferer yet retains
a fellow-feeling of our pains;
and still remembers in the skies
his tears, his agonies, and cries.

5   In every pang that rends the heart
the Man of Sorrows has a part;
he sympathizes with our grief,
and to the sufferer sends relief.

6   With boldness, therefore, at the throne,
let us make all our sorrows known;
and ask the aid of heavenly power
to help us in the evil hour.

Scottish Paraphrases, 1781
Hebrews 4: 14–16

Music German melody, fifteenth century
adapted Michael Praetorius (1571–1621)
harmonised George Ratcliffe Woodward (1848–1934)

HALLEY   12 12 12

1   Great ring of light, true circle with no ending;
    clear beam so bright, whose purpose knows no bending;
    O Word of God, in darkness always shining out.

2   A man who cried upon a cross at Calvary;
    for him who died an empty tomb, a mystery;
    O risen Christ, all pain and loss transcending.

3   Immortal fire of love for ever yearning;
    flame of desire for our salvation burning;
    Spirit divine, our friend and present comforter.

4   The light shines still, the eternal Word has spoken;
    on Calvary's hill the power of death is broken;
    and I receive the life, the joy, the loving.

                                   Colin Alexander Gibson (*b.* 1933)

Music Colin Alexander Gibson (*b.* 1933)

JOEL   87 87 D

1   Christ, of God unseen the image,
        born before creation's birth;
        through whom all things were created,
        all that live in heaven and earth —
        realms and rulers, thrones, dominions,
        powers great and forces small
        through and for him made and fashioned —
        he is in and over all.

2   Christ the firstborn of creation,
        Christ in whom all things cohere,
        all things' Maker, seen and unseen,
        low and lofty, far and near.
        Christ the head of his dear body,
        of his Church the living core,
        risen from the dead before us —
        him we gladly now adore.

3   Christ in whom the very fullness
        of the living God is found,
        Christ who reconciles creation
        turning earth to holy ground,
        Christ the home of God's good pleasure
        through whose blood is made our peace,
        in whose cross, beyond all measure
        is our freedom and release.

Leith Fisher (b.1941)
based on *Colossians 1: 15-20*

Music Sally Ann Morris (b.1952)

453   Words: © Leith Fisher.
453   Music: © The Pilgrim Press, 700 Prospect Avenue East, Cleveland, OH 44115-1100, USA. Permission applied for.

EIN' FESTE BURG   87 87 66 66 7

Ein' feste Burg ist unser Gott

1   A safe stronghold our God is still,
a trusty shield and weapon;
he'll help us clear from all the ill
that hath us now o'ertaken.
The ancient prince of hell
hath risen with purpose fell;
strong mail of craft and power
he weareth in this hour;
on earth is not his fellow.

2   With force of arms we nothing can,
full soon were we down-ridden;
but for us fights the proper Man,
whom God himself hath bidden.
Ask ye who is this same?
Christ Jesus is his name,
the Lord Sabaoth's Son;
he, and no other one,
shall conquer in the battle.

Music Melody by Martin Luther (1483–1546)
harmonised Johann Sebastian Bach (1685–1750)

3 And were this world all devils o'er,
   and watching to devour us,
   we lay it not to heart so sore;
   they cannot overpower us.
   And let the prince of ill
   look grim as e'er he will,
   he harms us not a whit;
   for why? — his doom is writ;
   a word shall quickly slay him.

4 God's word, for all their craft and force,
   one moment will not linger,
   but, spite of hell, shall have its course;
   'tis written by his finger.
   And, though they take our life,
   goods, honour, children, wife,
   yet is their profit small;
   these things shall vanish all:
   the city of God remaineth.

Martin Luther (1483–1546)
translated Thomas Carlyle (1795–1881)

TAKE UP THE SONG   10 10 10 10

Je te salue, mon certain Redempteur

1   I greet thee, who my sure Redeemer art,
      my only Trust and Saviour of my heart,
      who pain didst undergo for my poor sake;
      I pray thee from our hearts all cares to take.

2   Thou art the King of mercy and of grace,
      reigning omnipotent in every place:
      so come, O King, and our whole being sway;
      shine on us with the light of thy pure day.

3   Thou art the life, by which alone we live,
      and all our substance and our strength receive;
      sustain us by thy faith and by thy power,
      and give us strength in every trying hour.

4   Thou hast the true and perfect gentleness,
      no harshness hast thou, and no bitterness:
      oh, grant to us the grace we find in thee,
      that we may dwell in perfect unity.

5   Our hope is in no other save in thee;
      our faith is built upon thy promise free;
      Lord, give us peace, and make us calm and sure,
      that in thy strength we evermore endure.

attributed to John Calvin (1509–1564)
translated Elizabeth Lee Smith (1817–1898)

Music Alfred Victor Fedak (*b.* 1953)

RINKART (KOMMT SEELEN)   6767 6666

An alternative tune NUN DANKET *is found at 182.*

1   Christ is the world's true light,
      its captain of salvation,
      the daystar clear and bright
      of every race and nation;
      new life, new hope awakes,
      where people own his sway:
      from bondage freedom breaks,
      and night is turned to day.

2   In Christ all races meet,
      their ancient feuds forgetting,
      the whole round world complete,
      from sunrise to its setting:
      when Christ is throned as Lord,
      we shall forsake our fear,
      to ploughshare beat the sword,
      to pruning-hook the spear.

3   One Lord, in one great name
      unite us all who own you;
      cast out our pride and shame
      that hinder to enthrone you;
      the world has waited long,
      has travailed long in pain:
      come, heal its ancient wrong,
      come, Prince of Peace, and reign.

                    *George Wallace Briggs (1875–1959)

Music Melody and figured bass by
Johann Sebastian Bach (1685–1750)

MILES LANE   CM Irregular

crown him,

crown him,   crown him,   crown him   Lord   of   all.

457 2

DIADEM   CM extended

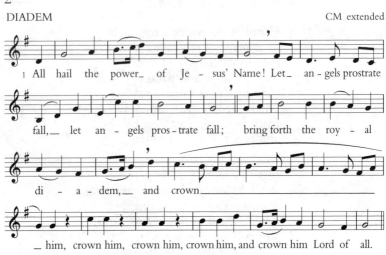

1 All hail the power_ of Je - sus' Name! Let_ an - gels prostrate

fall,_ let an - gels pros - trate fall; bring forth the roy - al

di - a - dem,_ and crown_____

_ him, crown him, crown him, crown him, and crown him Lord of all.

Music Tune 1 William Shrubsole (1759–1806)

Music Tune 2 James Ellor (1819–1899)

1   All hail the power of Jesus' Name!
Let angels prostrate fall;
bring forth the royal diadem,
* and crown him Lord of all.

2   Crown him, you martyrs of your God,
who from his altar call;
praise him whose path of pain you trod,
and crown him Lord of all.

3   Let every tongue and every tribe,
responsive to the call,
to him all majesty ascribe,
and crown him Lord of all.

4   Oh, that with yonder sacred throng,
we at his feet may fall;
join in the everlasting song,
and crown him Lord of all!

* *When using* MILES LANE *the words 'crown him' are
sung four times in each verse.*

Edward Perronet (1726–1792)

CUDDESDON   65 65 D
Unison

458 2

CAMBERWELL   65 65 D

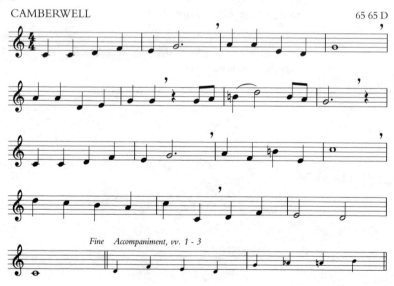

Fine   Accompaniment, vv. 1 - 3

Music Tune 1 William Harold Ferguson (1874–1950)
Music Tune 2 Michael Brierley (b. 1932)

1   At the name of Jesus
    every knee shall bow,
    every tongue confess him
    King of glory now;
    'tis the Father's pleasure
    we should call him Lord,
    who from the beginning
    was the mighty Word.

2   Brothers, sisters, name him
    with love strong as death,
    but with awe and wonder
    and with bated breath!
    He is God the Saviour,
    he is Christ the Lord,
    ever to be worshipped,
    trusted, and adored.

3   In your hearts enthrone him;
    there let him subdue
    all that is not holy,
    all that is not true:
    let his grace support you
    in temptation's hour;
    and his will enfold you
    in its light and power.

4   In his Father's glory
    Christ shall come again,
    angel hosts proclaiming
    his return to reign.
    For all wreaths of empire
    meet upon his brow,
    and our hearts confess him
    King of glory now.

*Caroline Maria Noel (1817–1877)

DIADEMATA   DSM

1   Crown him with many crowns,
     the Lamb upon his throne;
     Hark! how the heavenly anthem drowns
     all music but its own.
     Awake, my soul, and sing
     of him who died for thee,
     and hail him as thy matchless King
     through all eternity.

2   Crown him the Lord of life,
     who triumphed o'er the grave,
     and rose victorious in the strife
     for those he came to save.
     His glories now we sing
     who died and rose on high,
     who died eternal life to bring,
     and lives that death may die.

3   Crown him the Lord of love;
     behold his hands and side,
     rich wounds yet visible above,
     in beauty glorified.
     All hail, Redeemer, hail!
     for thou hast died for me:
     thy praise shall never, never fail
     throughout eternity.

                    Matthew Bridges (1800–1894)
                    and Godfrey Thring (1823–1903)

Music George Job Elvey (1816–1893)

CROFT'S 136th   6666 88

1   Join all the glorious names
         of wisdom, love, and power,
         that mortals ever knew,
         that angels ever bore:
         all are too mean to speak his worth,
         too mean to set my Saviour forth.

2   Great Prophet of my God,
         my tongue would bless your name;
         by you the joyful news
         of our salvation came:
         the joyful news of sins forgiven,
         of hell subdued, and peace with heaven.

3   Jesus, my great High Priest,
         offered his blood and died;
         my guilty conscience seeks
         no sacrifice beside:
         his powerful blood did once atone,
         and now it pleads before the throne.

4   My dear Almighty Lord,
         my Conqueror and my King,
         your sceptre and your sword,
         your reigning grace, I sing:
         yours is the power: behold I sit
         in willing service at your feet.

5   Now let my soul arise,
         and tread the tempter down:
         my Captain leads me forth
         to conquest and a crown:
         a feeble saint shall win the day,
         though death and hell obstruct the way.

                                       Isaac Watts (1674–1748)

Music Melody by William Croft (1678–1727)

ST PETER   CM

1   How sweet the name of Jesus sounds
in a believer's ear!
It soothes our sorrows, heals our wounds,
and drives away our fear.

2   It makes the wounded spirit whole,
and calms the troubled breast;
'tis manna to the hungry soul,
and to the weary rest.

3   Dear name! the rock on which I build,
my shield and hiding place,
my never-failing treasury, filled
with boundless stores of grace.

4   Jesus, my Shepherd, Husband, Friend,
my Prophet, Priest, and King,
my Lord, my Life, my Way, my End,
accept the praise I bring.

5   Weak is the effort of my heart,
and cold my warmest thought;
but, when I see thee as thou art,
I'll praise thee as I ought.

6   Till then I would thy love proclaim
with every fleeting breath;
and may the music of thy name
refresh my soul in death.

John Newton (1725–1807)

Music Alexander Robert Reinagle (1799–1877)

DOMINUS REGIT ME   87 87

1   The King of Love my Shepherd is,
     whose goodness faileth never;
     I nothing lack if I am his
     and he is mine for ever.

2   Where streams of living water flow
     my ransomed soul he leadeth,
     and where the verdant pastures grow
     with food celestial feedeth.

3   Perverse and foolish oft I strayed;
     but yet in love he sought me,
     and on his shoulder gently laid,
     and home rejoicing brought me.

4   In death's dark vale I fear no ill,
     with thee, dear Lord, beside me;
     thy rod and staff my comfort still,
     thy cross before to guide me.

5   Thou spread'st a table in my sight;
     thy unction grace bestoweth;
     and oh, what wonder and delight
     from thy pure chalice floweth!

6   And so through all the length of days
     thy goodness faileth never;
     Good Shepherd, may I sing thy praise
     within thy house for ever!

                    *Henry Williams Baker (1821–1877)
                              from *Psalm 23*

Music John Bacchus Dykes (1823–1876)

SCHÖNSTER HERR JESU (ST ELISABETH)

Irregular

Schönster Herr Jesu

1   Fairest Lord Jesus,
      ruler of all nature,
      O thou of God and Man the Son;
      thee will I cherish,
      thee will I honour,
      thou my soul's glory, joy, and crown.

2   Fair are the meadows,
      fairer still the woodlands,
      robed in the verdure and bloom of spring.
      Jesus is fairer,
      Jesus is purer,
      he makes the saddest heart to sing.

3   Fair is the sunshine,
      fairer still the moonlight,
      and fair the twinkling starry host;
      Jesus shines brighter,
      Jesus shines purer
      than all the stars that heaven can boast.

Münster Gesangbuch, 1677
translated Lilian Stevenson (1870–1960)
and others

Music Silesian melody from *Schlesische Volkslieder,* Leipzig, 1842
harmonised Compilers of *Rejoice and Sing,* 1991

CALABRIA   SM

Slowly

1   Though hope desert my heart,
     though strangeness fill my soul,
     though truth torment my troubled mind,
     you have been here before.

2   Though confidence run dry,
     though weary flesh be sore,
     though conversation bear no fruit,
     you have been here before.

3   There is no threatening place,
     no trial I could know
     which has not known your presence first:
     you have been here before.

4   In Christ who, on the cross,
     felt all our hurt and more,
     and cried in deep abandonment,
     you have been here before.

5   I will not dread the dark,
     the fate beyond control,
     nor fear what reigns in frightening things:
     you will be there before.

John L. Bell *(b.1949)*

Music John L. Bell *(b.1949)*

SLANE

10 10 10 10 Irregular

Music Irish traditional melody
harmonised David Evans (1874–1948)

Rop τú mo baile, a Choіндіu спіде

1   Be thou my Vision, O Lord of my heart;
    naught be all else to me, save that thou art;
    thou my best thought in the day or the night,
    waking or sleeping, thy presence my light.

2   Be thou my Wisdom, be thou my true Word;
    I ever with thee, and thou with me, Lord;
    thou my great Father: thine own I would be;
    thou in me dwelling, and I one with thee.

3   Be thou my breastplate, my sword for the fight;
    be thou my dignity, thou my delight,
    thou my soul's shelter, and thou my high tower;
    raise thou me heavenward, O Power of my power.

4   Riches I heed not, nor earth's empty praise,
    thou mine inheritance, now and always;
    thou, and thou only, the first in my heart,
    High King of Heaven, my treasure thou art.

5   High King of Heaven, after victory won,
    may I reach heaven's joys, O bright heaven's sun!
    Heart of my own heart, whatever befall,
    still be my Vision, O Ruler of all.

Irish, 8th century
translated Mary Elizabeth Byrne (1880–1931)
revised *Eleanor Henrietta Hull (1860–1935)

465   Words: © Estate of Eleanor Hull. From *The Poem Book of the Gael* translated by M. E. Byrne and edited by Eleanor Hull. Originally published by Chatto & Windus. Reprinted by permission of the Random House Group Ltd.

BEFORE THE THRONE OF GOD ABOVE　　　　　　　　　DLM extended

1 Be-fore the throne of God a-bove   I have a strong, a per-fect

plea, a great High Priest, whose name is Love, who ever lives and pleads for

me. My name is gra-ven on his hands, my name is writ-ten on his

heart;   I know that while   in   heaven he stands   no tongue can

bid me thence de - part,   no tongue can bid me thence de - part.

Music Vikki Cook

466   Music: © 1993 PDI, Worship. Administered by CopyCare Ltd,
PO Box 77, Hailsham, East Sussex, BN27 3EF, United Kingdom. <music@copycare.com>   Used by permission.

1   Before the throne of God above
    I have a strong, a perfect plea,
    a great High Priest, whose name is Love,
    who ever lives and pleads for me.
    My name is graven on his hands,
    my name is written on his heart;
    I know that while in heaven he stands
    no tongue can bid me thence depart.

2   When Satan tempts me to despair,
    and tells me of the guilt within,
    upward I look, and see him there
    who made an end of all my sin.
    Because the sinless Saviour died,
    my sinful soul is counted free;
    for God the just is satisfied
    to look on him and pardon me.

3   Behold him there! the risen Lamb,
    my perfect, spotless righteousness,
    the great unchangeable I AM,
    the King of glory and of grace!
    One with himself, I cannot die;
    my soul is purchased by his blood;
    my life is hid with Christ on high,
    with Christ my Saviour and my God.

The last line of each verse is repeated.

Charitie L. De Chenez (1841–1923)

BEAUTIFUL SAVIOUR   Irregular

1 All__ my days I will sing this song of glad - ness,
give__ my praise to the foun - tain of de - lights; for
in my help - less - ness you heard my__ cry, and
waves of mer - cy poured down on my life.__

Beau - ti - ful Sa - viour, won - der - ful Coun - - sel -
lor, clothed in ma - jes - ty, Lord of his - to - ry, you're the Way, the Truth, the
Life. Star__ of Morn - ing, glo - rious in ho - - li -
ness, you're the ri - sen one, hea - ven's cham - pi - on, and you reign, you
reign ov - er__ all!

Music Stuart Townend

1   All my days I will sing this song of gladness,
give my praise to the fountain of delights;
for in my helplessness you heard my cry,
and waves of mercy poured down on my life.

2   I will trust in the cross of my Redeemer,
I will sing of the blood that never fails,
of sins forgiven, of conscience cleansed,
of death defeated and life without end.
Beautiful Saviour, wonderful Counsellor,
clothed in majesty, Lord of history,
you're the Way, the Truth, the Life.
Star of Morning, glorious in holiness,
you're the risen one, heaven's champion,
and you reign, you reign over all!

3   I long to be where the praise is never-ending,
yearn to dwell where the glory never fades,
where countless worshippers will share one song,
and cries of 'worthy' will honour the Lamb!

Stuart Townend

BLAENWERN   87 87 D

A higher setting is found at 702.

1   Son of God, eternal Saviour,
     source of life and truth and grace,
     Son of Man, whose birth incarnate
     hallows all our human race;
     great High Priest who, throned in glory,
     for your own will ever plead,
     fill us with your love and pity,
     heal our wrongs, and help our need.

2   Lord, as you have lived for others,
     so may we for others live;
     freely have your gifts been granted,
     freely may your servants give.
     Yours the gold and yours the silver,
     yours the wealth of sea and land,
     we but stewards of your bounty
     held in trust at your command.

3   Come, Lord Jesus, reign among us,
     King of Love, and Prince of Peace;
     hush the storm of strife and passion,
     bid its cruel discords cease.
     Yours the prayer, and yours the purpose,
     that your people should be one;
     grant from heaven our hope's fruition:
     here on earth your will be done.

                              *Somerset Corry Lowry (1855–1932)

Music William Penfro Rowlands (1860–1937)

RESTORE, O LORD   Irregular

Re - store, O Lord, the hon - our of your name! In

works of sovereign pow – er come shake the earth a - gain, that all may

see, and come with rev - erent fear to the liv - ing God, _

_____ whose king - dom shall out – last the years. _____

1   Restore, O Lord, the honour of your name!
In works of sovereign power
come shake the earth again,
that all may see, and come with reverent fear
to the living God,
whose kingdom shall outlast the years.

2   Restore, O Lord, in all the earth your fame,
and in our time revive
the Church that bears your name,
and in your anger, Lord, remember mercy,
O living God,
whose mercy shall outlast the years.

3   Bend us, O Lord, where we are hard and cold,
in your refiner's fire;
come purify the gold:
though suffering comes, and evil crouches near,
still our living God
is reigning, he is reigning here.

Graham Kendrick (*b.* 1950)
and *Chris Rolinson* (*b.* 1958)

Music Graham Kendrick (*b.* 1950)
and Chris Rolinson (*b.* 1958)

WARRINGTON   LM

1   Jesus shall reign where'er the sun
does its successive journeys run;
his Kingdom stretch from shore to shore,
till moons shall wax and wane no more.

2   People and realms of every tongue
declare his love in sweetest song;
and infant voices shall proclaim
their early blessings on his name.

3   Blessings abound where Jesus reigns:
the prisoners leap to lose their chains,
the weary find eternal rest,
and all who suffer want are blessed.

4   Let every creature rise and bring
the highest honours to our King;
angels descend with songs again,
and earth repeat the loud Amen.

*Isaac Watts (1674–1748)

Music Adapted from Ralph Harrison (1748–1810)

471

TANTUM ERGO SACRAMENTUM   87 87 87

Gloriosi Salvatoris

1   To the name of our salvation
    laud and honour let us pay,
    which for many a generation
    hid in God's foreknowledge lay,
    but with holy exultation
    we may sing aloud today.

2   Jesus is the name we treasure,
    name beyond what words can tell,
    name of gladness, name of pleasure,
    ear and heart delighting well;
    name of power beyond all measure,
    saving us from sin and hell.

3   Jesus is the name exalted
    over every other name;
    in this name, whene'er assaulted
    we can put our foes to shame:
    strength to those who would have halted,
    eyes to blind, and feet to lame.

4   Therefore we in love adoring
    this most blessèd name revere,
    Holy Jesus, thee imploring
    so to write it in us here,
    that hereafter, heavenward soaring,
    we may sing with angels there.

15th century
translated *Compilers of
Hymns Ancient and Modern, 1861
based on the translation by
John Mason Neale (1818–1866)

Music French church melody from
Chants Ordinaires de l'Office Divin, Paris, 1881
harmonised David Evans (1874–1948)

Also suitable
The Lord is King! Lift up your voice   129
'Lift up your hearts': I hear the summons calling   654

**CHRIST RISEN
COMING AGAIN**

STUTTGART   87 87

1   Come, thou long-expected Jesus,
    born to set thy people free;
    from our fears and sins release us;
    let us find our rest in thee.

2   Israel's strength and consolation,
    hope of all the earth thou art,
    dear desire of every nation,
    joy of every longing heart.

3   Born thy people to deliver,
    born a child, and yet a King,
    born to reign in us for ever,
    now thy gracious kingdom bring.

4   By thine own eternal Spirit
    rule in all our hearts alone;
    by thine all-sufficient merit
    raise us to thy glorious throne.

                    Charles Wesley (1707–1788)

Music Melody in C.F. Witt's *Psalmodia Sacra*,
Gotha, 1715, *adapted*

IRISH CM

1 'Thy kingdom come!' — on bended knee
   the passing ages pray;
and faithful souls have yearned to see
   on earth that kingdom's day.

2 But the slow watches of the night
   not less to God belong;
and for the everlasting right
   the silent stars are strong.

3 And lo, already on the hills
   the flags of dawn appear;
gird up your loins, ye prophet souls,
   proclaim the day is near:

4 The day in whose clear-shining light
   all wrong shall stand revealed,
when justice shall be throned with might,
   and every hurt be healed:

5 When knowledge, hand in hand with peace,
   shall walk the earth abroad,
the day of perfect righteousness,
   the promised day of God.

Frederick Lucian Hosmer (1840–1929)

Music Melody from *A Collection of Hymns and Sacred Poems,*
Dublin, 1749, *harmonised* Compilers of *English Hymnal,* 1906

ES IST EIN ROS' ENTSPRUNGEN   7676 D

1   Hail to the Lord's Anointed,
          great David's greater Son!
          Hail, in the time appointed,
          his reign on earth begun!
          He comes to break oppression,
          to set the captive free,
          to take away transgression,
          and rule in equity.

2   He comes with succour speedy
          to those who suffer wrong,
          to help the poor and needy,
          and bid the weak be strong,
          to give them songs for sighing,
          their darkness turn to light
          whose souls, condemned and dying,
          are precious in his sight.

Music German melody, 16th-century or earlier
adapted James Smith Anderson (1853–1945)

3   He shall come down like showers
upon the fruitful earth,
and love, joy, hope, like flowers,
spring in his path to birth.
Before him, on the mountains,
shall peace, the herald, go;
and righteousness in fountains
from hill to valley flow.

4   For him shall prayer unceasing
and daily vows ascend,
his kingdom still increasing,
a kingdom without end.
The mountain dews shall nourish
a seed, in weakness sown,
whose fruit shall spread and flourish
and shake like Lebanon.

5   O'er every foe victorious,
he on his throne shall rest,
from age to age more glorious,
all blessing and all-blest.
The tide of time shall never
his covenant remove;
his name shall stand for ever;
that name to us is Love.

James Montgomery (1771–1854)

NEANDER (UNSER HERRSCHER)   87 87 87

1   Christ is coming! let creation
    from her groans and travail cease;
    let the glorious proclamation
    hope restore and faith increase:
    Christ is coming! Christ is coming!
    Come now, blessèd Prince of Peace.

2   Earth can now but tell the story
    of your bitter cross and pain;
    she shall yet behold your glory,
    Lord, when you return to reign:
    Christ is coming! Christ is coming!
    'Come, Lord Jesus, come again!'

3   Long your exiles have been pining,
    far from you, and rest, and home:
    but, in heavenly glory shining,
    soon their loving Lord shall come:
    Christ is coming! Christ is coming!
    Haste the joyous jubilee.

4   With that blessèd hope before us,
    harps be played and songs be sung;
    let the mighty advent chorus
    onward roll from tongue to tongue:
    'Christ is coming! Christ is coming!
    Come, Lord Jesus, quickly come!'

                        *John Ross Macduff (1818–1895)

Music Melody from Neander's *Alpha und Omega,* 1680

76

BATTLE HYMN OF THE REPUBLIC

Irregular

Unison

Harmony

1   Mine eyes have seen the glory of the coming of the Lord:
he is trampling out the vintage where the grapes of wrath
 are stored;
he hath loosed the fatal lightning of his terrible swift sword:
his truth is marching on.
  Glory, glory, Hallelujah,
  glory, glory, Hallelujah,
  glory, glory, Hallelujah,
  his truth is marching on.

2   He hath sounded forth the trumpet that shall never
 call retreat;
he is sifting out all human hearts before his judgment-seat;
O, be swift, my soul, to answer him; be jubilant, my feet!
Our God is marching on.
  Glory, glory, Hallelujah,
  glory, glory, Hallelujah,
  glory, glory, Hallelujah,
  our God is marching on.

continued overleaf

Music William Steffe c. 1852

3 In the beauty of the lilies Christ was born across the sea,
with a glory in his bosom that transfigures you and me:
as he died to make us holy, let us live to make all free,
while God is marching on.
 Glory, glory, Hallelujah,
 glory, glory, Hallelujah,
 glory, glory, Hallelujah,
 while God is marching on.

4 He is coming like the glory of the morning on the wave;
he is wisdom to the mighty; he is succour to the brave;
so the world shall be his footstool, and the soul of time
  his slave:
our God is marching on.
 Glory, glory, Hallelujah,
 glory, glory, Hallelujah,
 glory, glory, Hallelujah,
 our God is marching on.

*Julia Ward Howe (1819–1810)
and others

77

87 87 12 7

1   Lo, he comes with clouds descending,
      Christ, the Lamb, for sinners slain;
      thousand thousand saints attending
      join to sing the glad refrain:
      Alleluia! Alleluia! Alleluia!
      God appears on earth to reign.

2   Every eye shall now behold him,
      robed in dreadful majesty;
      those who set at naught and sold him,
      pierced, and nailed him to the tree,
      deeply wailing, deeply wailing, deeply wailing,
      shall the true Messiah see.

3   Those deep wounds of cross and passion
      still his glorious body bears;
      cause of endless exultation
      to his ransomed worshippers:
      Alleluia! Alleluia! Alleluia!
      See! the day of God appears.

4   Yea, amen, let all adore you,
      high on your eternal throne;
      Saviour, take the power and glory,
      claim the kingdom for your own:
      oh, come quickly, oh, come quickly, oh, come quickly,
      Alleluia! come, Lord, come!

*Charles Wesley (1707–1788)
based on a hymn by John Cennick (1718–1755)

Music Melody in John Wesley's
Select Hymns with Tunes Annext, 1765, adapted

ST STEPHEN (NEWINGTON)   CM

PARAPHRASE 63

1   Behold the amazing gift of love
       the Father hath bestowed
       on us, in calling us his own,
       the children of our God!

2   Concealed as yet this honour lies,
       by this dark world unknown,
       a world that knew not when he came,
       even God's eternal Son.

3   High is the rank we now possess;
       but higher we shall rise,
       though what we shall hereafter be
       is hid from mortal eyes.

4   Our souls, we know, when he appears,
       shall bear his image bright;
       for all his glory, full disclosed,
       shall open to our sight.

5   A hope so great and so divine
       may trials well endure;
       and purge the soul from sense and sin,
       as Christ himself is pure.

Scottish Paraphrases, 1781
1 John 3: 1-3

Music William Jones (1726–1800)
Ten Church Pieces for the Organ, Nayland, 1789

FRANKLIN PARK   85 85 88 85

1   View the present through the promise,
Christ will come again.
Trust despite the deepening darkness,
Christ will come again.
Lift the world above its grieving
through your watching and believing
in the hope past hope's conceiving:
Christ will come again.

2   Probe the present with the promise,
Christ will come again.
Let your daily actions witness,
Christ will come again.
Let your loving and your giving
and your justice and forgiving
be a sign to all the living:
Christ will come again.

3   Match the present to the promise,
Christ will come again.
Make this hope your guiding premise,
Christ will come again.
Pattern all your calculating
and the world you are creating
to the advent you are waiting:
Christ will come again.

Thomas H. Troeger (b. 1945)

Music Roy Hopp (b. 1951)

480

COME, LORD, COME

Word of the Fa - ther, *Come, Lord, come;* *and take our fear a-way,*

and take our fear a-way; *re-place it with your love.*

1 CANTOR:
   Word of the Father,
   ALL:
   Come, Lord, come;
   and take our fear away,
   and take our fear away;
   replace it with your love.

2 Firstborn of Mary,

3 Healer and helper,

4 Servant and sufferer,

5 Jesus, Redeemer,

6 Christ, resurrected,

7 Maranatha!

John L. Bell (*b.*1949)

Music John L. Bell (*b.*1949)

481

Je - sus   is the name we ho - nour;

Je - sus   is the name we praise._____   Ma-jes-tic

name above_ all other names, the highest heaven and earth proclaim that

Je - sus   is   our   God._____   *We will*

glo - - ri-fy,_____   we will   lift   him high,_____   we will

give   him   ho - nour_ and_ praise._____   We will

glo - ri - fy,___ we will lift him high,___ we will
give him ho - nour_ and_ praise._____

1   Jesus is the name we honour;
    Jesus is the name we praise.
    Majestic name above all other names,
    the highest heaven and earth proclaim
    that Jesus is our God.
        We will glorify,
        we will lift him high,
        we will give him honour and praise.
        We will glorify,
        we will lift him high,
        we will give him honour and praise.

2   Jesus is the name we worship;
    Jesus is the name we trust.
    He is the King above all other kings,
    let all creation stand and sing
    that Jesus is our God.

3   Jesus is the Father's splendour;
    Jesus is the Father's joy.
    He will return to reign in majesty,
    and every eye at last will see
    that Jesus is our God.

Phil Lawson-Johnston

Music Phil Lawson-Johnston

481 Words and Music: © 1991, Thankyou Music. Administered (UK and Europe) by kingswaysongs.com <tym@kingsway.co.uk>.
Remaining territories administered by worshiptogether.com songs. Used by permission.

Also suitable

482 1

OUR RESPONSE TO CHRIST
IN PENITENCE

KILMARNOCK　　　　　　　　　　　　　　　　　CM

482 2

KEDRON　　　　　　　　　　　　　　　　　CM

Music Tune 1 Melody, and most of the harmony,
by Neill Dougall (1776–1862)
from Clarke's *Parochial Psalmody,* 2nd edition, 1831

Music Tune 2 Source unknown
arranged Hugh S. Roberton (1874–1952) and Compilers

PARAPHRASE 30

1   Come, let us to the Lord our God
    with contrite hearts return;
    our God is gracious, nor will leave
    the desolate to mourn.

2   His voice commands the tempest forth,
    and stills the stormy wave;
    his arm is sure and strong to smite,
    but also strong to save.

3   Long has the night of sorrow reigned,
    the dawn shall bring us light:
    God shall appear, and we shall rise
    with gladness in his sight.

4   Our hearts, if God we seek to know,
    shall know him, and rejoice;
    his coming like the morn shall be,
    like morning songs his voice.

5   As dew upon the tender herb
    diffusing fragrance round;
    as showers that usher in the spring,
    and cheer the thirsty ground:

6   So shall his presence bless our souls,
    and shed a joyful light;
    that hallowed morn shall chase away
    the sorrows of the night.

Scottish Paraphrases, 1781
Hosea 6: 1-4

RIVAULX

LM

1 Father of heaven, whose love profound
   a ransom for our souls has found,
   before your throne we sinners bend:
   to us your pardoning love extend.

2 Almighty Son, incarnate Word,
   our Prophet, Priest, Redeemer, Lord,
   before your throne we sinners bend:
   to us your saving grace extend.

3 Eternal Spirit, by whose breath
   our souls are raised from sin and death,
   before your throne we sinners bend:
   to us your quickening power extend.

4 Jehovah — Father, Spirit, Son —
   mysterious Godhead, Three in One,
   before your throne we sinners bend:
   grace, pardon, life to us extend.

*Edward Cooper (1770–1833)

Music John Bacchus Dykes (1823–1876)

484

MELITA

8888 88

An alternative tune ST PETERSBURG *is found at 188.*

1   Great God, your love has called us here,
as we, by love for love were made.
Your living likeness still we bear,
though marred, dishonoured, disobeyed.
We come, with all our heart and mind
your call to hear, your love to find.

2   We come with self-inflicted pains
of broken trust and chosen wrong,
half-free, half-bound by inner chains,
by social forces swept along,
by powers and systems close confined
yet seeking hope for humankind.

3   Great God, in Christ you call our name
and then receive us as your own,
not through some merit, right or claim,
but by your gracious love alone.
We strain to glimpse your mercy-seat
and find you kneeling at our feet.

4   Then take the towel, and break the bread,
and humble us, and call us friends.
Suffer and serve till all are fed,
and show how grandly love intends
to work till all creation sings,
to fill all worlds, to crown all things.

5   Great God, in Christ you set us free
your life to live, your joy to share.
Give us your Spirit's liberty
to turn from guilt and dull despair
and offer all that faith can do
while love is making all things new.

Brian Wren (b. 1936)

Music John Bacchus Dykes (1823–1876)

484 Words: © 1975, 1995, Stainer & Bell Ltd, PO Box 110

REPTON

Unison

86 886 (6)

1   Dear Lord and Father of mankind,
forgive our foolish ways;
reclothe us in our rightful mind;
in purer lives thy service find,
*   in deeper reverence, praise.

2   In simple trust like theirs who heard,
beside the Syrian sea,
the gracious calling of the Lord,
let us, like them, without a word
rise up and follow thee.

3   O Sabbath rest by Galilee!
O calm of hills above,
where Jesus knelt to share with thee
the silence of eternity,
interpreted by love!

4   With that deep hush subduing all
our words and works that drown
the tender whisper of thy call,
as noiseless let thy blessing fall
as fell thy manna down.

5   Drop thy still dews of quietness,
till all our strivings cease;
take from our souls the strain and stress,
and let our ordered lives confess
the beauty of thy peace.

rles Hubert Hastings Parry (1848–1918)
Judith

6   Breathe through the heats of our desire
     thy coolness and thy balm;
     let sense be dumb, let flesh retire;
     speak through the earthquake, wind and fire,
     O still small voice of calm!

* *The last line of each verse is repeated.*

John Greenleaf Whittier (1807–1892)

86

DETROIT   CM

1   'Forgive our sins as we forgive',
     you taught us, Lord, to pray;
     but you alone can grant us grace
     to live the words we say.

2   How can your pardon reach and bless
     the unforgiving heart
     that broods on wrongs, and will not let
     old bitterness depart?

3   In blazing light your cross reveals
     the truth we dimly knew:
     what trivial debts are owed to us,
     how great our debt to you!

4   Lord, cleanse the depths within our souls,
     and bid resentment cease.
     Then, bound to all in bonds of love,
     our lives will spread your peace.

Rosamond Eleanor Herklots (1905–1987)

Music North American folk hymn melody in
A Supplement to the Kentucky Harmony, 1820
harmonised Russell Schulz-Widmar (*b.* 1944)

CHILEMA   995

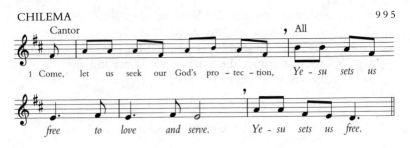

1 Come, let us seek our God's pro - tec - tion, Ye - su sets us
free to love and serve. Ye - su sets us free.

1   Come, let us seek our God's protection,
     Yesu sets us free to love and serve.
     Yesu sets us free.

2   Our foes are gathered all around us,

3   See fear, despair, and guile enslave us,

4   Our eyes are tired from too much weeping,

5   God knows our suffering, sees our trouble,

6   God is our refuge and defender,

7   How wonderful God's constant love is,

8   Our God unites us as one people,

9   Let's dance and sing to God our Saviour,

10   And shout for joy with all God's children,

11   Haleluya, yes, Haleluya,
     Yesu sets us free to love and serve.
     Yesu sets us free.

Tom Colvin (1925–2000)

Music Malawian folk melody
arranged Tom Colvin (1925–2000)

KHANDALLAH   CM

1 Teach us, O lov-ing heart_ of Christ, what on-ly love__ can say: 'Fa – ther, for - give'_ and still__ for - give the blind-ness of our way.

1   Teach us, O loving heart of Christ,
     what only love can say:
     'Father, forgive' and still forgive
     the blindness of our way.

2   Torn is the world you came to save,
     it bleeds from hands and side:
     slow is your Church to bear the scars
     of suffering love that died.

3   We have not found your way of peace,
     though lack of peace is death:
     we have not fed with word or bread
     the hungry of the earth.

4   Christ in whose hands were thrust the nails,
     who yet for us could pray:
     forgive the things we have not done,
     the words we do not say.

                          Shirley Erena Murray *(b. 1931)*

Music Jillian Bray

DOWN AMPNEY   66 11 D

Discendi, Amor santo

1   Come down, O Love Divine,
     seek out this soul of mine,
     and visit it with your own ardour glowing;
     O Comforter, draw near,
     within my heart appear,
     and kindle it, your holy flame bestowing.

2   O let it freely burn,
     till earthly passions turn
     to dust and ashes, in its heat consuming;
     and let your glorious light
     shine ever on my sight,
     and clothe me round, the while my path illuming.

3   Let holy charity
     my outward vesture be,
     and lowliness become my inner clothing;
     true lowliness of heart,
     which takes the humbler part,
     and o'er its own shortcomings weeps with loathing.

4   And so the yearning strong,
     with which the soul will long,
     shall far outpass the power of human telling;
     we cannot guess its grace,
     till we become the place
     wherein the Holy Spirit makes a dwelling.

Bianco da Siena (*d.* 1434)
translated *Richard Frederick Littledale (1833–1890)

Music Ralph Vaughan Williams (1872–1958)

489 Music: From *The English Hymnal*, 1906, Oxford University Press, Great Clarendon Street, Oxford. OX2 6DP.
Reproduced by permission.

ABERYSTWYTH   7777 D

1 Jesus, lover of my soul,
   let me to thy bosom fly,
   while the nearer waters roll,
   while the tempest still is high.
   Hide me, O my Saviour, hide,
   till the storm of life is past;
   safe into the haven guide,
   oh, receive my soul at last!

2 Other refuge have I none,
   hangs my helpless soul on thee;
   leave, ah! leave me not alone,
   still support and comfort me.
   All my trust on thee is stayed,
   all my help from thee I bring;
   cover my defenceless head
   with the shadow of thy wing.

3 Thou, O Christ, art all I want;
   more than all in thee I find!
   Raise the fallen, cheer the faint,
   heal the sick, and lead the blind.
   Just and holy is thy name,
   I am all unrighteousness;
   false and full of sin I am,
   thou art full of truth and grace.

4 Plenteous grace with thee is found,
   grace to cover all my sin;
   let the healing streams abound,
   make and keep me pure within.
   Thou of life the fountain art,
   freely let me take of thee;
   spring thou up within my heart,
   rise to all eternity.

Charles Wesley (1707–1788)

Music Joseph Parry (1841–1903)

HOLLINGSIDE   7777 D

1   Jesus, lover of my soul,
let me to thy bosom fly,
while the nearer waters roll,
while the tempest still is high.
Hide me, O my Saviour, hide,
till the storm of life is past;
safe into the haven guide,
oh, receive my soul at last!

2   Other refuge have I none,
hangs my helpless soul on thee;
leave, ah! leave me not alone,
still support and comfort me.
All my trust on thee is stayed,
all my help from thee I bring;
cover my defenceless head
with the shadow of thy wing.

3   Thou, O Christ, art all I want;
more than all in thee I find!
Raise the fallen, cheer the faint,
heal the sick, and lead the blind.
Just and holy is thy name,
I am all unrighteousness;
false and full of sin I am,
thou art full of truth and grace.

4   Plenteous grace with thee is found,
grace to cover all my sin;
let the healing streams abound,
make and keep me pure within.
Thou of life the fountain art,
freely let me take of thee;
spring thou up within my heart,
rise to all eternity.

Charles Wesley (1707–1788)

Music John Bacchus Dykes (1823–1876)

SOUTHWELL

SM

Μνώεο Χριστέ

1 Lord Jesus, think on me,
    and purge away my sin;
    from earthborn passions set me free,
    and make me pure within.

2 Lord Jesus, think on me,
    with care and woe oppressed;
    let me thy loving servant be,
    and taste thy promised rest.

3 Lord Jesus, think on me,
    amid the battle's strife;
    in all my pain and misery
    be thou my health and life.

4 Lord Jesus, think on me,
    nor let me go astray;
    through darkness and perplexity
    point thou the heavenly way.

5 Lord Jesus, think on me,
    when flows the tempest high:
    when on doth rush the enemy
    O Saviour, be thou nigh.

6 Lord Jesus, think on me,
    that when the flood is past,
    I may the eternal brightness see,
    and share thy joy at last.

Synesius of Cyrene (*c.* 365–414)
translated Allen William Chatfield (1808–1896)

Music Melody for Psalm 45 in Daman's
The Psalmes of David, 1579, *altered*

SOUTHWELL   SM

Μνώεο Χριστέ

1   Lord Jesus, think of me
     and take away my fear;
     in my depression, may I be
     assured that you are near.

2   Lord Jesus, think of me,
     by many cares oppressed;
     in times of great anxiety
     give me your promised rest.

3   Lord Jesus, think of me,
     when darker grows the day;
     and in my sad perplexity
     show me the heavenly way.

4   Lord Jesus, think of me,
     when night's dark shadows spread;
     restore my lost serenity,
     and show me light ahead.

5   Lord Jesus, think of me,
     that when the night is past
     I may the glorious morning see
     and share your joy at last!

Synesius of Cyrene (*c.*365–414)
adapted Jubilate Hymns

Music Melody for Psalm 45 in Daman's
The Psalmes of David, 1579, *altered*

IT'S ME, O LORD

It's me, it's me, O Lord,
standing in the need of prayer.
It's me, it's me, O Lord,
standing in the need of prayer.

1   Not my mother or my father, but it's me, O Lord,
     standing in the need of prayer;
     not my mother or my father, but it's me, O Lord,
     standing in the need of prayer.

2   Not my brother or my sister, but it's me, O Lord,
     standing in the need of prayer;
     not my brother or my sister, but it's me, O Lord,
     standing in the need of prayer.

3   Not the stranger or the neighbour, but it's me, O Lord,
     standing in the need of prayer;
     not the stranger or the neighbour, but it's me, O Lord,
     standing in the need of prayer.

African–American Spiritual

Music African–American Spiritual
arranged John L. Bell (*b.* 1949)

INTERCESSOR   11 10 11 10

1   Spirit of God, in all that's true I know you;
       yours is the light that shines through thoughts and words.
       Forgive my mind, slow as it is to read you,
       my mouth so slow to speak the truth you are.

2   Spirit of God, in beauty I behold you;
       yours is the loveliness of all that's fair.
       Forgive my heart, slow as it is to love you,
       my soul so slow to wonder at your grace.

3   Spirit of God, in all that's good I meet you;
       yours is the rightness in each deed of love.
       Forgive my will, slow as it is to serve you,
       my feet so slow to go, my hands to do.

4   Spirit of God, in Jesus Christ you find me;
       in him you enter through the door of faith;
       from deep within me take possession of me —
       my will, my heart, my mind all matched to his.

Reginald Thomas Brooks (1918–1985)

Music Charles Hubert Hastings Parry (1848–1918)

SONG 22   10 10 10 10

1   Spirit of God, descend upon my heart;
        wean it from earth; through all its pulses move;
        stoop to my weakness, mighty as thou art,
        and make me love thee as I ought to love.

2   I ask no dream, no prophet-ecstasies,
        no sudden rending of the veil of clay,
        no angel-visitant, no opening skies;
        but take the dimness of my soul away.

3   Hast thou not bid me love thee, God and King —
        all, all thine own, soul, heart, and strength, and mind?
        I see thy cross — there teach my heart to cling:
        oh, let me seek thee, and oh, let me find!

4   Teach me to feel that thou art always nigh;
        teach me the struggles of the soul to bear,
        to check the rising doubt, the rebel sigh;
        teach me the patience of unanswered prayer.

5   Teach me to love thee as thine angels love,
        one holy passion filling all my frame —
        the baptism of the heaven-descended Dove,
        my heart an altar, and thy love the flame.

George Croly (1780–1860)

Music Melody and bass by Orlando Gibbons (1583–1625), *adapted*

LIFE IN CHRIST
OUR RESPONSE TO CHRIST
IN DEDICATION

TIZA PANTAZI PINU   11 11

Tiza pantazi pinu

1   Humbly in your sight we come together, Lord;
    grant us now the blessing of your presence here.

2   These, our hearts, are yours, we give them to you, Lord;
    purify our love to make it like your own.

3   These, our eyes, are yours, we give them to you, Lord;
    may we always see your world as with your sight.

4   These, our hands, are yours, we give them to you, Lord;
    give them strength and skill to do all work for you.

5   These, our feet, are yours, we give them to you, Lord;
    may we always walk the path of life with you.

6   These, our tongues, are yours, we give them to you, Lord;
    may we speak your healing words of life and truth.

7   These, our ears, are yours, we give them to you, Lord;
    open them to hear the Gospel as from you.

8   Our whole selves are yours, we give them to you, Lord;
    take us now and keep us yours for evermore.

Tumbuka (Malawian) hymn
J. P. Chirwa (*d.* 1940)
translated and adapted Tom Colvin (1925–2000)

Music Traditional North Malawian melody
adapted Tom Colvin (1925–2000)
arranged John L. Bell (*b.* 1949)

CHILTON FOLIAT 10 10 10 10

1   Almighty Father of all things that be,
     our life, our work, we consecrate to thee,
     whose heavens declare thy glory from above,
     whose earth below is witness to thy love.

2   For well we know this weary, fallen earth
     is yet thine own by right of its new birth,
     since that great cross upreared on Calvary
     redeemed it from its fault and shame to thee.

3   Thine still the changeful beauty of the hills,
     the purple valleys flecked with silver rills,
     the ocean glistening 'neath the golden rays;
     they all are thine, and voiceless speak thy praise.

4   Thou dost the strength to worker's arm impart;
     from thee the skilled musician's mystic art,
     the grace of poet's pen or painter's hand
     to teach the loveliness of sea and land.

5   Then grant us, Lord, in all things thee to own,
     to dwell within the shadow of thy throne,
     to speak and work, to think, and live, and move,
     reflecting thine own nature which is love;

6   That so, by Christ redeemed from sin and shame,
     and hallowed by thy Spirit's cleansing flame,
     ourselves, our work, and all our powers may be
     a sacrifice acceptable to thee.

*Ernest Edward Dugmore (1843–1925)

Music George Clement Martin (1844–1916)

ANGEL VOICES

8585 843

1   Angel voices ever singing
round your throne of light,
angel harps for ever ringing,
rest not day nor night;
thousands only live to bless you
and confess you
Lord of might.

2   Lord, we know your heart rejoices
in each work divine,
you did ears and hands and voices
for your praise design;
craftsman's art and music's measure
for your pleasure
all combine.

Music Edwin George Monk (1819–1900)

3   In your house our gifts we offer
from your love so free;
and for your acceptance proffer
all unworthily,
hearts and minds and hands and voices
   in our choicest
   psalmody.

4   Honour, glory, might, and merit
yours shall ever be,
Father, Son, and Holy Spirit,
blessèd Trinity.
Earth and heaven join in praising,
   voices raising
   joyfully.

                           *Francis Pott (1832–1909)

All

D   **A**   **Bm**   **F#m**

1, 3 Lord God   Al - might - y,   Sav - iour,   Re - deem - er,
5 Fa - ther,   we praise you ;   Je - sus,   we love you ;

G   **D/F#**   **Em D/F# Bm**   **A**

on - ly   true God___   to be   wor-shipped and   praised :
Spi - rit,   we thank you   for the   gifts   of   new   life :

D   **A/C#**   **Bm**   **F#m**

how   can   we   tell   you   how   much   we   love   you?

G   **D**   **F#m7 G**   **D**   *Fine*

Take   now   our   lives, Lord,   and   teach   us   to   love.

Cantor or Group

D   **A**   **Bm**

2 'Do   not   fear, for   I   have re-deemed you. You are   mine, by name   I have

F#m   **G**   **D**   **Em7**   **A**

called you. When you walk through   the   wa - ters,   I will be   there with   you.

D   **A**   **Bm**   **F#m**

You   are   my   wit - ness - es,   cre - a - ted   for   my   glo - ry.   Tell the

G   **D**   **Em7**   **A** *D.C.*

na - tions   I   am the   Sav - iour.   Tell them   I   am   the   Lord.'

D   **A**   **Bm**   **F#m**

4 Shout for   joy,   O   heav - ens,   and re - joice,   O   earth!   In - to

G   **D**   **Em7**   **A**

joy - ful   shout - ing   let the moun - tains   break   forth!   For the

499   Words and Music: © Coni Huisman, Grand Rapids, Michigan, USA.

Our Response to Christ – In Dedication

Lord will com - fort his peo - ple, show com - pas-sion to those af - flict - ed.

He will not leave to shame those who trust in his Word.

To be hummed or played under cantor

1 ALL:
Lord God Almighty, Saviour, Redeemer,
only true God to be worshipped and praised:
how can we tell you how much we love you?
Take now our lives, Lord, and teach us to love.

2 CANTOR or GROUP:
'Do not fear, for I have redeemed you.
You are mine, by name I have called you.
When you walk through the waters,
I will be there with you.
You are my witnesses, created for my glory.
Tell the nations I am the Saviour.
Tell them I am the Lord.'

3 ALL:
Lord God Almighty, Saviour, Redeemer,
only true God to be worshipped and praised:
how can we tell you how much we love you?
Take now our lives, Lord, and teach us to love.

4 CANTOR or GROUP:
Shout for joy, O heavens, and rejoice, O earth!
Into joyful shouting let the mountains break forth!
For the Lord will comfort his people,
show compassion to those afflicted.
He will not leave to shame those who trust in his Word.

5 ALL:
Father, we praise you; Jesus, we love you;
Spirit, we thank you for the gifts of new life:
how can we tell you how much we love you?
Take now our lives, Lord, and teach us to love.

Coni Huisman

Music Coni Huisman

SLANE

10 11 11 11 Irregular

1   Lord of creation, to you be all praise!
Most mighty your working, most wondrous your ways!
Your glory and power are beyond us to tell,
and yet in the heart of the humble you dwell.

2   Lord of all power, I give you my will,
in joyful obedience your tasks to fulfil.
Your bondage is freedom; your service is song;
and, held in your keeping, my weakness is strong.

3   Lord of all wisdom, I give you my mind,
rich truth that surpasses our knowledge to find.
What eye has not seen and what ear has not heard
is taught by your Spirit and shines from your Word.

4   Lord of all bounty, I give you my heart;
I praise and adore you for all you impart;
your love to inflame me, your counsel to guide,
your presence to shield me, whatever betide.

5   Lord of all being, I give you my all;
if I should disown you, I'd stumble and fall;
but, sworn in your service your word I'll obey,
and walk in your freedom to the end of the way.

*John Copley Winslow (1882–1974)

Music Irish traditional melody
harmonised Erik Routley (1917–1982)

TAKE THIS MOMENT   75 75

1   Take this moment, sign, and space;
take my friends around;
here among us make the place
where your love is found.

2   Take the time to call my name,
take the time to mend
who I am and what I've been,
all I've failed to tend.

3   Take the tiredness of my days,
take my past regret,
letting your forgiveness touch
all I can't forget.

continued overleaf

Music John L. Bell (*b.*1949)

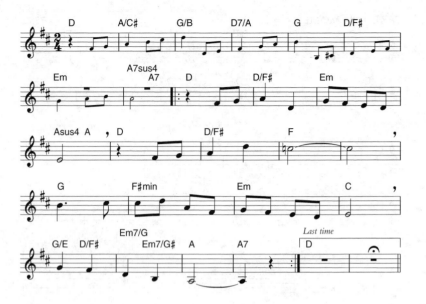

4   Take the little child in me,
scared of growing old;
help me here to find my worth
made in Christ's own mould.

5   Take my talents, take my skills,
take what's yet to be;
let my life be yours, and yet,
let it still be me.

John L. Bell (b. 1949)
and Graham Maule (b. 1958)

NOTTINGHAM   77 77

An alternative tune ST BEES *is found at 51.*

1   Take my life, Lord, let it be
        consecrated, glad, and free;
        take my moments and my days,
        let them flow in ceaseless praise.

2   Take my hands, and let them move
        at the impulse of your love;
        take my feet, that I may run
        bearing news of Christ your Son.

3   Take my voice, and let me sing
        always, only, for my King;
        take my intellect and use
        every power as you shall choose.

4   Take my will — your will be done,
        may my will and yours be one;
        take my heart — it is your own,
        it shall be your royal throne.

5   Take my love — my Lord, I pour
        at your feet its treasure-store;
        take myself, and I will be
        all for you, eternally.

           *Frances Ridley Havergal (1836–1879)

Music Wenzel Müller (1747–1835)

1 I will of-fer up my life in spi-rit and truth_ pour-ing

out the oil of love as my wor-ship to you._ In sur-rend-er I must

give my ev - ery part;_ Lord, re-ceive the sac-ri-fice of a

bro - ken heart._ *Je-sus, what can I give,_ what can I bring_*

_ to so faith-ful a friend,_ to so lov-ing a king?_ Sav-iour,

*what can be said?_ What can be sung_ as a praise of your name_*

_ for the things you have done?_ Oh, my words could not tell,_ not

*ev - en in part,_ of the debt of love that is owed_*

_ by this thank-ful heart._

503   Words and Music: © 1994, Thankyou Music. Administered (UK and Europe) by kingswaysongs.com <tym@kingsway.co.uk>. Remaining territories administered by worshiptogether.com songs. Used by permission.

1 I will offer up my life in spirit and truth,
   pouring out the oil of love as my worship to you.
   In surrender I must give my every part;
   Lord, receive the sacrifice of a broken heart.
   Jesus, what can I give, what can I bring
   to so faithful a friend, to so loving a king?
   Saviour, what can be said?   What can be sung
   as a praise of your name for the things you have done?
   Oh, my words could not tell, not even in part,
   of the debt of love that is owed by this thankful heart.

2 You deserve my every breath, for you've paid the great cost;
   giving up your life to death, even death on a cross.
   You took all my shame away, there defeated my sin,
   opened up the gates of heaven and have beckoned me in.

                                        Matt Redman

Music Matt Redman

ALL THAT I HAVE

Two lit-tle fish-es, five loaves of bread, five thou-sand peo-ple by Je-sus were fed. This is what hap-pened when one lit-tle lad glad-ly gave Je-sus all that he had. *All that I have, all that I have, I will give Je-sus all that I have.*

1   Two little fishes, five loaves of bread,
     five thousand people by Jesus were fed.
     This is what happened when one little lad
     gladly gave Jesus all that he had.
         All that I have, all that I have,
         I will give Jesus all that I have.

2   One lonely widow, two coins so small,
     Jesus was watching when she gave her all,
     and Jesus said, as his heart was made glad,
     that she had given all that she had.

                        Dorothy G. Montgomery

Music Dorothy G. Montgomery
arranged Compilers

ALL THAT I AM

1   All that I am, all that I do,
     all that I'll ever have I offer now to you.
     Take and sanctify these gifts for your honour, Lord.
     Knowing that I love and serve you is enough reward.
     All that I am, all that I do,
     all that I'll ever have I offer now to you.

2   All that I dream, all that I pray,
     all that I'll ever make I give to you today.
     Take and sanctify these gifts for your honour, Lord.
     Knowing that I love and serve you is enough reward.
     All that I am, all that I do,
     all that I'll ever have I offer now to you.

Sebastian Temple (1928–1997)

Music Sebastian Temple (1928–1997)
arranged John Ballantine

KNOWING YOU

1 All I once held dear, built my life up - on, all this world re -
veres, and wars to own, all I once thought gain I have
coun - ted loss; spent and worth - less now, com - pared to
this: Know - ing you, Je - sus, know - ing
you, there is no great - er thing. You're my
all, you're the best, you're my joy, my right - eous - ness, and I
love you, Lord. 2 Now my love you, Lord,
love you, Lord.

Music **Graham Kendrick** (*b.* 1950)

1   All I once held dear, built my life upon,
     all this world reveres, and wars to own,
     all I once thought gain I have counted loss;
     spent and worthless now, compared to this:
          Knowing you, Jesus, knowing you,
          there is no greater thing.
          You're my all, you're the best,
          you're my joy, my righteousness,
          and I love you, Lord.

2   Now my heart's desire is to know you more,
     to be found in you and known as yours,
     to possess by faith what I could not earn,
     all-surpassing gift of righteousness.

3   Oh, to know the power of your risen life,
     and to know you in your sufferings,
     to become like you in your death, my Lord,
     so with you to live and never die.

                    Graham Kendrick (*b.* 1950)

LITTLE VENICE   99 99

1 Je-sus, I come trust-ing your kind-ness, know-ing my need, lost in my blind-ness: you are the sense giv-ing life its mean-ing, you are the truth from the be-gin - ning.

1   Jesus, I come trusting your kindness,
       knowing my need, lost in my blindness:
       you are the sense, giving life its meaning,
       you are the truth from the beginning.

2   Now as I grow, use and affirm me,
       and when I doubt, touch me, reclaim me;
       when there is pain, heal me and hold me —
       cloak of your love, cover, enfold me.

3   All that I am, Jesus, I offer,
       all I achieve, all I may suffer,
       all whom I love for your compassion,
       all I hold dear for your possession.

                                  Shirley Erena Murray (*b.* 1931)

Music Gerald Hocken Knight (1908–1979)

UNION   67 77

1   I bind my heart this tide
     to the Galilean's side,
     to the wounds of Calvary,
     to the Christ who died for me.

2   I bind my soul this day
     to the neighbour far away,
     and the stranger near at hand,
     in this town, and in this land.

3   I bind my heart and soul
     to the God, the Lord of all,
     to the God, the poor one's friend,
     and the Christ whom he did send.

4   I bind myself to peace,
     to make strife and envy cease.
     My God, fasten sure the cord
     of my service to the Lord!

              Lauchlan McLean Watt (1867–1957)

Music J. Randall Zercher (*b.* 1940)

508   Music: © J. Randall Zercher, Houston, Texas, USA.

Also suitable
Worship the Lord in the beauty of holiness   201

509

OUR RESPONSE TO CHRIST
IN DISCIPLESHIP

ST ANDREW   87 87

1   Jesus calls us! O'er the tumult
of our life's wild restless sea,
day by day his voice is sounding,
saying, 'Christian, follow me'.

2   As, of old, Saint Andrew heard it
by the Galilean lake,
turned from home and toil and kindred,
leaving all for his dear sake.

3   Jesus calls us from the worship
of the vain world's golden store,
from each idol that would keep us,
saying, 'Christian, love me more'.

4   In our joys and in our sorrows,
days of toil and hours of ease,
still he calls, in cares and pleasures,
'Christian, love me more than these'.

5   Jesus calls us! By your mercy,
Saviour, make us hear your call,
give our hearts to your obedience,
serve and love you best of all.

*Cecil Frances Alexander (1818–1895)

Music Edward Henry Thorne (1834–1916)

LEWIS FOLK MELODY   87 87 D

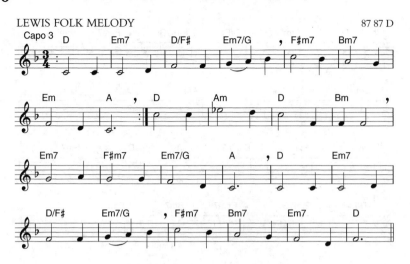

1   Jesus calls us here to meet him
       as, through word and song and prayer,
       we affirm God's promised presence
       where his people live and care.
       Praise the God who keeps his promise;
       praise the Son who calls us friends;
       praise the Spirit who, among us,
       to our hopes and fears attends.

2   Jesus calls us to confess him
       Word of life and Lord of all,
       sharer of our flesh and frailness,
       saving all who fail or fall.
       Tell his holy human story;
       tell his tales that all may hear;
       tell the world that Christ in glory
       came to earth to meet us here.

continued overleaf

Music Lewis Folk Melody
arranged John L. Bell (*b.* 1949)

LIFE IN CHRIST

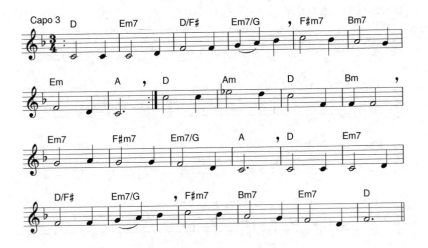

3   Jesus calls us to each other,
      vastly different though we are;
      creed and colour, class and gender
      neither limit nor debar.
      Join the hand of friend and stranger;
      join the hands of age and youth;
      join the faithful and the doubter
      in their common search for truth.

4   Jesus calls us to his table
      rooted firm in time and space,
      where the Church in earth and heaven
      finds a common meeting place.
      Share the bread and wine, his body;
      share the love of which we sing;
      share the feast for saints and sinners
      hosted by our Lord and King.

*Verse 4 may be omitted when there is no celebration
of Holy Communion.*

John L. Bell *(b. 1949)*
and Graham Maule *(b. 1958)*

THORNBURY   76 76 76 7 and refrain

1   Your hand, O God, has guided
your flock, from age to age;
the wondrous tale is written,
full clear, on every page;
your people owned your goodness,
and we their deeds record;
and both of this bear witness:
one Church, one Faith, one Lord.

2   Your heralds brought glad tidings
to greatest as to least;
they summoned all to hasten
and share the great King's feast;
and this was all their teaching,
in every deed and word,
to all alike proclaiming:
one Church, one Faith, one Lord.

continued overleaf

Music Basil Harwood (1859–1949)

3   Through many a day of darkness,
    through many a scene of strife,
    the faithful few fought bravely
    to guard the nation's life.
    Their Gospel of redemption,
    sin pardoned, life restored,
    was all in this enfolded:
    one Church, one Faith, one Lord.

4   Your mercy will not fail us,
    nor leave your work undone;
    with your right hand to help us,
    your victory shall be won;
    by mortals and by angels
    your name shall be adored,
    and this shall be their anthem:
    one Church, one Faith, one Lord.

        *Edward Hayes Plumptre (1821–1891)

TO GOD BE THE GLORY

11 11 11 11 and refrain

Refrain

1   To God be the glory, great things he has done!
    So loved he the world that he gave us his Son,
    who yielded his life an atonement for sin,
    and opened the life-gate that all may go in.
        Praise the Lord! Praise the Lord!
        Let the earth hear his voice!
        Praise the Lord! Praise the Lord!
        Let the people rejoice!
        Oh, come to the Father, through Jesus the Son,
        and give him the glory! Great things he has done!

2   O perfect redemption, the purchase of blood,
    to every believer the promise of God;
    for every offender who truly believes,
    that moment from Jesus a pardon receives.

3   Great things he has taught us, great things he has done,
    and great our rejoicing through Jesus the Son:
    but purer, and higher, and greater will be
    our joy and our wonder, when Jesus we see.

*Frances (Fanny) Jane Crosby (1820–1915)

Music William H. Doane (1832–1906), *adapted*

COURAGE BROTHER   87 87 D

trust   in God,   trust   in   God,   and____   do   the   right.

1   Courage, brother! do not stumble,
      though your path be dark as night;
      there's a star to guide the humble:
      trust in God, and do the right.
      Let the road be rough and dreary,
      and its end far out of sight;
      foot it bravely; strong or weary,
   * trust in God, and do the right.

2   Perish policy and cunning,
      perish all that fears the light!
      Whether losing, whether winning,
      trust in God, and do the right.
      Some will hate you, some will love you,
      some will flatter, some will slight;
      heed them not, and look above you:
      trust in God, and do the right.

3   Simple rule and safest guiding,
      inward peace and inward might,
      star upon our path abiding,
      trust in God and do the right.
      Courage, sister! do not stumble,
      though your path be dark as night;
      there's a star to guide the humble:
      trust in God, and do the right.

   * *The words 'trust in God' are sung three times.*

                          *Norman Macleod (1812–1872)

Music Arthur Seymour Sullivan (1842–1900)

ST GERTRUDE

6565 D and refrain

1. Onward! Christian soldiers,
marching as to war,
with the cross of Jesus
going on before.
Christ, the royal Master
leads against the foe;
forward into battle,
see! his banners go:
  Onward! Christian soldiers,
  marching as to war,
  with the cross of Jesus
  going on before.

2. At the sign of triumph
Satan's legions flee;
on then, Christian soldiers,
on to victory!
Hell's foundations quiver
at the shout of praise;
lift your hearts and voices,
loud your anthems raise:

3. Crowns and thrones may perish,
kingdoms rise and wane,
but the Church of Jesus
constant will remain;
gates of hell can never
'gainst that Church prevail;
we have Christ's own promise,
and that cannot fail:

4. Onward, then, you people,
join our happy throng;
blend with ours your voices
in the triumph song:
'Glory, laud and honour
unto Christ the King!'
This, through countless ages,
we with angels sing:

*Sabine Baring-Gould (1834–1924)

Music Arthur Seymour Sullivan (1842–1900), *adapted*

FROM STRENGTH TO STRENGTH   DSM

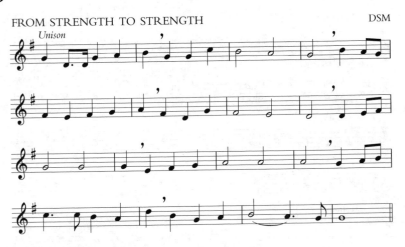

1   Soldiers of Christ, arise,
     and put your armour on,
     strong in the strength which God supplies
     through his eternal Son;
     strong in the Lord of hosts,
     and in his mighty power;
     who in the strength of Jesus trusts
     is more than conqueror.

2   Stand, then, in his great might,
     with all his strength endued;
     and take, to arm you for the fight,
     the panoply of God.
     To keep your armour bright
     attend with constant care,
     still walking in your Captain's sight,
     and watching unto prayer.

3   From strength to strength go on,
     wrestle, and fight, and pray;
     tread all the powers of darkness down,
     and win the well-fought day,
     that, having all things done
     and all your conflicts passed,
     you may o'ercome through Christ alone,
     and stand complete at last.

                         Charles Wesley (1707–1788)

Music Edward Woodall Naylor (1867–1934)

SIYAHAMBA

We are marching in the light of God,
we are marching in the light of God.
We are marching in the light of God,
we are marching in the light of God.
We are marching, O-o,
we are marching in the light of God,
we are marching, O-o,
we are marching in the light of God.

Original Xhosa text:
Siyahamb' ekukhanyen' kwenkhos',
siyahamb' ekukhanyen' kwenkhos'.
Siyahamb' ekukhanyen' kwenkhos',
siyahamb' ekukhanyen' kwenkhos'.
Siyahamba, O-o,
siyahamb' ekukhanyen' kwenkhos',
siyahamba, O-o,
siyahamb' ekukhanyen' kwenkhos'.

Xhosa (South African) traditional hymn
adapted Anders Nyberg (*b.* 1955)

Music South African traditional melody
arranged Anders Nyberg (*b.* 1955)

DUKE STREET　　　　　　　　　　　　　　　　　　　　LM

1　Fight the good fight with all your might;
　Christ is your strength, and Christ your right;
　lay hold on life, and it shall be
　your joy and crown eternally.

2　Run the straight race through God's good grace,
　lift up your eyes, and seek his face;
　life with its path before us lies;
　Christ is the way, and Christ the prize.

3　Cast care aside, lean on your Guide;
　his boundless mercy will provide.
　Trust, and your trusting soul shall prove
　Christ is its life, and Christ its love.

4　Faint not, nor fear; his arm is near;
　he does not change, and you are dear;
　only believe, and Christ shall be
　your all in all eternally.

*John Samuel Bewley Monsell (1811–1875)

Music Melody attributed to John L. Hatton (*d.*1793)
from Boyd's *Psalm and Hymn Tunes,* 1793
harmonised David Evans (1874–1948)

WOODLANDS   10 10 10 10

A simpler version is found at 286.

1   'Lift up your hearts!' We lift them, Lord, to thee;
here at thy feet none other may we see:
'Lift up your hearts!' Even so, with one accord,
we lift them up, we lift them to the Lord.

2   Above the level of the former years,
the mire of sin, the slough of guilty fears,
the mist of doubt, the blight of love's decay,
O Lord of light, lift all our hearts today!

3   Lift every gift that thou thyself hast given;
low lies the best till lifted up to heaven:
low lie the bounding heart, the teeming brain,
till, sent from God, they mount to God again.

4   Then, as the trumpet-call in after years,
'Lift up your hearts!' rings pealing in our ears,
still shall our hearts respond with full accord,
'We lift them up, we lift them to the Lord!'

Henry Montagu Butler (1833–1918)

Music Walter Greatorex (1877–1949)

HYFRYDOL

87 87 D

An alternative tune BLAENWERN *is found at 468.*

1   Love divine, all loves excelling,
    joy of heaven, to earth come down,
    fix in us thy humble dwelling,
    all thy faithful mercies crown.
    Jesus, thou art all compassion,
    pure, unbounded love thou art;
    visit us with thy salvation,
    enter every trembling heart.

2   Come, almighty to deliver;
    let us all thy life receive;
    suddenly return, and never,
    never more thy temples leave.
    Thee we would be always blessing,
    serve thee as thy hosts above,
    pray, and praise thee, without ceasing,
    glory in thy perfect love.

3   Finish then thy new creation:
    pure and spotless let us be;
    let us see thy great salvation
    perfectly restored in thee,
    changed from glory into glory,
    till in heaven we take our place,
    till we cast our crowns before thee,
    lost in wonder, love, and praise.

Charles Wesley (1707–1788)

Music Melody by Rowland Hugh Pritchard (1811–1887)
harmonised David Evans (1874–1948)

ST ANNE   CM

An alternative tune ST PETER *is found at 461.*

PARAPHRASE 52, verses 1, 3–6

1   Ye who the name of Jesus bear,
     his sacred steps pursue;
     and let that mind which was in him
     be also found in you.

2   His greatness he for us abased,
     for us his glory veiled;
     in human likeness dwelt on earth,
     his majesty concealed:

3   Nor only as a man appears,
     but stoops a servant low;
     submits to death, nay, bears the cross,
     in all its shame and woe.

4   Hence God this generous love to all
     with honours just hath crowned,
     and raised the name of Jesus far
     above all names renowned:

5   That at this name, with sacred awe,
     each humble knee should bow,
     of hosts immortal in the skies,
     and nations spread below.

Scottish Paraphrases, 1781
Phil. 2: 5, 7-10

Music Modern form of melody, 1708,
probably by William Croft (1678–1737)

INTERCESSOR   11 10 11 10

1   Children of God, reach out to one another!
Where pity dwells, the peace of God is there;
to worship rightly is to love each other,
each smile a hymn, each kindly deed a prayer.

2   For he whom Jesus loved has truly spoken:
the holier worship which God deigns to bless
restores the lost, and binds the spirit broken,
and feeds the widow and the fatherless.

3   Follow with reverent steps the great example
of him whose holy work was doing good;
so shall the wide earth seem our Father's temple,
each loving life a psalm of gratitude.

4   Then shall all shackles fall; the stormy clangour
of wild war-music o'er the earth shall cease;
love shall tread out the baleful fire of anger,
and in its ashes plant the tree of peace.

*John Greenleaf Whittier (1807–1892)

Music Charles Hubert Hastings Parry (1848–1918)

THE BARD OF ARMAGH   12 10 12 11 Irregular

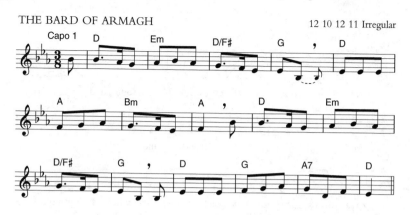

1   The Church is wherever God's people are praising,
knowing they're wanted and loved by their Lord.
The Church is wherever Christ's followers are trying
to live and to share out the good news of God.

2   The Church is wherever God's people are loving,
where all are forgiven and start once again,
where all are accepted, whatever their background,
whatever their past and whatever their pain.

3   The Church is wherever God's people are seeking
to reach out and touch folk wherever they are —
conveying the Gospel, its joy and its comfort,
to challenge, refresh, and excite and inspire.

4   The Church is wherever God's people are praising,
knowing we're wanted and loved by our Lord.
The Church is where we as Christ's followers are trying
to live and to share out the good news of God.

     Carol Rose Ikeler (*b.* 1920)

Music American cowboy melody, derived from Irish folk
melody, collected by John A. Lomax

CAREY'S FANCY   77 79

1   Hands to work and feet to run,
God's good gifts to me and you;
hands and feet he gave to us
to help each other the whole day through.

2   Eyes to see and ears to hear,
God's good gifts to me and you;
eyes and ears he gave to us
to help each other the whole day through.

3   Minds to think and hearts to love,
God's good gifts to me and you;
minds and hearts he gave to us
to help each other the whole day through.

Hilda Margaret Dodd
from *Child Songs,* 1910,
National Sunday School Union

Music Caribbean folk melody *arranged* Compilers

SANDOR
777 47

1   Jesus Christ, our living Lord,
       we believe you keep your word.
       Whatever may befall us,
         stretch or stall us,
       we'll trust your voice to call us.

2   In the humblest things we do,
       we'll account ourselves to you,
       making your love our measure,
         truth and treasure;
       your will our joy and pleasure.

3   Food enough that all may feed,
       grace enough for each one's need:
       here as we praise you, singing,
         you come bringing
       gifts at the day's beginning.

4   Lord in all we do today,
       let our lives prepare your way.
       May peace and love befriend us
         and defend us
       where you require and send us.

                       John L. Bell (*b.* 1949)

Music Sandor Szokolay (*b.* 1931)

HAVE YOU HEARD THE RAINDROPS

12 11 12 9 and refrain

1 Have you heard the rain-drops drum-ming on the roof-tops?
Have you heard the rain-drops drip-ping on the ground?
Have you heard the rain-drops splash-ing in the streams and
run-ning to the ri-vers all a-round? *There's wa--ter,
wa-ter of life. Je--sus gives us the wa-ter of life; there's
wa--ter, wa-ter of life, Je--sus gives us the wa-ter of life.*

Music Martyn Christian Tinne Strover (*b.*1932)

525 Words and Music: © Christian Strover / Jubilate Hymns, 4 Thorne Park Road, Chelston, Torquay TQ2 6RX
<enquiries@jubilate.co.uk> Used by permission.

1   Have you heard the raindrops drumming on the rooftops?
    Have you heard the raindrops dripping on the ground?
    Have you heard the raindrops splashing in the streams and
    running to the rivers all around?
      There's water, water of life,
      Jesus gives us the water of life;
      there's water, water of life,
      Jesus gives us the water of life.

2   There's a busy workman digging in the desert,
    digging with a spade that flashes in the sun;
    soon there will be water rising in the wellshaft,
    spilling from the bucket as it comes.

3   Nobody can live who hasn't any water,
    when the land is dry then nothing much grows;
    Jesus gives us life if we drink the living water,
    sing it so that everybody knows.

                    Martyn Christian Tinne Strover (*b.* 1932)

CANONMILLS   98 98

1 This is a day   of new be-gin-nings, time to re-mem – ber and move on,

time to   believe what love is bring-ing,   laying to rest the pain – that's gone.

1   This is a day of new beginnings,
     time to remember, and move on,
     time to believe what love is bringing,
     laying to rest the pain that's gone.

2   For by the life and death of Jesus,
     love's mighty Spirit, now as then,
     can make for us a world of difference
     as faith and hope are born again.

3   Then let us, with the Spirit's daring,
     step from the past and leave behind
     our disappointment, guilt and grieving,
     seeking new paths, and sure to find.

4   Christ is alive, and goes before us
     to show and share what love can do.
     This is a day of new beginnings —
     our God is making all things new.

*   In faith we'll gather round the table
     to show and share what love can do.
     This is a day of new beginnings —
     our God is making all things new.

*   *Alternative text (v. 4) for Holy Communion*

                         Brian Wren (*b.* 1936)

Music Douglas Galbraith (*b.* 1940)

526   Words: © 1983, 1987, Stainer & Bell Ltd, PO Box 110, Victoria House, 23 Gruneisen Road, London N3 1DZ
526   Music: © Douglas Galbraith

O WALY WALY   LM

1   Lord, make us servants of your peace:
     where there is hate, may we sow love;
     where there is hurt, may we forgive;
     where there is strife, may we make one.

2   Where all is doubt, may we sow faith;
     where all is gloom, may we sow hope;
     where all is night, may we sow light;
     where all is tears, may we sow joy.

3   Jesus, our Lord, may we not seek
     to be consoled, but to console,
     nor look to understanding hearts,
     but look for hearts to understand.

4   May we not look for love's return,
     but seek to love unselfishly,
     for in our giving we receive,
     and in forgiving are forgiven.

5   Dying, we live, and are reborn
     through death's dark night to endless day;
     Lord, make us servants of your peace
     to wake at last in heaven's light.

                              James Quinn (*b.* 1919)

Music English traditional melody
arranged Compilers of *Church Hymnary,* 3rd edition, 1973

528

PRAYER OF ST FRANCIS (CHANNEL OF PEACE)   irregular

1 Make me a chan-nel of your peace.____ Where there is ha-tred let me bring your love;____ where there is in-ju-ry, your par-don, Lord;____ and__ where there's doubt, true faith____ in__ you.____ Oh, Mas-ter, grant that I may ne-ver seek____ so much to be con-soled as to con-sole;____ to be un-der-stood as to un-der-stand;____ to be loved, as to love with all my soul.____

Music Sebastian Temple (1928–1997)
arranged Betty Jane Pulkingham (*b.* 1928)

1 Make me a channel of your peace.
   Where there is hatred let me bring your love;
   where there is injury, your pardon, Lord;
   and where there's doubt, true faith in you.
       Oh, Master, grant that I may never seek
       so much to be consoled as to console;
       to be understood as to understand;
       to be loved, as to love with all my soul.

2 Make me a channel of your peace.
   Where there's despair in life let me bring hope;
   where there is darkness, only light;
   and where there's sadness, ever joy.

3 Make me a channel of your peace.
   It is in pardoning that we are pardoned,
   in giving of ourselves that we receive;
   and in dying that we're born to eternal life.

Sebastian Temple (1928–1997)
from the *Prayer of St Francis*

KILLIBEGS   LM
Steadily

An alternative tune WARRINGTON *is found at 470.*

1   Forth in thy name, O Lord, I go,
my daily labour to pursue,
thee, only thee, resolved to know
in all I think, or speak, or do.

2   The task thy wisdom hath assigned
oh, let me cheerfully fulfil,
in all my works thy presence find,
and prove thy good and perfect will.

3   Thee may I set at my right hand,
whose eyes my inmost substance see,
and labour on at thy command,
and offer all my works to thee.

4   Give me to bear thy easy yoke,
and every moment watch and pray,
and still to things eternal look,
and hasten to thy glorious day;

5   For thee delightfully employ
whate'er thy bounteous grace has given,
and run my course with even joy,
and closely walk with thee to heaven.

Charles Wesley (1707–1788)

Music William Davies (*b.* 1921)

SOUTHCOTE   99 79 and refrain
Unison

1. One more step along the world I go,
    one more step along the world I go;
    from the old things to the new
    keep me travelling along with you:
        And it's from the old I travel to the new;
        keep me travelling along with you.

2. Round the corners of the world I turn,
    more and more about the world I learn;
    all the new things that I see
    you'll be looking at along with me:

3. As I travel through the bad and good,
    keep me travelling the way I should;
    where I see no way to go
    you'll be telling me the way, I know:

4. Give me courage when the world is rough,
    keep me loving though the world is tough;
    leap and sing in all I do,
    keep me travelling along with you:

5. You are older than the world can be,
    you are younger than the life in me;
    ever old and ever new,
    keep me travelling along with you:

Sydney Bertram Carter (1915–2004)

Music Sydney Bertram Carter (1915–2004)

My Je-sus, my Sav-iour, Lord there is none like you.
All of my days I want to praise the won-ders of your
migh-ty love. My com-fort, my shel-ter,
tow-er of re-fuge and strength, let ev-ery breath, all that I am,
never cease to wor-ship you.

Refrain

Shout to the Lord all the earth, let us sing, pow-er and ma-
I sing for joy at the work of your hands. For ev-er I'll love

- jes-ty, praise to the King. Moun-tains bow down and the seas
you, for ev - - er I'll stand. No-thing com-pares to the pro-

will roar at the sound of your name.

- - mise I have in you.

My Jesus, my Saviour,
Lord, there is none like you.
All of my days I want to praise
the wonders of your mighty love.
My comfort, my shelter,
tower of refuge and strength,
let every breath, all that I am,
never cease to worship you.

Shout to the Lord all the earth, let us sing,
power and majesty, praise to the King.
Mountains bow down and the seas will roar
at the sound of your name.
I sing for joy at the work of your hands,
for ever I'll love you, for ever I'll stand.
Nothing compares to the promise I have in you.

Darlene Zschech

Music and words Darlene Zschech

PESCADOR DE HOMBRES

1 Lord, you have come to the sea - shore, nei - ther search - ing for the rich nor the wise, de - sir - ing on - ly that I should fol - low.

Refrain

O Lord, *with your eyes set up - on me, gent - ly smil - ing, you have spo - ken my* name. *All I longed for I have found by the wa - ter, at your* side *I will seek o - ther shores.*

Music Cesáreo Gabaráin (1936–1991)

Tú has venido a la orilla

1 Lord, you have come to the seashore,
neither searching for the rich nor the wise,
desiring only that I should follow.
  O Lord, with your eyes set upon me,
  gently smiling, you have spoken my name.
  All I longed for I have found by the water,
  at your side I will seek other shores.

2 Lord, see my goods, my possessions;
in my boat you find no power, no wealth.
Will you accept, then, my nets and labour?

3 Lord, take my hands, and direct them.
Help me spend myself in seeking the lost,
returning love for the love you gave me.

4 Lord, as I drift on the waters,
be the resting-place of my restless heart,
my life's companion, my friend and refuge.

Cesáreo Gabaráin (1936–1991)
translated Robert Trupia

KELVINGROVE

This may be sung in duple time by treating minims as crotchets.

1   Will you come and follow me
    if I but call your name?
    Will you go where you don't know
    and never be the same?
    Will you let my love be shown,
    will you let my name be known,
    will you let my life be grown
    in you and you in me?

2   Will you leave yourself behind
    if I but call your name?
    Will you care for cruel and kind
    and never be the same?
    Will you risk the hostile stare
    should your life attract or scare?
    Will you let me answer prayer
    in you and you in me?

Music Scottish folk melody
arranged John L. Bell (*b.*1949)

3   Will you let the blinded see
     if I but call your name?
     Will you set the prisoners free
     and never be the same?
     Will you kiss the leper clean,
     and do such as this unseen,
     and admit to what I mean
     in you and you in me?

4   Will you love the 'you' you hide
     if I but call your name?
     Will you quell the fear inside
     and never be the same?
     Will you use the faith you've found
     to reshape the world around,
     through my sight and touch and sound
     in you and you in me?

5   Lord, your summons echoes true
     when you but call my name.
     Let me turn and follow you
     and never be the same.
     In your company I'll go
     where your love and footsteps show.
     Thus I'll move and live and grow
     in you and you in me.

The first four verses may be sung by a solo voice,
to which the congregation responds by singing verse 5.

John L. Bell *(b. 1949)*
and Graham Maule *(b. 1958)*

LEOMINSTER   DSM

1 Make me a captive, Lord,
   and then I shall be free;
   force me to render up my
      sword,
   and I shall conqueror be.
   I sink in life's alarms
   when by myself I stand;
   imprison me within thine
      arms,
   and strong shall be my hand.

2 My heart is weak and poor
   until it master find;
   it has no spring of action sure,
   it varies with the wind.
   It cannot freely move
   till thou hast wrought its chain;
   enslave it with thy matchless
      love,
   and deathless it shall reign.

3 My power is faint and low
   till I have learned to serve;
   it wants the needed fire to
      glow,
   it wants the breeze to nerve;
   it cannot drive the world,
   until itself be driven;
   its flag can only be unfurled
   when thou shalt breathe from
      heaven.

4 My will is not my own
   till thou hast made it thine;
   if it would reach a monarch's
      throne
   it must its crown resign;
   it only stands unbent,
   amid the clashing strife,
   when on thy bosom it has leant
   and found in thee its life.

George Matheson (1842–1906)

Music George William Martin (1828–1881)
arranged Arthur Seymour Sullivan (1842–1900)

MONKS GATE   6565 6665

1   Who would true valour see,
let him come hither;
one here will constant be,
come wind, come weather;
there's no discouragement
shall make him once relent
his first avowed intent
to be a pilgrim.

2   Whoso beset him round
with dismal stories,
do but themselves confound;
his strength the more is.
No lion can him fright;
he'll with a giant fight,
but he will have a right
to be a pilgrim.

3   Hobgoblin nor foul fiend
can daunt his spirit;
he knows he at the end
shall life inherit.
Then fancies fly away;
he'll fear not what men say;
he'll labour night and day
to be a pilgrim.

John Bunyan (1628–1688)

Music English traditional melody
adapted Ralph Vaughan Williams (1872–1958)

535 Adaptation: From *The English Hymnal*, 1906, Oxford University Press, Great Clarendon Street, Oxford. OX2 6DP.
Reproduced by permission.

CANDLEBEAM   87 85

1 May the mind of Christ my Sa-viour live in me from day to day,

by his love and power con-trol - ling all I do or say.

1   May the mind of Christ my Saviour
        live in me from day to day,
        by his love and power controlling
        all I do or say.

2   May the word of God dwell richly
        in my heart from hour to hour,
        so that all may see I triumph
        only through his power.

3   May the peace of God my Father
        in my life for ever reign;
        that I may be calm to comfort
        those in grief, or pain.

4   May the love of Jesus fill me,
        as the waters fill the sea;
        him exalting, self denying,
        this is victory.

5   May I run the race before me,
        strong and brave to face the foe,
        drawing all my strength from Jesus
        as I onward go.

*Katie Barclay Wilkinson (1859–1928)

Music Alison M. Robertson (*b.* 1940)

MARY MORISON   DLM

1   We do not hope to ease our minds
by simple answers, shifted blame,
while Christ is homeless, hungry, poor,
and we are rich who bear his name.
As long as justice is a dream
and human dignity denied,
we stand with Christ; disturb us still
till every need is satisfied.

2   We cannot ask to live at peace
in comfort and security
while Christ is tried in Pilate's hall
and drags his cross to Calvary.
As long as hatred stifles truth
and freedom is betrayed by fear,
we stand with Christ; give us no peace
till his peace reigns in triumph here.

3   We will not pray to be preserved
from any depths of agony
while Christ's despairing cry rings out:
God, why have you abandoned me?
As long as we have hope to share
of life renewed beyond the pain,
we stand with Christ all through the night
till Easter morning dawns again.

Marnie Barrell (*b.* 1952)

Music Scottish folk melody
arranged John L. Bell (*b.* 1949)

GOD BE IN MY HEAD

Irregular

God be in my head,
and in my un - der - stand - ing; God be in mine
eyes, and in my look - ing; God be in my
mouth, and in my speak - ing; God be in my
heart, and in my think - - ing;
God be at mine _ end, and at my de - part - ing.

God be in my head, and in my understanding;
God be in mine eyes, and in my looking;
God be in my mouth, and in my speaking;
God be in my heart, and in my thinking;
God be at mine end, and at my departing.

Book of Hours 1514

Music Henry Walford Davies (1869–1941)

SOJOURNER   88 89

Slowly

1 I want Je - sus to walk with me;
I want Je - sus to walk with me;
all a - long my pil - grim jour - ney,
oh, I want Je - sus to walk with me.

1   I want Jesus to walk with me;
      I want Jesus to walk with me;
      all along my pilgrim journey,
      oh, I want Jesus to walk with me.

2   In my trials, Lord, walk with me;
      in my trials, Lord, walk with me;
      when my heart is almost breaking,
      oh, I want Jesus to walk with me.

3   When I'm troubled, Lord, walk with me;
      when I'm troubled, Lord, walk with me;
      when my head is bowed in sorrow,
      oh, I want Jesus to walk with me.

                          African–American spiritual

Music African-American spiritual
harmonised Judge Jefferson Cleveland (1937–1986) and Verolga Nix

THE ROWAN TREE
DCM irregular

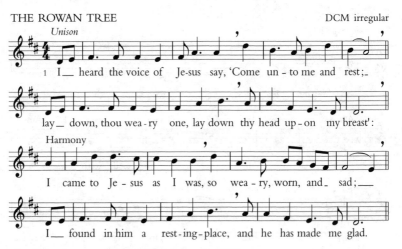

1 I heard the voice of Jesus say, 'Come unto me and rest;
lay down, thou weary one, lay down thy head upon my breast':
I came to Jesus as I was, so weary, worn, and sad;
I found in him a resting-place, and he has made me glad.

An alternative tune KINGSFOLD is found at 291.

1   I heard the voice of Jesus say,
    'Come unto me and rest;
    lay down, thou weary one, lay down
    thy head upon my breast':
    I came to Jesus as I was,
    so weary, worn, and sad;
    I found in him a resting-place,
    and he has made me glad.

2   I heard the voice of Jesus say,
    'Behold, I freely give
    the living water; thirsty one,
    stoop down and drink, and live':
    I came to Jesus, and I drank
    of that life-giving stream;
    my thirst was quenched, my soul revived,
    and now I live in him.

3   I heard the voice of Jesus say,
    'I am this dark world's Light;
    Look unto me, thy morn shall rise,
    and all thy day be bright':
    I looked to Jesus, and I found
    in him my Star, my Sun;
    and in that light of life I'll walk,
    till travelling days are done.

Horatius N. Bonar (1808–1889)

Music Scottish traditional melody, *arranged* Compilers

KLOKJE KLINKT   67 67

1   Lord, I pray, if today
    someone wrongs or troubles me,
    make me kind; bring to mind
    that forgiveness makes us free.

2   Lord, I pray, if today
    joy should fill my heart with song,
    help me raise thanks and praise
    for your goodness, sure and strong.

3   Lord, today if I stray,
    show the road I ought to take.
    When I fear, Lord, be near;
    hear my prayer for your love's sake.

                    Jean C. Keegstra-DeBoer

Music Dutch melody
arranged Grace Schwanda

WINSCOTT   LM

1   Lord, speak to me, that I may speak
in living echoes of your tone;
as you have sought, so let me seek
your erring children lost and lone.

2   O lead me, Lord, that I may lead
the wandering and the wavering feet;
O feed me, Lord, that I may feed
your hungering ones with manna sweet.

3   O strengthen me, that, while I stand
firm on the rock, secure and free,
I may stretch out a loving hand
to wrestlers with the troubled sea.

4   O teach me, Lord, that I may teach
the precious things which you impart;
and wing my words, that they may reach
the hidden depths of many a heart.

5   O fill me with your fullness, Lord,
until my very heart o'erflow
in kindling thought and glowing word,
your love to tell, your praise to show.

6   O use me, Lord, use even me,
just as you will, and when, and where,
until at last your face I see,
your rest, your joy, your glory share.

Frances Ridley Havergal (1836–1879)

Music Samuel Sebastian Wesley (1810–1876)

CHRIST BE OUR LIGHT   98 96 and refrain

1 Longing for light, we wait in darkness;
  longing for truth we turn to you.
  Make us your own, your holy people,
  light for the world to see.

*Christ, be our light! Shine in our hearts.
Shine through the darkness. Christ, be our light!
Shine in your Church gathered today.*

1   Longing for light, we wait in darkness.
     Longing for truth, we turn to you.
     Make us your own, your holy people,
     light for the world to see.
         Christ, be our light!
         Shine in our hearts.
         Shine through the darkness.
         Christ, be our light!
         Shine in your Church gathered today.

2   Longing for peace, our world is troubled.
     Longing for hope, many despair.
     Your word alone has power to save us.
     Make us your living voice.

continued overleaf

Music Bernadette Farrell (*b.* 1957)

LIFE IN CHRIST

Christ,   be   our   light!   Shine   in   our   hearts.

Shine through the   dark - - ness.   Christ,   be   our   light!

Shine   in   your Church   gath - ered   to - day.

3   Longing for food, many are hungry.
     Longing for water, many still thirst.
     Make us your bread, broken for others,
     shared until all are fed.

4   Longing for shelter, many are homeless.
     Longing for warmth, many are cold.
     Make us your building, sheltering others,
     walls made of living stone.

5   Many the gifts, many the people,
     many the hearts that yearn to belong.
     Let us be servants to one another,
     making your kingdom come.

Bernadette Farrell (*b.*1957)

NEIGHBOUR

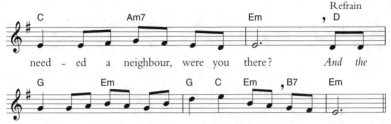

1. When I needed a neighbour, were you there, were you there?
When I needed a neighbour, were you there?
And the creed and the colour and the name won't matter,
were you there?

2. I was hungry and thirsty, were you there, were you there?
I was hungry and thirsty, were you there?

3. I was cold, I was naked, were you there, were you there?
I was cold, I was naked, were you there?

4. When I needed a shelter, were you there, were you there?
When I needed a shelter, were you there?

5. When I needed a healer, were you there, were you there?
When I needed a healer, were you there?

6. Wherever you travel I'll be there, I'll be there,
wherever you travel I'll be there.
And the creed and the colour and the name won't matter,
I'll be there.

Sydney Bertram Carter (1915–2004)

Music Sydney Bertram Carter (1915–2004)

Also suitable

Lord, can this really be?	205
As a fire is meant for burning	252
Jesus Christ is waiting	360
View the present through the promise	479
Thuma mina	800

545

OUR RESPONSE TO CHRIST
IN DEVOTION

EDGBASTON   CM

1   Lord, teach us how to pray aright
    with reverence and with fear;
    though fallen sinners in thy sight,
    we may, we must, draw near.

2   Our spirits fail through lack of prayer:
    oh, grant us power to pray;
    and, when to meet thee we prepare,
    Lord, meet us by the way.

3   God of all grace, we bring to thee
    a broken, contrite heart;
    give what thine eye delights to see —
    truth in the inward part;

4   Trust in the only sacrifice
    that can for sin atone,
    to cast our hopes, to fix our eyes,
    on Christ, on Christ alone;

5   Patience to watch and wait and weep,
    though mercy long delay;
    and courage our faint souls to keep,
    with faith in thee alway.

6   Give these, and then thy will be done;
    thus, strengthened with all might,
    we, through thy Spirit and thy Son,
    shall pray and pray aright.

                    *James Montgomery (1771–1854)

Music John Joubert (*b.* 1927)

COLESHILL   CM

1   Prayer is the soul's sincere desire,
        unuttered or expressed,
        the motion of a hidden fire
        that trembles in the breast.

2   Prayer is the burden of a sigh,
        the falling of a tear,
        the upward glancing of an eye
        when none but God is near.

3   Prayer is the simplest form of speech
        that infant lips can try;
        prayer the sublimest strains that reach
        the Majesty on high.

4   Prayer is the Christian's vital breath,
        the Christian's native air,
        our watchword at the gates of death,
        we enter heaven with prayer.

5   Prayer is not made by us alone:
        the Holy Spirit pleads,
        and Jesus, on the eternal throne,
        for sinners intercedes.

6   O Christ, by whom we come to God,
        the Life, the Truth, the Way,
        the path of prayer yourself have trod,
        Lord, teach us how to pray.

James Montgomery (1771–1854)

Music Melody from Barton's *The Psalms of David in Metre*,
Dublin, 1706, later form
harmonised Compilers of *Church Hymnary*, 3rd edition, 1973

CONVERSE

87 87 D

An alternative tune WHITE ROSETTES *is found at 295.*

1   What a friend we have in Jesus,
    all our sins and griefs to bear!
    What a privilege to carry
    everything to God in prayer!
    Oh, what peace we often forfeit,
    oh, what needless pain we bear,
    all because we do not carry
    everything to God in prayer!

2   Have we trials and temptations,
    is there trouble anywhere?
    We should never be discouraged:
    take it to the Lord in prayer.
    Can we find a friend so faithful,
    who will all our sorrows share?
    Jesus knows our every weakness:
    take it to the Lord in prayer.

3   Are we weak and heavy-laden,
    cumbered with a load of care?
    Jesus is our only refuge:
    take it to the Lord in prayer.
    Do your friends despise, forsake you?
    Take it to the Lord in prayer!
    In his arms he'll take and shield you;
    you will find a solace there.

                    Joseph Scriven (1819–1886)

Music Charles Crozat Converse (1832–1918)

STRACATHRO   CM

A lower setting is found at 637.

1   Approach, my soul, the mercy-seat,
         where Jesus answers prayer;
         there humbly fall before his feet,
         for none can perish there.

2   Thy promise is my only plea;
         with this I venture nigh:
         thou callest burdened souls to thee,
         and such, O Lord, am I.

3   Bowed down beneath a load of sin,
         by Satan sorely pressed,
         by war without and fears within,
         I come to thee for rest.

4   Be thou my shield and hiding-place,
         that, sheltered near thy side,
         I may my fierce accuser face,
         and tell him thou hast died.

5   O wondrous love! to bleed and die,
         to bear the cross and shame,
         that guilty sinners, such as I,
         might plead thy gracious name!

                                     John Newton (1725–1807)

Music Charles Hutcheson (1792–1860)
harmonised David Evans (1874–1948)

HOW DEEP THE FATHER'S LOVE 87 87 D

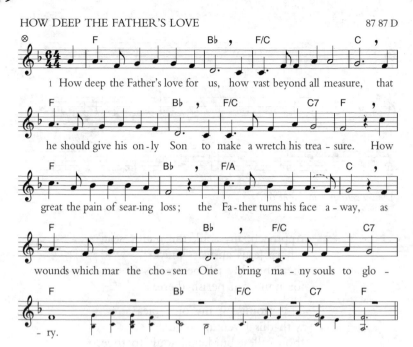

1 How deep the Father's love for us, how vast beyond all measure, that he should give his on-ly Son to make a wretch his trea-sure. How great the pain of sear-ing loss; the Fa-ther turns his face a-way, as wounds which mar the cho-sen One bring ma-ny souls to glo-ry.

Music Stuart Townend

549 Words and Music: © 1995, Thankyou Music. Administered (UK and Europe) by kingswaysongs.com <tym@kingsway.co.uk>. Remaining territories administered by worshiptogether.com songs. Used by permission.

1 How deep the Father's love for us,
   how vast beyond all measure,
   that he should give his only Son
   to make a wretch his treasure.
   How great the pain of searing loss;
   the Father turns his face away,
   as wounds which mar the chosen One
   bring many souls to glory.

2 Behold the man upon a cross,
   my sin upon his shoulders;
   ashamed, I hear my mocking voice
   call out among the scoffers.
   It was my sin that held him there,
   my pardon he accomplished;
   his dying breath has brought me life —
   I know that 'it is finished'.

3 I will not boast in anything,
   no gifts, no power, no wisdom;
   but I will boast in Jesus Christ,
   his death and resurrection.
   Why should I gain from all of this?
   I cannot give an answer;
   but this I know with all my heart,
   his wounds have paid my ransom.

                              Stuart Townend

AS THE DEER PANTS 87 87 89 87

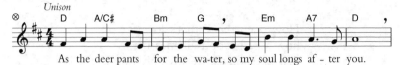

As the deer pants for the wa-ter, so my soul longs af – ter you.

You a – lone are my heart's de – sire, _ and I long to wor – ship you.

You a – lone are my strength, my shield, to you a – lone may my spi – rit yield.

You a – lone are my heart's de – sire, _ and I long to wor – ship you.

1. As the deer pants for the water,
   so my soul longs after you.
   You alone are my heart's desire,
   and I long to worship you.
   You alone are my strength, my shield,
   to you alone may my spirit yield.
   You alone are my heart's desire,
   and I long to worship you.

2. I want you more than gold or silver;
   only you can satisfy.
   You alone are the real joy-giver,
   and the apple of my eye.

3. You're my friend and you are my brother,
   even though you are a King.
   I love you more than any other,
   so much more than anything.

Martin J. Nystrom (b. 1956)

Music Martin J. Nystrom (b. 1956)
adapted Compilers

PENLAN   76 76 D

1   In heavenly love abiding,
       no change my heart shall fear;
       and safe is such confiding,
       for nothing changes here:
       the storm may roar without me,
       my heart may low be laid;
       but God is round about me,
       and can I be dismayed?

2   Wherever he may guide me,
       no want shall turn me back;
       my Shepherd is beside me,
       and nothing can I lack.
       His wisdom ever waketh,
       his sight is never dim:
       he knows the way he taketh,
       and I will walk with him.

3   Green pastures are before me,
       which yet I have not seen;
       bright skies will soon be o'er me,
       where darkening clouds have been.
       My hope I cannot measure:
       my path to life is free:
       my Saviour has my treasure,
       and he will walk with me.

Anna Laetitia Waring (1823–1910)

Music David Jenkins (1849–1915)

MARTYRDOM (FENWICK) CM

THE FLOWER O' THE QUERN DCM

Slowly

Music Tune 1 Hugh Wilson (1766–1824)
adapted Robert Archibald Smith (1780–1829)

Music Tune 2 J. Scott Skinner (1843–1927)
arranged John P. Kitchen (b. 1950)

1   Oh, for a closer walk with God,
    a calm and heavenly frame,
    a light to shine upon the road
    that leads me to the Lamb!

2   Where is the blessedness I knew
    when first I saw the Lord?
    Where is the soul-refreshing view
    of Jesus and his word?

3   What peaceful hours I once enjoyed!
    How sweet their memory still!
    But they have left an aching void
    the world can never fill.

4   Return, O Holy Dove! return,
    sweet messenger of rest!
    I hate the sins that made thee mourn,
    and drove thee from my breast.

5   The dearest idol I have known,
    whate'er that idol be,
    help me to tear it from thy throne,
    and worship only thee.

6   So shall my walk be close with God,
    calm and serene my frame;
    so purer light shall mark the road
    that leads me to the Lamb.

When sung to THE FLOWER OF THE QUERN,
two verses of text are sung to each verse of music.

William Cowper (1731–1800)

SAFFRON WALDEN   8886

553 2

MISERICORDIA   8886

Music Tune 1 Arthur Henry Brown (1830–1926)
Music Tune 2 Henry Thomas Smart (1813–1879)

1   Just as I am, without one plea
    but that your blood was shed for me,
    and that you call us, 'Come to me',
    O Lamb of God, I come.

2   Just as I am, though tossed about
    with many a conflict, many a doubt,
    fightings and fears within, without,
    O Lamb of God, I come.

3   Just as I am you will receive,
    will welcome, pardon, cleanse, relieve;
    because your promise I believe,
    O Lamb of God, I come.

4   Just as I am — your love unknown
    has broken every barrier down —
    now to be yours, and yours alone,
    O Lamb of God, I come.

5   Just as I am, of that free love
    the breadth, length, depth, and height to prove,
    here for a season, then above —
    O Lamb of God, I come.

                    Charlotte Elliott (1789–1871)

PETRA (REDHEAD No. 76)   7777 77

1   Rock of ages cleft for me,
    let me hide myself in thee;
    let the water and the blood,
    from thy riven side which flowed,
    be of sin the double cure,
    cleanse me from its guilt and power.

2   Not the labours of my hands
    can fulfil thy law's demands;
    could my zeal no respite know,
    could my tears for ever flow,
    all for sin could not atone:
    thou must save, and thou alone.

3   Nothing in my hand I bring,
    simply to thy cross I cling;
    naked, come to thee for dress;
    helpless, look to thee for grace;
    stained by sin, to thee I fly;
    wash me, Saviour, or I die.

4   While I draw this fleeting breath,
    when my eyelids close in death,
    when I soar through realms unknown,
    see thee on thy judgement throne,
    Rock of ages, cleft for me,
    let me hide myself in thee.

        Augustus Montague Toplady (1740–1778)

Music Richard Redhead (1820–1901)
Church Hymn Tunes, 1853

AMAZING GRACE (NEW BRITAIN)   CM

55 2

AMAZING GRACE (NEW BRITAIN)   CM

1   Amazing grace! how sweet the sound
that saved a wretch like me!
I once was lost, but now am found,
was blind, but now I see.

2   'Twas grace that taught my heart to fear,
and grace my fears relieved;
how precious did that grace appear
the hour I first believed!

3   Through many dangers, toils, and snares
I have already come;
'tis grace has brought me safe thus far,
and grace will lead me home.

4   The Lord has promised good to me,
his word my hope secures;
he will my shield and portion be
as long as life endures.

John Newton (1725–1807)

Music Tunes 1 & 2 Scottish traditional melody
arranged John L. Bell (b. 1949)

I NEED THEE

64 64 and refrain

Refrain

1   I need thee every hour,
    most gracious Lord;
    no tender voice but thine
    can peace afford.
      I need thee, oh, I need thee,
      every hour I need thee;
      O bless me now, my Saviour,
      I come to thee.

2   I need thee every hour,
    stay thou near by;
    temptations lose their power
    when thou art nigh.

3   I need thee every hour,
    in joy or pain;
    come quickly and abide,
    or life is vain.

4   I need thee every hour,
    teach me thy will;
    and thy rich promises
    in me fulfil.

          Annie Sherwood Hawks (1835–1918)

Music Robert Lowry (1826–1899)

ST MARGARET   88 886

1   O Love that wilt not let me go,
       I rest my weary soul in thee:
       I give thee back the life I owe,
       that in thine ocean depths its flow
       may richer, fuller be.

2   O Light that followest all my way,
       I yield my flickering torch to thee:
       my heart restores its borrowed ray,
       that in thy sunshine's blaze its day
       may brighter, fairer be.

3   O Joy that seekest me through pain,
       I cannot close my heart to thee:
       I trace the rainbow through the rain,
       and feel the promise is not vain,
       that morn shall tearless be.

4   O Cross that liftest up my head,
       I dare not ask to fly from thee:
       I lay in dust life's glory dead,
       and from the ground there blossoms red
       life that shall endless be.

George Matheson (1842–1906)

Music Albert Lister Peace (1844–1912)

Lord, I lift your name on high,
Lord, I love to sing your praises;
I'm so glad you're in my life,
I'm so glad you came to save us.
You came from heaven to earth to show the way,
from the earth to the cross my debt to pay,
from the cross to the grave, from the grave to the sky:
Lord, I lift your name on high.

Rick Founds

Music Rick Founds

6585

1 There is a Re-deem-er, Je-sus, God's own Son,___ pre-cious Lamb of God, Mes-si-ah, Ho - - - ly One. *Thank you, O my Fa- -ther, for giv-ing us your Son,___ and leav-ing us your Spi-rit till your work on___ earth is done. done.*

1   There is a Redeemer,
     Jesus, God's own Son,
     precious Lamb of God, Messiah,
     Holy One.
          Thank you, O my Father,
          for giving us your Son,
          and leaving us your Spirit
          till your work on earth is done.

2   Jesus, my Redeemer,
     name above all names,
     precious Lamb of God, Messiah,
     once for sinners slain:

3   When I stand in glory
     I will see his face,
     and there I'll serve my King for ever
     in that holy place.

Melody Green (b. 1946)

Music Melody Green (b. 1946)

ST AGNES (DYKES)

CM

Jesu dulcis memoria

1   Jesus, the very thought of thee
with sweetness fills my breast;
but sweeter far thy face to see,
and in thy presence rest.

2   Nor voice can sing, nor heart can frame,
nor can the memory find
a sweeter sound than thy blest name,
Saviour of humankind!

3   O hope of every contrite heart,
O joy of all the meek,
to those who fall how kind thou art!
how good to those who seek!

4   But what to those who find? Ah, this
nor tongue nor pen can show;
the love of Jesus, what it is
none but his loved ones know.

5   Jesus, our only joy be thou,
as thou our prize wilt be;
Jesus, be thou our glory now,
and through eternity.

Probably 12th century
translated *Edward Caswell (1814–1878)
Lyra Catholica, 1849

Music John Bacchus Dykes (1823–1876)

BLESSED ASSURANCE   99 99 and refrain

1   Blessed assurance, Jesus is mine!
Oh, what a foretaste of glory divine!
Heir of salvation, purchase of God;
born of his Spirit, washed in his blood.
     This is my story, this is my song,
     praising my Saviour all the day long.
     This is my story, this is my song,
     praising my Saviour all the day long.

2   Perfect submission, perfect delight,
visions of rapture burst on my sight;
angels descending bring from above
echoes of mercy, whispers of love.

3   Perfect submission, all is at rest,
I in my Saviour am happy and blest;
watching and waiting, looking above,
filled with his goodness, lost in his love.

Frances (Fanny) Jane Crosby (1820–1915)

Music Phoebe Palmer Knapp (1839–1908)

AR HYD Y NOS   84 84 88 84

1   Through the love of God, our Saviour,
all will be well.
Free and changeless is his favour;
all, all is well.
Precious is the blood that healed us,
perfect is the grace that sealed us,
strong the hand stretched forth to shield us;
all must be well.

2   Though we pass through tribulation,
all will be well.
Ours is such a full salvation,
all, all is well.
Happy still in God confiding,
fruitful, if in Christ abiding,
holy, through the Spirit's guiding;
all must be well.

3   We expect a bright tomorrow;
all will be well.
Faith can sing through days of sorrow,
'All, all is well.'
On our Father's love relying,
Jesus every need supplying,
in our living, in our dying,
all must be well.

Mary Peters (1813–1856)

Music Welsh traditional melody
harmonised Compilers of *English Hymnal,* 1906

GAELIC LULLABY 7777 and refrain

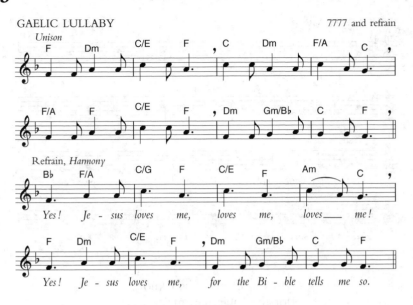

Yes! Je - sus loves me, loves me, loves____ me!

Yes! Je - sus loves me, for the Bi - ble tells me so.

1   Jesus loves me! this I know,
    for the Bible tells me so;
    little ones to him belong;
    they are weak, but he is strong.
        Yes! Jesus loves me, loves me, loves me!
        Yes! Jesus loves me,
        for the Bible tells me so.

2   Jesus loves me! this I know:
    he loved children long ago;
    he can always make me glad,
    even when I'm feeling sad.

3   Jesus loves me! he will stay
    close beside me all the way;
    he will always be my friend,
    and his love will never end.

                    *Anna Bartlett Warner (1820–1915)

Music Gaelic traditional melody
arranged Compilers of *Church Hymnary,* 3rd edition, 1973

JESUS LOVES ME   7777 and refrain

Yes! Je - sus loves me! Yes! Je - sus loves me!

Yes! Je - sus loves me! The Bi - ble tells me so.

1   Jesus loves me! this I know,
for the Bible tells me so;
little ones to him belong;
they are weak, but he is strong.
Yes! Jesus loves me!
Yes! Jesus loves me!
Yes! Jesus loves me!
The Bible tells me so.

2   Jesus loves me! this I know
he loved children long ago;
he can always make me glad,
even when I'm feeling sad.

3   Jesus loves me! he will stay
close beside me all the way;
he will always be my friend,
and his love will never end.

*Anna Bartlett Warner (1820–1915)

Music William Batchelder Bradbury (1816–1868)

HOW CAN I KEEP FROM SINGING   87 87 and refrain

1. My life flows on in endless song above earth's lamentation: I catch the sweet, though far off hymn that hails a new creation. No storm can shake my inmost calm while to that Rock I'm clinging. Since love is Lord of heaven and earth, how can I keep from singing?

1.   My life flows on in endless song
    above earth's lamentation:
    I catch the sweet, though far off, hymn
    that hails a new creation.
        No storm can shake my inmost calm
        while to that Rock I'm clinging.
        Since love is Lord of heaven and earth,
        how can I keep from singing?

2.   Through all the tumult and the strife,
    I hear that music ringing.
    It finds an echo in my soul —
    how can I keep from singing?

3.   What though my joys and comforts die?
    The Lord, my Saviour, liveth.
    What though the darkness round me close?
    Songs in the night he giveth.

4.   The peace of Christ makes fresh my heart,
    a fountain ever springing.
    All things are mine since I am his!
    How can I keep from singing?

Robert Lowry (1822–1899)
and Doris Plenn

Music American traditional melody
arranged Compilers of *Common Ground,* 1998

SEVEN JOYS OF MARY   87 87 D

1   When I receive the peace of Christ
my loneliness shall end;
and I must reach a hand and take
my brother as a friend —
my brother as a friend indeed
who has an honoured place
where he may stand before the Lord
in dignity and grace.

2   When I receive the peace of Christ
my loneliness shall end;
and I must reach a hand and take
my sister as a friend —
my sister as a friend indeed
who has an honoured place
where she may stand before the Lord
in dignity and grace.

3   When I receive the peace of Christ
my loneliness shall end;
and I must reach a hand and take
my own self as a friend —
my own self as a friend indeed
who has an honoured place
where I may stand before the Lord
in dignity and grace.

Music English carol melody
arranged John L. Bell (*b.* 1949)

4 When I receive the peace of Christ
my loneliness shall end;
and I must reach a hand and take
Christ Jesus as a friend —
Christ Jesus as a friend indeed
who has an honoured place
where now he stands among us all
in dignity and grace.

Michael Mair (b. 1942)

67

FOCUS MY EYES

Slowly

1 Focus my eyes on you, O Lord, focus my eyes on you; to worship in spi - rit and in truth, focus my eyes on you.

1 Focus my eyes on you, O Lord,
focus my eyes on you;
to worship in spirit and in truth,
focus my eyes on you.

2 Turn round my life to you, O Lord,
turn round my life to you;
to know from this time you've made me new,
turn round my life to you.

3 Fill up my heart with praise, O Lord,
fill up my heart with praise;
to speak of your love in every place,
fill up my heart with praise.

Ian White (b. 1956)

Music Ian White (b. 1956)

DUMPS   77 83

When I'm feel-ing down and sad, no-thing much to make me glad,

help me to re-mem-ber, you are there for me.

Last time

568 2

WHEN I'M FEELING DOWN AND SAD   77 83

1 When I'm feel-ing down and sad, no-thing much to make me glad,

help me to re-mem-ber, you are there for me.

1   When I'm feeling down
      and sad,
nothing much to make
      me glad,
help me to remember,
you are there for me.

2   When things seem so
      different, and
very hard to understand,
help me to remember,
you are close to me.

3   When no one has time
      for me,
nothing's as it used to be,
help me to remember,
you are still with me.

4   When I'm crying, deep
      inside,
harder than I've ever cried,
help me to remember,
you are loving me.

Joy Webb (*b.* 1932)

Music Tune 1 Douglas Galbraith (*b.* 1940)
Music Tune 2 Joy Webb (*b.* 1932)

HE'S ALWAYS THERE   Irregular

1 When I'm feel-ing sad, I can call out to him. When it hurts in-side he feels ev - ery tear. When no-one un-der-stands just__ what I'm think-ing,

Refrain

Je - - sus,   he's   al - ways   there _____ __ he's al - ways   there. _____

1   When I'm feeling sad, I can call out to him.
     When it hurts inside, he feels every tear.
     When no one understands just what I'm thinking,
     Jesus, he's always there,
     he's always there.

2   When I'm feeling fine, we can talk together.
     Everyone around me seems to care.
     Walking in the sun, I can feel him smiling.

                         Stephen Fischbacher (*b.* 1960)

Music Stephen Fischbacher (*b.* 1960)

569   Words and Music: © Stephen Fischbacher, Fischy Music, 45 Queensferry Lane, Edinburgh. EH2 4PF.

STAND BY ME

83 83 77 83

1 When the storms of life are ra-ging, stand by me; when the
storms of life are ra-ging, stand by me. When the
world is pound-ing me, like a ship up-on the sea, Lord, who
rules the wind and wa-ter, stand by me.

1   When the storms of life are raging, stand by me;
    when the storms of life are raging, stand by me.
    When the world is pounding me,
    like a ship upon the sea,
    Lord, who rules the wind and water, stand by me.

2   In the midst of tribulation, stand by me;
    in the midst of tribulation, stand by me.
    When the hosts of hell assail,
    and my strength begins to fail,
    Lord, who never lost a battle, stand by me.

3   In the midst of faults and failures, stand by me;
    in the midst of faults and failures, stand by me.
    When I've done the best I can,
    and my friends misunderstand,
    Lord, who knows all about me, stand by me.

4   In the midst of persecution, stand by me;
    in the midst of persecution, stand by me.
    When my foes in war array
    undertake to stop my way,
    Lord, who saved Paul and Silas, stand by me.

5   When I'm growing old and feeble, stand by me;
    when I'm growing old and feeble, stand by me.
    When my life becomes a burden
    and I'm nearing chilly Jordan,
    Lord, the Lily of the Valley, stand by me.

Charles Albert Tindley (1851–1933)

Music Charles Albert Tindley (1851–1933)
arranged William Farley Smith (1941–1997)

PRABHOO LAY LAY

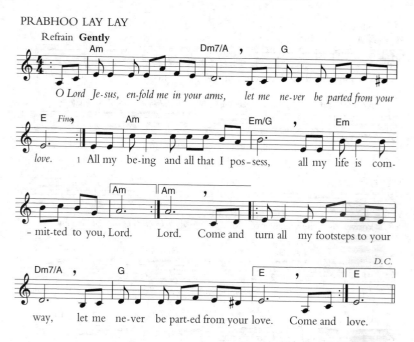

O Lord Jesus, enfold me in your arms,
let me never be parted from your love.

1.   All my being and all that I possess,
   all my life is committed to you, Lord.
   Come and turn all my footsteps to your way,
   let me never be parted from your love.

2.   Let your Spirit be always in my heart,
   and let only your spirit live within.
   Come and turn all my footsteps to your way,
   let me never be parted from your love.

3.   Let me bring to you others who are lost,
   in their sadness, may they discover joy.
   In believing they'll witness to your truth,
   let them never be parted from your love.

In the refrain and verses, each pair of lines is repeated.

Author unknown

Music Pakistani traditional melody
arranged Compilers

1 So much wrong and so much in-jus-tice, so you shoul-dered a wood-en cross. Now like you,— my best dreams are shat-tered; all I know is the weight of loss. *My be-lov-ed, my be-lov-ed, tell me, where can you be found? You drank deep of the cup of suf-fer-ing, and your death is our ho-ly ground.*

Music French 16th-century melody
adapted John L. Bell (*b.* 1949)

1   So much wrong and so much injustice,
    so you shouldered a wooden cross.
    Now like you, my best dreams are shattered;
    all I know is the weight of loss.
        My beloved, my beloved,
        tell me, where can you be found?
        You drank deep of the cup of suffering,
        and your death is our holy ground.

2   Olive trees showed the pain of sorrow;
    they were grieving for their Lord.
    Round Jerusalem the hills were mourning,
    as the city denied its God.

3   No fine song, no impressive music
    can attempt to relieve my heart;
    in this hour I am called to grieving,
    lest no other will play this part.

4   Everything I could ever offer
    could not pay for what God has done;
    but my life shall be spent in honour
    of my Saviour, God's only Son.

                            Arabic text
        English version John L. Bell (*b.*1949)

SARANAM   Irregular

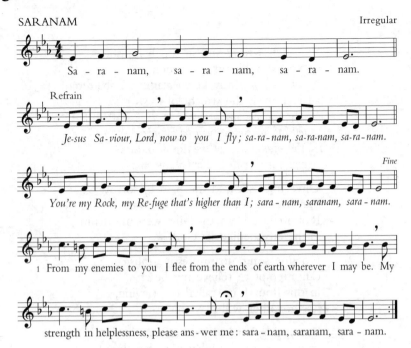

Sa - ra - nam,   sa - ra - nam,   sa - ra - nam.

Refrain

Je-sus Sa-viour, Lord, now to you I fly; sa-ra-nam, sa-ra-nam, sa-ra-nam.

Fine

You're my Rock, my Re-fuge that's higher than I; sara-nam, saranam, sara-nam.

1 From my enemies to you I flee from the ends of earth wherever I may be. My

strength in helplessness, please ans-wer me: sara-nam, saranam, sara-nam.

Music Indian melody
arranged Compilers

* Saranam, saranam, saranam.

Jesus Saviour, Lord, now to you I fly;
saranam, saranam, saranam.
You're my Rock, my Refuge that's higher than I;
saranam, saranam, saranam.

1 From my enemies to you I flee
from the ends of earth wherever I may be.
My strength in helplessness, please answer me:
saranam, saranam, saranam.

2 In your tent give me a dwelling place,
and beneath your wings may I find sheltering grace,
and may I feel the sunshine of your face:
saranam, saranam, saranam.

3 May I keep my vows to you each day
and depend upon your love along the way,
and on your faithful strength my burdens lay:
saranam, saranam, saranam.

4 Yesterday, today, for e'er the same,
Lord, you give your grace to all who bear your name;
you ransomed us from sin and took the blame:
saranam, saranam, saranam.

* *This line is sung before the first verse only.*

'Saranam' means 'I surrender'.

Sri Lankan text
English version by Compilers

THE CLOUD'S VEIL

Irregular

Even though the rain hides the stars, even though the mist swirls the hills, even when the dark clouds veil the sky, God is by my side. Even when the sun shall fall in sleep, e-ven when at dawn the sky shall weep, even in the night when storms shall rise, God is by my side, God is by my side.

1 *Bright the stars at night that mir-ror hea-ven's way to you. Bright the saints in light who dwell with God in love and truth.*

Music Liam Lawton, *arranged* Compilers

Even though the rain hides the stars,
even though the mist swirls the hills,
even when the dark clouds veil the sky,
God is by my side.
Even when the sun shall fall in sleep,
even when at dawn the sky shall weep,
even in the night when storms shall rise,
God is by my side,
God is by my side.

1   Bright the stars at night
that mirror heaven's way to you.
Bright the saints in light
who dwell with God in love and truth.

2   Blest are they who sing
in fellowship with saints in light.
Blest is heaven's King.
Let all adore the Lord most high.

Liam Lawton
The Cloud's Veil

OVER MY HEAD

Refrain

Ov-er my head,— I hear mu-sic in the air;— ov-er my head,— I hear mu-sic in the air;— ov-er my head,— I hear mu-sic in the air:— there must be a God some-where. *Fine*

Cantor
1 Oh, when the world is si-lent,_____ oh,

All: *(Hum)* I hear mu-sic in the air:—

when the world is si-lent,_____ oh,

(Hum) I hear mu-sic in the air;—

when the world is si-lent,_____

(Hum) I hear mu-sic in the air:—

D.C.

there must be a God some-where.

Music African-American Spiritual *arranged* Pamela Warrick Smith

Over my head, I hear music in the air;
over my head, I hear music in the air;
over my head, I hear music in the air;
there must be a God somewhere.

1   CANTOR: Oh, when the world is silent,
    ALL: I hear music in the air;
    CANTOR: oh, when the world is silent,
    ALL: I hear music in the air;
    CANTOR: oh, when the world is silent,
    ALL: I hear music in the air;
    there must be a God somewhere.

2   And when I'm feeling lonely,
    and when I'm feeling lonely,
    and when I'm feeling lonely,
    there must be a God somewhere.

3   Now when I think on Jesus,
    now when I think on Jesus,
    now when I think on Jesus,
    there must be a God somewhere.

*Pamela Warrick Smith

CIRCLE ME, LORD

10 10 and refrain

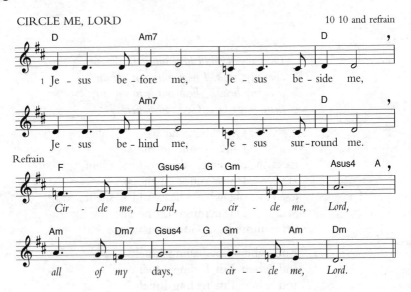

1 Jesus before me, Jesus beside me,
Jesus behind me, Jesus surround me.

Refrain: Circle me, Lord, circle me, Lord,
all of my days, circle me, Lord.

1   Jesus before me, Jesus beside me,
Jesus behind me, Jesus surround me.
Circle me, Lord, circle me, Lord,
all of my days, circle me, Lord.

2   Jesus above me, Jesus below me,
Jesus within me, Jesus enfold me.

3   Jesus for our time, Jesus for all time,
Jesus eternal, Jesus immortal.

Andy Moss

Music Andy Moss

BUNESSAN   55 54 D

An alternative arrangement is found at 212.

1   Christ be beside me,
    Christ be before me,
    Christ be behind me,
    King of my heart.
    Christ be within me,
    Christ be below me,
    Christ be above me,
    never to part.

2   Christ on my right hand,
    Christ on my left hand,
    Christ all around me,
    shield in the strife.
    Christ in my sleeping,
    Christ in my sitting,
    Christ in my rising,
    light of my life.

3   Christ be in all hearts
    thinking about me,
    Christ be in all tongues
    telling of me.
    Christ be the vision
    in eyes that see me,
    in ears that hear me,
    Christ ever be.

from *St Patrick's Breastplate,* 8th century
adapted James Quinn (*b.* 1919)

Music Gaelic traditional melody *arranged* David Evans (1874–1948)

SKIES OF GLORY   77 77 77

578 2

PSALM 135 (MINISTRES DE L'ÉTERNEL)   77 77 77

Music Tune 1 Malcolm Williamson (1931–2003)
Music Tune 2 Melody from *French Psalter,* 1562,
set by Claude Goudimel, 1565

1   Christ, whose glory fills the skies,
     Christ, the true, the only Light,
     Sun of Righteousness, arise,
     triumph o'er the shades of night.
     Dayspring from on high, be near;
     Daystar, in my heart appear.

2   Dark and cheerless is the morn
     unaccompanied by thee;
     joyless is the day's return,
     till thy mercy's beams I see,
     till they inward light impart,
     glad my eyes, and warm my heart.

3   Visit, then, this soul of mine;
     pierce the gloom of sin and grief;
     fill me, Radiancy Divine;
     scatter all my unbelief;
     more and more thyself display,
     shining to the perfect day.

                    Charles Wesley (1707–1788)

579

Come my Way, my Truth,__ my Life: such a
way as gives__ us breath; such a truth as ends all
strife; such a life as con - - - quers death.

1   Come, my Way, my Truth, my Life:
      such a way as gives us breath;
      such a truth as ends all strife;
      such a life as conquers death.

2   Come, my Light, my Feast, my Strength:
      such a light as shows a feast;
      such a feast as mends in length;
      such a strength as makes a guest.

3   Come, my Joy, my Love, my Heart:
      such a joy as none can move;
      such a love as none can part;
      such a heart as joys in love.

                        George Herbert (1593–1633)

Music Ralph Vaughan Williams (1872–1958)
adapted E. Harold Greer (1886–1957)

580

1   Abide with me: fast falls the eventide;
the darkness deepens; Lord, with me abide:
when other helpers fail, and comforts flee,
help of the helpless, O abide with me.

2   Swift to its close ebbs out life's little day;
earth's joys grow dim, its glories pass away;
change and decay in all around I see:
O thou who changest not, abide with me.

3   I need thy presence every passing hour;
what but thy grace can foil the tempter's power?
Who like thyself my guide and stay can be?
Through cloud and sunshine, Lord, abide with me.

4   I fear no foe with thee at hand to bless;
ills have no weight, and tears no bitterness:
where is death's sting? where, grave, thy victory?
I triumph still if thou abide with me.

5   Hold thou thy cross before my closing eyes,
shine through the gloom, and point me to the skies;
heaven's morning breaks, and earth's vain shadows flee:
in life, in death, O Lord, abide with me.

Henry Francis Lyte (1793–1847)

Music William Henry Monk (1823–1889)

Also suitable

THE HOLY SPIRIT

SALVE FESTA DIES   Irregular

Refrain, Unison

1 Hail thee, Fe - sti - val Day! blest day that art hal-lowed for

ev - - er; day when the Lord from heaven shone on the

Fine   vv. 2, 4

world with his grace.   2 Lo! in the like - ness of fire,   on
                          4 Hark! in a hun - dred_ tongues Christ's

those who a - wait his ap - pear - ing,   he   whom the __
own, his   cho - sen a - post - les,   preach   to   a __

                                                              D.C.

Lord fore - told __   sud - den - ly, swift - ly,   de - scends.
hun - dred tribes __   Christ and his won-der - ful   works.

vv. 3, 5

3 Forth from the Fa - ther he comes with his seven - fold_
5 Praise to the Spi - rit of life, all __ praise to the

mys - - ti - cal dow - ry,   pour-ing on hu - - man
fount   of our be - ing,   light that now light - ens

                                                              D.C.

souls   in - fi - nite rich - es   of God. __
all,   life that in   all   now   a - bides. __

Music Ralph Vaughan Williams (1872–1958)

581 Words and Music: From *The English Hymnal*, 1906, Oxford University Press, Great Clarendon Street, Oxford. OX2 6DP.
Reproduced by permission.

Salve, festa dies, toto venerabilis aevo

*1   *Hail thee, Festival Day!*
blest day that art hallowed for ever;
day when the Lord from heaven
shone on the world with his grace.

2   Lo! in the likeness of fire,
on those who await his appearing,
he whom the Lord foretold
suddenly, swiftly, descends.

3   Forth from the Father he comes
with his sevenfold mystical dowry,
pouring on human souls
infinite richness of God.

4   Hark! in a hundred tongues
Christ's own, his chosen apostles,
preach to a hundred tribes
Christ and his wonderful works.

5   Praise to the Spirit of life,
all praise to the fount of our being,
light that now lightens all,
life that in all now abides.

*   *Verse 1 is also sung as a refrain after each verse.*

c. 14th century (York Processional)
translated Gabriel Gillett (1873–1948)

ES IST EIN ROS' ENTSPRUNGEN   76 76 D

1   O Day of joy and wonder!
      Christ's promise now fulfilled!
      The coming of his Spirit
      the Father's love has willed;
      our Lord in human body
      to mortal eye is lost,
      yet he returns for ever
      at blessèd Pentecost!

2   The world, in sheer amazement,
      the truth must now declare:
      that men, who once were cowards,
      are brave beyond compare;
      and tongues, which could not utter
      their faith in Jesus' name,
      defy all persecution
      his glory to proclaim!

3   We too may know your power,
      your courage makes us strong,
      your love, your joy, your patience
      can all to us belong.
      Come now and dwell within us,
      O Comforter divine,
      come to our hearts, and keep them;
      there let your brightness shine.

            Violet Nita Buchanan (1891–1975)

Music German melody, 16th century, or earlier.
adapted James Smith Anderson (1853–1945)

MARTYRS   CM

1   Spirit divine, attend our prayers,
     and make this house your home;
     descend with all your gracious powers;
     come now, great Spirit, come!

2   Come as the fire: and purge our hearts
     like sacrificial flame;
     let our whole life an offering be
     to our Redeemer's name.

3   Come as the dove: and spread your wings,
     the wings of peaceful love;
     and let your Church on earth become
     blest as the Church above.

4   Come as the wind, with rushing sound
     and Pentecostal grace,
     that all of woman born may see
     the glory of your face.

5   Spirit divine, attend our prayers;
     and make this world your home;
     descend with all your gracious powers;
     come now, great Spirit, come!

                              Andrew Reed (1787–1862)

Music Melody from *Scottish Psalter* 1615 (1635 rhythm)
harmonised David Evans (1874–1948)

ST JOHN (Havergal)   6666 4444

1   Like fireworks in the night
     the Holy Spirit came;
     disciples' fears took flight
     when touched by fronds of flame:
       and suddenly the world was young
       as hope embraced a Saviour's claim.

2   For Jesus bade them dare
     to venture, as they should;
     his love taught them to share
     their homes, possessions, food:
       the mind of Jesus gave them speech
       all tribes and peoples understood.

3   Thus God our spirits lifts
     fresh daring to inspire;
     as common folk get gifts
     to change the world entire:
       the tongues of flame at Pentecost
       ran through the world like forest fire.

Ian Masson Fraser (*b.* 1917)

Music The Parish Choir, vol. III, 1851
sometimes attributed to William Henry Havergal (1793–1870)

584   Words: © 2001, Stainer & Bell Ltd, PO Box 110, Victoria House, 23 Gruneisen Road, London N3 1DZ

NYOHENE

99 and refrain

1 When our Sa-viour Ye - su went a-way, he sent here a friend with us to stay. *Come, Guide on earth, our Spi-rit friend; come to in-spire, di-rect, de-fend.*

1   When our Saviour Yesu went away,
     he sent here a friend with us to stay.
     Come, Guide on earth, our Spirit-friend;
     come to inspire, direct, defend.

2   In all Yesu's friends the Spirit lives,
     it is Yesu's power that moulds and saves.

3   O great Spirit, fill us all with love
     for the neighbours God gives us to serve.

4   Come, great Spirit, fire the Church on earth,
     to your whole creation give new birth.

5   Praise be to our Maker, and the Son,
     with whom now and ever you are one.

Tom Colvin (1925–2000)

Music Ghanaian (Dagomba) melody
adapted Tom Colvin (1925–2000)
arranged John L. Bell (b. 1949)

VENI CREATOR   Irregular

'Praise ___ to thine e - ter - nal me - rit, Fa - ther,

Son, ___ and Ho - ly Spi - rit.' A - - men.

Veni, Creator Spiritus

1   Come, Holy Ghost, our souls inspire,
    and lighten with celestial fire;
    thou the anointing Spirit art,
    who dost thy sevenfold gifts impart.

2   Thy blessèd unction from above
    is comfort, life, and fire of love;
    enable with perpetual light
    the dullness of our blinded sight.

3   Anoint and cheer our soilèd face
    with the abundance of thy grace;
    keep far our foes; give peace at home:
    where thou art guide no ill can come.

4   Teach us to know the Father, Son,
    and thee, of both to be but One,
    that through the ages all along
    this may be our endless song,
        'Praise to thine eternal merit,
        Father, Son, and Holy Spirit.' Amen.

9th century
translated John Cosin (1594–1672)

Music Plainsong melody, metrical version, Mechlin 1848

VERBUM SUPERNUM   LM

1   Come, gracious Spirit, heavenly Dove,
    with light and comfort from above;
    come, be our Guardian, be our Guide,
    o'er every thought and step preside.

2   The light of truth to us display,
    and make us know and choose your way;
    plant holy fear in every heart,
    that we from God may ne'er depart.

3   Lead us to Christ, the living Way,
    nor let us from his pastures stray;
    lead us to holiness, the road
    that we must take to dwell with God.

4   Lead us to heav'n, that we may share
    fullness of joy for ever there;
    lead us to God, our final rest,
    to be with him for ever blest.

                          Simon Browne (1680–1732)

Music 8th mode plainsong melody
as in *Antiphonarium Monasticum,* Mechlin, 1848
harmonised Compilers

JULION   87 87 87

1
Praise the Spirit in creation,
breath of God, life's origin:
Spirit, moving on the waters,
forming order deep within,
source of breath for all things breathing,
life in whom all lives begin.

2
Praise the Spirit, close companion
of our inmost thoughts and ways;
who, in showing us God's wonders,
moves our hearts to love and praise;
and God's will, to those who listen,
by a still small voice conveys.

3
Praise the Spirit, who enlightened
priests and prophets with the word;
hidden truth behind the wisdoms
which as yet know not their Lord;
by whose love and power in Jesus
God himself is seen and heard.

4
Praise the Spirit, sent by Jesus
when ascended to his throne,
who pours out on men and women
power for turning upside down
all the world and every people
as the gospel is made known.

Music David Hurd (*b.* 1950)

5   Pray we now, Lord, Holy Spirit,
    on our lives descend in might;
    let your flame burn bright within us,
    fire our hearts and clear our sight,
    till, consumed with your compassion,
    we too set the world alight.

Michael Hewlett (1916–2000)

589

BREATH OF HEAVEN   5 4 4 8

1 Come, Holy Spirit, descend on us, descend on us. We gather here in Jesus' name. *(Hum)*

2 Come, Breath of Heaven.

2 Come, Breath of name.

1   Come, Holy Spirit,
        descend on us,
        descend on us.
        We gather here in Jesus' name.

2   Come, Breath of Heaven,

3   Come, Word of Mercy,

4   Come, Fire of Judgement,

5   Come, Great Creator,

6   Come to unite us,

7   Come to disturb us,

8   Come to inspire us,

John L. Bell (*b.* 1949)

Music John L. Bell (*b.* 1949)

YR HUN GÂN

87 87 D

1 Holy Spirit, gift bestower,
 breathe into our hearts today.
 Flowing water, dove that hovers,
 Holy Spirit, guide our way.
 Love inspirer, joy releaser,
 Spirit, take our fears away.
 Reconciler, peace restorer,
 move among us while we pray.

2 Holy Spirit, Christ proclaimer,
 wisdom bringer, light our way.
 Fire that dances, wind that whispers,
 Holy Spirit, come today.
 Ease disturber, comfort bearer,
 move among us while we pray.
 Truth revealer, faith confirmer,
 rest within our hearts today.

Author unknown

Music Welsh traditional melody
arranged Compilers

LOIS

99 96

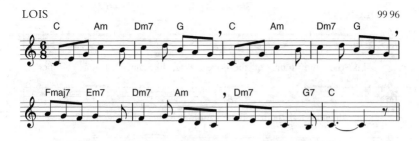

1   O holy dove of God descending,
    you are the love that knows no ending,
    all of our shattered dreams you're mending:
    Spirit, now live in me.

2   O holy wind of God now blowing,
    bearing the seed that God is sowing,
    you are the life that starts us growing:
    Spirit, now live in me.

3   O holy flame of God now burning,
    you are the power of Christ returning,
    you are the answer to our yearning:
    Spirit, now live in me.

Bryan Jeffery Leech (*b.* 1931)

Music Bryan Jeffery Leech (*b.* 1931)
arranged Compilers

BRIDEGROOM   87 87 6

1 Like the mur-mur of the dove's song, like the chal-lenge of her flight, like the vi-gour of the wind's rush, like the new flame's ea-ger might: come,___ Ho - ly Spi - - rit, come.

1   Like the murmur of the dove's song,
    like the challenge of her flight,
    like the vigour of the wind's rush,
    like the new flame's eager might:
    come, Holy Spirit, come.

2   To the members of Christ's body,
    to the branches of the vine,
    to the Church in faith assembled,
    to our midst as gift and sign:
    come, Holy Spirit, come.

3   With the healing of division,
    with the ceaseless voice of prayer,
    with the power to love and witness,
    with the peace beyond compare:
    come, Holy Spirit, come.

                    Carl P. Daw, Jr *(b.* 1944)

Music Peter Warwick Cutts *(b.* 1937)

THAINAKY   11 11 D

1 She sits like a bird, brooding on the waters, hovering on the chaos of the world's first day: she sighs and she sings, mo-ther-ing cre-a-tion, wait-ing to give birth to all the Word— will say.

1   She sits like a bird, brooding on the waters,
     hovering on the chaos of the world's first day;
     she sighs and she sings, mothering creation,
     waiting to give birth to all the Word will say.

2   She wings over earth, resting where she wishes,
     lighting close at hand or soaring through the skies;
     she nests in the womb, welcoming each wonder,
     nourishing potential hidden to our eyes.

3   She dances in fire, startling her spectators,
     waking tongues of ecstasy where dumbness reigned;
     she weans and inspires all whose hearts are open,
     nor can she be captured, silenced, or restrained.

4   For she is the Spirit, one with God in essence,
     gifted by the Saviour in eternal love;
     and she is the key opening the scriptures,
     enemy of apathy and heavenly dove.

John L. Bell (b. 1949)
and Graham Maule (b. 1958)

Music John L. Bell (b. 1949)

DIADEMATA   DSM

1   Come, Holy Spirit, come!
　　　 Inflame our souls with love,
　　　 transforming every heart and home
　　　 with wisdom from above.
　　　 Let none of us despise
　　　 the humble path Christ trod,
　　　 but choose, to shame the worldly wise,
　　　 the foolishness of God.

2   All-knowing Spirit, prove
　　　 the poverty of pride,
　　　 by knowledge of the Father's love
　　　 in Jesus crucified.
　　　 And grant us faith to know
　　　 the glory of that sign,
　　　 and in our very lives to show
　　　 the marks of love divine.

Music George Job Elvey (1816–1893)

3   Come with the gift to heal
the wounds of guilt and fear,
and to oppression's face reveal
the kingdom drawing near.
Where chaos longs to reign,
descend, O holy Dove,
and free us all to work again
the miracles of love.

4   Spirit of truth, arise;
inspire the prophet's voice:
expose to scorn the tyrant's lies,
and bid the poor rejoice.
O Spirit, clear our sight,
all prejudice remove,
and help us to discern the right,
and covet only love.

5   Give us the tongues to speak
the word of love and grace
to rich and poor, to strong and weak,
in every time and place.
Enable us to hear
the words that others bring,
interpreting with open ear
the special song they sing.

6   Come, Holy Spirit, dance
within our hearts today,
our earthbound spirits to entrance,
our mortal fears allay.
And teach us to desire,
all other things above,
that self-consuming holy fire,
the perfect gift of love.

Michael Forster (b. 1946)

594 Words: © 1992 Kevin Mayhew Ltd, Buxhall, Stowmarket, Suffolk. IP14 3BW,

SUNSET   98 98

1   O Breath of life, come sweeping through us,
    revive your Church with life and power;
    O Breath of life, come, cleanse, renew us,
    and fit your Church to meet this hour.

2   O Wind of God, come bend us, break us,
    till humbly we confess our need;
    then in your tenderness remake us,
    revive, restore; for this we plead.

3   O Breath of love, come breathe within us,
    renewing thought and will and heart:
    come, Love of Christ, afresh to win us,
    revive your Church in every part.

4   Revive us, Lord! is zeal abating
    while harvest fields are vast and white?
    Revive us, Lord, the world is waiting,
    equip your Church to spread the light.

Elizabeth Ann Head (1850–1936)

Music George Gilbert Stocks (1877–1960)

VENI SPIRITUS   SM

1   Breathe on me, Breath of God;
        fill me with life anew,
        that I may love the way you love,
        and do what you would do.

2   Breathe on me, Breath of God,
        until my heart is pure,
        until with you I will one will,
        to do and to endure.

3   Breathe on me, Breath of God,
        direct my heart's desire,
        till every earthly part of me
        glows with your holy fire.

4   Breathe on me, Breath of God;
        so shall I never die,
        but live with you the perfect life
        of your eternity.

                 *Edwin Hatch (1835–1889)

Music John Stainer (1840–1901)

ELLEN

87 87

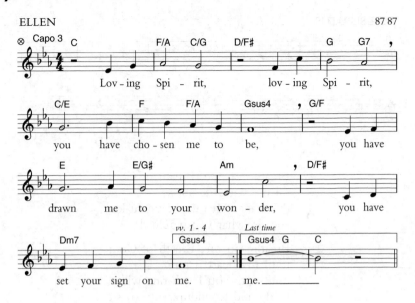

1   Loving Spirit, loving Spirit,
you have chosen me to be,
you have drawn me to your wonder,
you have set your sign on me.

Music David Dell (*b.* 1959)

2   Like a mother, you enfold me,
hold my life within your own,
feed me with your very body,
form me of your flesh and bone.

3   Like a father, you protect me,
teach me the discerning eye,
hoist me up upon your shoulder,
let me see the world from high.

4   Friend and lover, in your closeness
I am known and held and blest,
in your promise is my comfort,
in your presence I may rest.

5   Loving Spirit, loving Spirit,
you have chosen me to be,
you have drawn me to your wonder,
you have set your sign on me.

Shirley Erena Murray (*b.* 1931)

Also suitable

I am the Church! You are the Church   204
Come down, O Love Divine   489
Spirit of God, descend upon my heart   495
Come, Holy Spirit   758

598

THE HOLY SPIRIT IN THE CHURCH
ILLUMINATION OF GOD'S WORD

ST COLUMBA (ERIN)   CM

1   Come, Holy Ghost, our hearts inspire,
     let us thine influence prove;
     source of the old prophetic fire,
     fountain of life and love.

2   Come, Holy Ghost, for moved by thee
     the prophets wrote and spoke;
     unlock the truth, thyself the key;
     unseal the sacred book.

3   Expand thy wings, celestial Dove,
     brood o'er our nature's night;
     on our disordered spirits move,
     and let there now be light.

4   God through himself we then shall know,
     if thou within us shine,
     and sound, with all thy saints below,
     the depths of love divine.

Charles Wesley (1707–1788)

Music Petrie *Collection of Irish Melody*
harmonised Compilers of Irish *Church Hymnal,* 1874

GLENFINLAS   65 65

Unison

1   Holy Spirit, hear us;
help us while we sing;
breathe into the music
of the praise we bring.

2   Holy Spirit, prompt us
when we try to pray;
nearer come, and teach us
what we ought to say.

3   Holy Spirit, teach us
through the words we read;
bring to life the Bible
with the light we need.

4   Holy Spirit, give us
each a lively mind;
make us more like Jesus,
gracious, pure, and kind.

5   Holy Spirit, help us
daily, by your might,
what is wrong to conquer,
and to choose the right.

*William Henry Parker (1845–1929)

Music Kenneth George Finlay (1882–1974)
arranged Compilers of *Church Hymnary,* 3rd edition, 1973

SKYE BOAT SONG   86 86 and refrain

Spi - rit of God, un - seen as the wind, gen - tle as is the dove: teach us the truth and help us be - lieve, show us the Sa - viour's love.

1 You spoke to us long, long a - go, gave us the writ - ten word; we read it still, need-ing its truth, through it God's voice is heard.

Spirit of God, unseen as the wind,
gentle as is the dove,
teach us the truth and help us believe,
show us the Saviour's love.

1   You spoke to us long, long ago,
     gave us the written word;
     we read it still, needing its truth,
     through it God's voice is heard.

2   Without your help we fail our Lord,
     we cannot live his way;
     we need your power, we need your strength,
     following Christ each day.

                              Margaret V. Old (1932–2001)

Music Scottish folk melody
arranged Compilers of *Common Ground*, 1998

LIEBSTER JESU (DESSAU) 78 78 88

Liebster Jesu, wir sind hier

1 Look upon us, blessèd Lord,
   take our wandering thoughts and guide us:
   we have come to hear your word:
   with your teaching now provide us,
   that, from earth's distractions turning,
   we your message may be learning.

2 For your Spirit's radiance bright
   we, assembled here, are hoping:
   when we live without your light,
   in the dark our souls are groping:
   in word, deed, and thought direct us:
   only you, Lord, can correct us.

3 Brightness of the Father's face,
   Light of Light, from God proceeding,
   make us ready in this place:
   ear and heart await your leading.
   In our study, prayers, and praising,
   may our souls find their upraising.

Tobias Clausnitzer (1619–1684)
translated Robert Alexander Stewart
Macalister (1870–1950)

Music Melody by Johann Rudolph Ahle (1625–1673)
harmonised Johann Sebastian Bach (1685–1750)

GOD SPEAKS   Irregular

Is it spoo-ky, is it weird that God wants to talk to you and me?

Is it some-thing to be feared? No! God wants the best for you and

me!   God speaks through words in the

Bi - ble, through o - ther peo - ple too; and shows us the

right way we should live, in what we say and do. Oh, …

Is it spooky, is it weird
that God wants to talk to you and me?
Is it something to be feared?
No! God wants the best for you and me!

1 God speaks through words in the Bible,
   through other people too;
   and shows us the right way we should live,
   in what we say and do. Oh, …

2 He gives the Holy Spirit,
   to help us all to see,
   through people, words and pictures,
   his truth for you and me. Oh, …

3 Now we should learn to listen
   to all that God would say,
   and act on what we think he's said,
   so listen and obey. Oh, …

Captain Alan Price

Music Captain Alan Price
arranged Compilers

LAUS DEO (REDHEAD No. 46)   87 87

A higher setting is found at 139.

1   For your gift of God the Spirit,
    with us, in us, always true,
    pledge of life and hope of glory,
    Saviour, we would worship you.

2   He who in creation's dawning
    brooded o'er the pathless deep,
    still across our nature's darkness
    moves to wake our souls from sleep.

3   He it is, the living author,
    wakes to life the sacred word,
    reads with us the Bible story
    and reveals our risen Lord.

4   He it is who works within us,
    teaching rebel hearts to pray;
    he whose fervent intercessions
    rise for us both night and day.

5   Fill us with your grace and goodness,
    God the Father, Spirit, Son;
    in us, through us, now and always,
    may your perfect will be done.

                    *Edith Margaret Clarkson (*b.* 1915)

Music Richard Redhead (1820–1901)
Church Hymn Tunes, 1853

IN BABILONE

87 87 D

Brightly

1   Holy wisdom, lamp of learning,
bless the light that reason lends.
Teach us judgment as we kindle
sparks of thought your Spirit sends.
Sanctify our search for knowledge
and the truth that sets us free.
Come, illumine mind and spirit
joined in deepest unity.

2   Vine of truth, in you we flourish;
by your grace we learn and grow.
May the word of Christ among us
shape our life, your will to know.
Joined to Christ in living, dying,
may we help the Church convey
witness to the saving gospel,
bearing fruit of faith today.

3   Holy God, the hope of nations,
tune us to your righteous will,
as the symphony of ages
claims our best, our finest skill.
Shape our search for peace and justice
through prophetic deed and word.
Christ, conduct us, set our rhythm,
that God's praise be ever heard.

Ruth C. Duck (*b.* 1947)

Music Dutch dance melody, collected by
Julius Röntgen 1855-1932, *harmonised* Compilers

ST HELEN   87 87 87

1   Thanks to God whose word was spoken
     in the making of the earth.
     His the voice that called a nation,
     fired her vision, tried her worth.
   * God has spoken:
     praise him for his open word.

2   Thanks to God whose word incarnate
     came to save our human race.
     Deeds and words and death and rising
     testify to heaven's grace.
     God has spoken:
     praise him for his open word.

3   Thanks to God whose word was written
     in the Bible's sacred page,
     record of the revelation
     showing God to every age.
     God has spoken:
     praise him for his open word.

4   Thanks to God whose word is published
     in the tongues of every race.
     See its glory undiminished
     by the change of time or place.
     God has spoken:
     praise him for his open word.

   * *This line of each verse is repeated.*

continued overleaf

Music George Clement Martin (1844–1916)

5   Thanks to God whose word is answered
by the Spirit's voice within.
Here we drink of joy unmeasured,
life redeemed from death and sin.
God is speaking:
praise him for his open word.

Reginald Thomas Brooks (1918–1985)

STUTTGART   87 87

1   Lord, you sometimes speak in wonders,
   unmistakable and clear,
   mighty signs that show your presence,
   overcoming doubt and fear.

2   Lord, you sometimes speak in whispers,
   still and small and scarcely heard;
   only those who want to listen
   catch the all-important word.

3   Lord, you sometimes speak in silence,
   through our loud and noisy day;
   we can know and trust you better
   when we quietly wait and pray.

4   Lord, you sometimes speak in Scripture,
   words that summon from the page,
   shown and taught us by your Spirit
   with fresh light for every age.

5   Lord, you always speak in Jesus,
   always new yet still the same:
   teach us now more of our Saviour,
   make our lives display his Name.

Christopher Martin Idle (b. 1938)

Music adapted from a melody in Christian Friedrich Witt's
Psalmodia Sacra, Gotha, 1715

Also suitable

607

THE HOLY SPIRIT IN THE CHURCH
ENLIVENING AND RENEWING THE CHURCH

THE BRIGHT WIND OF HEAVEN   12 11 12 11

1 The bright wind is blowing, the bright wind of heaven, and
where it is going to, no one can say; but—
where it is passing our— hearts are awaking to
stretch from the darkness and reach for the day. way.

1   The bright wind is blowing, the bright wind of heaven,
     and where it is going to, no one can say;
     but where it is passing our hearts are awaking
     to stretch from the darkness and reach for the day.

2   The bright wind is blowing, the bright wind of heaven,
     and many old thoughts will be winnowed away;
     the husk that is blown is the chaff of our hating,
     the seed that is left is the hope for our day.

3   The bright wind is blowing, the bright wind of heaven,
     the love that it kindles will never betray;
     the fire that it fans is the warmth of our caring,
     so lean on the wind, it will show us the way.

                                        Cecily Taylor (b. 1930)

Music John Maynard (1925–1985)

DOWN AMPNEY   66 11 D

1   Spirit of truth and grace,
     come to us in this place
     as now in Jesus' name God's people gather.
     Open our eyes to see
     truths that will ever be,
     and in communion draw us close together.

2   Spirit of joy and peace,
     make all anxieties cease
     with knowledge of the Father's perfect caring.
     Then may God's children know
     love that won't let us go
     and joy that fills each day, beyond comparing.

3   Spirit of life and power,
     revive us in this hour
     and stir our hearts to praise with true devotion.
     Fill us with heavenly fire,
     and every heart inspire,
     that we may serve the world with your compassion.

                                   Iain D. Cunningham (*b.* 1954)

Music Ralph Vaughan Williams (1872–1958)

SUNSET   98 98

1   Come, living God, when least expected,
     when minds are dull and hearts are cold,
     through sharpening word and warm affection
     revealing truths as yet untold.

2   Break from the tomb in which we hide you
     to speak again in startling ways;
     break through the words in which we bind you
     to resurrect our lifeless praise.

3   Come now, as once you came to Moses
     within the bush alive with flame;
     or to Elijah on the mountain,
     by silence pressing home your claim.

4   So, let our minds be sharp to read you
     in sight or sound or printed page,
     and let us greet you in our neighbours,
     in ardent youth or mellow age.

5   Then, through our gloom, your Son will meet us
     as vivid truth and living Lord,
     exploding doubt and disillusion
     to scatter hope and joy abroad.

6   Then we will share his radiant brightness
     and, blazing through the dread of night,
     illuminate by love and reason,
     for those in darkness, faith's delight.

Alan Gaunt (*b.* 1935)

Music George Gilbert Stocks (1877–1960)

MAGDA   10 10 10 10

1   Love of the Father, Love of God the Son,
    from whom all came, in whom was all begun;
    who formest heavenly beauty out of strife,
    creation's whole desire and breath of life:

2   Thou the all-holy, thou supreme in might,
    thou dost give peace, thy presence maketh right;
    thou with thy favour all things dost enfold,
    with thine all-kindness free from harm wilt hold.

3   Purest and highest, wisest and most just,
    there is no truth save only in thy trust;
    thou dost the mind from earthly dreams recall,
    and bring, through Christ, to him for whom are all.

4   Eternal Glory, let all thee adore,
    who art and shalt be worshipped evermore:
    us whom thou madest, comfort with thy might,
    and lead us to enjoy thy heavenly light.

Robert Bridges (1844–1930)
based on *Amor Patris et Filii,* 12th century

Music Ralph Vaughan Williams (1872–1958)

610 Music: From *The English Hymnal,* 1906, Oxford University Press, Great Clarendon Street, Oxford. OX2 6DP.
Reproduced by permission.

Ho - ly Spi - rit, fill our hearts ov - er-flow-ing with love.

May we shine with the light of God; come, Spi - rit, come.

1   Holy Spirit, fill our hearts
     overflowing with love.
     May we shine with the light of God,
     come, Spirit, come.

2   Holy Spirit, fill our minds,
     understanding the truth.
     May we grow in the wisdom of God;
     Come, Spirit, come.

3   Holy Spirit, make us one,
     strong together in faith.
     May we live as the family of God;
     come, Spirit, come.

Author unknown

Music Source unknown
arranged Compilers

612

CASTLEWOOD   85 85 84 3

1 Come to us, ___ cre - a - tive Spi - rit, in our Fa - ther's house,

ev - ery hu - man tal - ent hal - low, hid - den skills a -

- rouse, that with-in ___ your earth - ly tem - ple,

wise and sim - ple may ___ re - joice.

1   Come to us, creative Spirit,
    in our Father's house,
    every human talent hallow,
    hidden skills arouse,
    that within your earthly temple,
    wise and simple
    may rejoice.

2   Poet, painter, music-maker,
    all your treasures bring;
    craftsman, actor, graceful dancer,
    make your offering:
    join your hands in celebration!
    Let creation
    shout and sing!

3   Word from God eternal springing,
    fill our minds, we pray,
    and in all artistic vision
    give integrity.
    May the flame within us burning
    kindle yearning
    day by day.

4   In all places and for ever
    glory be expressed
    to the Son, with God the Father,
    and the Spirit blessed.
    In our worship and our living
    keep us striving
    for the best.

                    David Mowbray (*b.* 1938)

Music Richard Proulx (*b.* 1937)

NJOO KWETU, ROHO MWEMA   86 86 and refrain

Come,____ come,____ come, Ho - ly Spi - rit, come.

1 Gracious Spirit, hear our pleading;
   fashion us all anew.
   It's your leading we are needing;
   help us to follow you.
       Come, come, come, Holy Spirit, come.
       Come, come, come, Holy Spirit, come.

2 Come to teach us; come to nourish
   those who believe in Christ.
   Bless the faithful; may they flourish,
   strengthened by grace unpriced.

3 Guide our thinking and our speaking
   done in your holy name.
   Motivate us in our seeking,
   freeing from guilt and shame.

4 Keep us fervent in our witness;
   unswayed by earth's allure.
   Ever grant us zeal and fitness,
   which you alone assure.

                           Wilson Niwagila
                 translated Howard S. Olson (*b.* 1922)

Music Tanzanian melody
arranged C. Michael Hawn (*b.* 1948)

SIGNUM 76 76 76 66

1 From the waiting comes the sign,
   come, Holy Spirit, come;
from the presence comes the peace,
   come, Holy Spirit, come;
from the silence comes the song,
   come, Holy Spirit, come;
   and be to us the truth,
   the sign, the peace, the song.

2 In the burning is the fire,
   come, Holy Spirit, come;
in the spending is the gift,
   come, Holy Spirit, come;
in the breaking is the life,
   come, Holy Spirit, come;
   and be to us in faith,
   the fire, the gift, the life.

Lines 1, 3 and 5 may be sung by a cantor.

Shirley Erena Murray *(b.* 1931)

Music Colin Alexander Gibson *(b.* 1933)

ABBOT'S LEIGH   87 87 D

A higher setting is found at 642.

1   Holy Spirit, ever living
   as the Church's very life;
   Holy Spirit, ever striving
   through her in a ceaseless strife;
   Holy Spirit, ever forming
   in the Church the mind of Christ;
   you we praise with endless worship
   for your fruit and gifts unpriced.

2   Holy Spirit, ever working
   through the Church's ministry;
   quickening, strengthening, and absolving,
   setting captive sinners free;
   Holy Spirit, ever binding
   age to age and soul to soul
   in a fellowship unending,
   you we worship and extol.

                                       Timothy Rees (1874–1939)

Music Cyril Vincent Taylor (1907–1991)

LAUDS   77 77

1   There's a spirit in the air,
    telling Christians everywhere:
    'Praise the love that Christ revealed,
    living, working in our world!'

2   Lose your shyness, find your tongue,
    tell the world what God has done:
    God in Christ has come to stay.
    Live tomorrow's life today!

3   When believers break the bread,
    when a hungry child is fed,
    praise the love that Christ revealed,
    living, working, in our world.

4   Still the Spirit gives us light,
    seeing wrong and setting right:
    God in Christ has come to stay.
    Live tomorrow's life today!

5   When a stranger's not alone,
    where the homeless find a home,
    praise the love that Christ revealed,
    living, working, in our world.

6   May the Spirit fill our praise,
    guide our thoughts and change our ways.
    God in Christ has come to stay.
    Live tomorrow's life today!

7   There's a Spirit in the air,
    calling people everywhere:
    praise the love that Christ revealed,
    living, working, in our world.

                              Brian Wren (*b.* 1936)

Music John Whitridge Wilson (1905–1992)

LUX TREMENDA   87 87 D

1   Great and deep the Spirit's purpose,
    hidden now in mystery;
    nature bursts with joyful promise,
    ripe with what is yet to be.
    In a wealth of rich invention,
    still God's work of art unfolds;
    barely have we seen, and faintly,
    what God's great salvation holds.

2   Great and deep the Spirit's purpose,
    making Jesus seen and heard.
    Every age of God's creation
    grasps new meaning from the Word.
    Show us, Holy Spirit, show us
    your new work begun today;
    eyes and ears and hearts are open,
    teach us what to do and say.

3   Great and deep the Spirit's purpose:
    all God's children brought to birth;
    freed from hunger, fear and evil
    every corner of the earth;
    and a million, million voices
    speak with joy the Saviour's name;
    every face reflects his image,
    never any two the same.

Music Alfred Victor Fedak (b. 1953)

4   Great and deep the Spirit's purpose:
     nothing shall be left to chance;
     all that lives will be united
     in the everlasting dance;
     all fulfilled and all perfected,
     each uniquely loved and known;
     Christ in glory unimagined
     once for all receives his own.

Marnie Barrell (*b.* 1952)

618

WEAVER   11 10 11 10

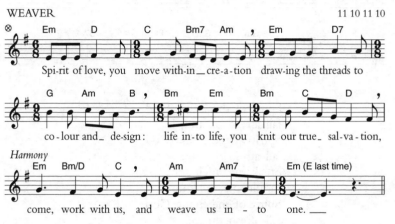

Spi-rit of love, you move with-in _ cre-a-tion draw-ing the threads to

co-lour and_ de-sign: life in-to life, you knit our true_ sal-va-tion,

Harmony

come, work with us, and weave us in - to one. __

1   Spirit of love, you move within creation
     drawing the threads to colour and design:
     life into life, you knit our true salvation,
         come, work with us,
         and weave us into one.

2   Though we have frayed the fabric of your making,
     tearing away from all that you intend,
     yet, to be whole, humanity is aching,
         come, work with us,
         and weave us into one.

3   Great loom of God, where history is woven,
     you are the frame that holds us to the truth,
     Christ is the theme, the pattern you have given,
         come, work with us,
         and weave us into one.

Shirley Erena Murray (*b.* 1931)

Music Colin Alexander Gibson (*b.* 1933), *adapted* Compilers

75 75 44 75

Spirit of the living God
fall afresh on me;
Spirit of the living God,
fall afresh on me:
break me, melt me,
mould me, fill me.
Spirit of the living God,
fall afresh on me.

Daniel Iverson (1890–1977)

620

Spirit of the living God,
move among us all;
make us one in heart and mind,
makes us one in love,
humble, caring,
selfless, sharing.
Spirit of the living God,
fill our lives with love.

Michael Baughen (*b.* 1930)

619 and 620 may be sung as one hymn.

Music Daniel Iverson (1890–1977)

MARK OF NAILS   11 10 11 10

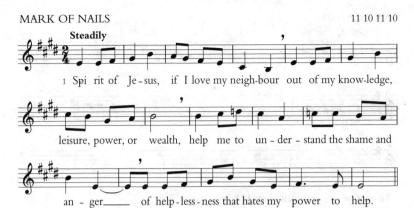

1 Spirit of Jesus, if I love my neighbour out of my knowledge, leisure, power, or wealth, help me to understand the shame and anger of helplessness that hates my power to help.

1   Spirit of Jesus, if I love my neighbour
    out of my knowledge, leisure, power, or wealth,
    help me to understand the shame and anger
    of helplessness that hates my power to help.

2   And if, when I have answered need with kindness,
    my neighbour rises, wakened from despair,
    keep me from flinching when the cry for justice
    requires of me the changes that I fear.

3   If I am hugging safety or possessions,
    uncurl my spirit, as your love prevails,
    to join my neighbours, work for liberation,
    and find my freedom at the mark of nails.

                                        Brian Wren (b. 1936)

Music John L. Bell (b. 1949)

622

WOODLANDS

10 10 10 10

Unison

The original version is found at 518.

1   We sing a love that sets all people free,
    that blows like wind, that burns like scorching flame,
    enfolds the earth, springs up like water clear:
    come, living love, live in our hearts today.

2   We sing a love that seeks another's good,
    that longs to serve and not to count the cost,
    a love that, yielding, finds itself made new:
    come, caring love, live in our hearts today.

3   We sing a love, unflinching, unafraid
    to be itself, despite another's wrath,
    a love that stands alone and undismayed:
    come, strengthening love, live in our hearts today.

4   We sing a love, that, wandering, will not rest
    until it finds its way, its home, its source,
    through joy and sadness pressing on refreshed:
    come, pilgrim love, live in our hearts today.

5   We sing the Holy Spirit, full of love,
    who seeks out scars of ancient bitterness,
    brings to our wounds the healing grace of Christ:
    come, radiant love, live in our hearts today.

June Boyce-Tillman (*b.* 1943)

Music Walter Greatorex (1877–1949)

GATHER US IN   Irregular

Brightly

1 Here in this place new light is stream-ing, now is the dark-ness van-ished a-way, see in this space our fears and our dream-ings, brought here to you in the light of this day._____ Gath-er us in — the lost and for-sak-en, gath-er us in — the blind and the lame: call to us now, and we shall a-wak-en, we shall a-rise at the sound of our name._____

1   Here in this place new light is streaming,
          now is the darkness vanished away,
          see in this space our fears and our dreamings,
          brought here to you in the light of this day.
          Gather us in — the lost and forsaken,
          gather us in — the blind and the lame;
          call to us now, and we shall awaken,
          we shall arise at the sound of our name.

2   We are the young — our lives are a mystery,
          we are the old who yearn for your face,
          we have been sung throughout all of history,
          called to be light to the whole human race.
          Gather us in — the rich and the haughty,
          gather us in — the proud and the strong;
          give us a heart so meek and so lowly,
          give us the courage to enter the song.

continued overleaf

Music Marty Haugen (b.1950)

3   Here we will take the wine and the water,
here we will take the bread of new birth,
here you shall call your sons and your daughters,
call us anew to be salt for the earth.
Give us to drink the wine of compassion,
give us to eat the bread that is you;
nourish us well, and teach us to fashion
lives that are holy and hearts that are true.

4   Not in the dark of buildings confining,
not in some heaven, light years away,
but here in this place the new light is shining,
now is the Kingdom, now is the day.
Gather us in and hold us for ever,
gather us in and make us your own;
gather us in — all peoples together,
fire of love in our flesh and our bone.

Marty Haugen (*b.* 1950)

McKEE   CM

1   In Christ there is no east or west,
    in him no south or north,
    but one great fellowship of love
    throughout the whole wide earth.

2   In Christ shall true hearts everywhere
    their high communion find,
    his service is the golden cord
    close-binding human kind.

3   Come, brothers, sisters of the faith,
    whate'er your race may be:
    whoever does my Father's will
    is surely kin to me.

4   In Christ now meet both east and west,
    in him meet south and north,
    all Christ-like souls are one in him,
    throughout the whole wide earth.

John Oxenham, pseud. (1852–1941)
*William Arthur Dunkerley (1852–1941)

Music Afro-American spiritual
adapted Henry Thacker Burleigh (1866–1949)

HEREFORD   LM

1   O thou who camest from above
the pure celestial fire to impart,
kindle a flame of sacred love
on the mean altar of my heart.

2   There let it for thy glory burn
with inextinguishable blaze,
and trembling to its source return,
in humble prayer and fervent praise.

3   Jesus, confirm my heart's desire
to work, and speak, and think for thee;
still let me guard the holy fire,
and still stir up thy gift in me:

4   Ready for all thy perfect will,
my acts of faith and love repeat,
till death thy endless mercies seal,
and make the sacrifice complete.

Charles Wesley (1707–1788)

Music Samuel Sebastian Wesley (1810–1876)

LAUDS   77 77

1   Holy Spirit, truth divine,
     dawn upon this soul of mine;
     Word of God, and inward light,
     wake my spirit, clear my sight.

2   Holy Spirit, love divine,
     glow within this heart of mine;
     kindle every high desire,
     perish self in your pure fire.

3   Holy Spirit, power divine,
     fill and nerve this will of mine;
     by you may I strongly live,
     bravely bear, and nobly strive.

4   Holy Spirit, right divine,
     King within my conscience reign;
     be my law, and I shall be
     firmly bound, for ever free.

5   Holy Spirit, peace divine,
     still this restless soul of mine;
     speak to calm this tossing sea,
     stayed in your tranquillity.

6   Holy Spirit, joy divine,
     gladden now this heart of mine;
     in the desert ways I sing,
     'Spring, O well, for ever spring!'

                Samuel Longfellow (1819–1892)

Music John Whitridge Wilson (1905–1992)

CHARITY

7775

1   Gracious Spirit, Holy Ghost,
    taught by you, we covet most,
    of your gifts at Pentecost,
    holy, heavenly love.

2   Faith that mountains could remove,
    tongues of earth or heaven above,
    knowledge, all things, empty prove
    without heavenly love.

3   Though I as a martyr bleed,
    give my goods the poor to feed,
    all is vain, if love I need;
    therefore give me love.

3   Love is kind, and suffers long;
    love is meek, and thinks no wrong,
    love than death itself more strong;
    therefore give us love.

5   Prophecy will fade away,
    melting in the light of day;
    love will ever with us stay;
    therefore give us love.

6   Faith and hope and love we see,
    joining hand in hand, agree;
    but the greatest of the three,
    and the best, is love.

Christopher Wordsworth (1807–1885)

Music John Stainer (1840–1901)

Also suitable
God, whose almighty word   112
This is a day of new beginnings   526
If you believe and I believe   771

THE CHURCH CELEBRATES
HOLY BAPTISM

The Apostles' Creed

I believe in God, the Father almighty,
creator of heaven and earth.

I believe in Jesus Christ, God's only Son, our Lord,
who was conceived by the Holy Spirit,
born of the Virgin Mary,
suffered under Pontius Pilate,
was crucified, died, and was buried;
he descended to the dead.
On the third day he rose again;
he ascended into heaven,
he is seated at the right hand of the Father,
and he will come to judge the living and the dead.

I believe in the Holy Spirit,
the holy catholic Church,
the communion of saints,
the forgiveness of sins,
the resurrection of the body,
and the life everlasting.
Amen.

Liturgical text, ELLC, 1998

PSALM 118 (RENDEZ A DIEU)   98 98 D

Briskly

An alternative harmonisation is found at 672.

1   Mark how the Lamb of God, self-offering,
     our human sinfulness takes on
     there in the waters of the Jordan,
     as Jesus is baptized by John.
     Hear how the voice from heaven is saying,
     'Lo, this is my belovèd Son.'
     See how in dovelike form the Spirit
     descends on God's Anointed One.

2   From this assurance of God's favour
     Christ goes into the wilderness,
     there to endure a time of testing,
     preparing him to teach and bless.
     So we, by water and the Spirit
     baptized into Christ's ministry,
     are often led to paths of service
     through mazes of adversity.

3   Grant us, O God, the strength and courage
     to live the faith our lips declare;
     bless us in our baptismal calling;
     Christ's royal priesthood help us share.
     Turn us from every false allegiance,
     that we may trust in Christ alone:
     make of us now a chosen people
     transformed by love to be your own.

                              Carl P. Daw, Jr (*b.* 1944)

Music Melody probably by Louis Bourgeois (*c.* 1510–1561)
harmonised Compilers

CAITHNESS   CM

PARAPHRASE 47, verses 2–4

1   When to the sacred font we came,
         did not the rite proclaim,
         that, washed from sin and all its stains,
         new creatures we became?

2   With Christ the Lord we died to sin;
         with him to life we rise,
         to life which, now begun on earth,
         is perfect in the skies.

3   Too long enthralled to Satan's sway,
         we now are slaves no more;
         for Christ hath vanquished death and sin,
         our freedom to restore.

Scottish Paraphrases, 1781
Romans 6: 2-7

Music Melody from *Scottish Psalter,* 1635
harmonised Compilers of *English Hymnal,* 1906

COMMANDMENTS   LM

1   A little child the Saviour came,
     the mighty God was still his name,
     and angels worshipped as he lay
     the seeming infant of a day.

2   He who, a little child, began
     to show the world God's loving plan,
     proclaims from heaven the message free,
     'Let little children come to me.'

3   We bring them, Lord, and with the sign
     of sprinkled water name them thine:
     their souls with saving grace endow;
     baptize them with thy Spirit now.

4   O give thine angels charge, good Lord,
     them safely in thy way to guard;
     thy blessing on their lives command,
     and write their names upon thy hand.

5   O thou, who by an infant's tongue
     dost hear thy perfect glory sung,
     may these, with all the heavenly host,
     praise Father, Son, and Holy Ghost.

                    *William Robertson (1820–1864)

Music Adapted from a melody in *La Forme des Prières et Chants
Ecclésiastiques,* Strasbourg, 1545
harmonised *David Evans (1874–1948)

BELMONT   CM

A lower setting is found at 688.

1   Our children, Lord, in faith and prayer,
     we now devote to you;
     let them your covenant mercies share,
     and your salvation true.

2   Such children you did once embrace,
     while dwelling here below;
     to us and ours, O God of grace,
     the same compassion show.

3   Dear Lord, your infant feet were found
     within your Father's shrine;
     your years, with changeless virtue crowned,
     were all alike divine.

4   Dependent on your bounteous breath,
     we seek your grace alone,
     in every stage of life and death,
     to keep us still your own.

                              *Thomas Haweis (1734–1820)
                    and *Reginald Heber (1783–1826)

Music Melody by William Gardiner (1770–1853)
harmonised Compilers of *Revised Church Hymnary,* 1927

SHIPSTON   87 87

1   Child of blessing, child of promise,
     God's you are, from God you came.
     In this sacrament God claims you:
     live as one who bears Christ's name.

2   Child of God, you bear God's image,
     learn to listen for God's call;
     grow to laugh and sing and worship,
     trust and love God more than all.

                    Ronald S. Cole-Turner (*b.* 1948)

Music English traditional melody
harmonised Ralph Vaughan Williams (1872–1958)

634

WAS LEBET, WAS SCHWEBET   11 10 11 10

1   Word of the Father, the life of creation,
     emptied of glory, among us you came;
     born as a servant, assuming our weakness,
     drank from the cup of our joy and our shame.

2   Each human child bears your image and likeness,
     yet all are heirs to the sins of our earth;
     once from death's flood you arose to redeem us,
     water and Spirit now seal our rebirth.

Music Melody from Rheinhardt MS, Üttingen, 1754
harmonised Ralph Vaughan Williams (1872–1958)

3   Searching, you found us before we could name you,
loving, you suffered our pain and our loss;
strengthen each child through the faith of your people,
born in the glory which streams from the Cross.

Colin Peter Thompson (b. 1945)

635

ENGELBERG   10 10 10 and Alleluia

1   We know that Christ is raised and dies no more.
Embraced by death, he broke its fearful hold,
and our despair he turned to blazing joy.
Alleluia!

2   We share by water in his saving death.
Reborn, we share with him an Easter life
as living members of a living Christ.

3   The God of splendour clothes the Son with life.
The spirit's fission shakes the church of God.
Baptized, we live with God the Three in One.

4   A new creation comes to life and grows
as Christ's new body takes on flesh and blood.
The universe restored and whole will sing:

John Brownlow Geyer (b. 1932)

Music Charles Villiers Stanford (1852–1924)
arranged Compilers of *BBC Hymn Book,* 1951

BAPTIZED IN WATER   5553 D

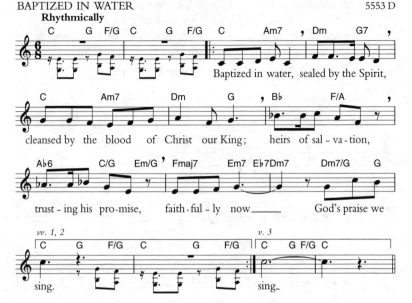

An alternative tune BUNESSAN *is found at* 212.

1   Baptized in water,
      sealed by the Spirit,
      cleansed by the blood of Christ our king;
      heirs of salvation,
      trusting his promise,
      faithfully now God's praise we sing.

2   Baptized in water,
      sealed by the Spirit,
      dead in the tomb with Christ our king;
      one with his rising,
      freed and forgiven,
      thankfully now God's praise we sing.

3   Baptized in water,
      sealed by the Spirit,
      marked with the sign of Christ our king;
      born of one Father,
      we are his children,
      joyfully now God's praise we sing.

Michael Saward (*b.* 1932)

Music Alistair Goudie
arranged Geoff Weaver (*b.* 1943)

STRACATHRO   CM

A higher setting is found at 548.

1   Now through the grace of God we claim
     this life to be his own,
     baptized with water in the name
     of Father, Spirit, Son.

2   For Jesus Christ the crucified,
     who broke the power of sin,
     now lives to plead for those baptized
     in unity with him.

3   So let us take him at his word,
     rejoicing in our faith,
     until we rise with Christ our Lord
     and triumph over death!

                    Michael Arnold Perry (1942–1996)

Music Charles Hutcheson (1792–1860)
arranged David Evans (1874–1948)

Also suitable
Here is the place, now is the time   678

EPIPHANY

11 10 11 10

Another version is found at 240.

1   Lord, we have come at your own invitation,
    chosen by you, to be counted your friends;
    yours is the strength that sustains dedication,
    ours a commitment we know never ends.

2   Here at your table, confirm our intention,
    give it your seal of forgiveness and grace;
    teach us to serve, without pride or pretension,
    Lord, in your kingdom, whatever our place.

3   When, at your table, each time of returning,
    vows are renewed and our courage restored,
    may we increasingly glory in learning
    all that it means to accept you as Lord.

4   So, in the world, where each duty assigned us
    gives us the chance to create or destroy,
    help us to make those decisions that bind us,
    Lord, to yourself, in obedience and joy.

                        Frederick Pratt Green (1903–2000)

Music Joseph Francis Thrupp (1827–1867)
arranged Compilers

ST PATRICK   DLM

Unison
vv. 1 - 4, 6

v. 1 ends here

Ατομριυς ιηδιύ ηιυρτ τρέη τοζαιρm τριηοιτ

1   I bind unto myself today
        the strong Name of the Trinity;
        by invocation of the same,
        the Three in One, and One in Three.

2   I bind this day to me for ever,
        by power of faith, Christ's Incarnation;
        his baptism in the Jordan river;
        his death on cross for my salvation;
        his bursting from the spicèd tomb;
        his riding up the heavenly way;
        his coming at the day of doom:
        I bind unto myself today.

continued overleaf

Music Irish traditional melody
arranged Charles Villiers Stanford (1852–1924)

3   I bind unto myself today
      the virtues of the star-lit heaven,
      the glorious sun's life-giving ray,
      the whiteness of the moon at even,
      the flashing of the lightning free,
      the whirling wind's tempestuous shocks,
      the stable earth, the deep salt sea
      around the old eternal rocks.

4   I bind unto myself today
      the power of God to hold and lead,
      his eye to watch, his might to stay,
      his ear to hearken to my need,
      the wisdom of my God to teach,
      his hand to guide, his shield to ward,
      the word of God to give me speech,
      his heavenly host to be my guard.

Either CLONMACNOISE *or* GARTAN *may be sung to verse 5.*
Turn over for GARTAN.

CLONMACNOISE   8888 D

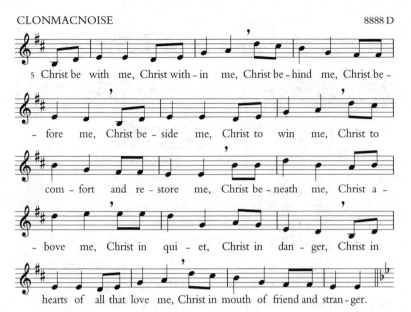

5 Christ be with me, Christ with - in me, Christ be - hind me, Christ be - fore me, Christ be - side me, Christ to win me, Christ to com - fort and re - store me, Christ be - neath me, Christ a - bove me, Christ in qui - et, Christ in dan - ger, Christ in hearts of all that love me, Christ in mouth of friend and stran - ger.

5 Christ be with me, Christ within me,
  Christ behind me, Christ before me,
  Christ beside me, Christ to win me,
  Christ to comfort and restore me,
  Christ beneath me, Christ above me,
  Christ in quiet, Christ in danger,
  Christ in hearts of all that love me,
  Christ in mouth of friend and stranger.

6 I bind unto myself the name,
  the strong Name of the Trinity,
  by invocation of the same,
  the Three in One, and One in Three,
  of whom all nature hath creation,
  Eternal Father, Spirit, Word.
  Praise to the Lord of my salvation:
  salvation is of Christ the Lord. Amen.

St Patrick (372–466)
version by Cecil Frances Alexander (1818–1895)

Music Ancient Irish melody
arranged Richard Runciman Terry (1865–1938)

639.ii Music: © Continuum International Publishing Group Ltd, The Tower Building, 11 York Road, London SE1 7NX.
Used by permission.

GARTAN   8888

5   Christ be with me, Christ within me,
Christ behind me, Christ before me,
Christ beside me, Christ to win me,
Christ to comfort and restore me,
Christ beneath me, Christ above me,
Christ in quiet, Christ in danger,
Christ in hearts of all that love me,
Christ in mouth of friend and stranger.

Turn back for verse 6.

Either CLONMACNOISE *or* GARTAN *may be sung to verse 5.*

Music Irish traditional melody, *harmonised* Compilers

640

ALL FOR JESUS   87 87

1   Holy Spirit, come, confirm us
in the truth that Christ makes known;
we have faith and understanding
through your helping gifts alone.

2   Holy Spirit, come, console us,
come as advocate to plead;
loving Spirit from the Father,
grant in Christ the help we need.

3   Holy Spirit, come, renew us,
come yourself to make us live;
keep us holy through your presence,
holy through the gifts you give.

William Brian Foley (1919–2000)

Music John Stainer (1840–1901)

SEEK YE FIRST

8 5 11 and Alleluias

1.   Seek ye first the kingdom of God
   and his righteousness;
   and all these things shall be added unto you;
   allelu, alleluia.
   Alleluia, alleluia, alleluia, alleluia!

2.   Ask, and it shall be given unto you,
   seek, and ye shall find;
   knock, and the door shall be opened unto you;
   allelu, alleluia.

3.   You shall not live by bread alone,
   but by every word
   that proceeds from the mouth of the Lord;
   allelu, alleluia.

The verses may be sung in canon with the refrain.

Karen Lafferty (*b.* 1948)

Music Karen Lafferty (*b.* 1948)

ABBOT'S LEIGH   87 87 D

A lower setting is found at 615.

1   Ye that know the Lord is gracious,
          ye for whom a corner stone
          stands, of God elect and precious,
          laid that ye may build thereon,
          see that on that sure foundation
          ye a living temple raise,
          towers that may tell forth salvation,
          walls that may re-echo praise.

2   Living stones, by God appointed
          each to an allotted place,
          kings and priests, by God anointed,
          shall ye not declare his grace?
          Ye, a royal generation,
          tell the tidings of your birth,
          tidings of a new creation
          to an old and weary earth.

Music Cyril Vincent Taylor (1907–1991)

3   Tell the praise of him who called you
out of darkness into light,
broke the fetters that enthralled you,
gave you freedom, peace and sight:
tell the tale of sins forgiven,
strength renewed and hope restored,
till the earth, in tune with heaven,
praise and magnify the Lord!

Cyril Argentine Alington (1872–1955)

643

ST MICHAEL (OLD 134TH)   SM

1   For me to live is Christ:
with him new life begins;
his loving touch renews my mind
and takes away my sins.

2   For me to live is Christ:
from him true living springs;
he comes, and with his radiant love
transforms all common things.

3   For me to live is Christ:
to serve is now my aim;
to help wherever there is need,
and care in Jesus' name.

4   For me to live is Christ:
for him my life I'll spend;
my strength, my aim, my hope, my Lord,
from now till my life's end.

Peter Henry Kelway Tongeman (b. 1929)

Music Derived from melody for 'Psalm 101' in
French-Genevan Psalter, 1551
adapted William Crotch (1775–1847)
arranged Compilers of *Revised Church Hymnary,* 1927

644 1

THORNBURY 76 76 D

644 2

WOLVERCOTE 76 76 D

Music Tune 1 Basil Harwood (1859–1949)
Music Tune 2 William Harold Ferguson (1874–1950)

1   O Jesus, I have promised
to serve you to the end;
be now and always near me,
my master and my friend:
I shall not fear the battle
if you are by my side,
nor wander from the pathway
if you will be my guide.

2   Oh, let me feel you near me:
the world is ever near;
I see the sights that dazzle,
the tempting sounds I hear;
my foes are ever near me,
around me, and within;
but, Jesus, draw still nearer,
and shield my soul from sin.

3   Oh, let me hear you speaking
in accents clear and still,
above the storms of passion,
the murmurs of self-will;
Oh, speak to reassure me,
to hasten or control;
O speak, and make me listen,
true guardian of my soul.

4   O Jesus, you have promised
to all who follow you,
that where you are in glory
your servant shall be too;
and, Jesus, I have promised
to serve you to the end:
now give me grace to follow,
my master and my friend.

*John Ernest Bode (1816–1874)

JACKSON (BYZANTIUM)   CM

PARAPHRASE 54

1   I'm not ashamed to own my Lord,
or to defend his cause,
maintain the glory of his cross,
and honour all his laws.

2   Jesus, my Lord! I know his name,
his name is all my boast;
he will not put my soul to shame,
nor let my hope be lost.

3   I know that safe with him remains,
protected by his power,
what I've committed to his trust,
till the decisive hour.

4   Then will he own his servant's name
before his Father's face,
and in the new Jerusalem
appoint my soul a place.

Scottish Paraphrases, 1781

Music Melody in *Twelve Psalm Tunes,* 1780 by
Thomas Jackson (1715–1781)
harmonised David Evans (1874–1948)

646

DUKE STREET   LM

1   Forth in the peace of Christ we go;
    Christ to the world with joy we bring;
    Christ in our minds, Christ on our lips,
    Christ in our hearts, the world's true king.

2   King of our hearts, Christ reigns in us;
    kingship with him his servants gain;
    with Christ, the Servant-Lord of all,
    Christ's world we serve to share Christ's reign.

3   Priests of the world, Christ sends us forth
    this world of time to consecrate,
    our world of sin by grace to heal,
    Christ's world in Christ to re-create.

4   Prophets of Christ, we hear his word:
    he claims our minds, to search his ways;
    he claims our lips, to speak his truth;
    he claims our hearts, to sing his praise.

5   We are his Church, he makes us one:
    here is one hearth for all to find;
    here is one flock, one Shepherd-King;
    here is one faith, one heart, one mind.

James Quinn *(b. 1919)*

Music Melody attributed to John L. Hatton *(d. 1793)*
from Boyd's *Psalm and Hymn Tunes,* 1793
harmonised David Evans (1874–1948)

Also suitable

Sent by the Lord am I	250
As a fire is meant for burning	252
Take this moment, sign, and space	501
This is a day of new beginnings	526
May the mind of Christ my Saviour	536
Holy Spirit, ever living	615
O thou who camest from above	625
Here is the place, now is the time	678

Gloria in excelsis

Glory to God in the highest,
and peace to God's people on earth.

Lord God, heavenly King,
almighty God and Father,
we worship you, we give you thanks,
we praise you for your glory.

Lord Jesus Christ, only Son of the Father,
Lord God, Lamb of God,
you take away the sin of the world:
have mercy on us;
you are seated at the right hand of the Father:
receive our prayer.

For you alone are the Holy One,
you alone are the Lord,
you alone are the Most High,
Jesus Christ,
with the Holy Spirit,
in the glory of God the Father.
Amen.

Liturgical text, ELLC, 1998

648

Kyrie eleison

Kyrie eleison

Lord, have mercy.
Christ, have mercy.
Lord, have mercy.

Music St Anne Mass, James MacMillan (*b.* 1959)

648 Music: © 1997 Boosey & Hawkes Music Publishers Ltd, 295 Regent Street, London W1B 2JH.

Nicene Creed

We believe in one God,
the Father, the Almighty,
maker of heaven and earth,
of all that is, seen and unseen.

We believe in one Lord, Jesus Christ,
the only Son of God,
eternally begotten of the Father,
God from God, Light from Light,
true God from true God,
begotten, not made,
of one Being with the Father;
through him all things were made.
For us and for our salvation he came down from heaven,
was incarnate of the Holy Spirit and the Virgin Mary
and became truly human.
For our sake he was crucified under Pontius Pilate;
he suffered death and was buried.
On the third day he rose again
in accordance with the Scriptures;
he ascended into heaven
and is seated at the right hand of the Father.
He will come again in glory to judge the living and the dead,
and his kingdom will have no end.

We believe in the Holy Spirit, the Lord, the giver of life,
who proceeds from the Father and the Son,
who with the Father and the Son is worshipped and glorified,
who has spoken through the prophets.
We believe in one holy catholic and apostolic Church.
We acknowledge one baptism for the forgiveness of sins.
We look for the resurrection of the dead,
and the life of the world to come.   Amen.

Liturgical text, ELLC, 1998

50

Sursum corda

The Lord be with you.
And also with you.

Lift up your hearts.
We lift them to the Lord.

Let us give thanks to the Lord our God.
It is right to give our thanks and praise.

Liturgical text, ELLC, 1998

Sanctus and *Benedictus qui venit*

Ho - ly, ho - ly, ho - ly Lord, God of power and might. heaven and earth are full of your glo - ry. Ho - san - na in the high - est. Bles - sed is he, O bles - sed is he who comes in the name of the Lord. Ho - san - na in the high - est. Ho - san - na in the high - est.

Sanctus and *Benedictus qui venit*

Holy, holy, holy Lord, God of power and might,
heaven and earth are full of your glory.
Hosanna in the highest.

Blessed is he who comes in the name of the Lord.
Hosanna in the highest.

Liturgical text, ELLC, 1998

Music St Anne Mass, James MacMillan (b. 1959)

652   *The Lord's Prayer*

First Form
Our Father in heaven,
hallowed be your name,
your kingdom come,
your will be done,
on earth as in heaven.

Give us today our daily bread.
Forgive us our sins
as we forgive those who sin against us.
Save us from the time of trial
and deliver us from evil.
For the kingdom, the power,
and the glory are yours
now and for ever.
Amen.

Liturgical text, ELLC, 1998

Second Form (a)
Our Father, who art in heaven,
hallowed be thy name;
thy kingdom come;
thy will be done;
on earth as it is in heaven.
Give us this day our daily bread.
And forgive us our debts,
as we forgive our debtors.
And lead us not into temptation;
but deliver us from evil.
For thine is the kingdom,
the power, and the glory,
for ever.
Amen.

Traditional version, modified

Second Form (b)
Our Father, who art in heaven,
hallowed be thy name;
thy kingdom come;
thy will be done;
on earth as it is in heaven.
Give us this day our daily bread.
And forgive us our trespasses,
as we forgive those who trespass against us.
And lead us not into temptation;
but deliver us from evil.
For thine is the kingdom,
the power, and the glory,
for ever and ever.
Amen.

Traditional version, modified

Agnus Dei

Lamb of God, you take a - way the sin___ of the___ world,___ have mer - cy___ on us. Lamb of God, you take a - way the sin___ of the___ world,___ have mer - cy___ on us. Lamb of God, you take a - way the sin___ of the world, grant___ us peace.

Agnus Dei

Lamb of God, you take away the sin of the world,
have mercy on us.

Lamb of God, you take away the sin of the world,
have mercy on us.

Lamb of God, you take away the sin of the world,
grant us peace.

Liturgical text, ELLC, 1998

Music St Anne Mass
James MacMillan (*b.* 1959)

GOVAN OLD 11 10 11 10

1   'Lift up your hearts': I hear the summons calling
      forth from the heavenly altar where he stands —
      our great High Priest, the Father's love revealing,
      in priestly act, with pleading outspread hands.

2   'Lift up your hearts': with hearts to heaven soaring
      the Church exulting makes her glad reply —
      'We lift them up unto the Lord', adoring;
      our God and thine, through thee, we glorify.

3   'Lift up your hearts': alas, O Lord, I cannot
      lift up aright my burdened heart to thee;
      thou knowest, Lord, the cares that weigh upon it,
      the chains that bind it struggling to be free.

4   O Love divine! thy promise comes to cheer me,
      O Voice of pity! blessing and thrice blest —
      'Come unto me, ye laden hearts and weary;
      take up my yoke, and learn: I pledge you rest'.

5   I dare not waver by such grace invited,
      I yield my heart, dear Lord: I close the strife.
      Lift thou my heart until, with thine united,
      I taste anew the joy of endless life.

John Macleod (1840–1898)

Music Douglas Galbraith (b. 1940)

HOLY MANNA   87 87 D

1   For your generous providing
     which sustains us all our days,
     for your Spirit here residing,
     we proclaim our heartfelt praise.
     Through the depths of joy and sorrow,
     though the road be smooth or rough,
     fearless, we can face tomorrow
     for your grace will be enough.

2   Hush our world's seductive noises
     tempting us to stand alone;
     save us from the siren voices
     calling us to trust our own.
     For those snared by earthly treasure,
     lured by false security,
     Jesus, true and only measure,
     spring the trap to set folk free.

3   Round your table, through your giving,
     show us how to live and pray
     till your kingdom's way of living
     is the bread we share each day:
     bread for us and for our neighbour,
     bread for body, mind, and soul,
     bread of heaven and human labour —
     broken bread that makes us whole.

                                        Leith Fisher (b. 1941)

Music The Columbian Harmony, Cincinatti, 1825
arranged Marty Haugen (b. 1950)

DOVE OF PEACE   86 86 6

1 I come with joy, a child of God, for-giv-en, loved and free,____ the life of Je - sus to re-call, in love laid down for me,____ in love laid down for me.____

vv. 1 - 4   v. 5

2 I

1   I come with joy, a child of God,
      forgiven, loved and free,
      the life of Jesus to recall,
   * in love laid down for me.

2   I come with Christians far and near
      to find, as all are fed,
      the new community of love
      in Christ's communion bread.

3   As Christ breaks bread, and bids us share,
      each proud division ends.
      The love that made us, makes us one,
      and strangers now are friends.

4   The Spirit of the risen Christ,
      unseen, but ever near,
      is in such friendship better known,
      alive among us here.

5   Together met, together bound
      by all that God has done,
      we'll go with joy, to give the world
      the love that makes us one.

   * *The last line of each verse is repeated.*

                              Brian Wren (b. 1936)

Music Southern Harmony, 1835, *adapted* Compilers

656 Words: © 1971, 1995, Stainer & Bell Ltd, PO Box 110, Victoria House, 23 Gruneisen Road, London N3 1DZ

CHRISTE SANCTORUM

11 11 11 5

1   Father most loving, listen to your children
    who as your family gladly come together,
    singing the praises of your Son, our Brother,
    Jesus beloved.

2   We stand attentive, listening to God's Gospel,
    welcoming Jesus as he speaks among us,
    mind and heart open, ready to receive him,
    lips to proclaim him.

3   Father in heaven, bless the gifts we offer,
    signs of our true love, hearts in homage given!
    Make them the one gift that is wholly worthy,
    Christ, spotless victim.

4   Father, we thank you for your Son's dear presence,
    coming to feed us as the Bread of heaven,
    making us one with him in true communion,
    one with each other.

5   Praised be our Father, lovingly inviting
    guests to his banquet, praised the Son who feeds us,
    praised too the Spirit, sent by Son and Father,
    making us Christ-like.

James Quinn (*b.* 1919)

Music Melody, *Paris Antiphoner,* 1681
harmonised David Evans (1874–1948)

LAYING DOWN

10 10 10 4

1   Before I take the body of my Lord,
     before I share his life in bread and wine,
     I recognise the sorry things within:
     these I lay down.

2   The words of hope I often failed to give,
     the prayers of kindness buried by my pride,
     the signs of care I argued out of sight:
     these I lay down.

3   The narrowness of vision and of mind,
     the need for other folk to serve my will,
     and every word and silence meant to hurt:
     these I lay down.

4   Of those around in whom I meet my Lord,
     I ask their pardon and I grant them mine,
     that every contradiction of Christ's peace
     might be laid down.

5   Lord Jesus Christ, companion at this feast,
     I empty now my heart and stretch my hands,
     and ask to meet you here in bread and wine
     which you lay down.

John L. Bell (*b.* 1949)
and Graham Maule (*b.* 1958)

Music John L. Bell (*b.* 1949)

VRIEDE IN HANDEN

87 87 (Iambic)

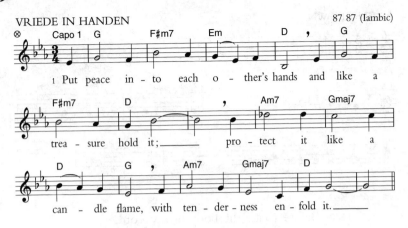

1 Put peace in-to each o-ther's hands and like a
trea-sure hold it;_____ pro-tect it like a
can-dle flame, with ten-der-ness en-fold it._____

1   Put peace into each other's hands
    and like a treasure hold it;
    protect it like a candle flame,
    with tenderness enfold it.

2   Put peace into each other's hands
    with loving expectation;
    be gentle in your words and ways,
    in touch with God's creation.

3   Put peace into each other's hands,
    like bread we break for sharing;
    look people warmly in the eye:
    our life is meant for caring.

4   And at communion, shape your hands
    into a waiting cradle;
    the gift of Christ, receive, revere,
    united round the table.

5   Put Christ into each other's hands,
    he is love's deepest measure;
    in love make peace, give peace a chance
    and share it like a treasure.

Fred Kaan (b. 1929)

Music John L. Bell (b. 1949)

659 Words: © 1989, Stainer & Bell Ltd, PO Box 110, Victoria House, 23 Gruneisen Road, London N3 1DZ
659 Music: © WGRG, The Iona Community

A VA DE   10 10

1   CANTOR: Come, let us eat, for now the feast is spread.
     ALL: Come, let us eat, for now the feast is spread.
     CANTOR: Our Lord's body let us take together.
     ALL: Our Lord's body let us take together.

2   Come, let us drink, for now the wine is poured.
     Jesus' blood now let us drink together.

3   In Jesus' presence now we meet and rest.
     In the presence of our Lord we gather.

4   Rise, let us share God's peace with everyone.
     At the table we are one together.

Verses 2, 3 and 4 are sung in the same way as verse 1.

Billema Kwilla (*b.* 1925)

Music Billema Kwilla (*b.* 1925)

EAT THIS BREAD   Irregular

Eat this bread, drink this cup, come to me and nev-er be hun-gry.
Eat this bread, drink this cup, trust in me and you will not thirst.

Eat this bread, drink this cup,
come to me and never be hungry.
Eat this bread, drink this cup,
trust in me and you will not thirst.

Taizé Community
from *John 6*

Music Jacques Berthier (1923–1994)

662

MARYTON   LM

Jesu, dulcedo cordium

1   Jesus, thou joy of loving hearts,
    thou light of life, thou fount of grace;
    from the best bliss that earth imparts
    we turn unfilled to seek thy face.

2   Thy truth unchanged has ever stood;
    thou savest those that on thee call:
    to those that seek thee thou art good,
    to those that find thee, all in all.

3   We taste thee, O thou living bread,
    and long to feast upon thee still;
    we drink of thee, the fountain-head,
    and thirst our souls from thee to fill.

4   Our restless spirits yearn for thee,
    where'er our changeful lot is cast,
    glad when thy gracious smile we see,
    blest when our faith can hold thee fast.

5   O Jesus, ever with us stay;
make all our moments calm and bright;
chase the dark night of sin away;
shed o'er the world thy holy light.

12th century
translated *Ray Palmer (1808–1887)

Music Henry Percy Smith (1825–1898)

63

BREAD OF LIFE   66 75 and refrain

*Bread of life, hope of the world,
Jesus Christ, our brother:
feed us now, give us life,
lead us to one another.*

1 As we proclaim your death,
as we recall your life,
we remember your promise
to return again.

2 This bread we break and
share
was scattered once as grain:
just as now it is gathered,
make your people one.

3 We eat this living bread,
we drink this saving cup:
sign of hope in our broken
world,
source of lasting love.

Music Bernadette Farrell (b. 1957)   Bernadette Farrell (b. 1957)

ST AGNES (LANGRAN)   10 10 10 10

664 2

KINGSBORO   10 10 10 10

Music Tune 1 James Langran (1835–1909)

Music Tune 2 M. Lee Suitor (b. 1942)
harmonised Marilyn Hauser Hamm (b. 1951)

before Communion

1   Here, O my Lord, I see thee face to face;
    here would I touch and handle things unseen,
    here grasp with firmer hand the eternal grace,
    and all my weariness upon thee lean.

2   Mine is the sin, but thine the righteousness;
    mine is the guilt, but thine the cleansing blood;
    here is my robe, my refuge, and my peace —
    thy blood, thy righteousness, O Lord my God.

3   Here would I feed upon the bread of God,
    here drink with thee the royal wine of heaven;
    here would I lay aside each earthly load,
    here taste afresh the calm of sin forgiven.

4   This is the hour of banquet and of song;
    this is the heavenly table spread for me;
    here let me feast, and, feasting, still prolong
    this hallowed hour of fellowship with thee.

after Communion

5   Too soon we rise; the symbols disappear;
    the feast, though not the love, is past and gone;
    the bread and wine remove, but thou art here,
    nearer than ever, still my Shield and Sun.

6   I have no help but thine; nor do I need
    another arm but thine to lean upon;
    it is enough, my Lord, enough indeed;
    my strength is in thy might, thy might alone.

7   Feast after feast thus comes and passes by,
    yet, passing, points to the glad feast above,
    giving sweet foretaste of the festal joy,
    the Lamb's great bridal feast of bliss and love.

                    Horatius N. Bonar (1808–1889)

The whole hymn is sung to either tune.

One bread, one body, one Lord of all,
one cup of blessing which we bless,
and we, though many, throughout the earth,
we are one body in this one Lord.

1   Gentile or Jew,
    servant or free,
    woman or man — no more.

2   Many the gifts,
    many the works,
    one in the Lord of all.

3   Grain for the fields,
    scattered and grown,
    gathered to one for all.

John Foley, SJ (b. 1939)

Music John Foley, SJ (b. 1939)

PICARDY   87 87 87

Σιγησάτω πᾶσα σὰρξ βροτεία

1   Let all mortal flesh keep silence,
and with fear and trembling stand;
ponder nothing earthly-minded,
for with blessing in his hand
Christ our God to earth descending,
comes our homage to demand.

2   King of kings, yet born of Mary,
as of old on earth he stood,
Lord of lords we now receive him
in the body and the blood,
as he gives to all the faithful
his own self for heavenly food.

3   Rank on rank the host of heaven
streams before him on the way,
as the Light of light descending
from the realms of endless day
conquers all the powers of darkness,
drives the gloom of hell away.

4   At his feet the six-winged seraph;
cherubim with sleepless eye,
veil their faces to the Presence,
as with ceaseless voice they cry,
'Alleluia, Alleluia,
Alleluia, Lord most high'.

Liturgy of St James
translated Gerard Moultrie (1829–1885)

Music French carol melody
harmonised Ralph Vaughan Williams (1872–1958)

PANGE LINGUA

87 87 87

Unison

A - - men.

An alternative tune PICARDY *is found at 666.*

Pange lingua gloriosi Corporis mysterium

1   Now, my tongue, the mystery telling
    of the glorious body sing,
    and the blood, all price excelling,
    which the world's great Lord and King,
    in a virgin's womb once dwelling,
    shed for this world's ransoming.

2   That last night, at supper lying,
    with the Twelve, his chosen band,
    Jesus, with the law complying,
    keeps the feast its rites demand;
    then, more precious food supplying,
    gives himself with his own hand.

Music Mode iii (Sarum form)
harmonised Compilers of *Church Hymnary,* 3rd edition, 1973

3   Word-made-flesh! his word is making
    earthly bread his flesh to be,
    wine his blood; and all partaking
    should from sinful thoughts be free.
    Faith alone, sight's limits breaking,
    shows true hearts the mystery.

4   Therefore we, before him bending,
    this great sacrament revere;
    older rituals have their ending,
    for the newer rite is here;
    faith, our outward sense befriending,
    makes our inner vision clear.

5   Unto God be praise and honour:
    to the Father, to the Son,
    to the mighty Spirit, glory,
    ever Three and ever One:
    power and glory in the highest
    while eternal ages run. Amen.

translated Edward Caswall (1814–1878),
*Compilers of *Hymns Ancient and Modern,* 1861

BALLERMA   CM

A higher setting is found at 30.

1   According to thy gracious word,
     in meek humility,
     this will I do, my dying Lord,
     I will remember thee.

2   Thy body broken for my sake,
     my bread from heaven shall be;
     thy testamental cup I take,
     and thus remember thee.

3   Gethsemane can I forget?
     or there thy conflict see,
     thine agony and bloody sweat,
     and not remember thee?

4   When to the cross I turn mine eyes
     and rest on Calvary,
     O Lamb of God, my sacrifice,
     I must remember thee:

5   Remember thee, and all thy pains,
     and all thy love to me;
     yea, while a breath, a pulse remains,
     will I remember thee.

6   And when these failing lips grow dumb,
     and mind and memory flee,
     when thou shalt in thy kingdom come,
     Jesus, remember me.

                              James Montgomery (1771–1854)

Music French song by
François Hyppolyte Barthélémon (1741–1808)
adapted Robert Simpson (1790–1832)

SONG 1   10 10 10 10 10 10

1   O thou, who at thy Eucharist didst pray
         that all thy Church might be for ever one,
         grant us at every eucharist to say,
         with longing heart and soul, 'Thy will be done.'
         Oh, may we all one bread, one body be,
         one through this sacrament of unity.

2   For all thy Church, O Lord, we intercede;
         make thou our sad divisions soon to cease;
         draw us the nearer each to each, we plead,
         by drawing all to thee, O Prince of Peace;
         thus may we all one bread, one body be,
         one through this sacrament of unity.

3   We pray thee too for wanderers from thy fold;
         O bring them back, good Shepherd of the sheep,
         back to the faith which saints believed of old,
         back to the Church which still that faith doth keep;
         soon may we all one bread, one body be,
         one through this sacrament of unity.

4   So, Lord, at length when sacraments shall cease,
         may we be one with all thy Church above,
         one with thy saints in one unbroken peace,
         one with thy saints in one unbounded love:
         more blessèd still, in peace and love to be
         one with the Trinity in Unity.

                          William Henry Turton (1856–1938)

Music Orlando Gibbons (1583–1625)

670

TAKE AND EAT

Irregular

Take and eat; take and eat: this is my bo-dy given up for you.

Take and drink; take and drink: this is my blood giv-en up for you.

1 I am the word that spoke and light was made; I am the

seed that died to be reborn; I am the bread that comes from

heaven a-bove; I am the vine that fills your cup with joy.

*This hymn may be sung **during** communion, the verses by a cantor,
and the refrain by the congregation.*

Music Michael Joncas (b. 1951)

Take and eat; take and eat:
this is my body given up for you.
Take and drink; take and drink:
this is my blood given up for you.

1   I am the word that spoke and light was made;
     I am the seed that died to be reborn;
     I am the bread that comes from heaven above;
     I am the vine that fills your cup with joy.

2   I am the way that leads the exile home;
     I am the truth that sets the captive free;
     I am the life that raises up the dead;
     I am your peace, true peace my gift to you.

3   I am the lamb that takes away your sin;
     I am the gate that guards you night and day;
     you are my flock; you know the shepherd's voice;
     you are my own: your ransom is my blood.

4   I am the cornerstone that God has laid;
     a chosen stone and precious in his eyes;
     you are God's dwelling place, on me you rest;
     like living stones, a temple for God's praise.

5   I am the light that came into the world;
     I am the light that darkness cannot hide;
     I am the morning star that never sets;
     lift up your face, in you my light will shine.

6   I am the first and last, the Living One;
     I am the Lord who died that you might live;
     I am the bridegroom, this my wedding song;
     you are my bride, come to the marriage feast.

*This hymn may be sung **during** communion, the verses by a*
cantor, and the refrain by the congregation.

verse text James Quinn (*b.* 1919)
refrain text Michael Joncas (*b.* 1951)

FINEST WHEAT (BICENTENNIAL)   86 86 and refrain

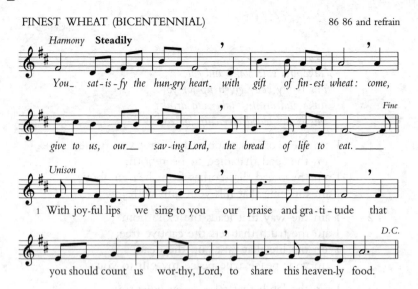

Harmony **Steadily**

You sat-is-fy the hun-gry heart with gift of fin-est wheat: come,

give to us, our sav-ing Lord, the bread of life to eat.

Unison

1 With joy-ful lips we sing to you our praise and gra-ti-tude that

you should count us wor-thy, Lord, to share this heaven-ly food.

You satisfy the hungry heart
with gift of finest wheat:
come give to us, our saving Lord,
the bread of life to eat.

1   With joyful lips we sing to you
     our praise and gratitude
     that you should count us worthy, Lord,
     to share this heavenly food.

2   Is not the cup we bless and share
     the blood of Christ out-poured?
     Do not one cup, one loaf, declare
     our one-ness in the Lord?

3   In gracious love you gave yourself;
     then selfless let us be,
     to serve each other in your name
     in truth and charity.

Omer Westendorf (*b.*1916)

Music Robert E. Kreutz (*b.*1922)

PSALM 118 (RENDEZ À DIEU)   98 98 D

An alternative harmonisation is found at 629.

1   Father, we thank you: for you planted
     your holy name within our hearts.
     Knowledge and faith and life immortal
     Jesus your Son to us imparts.
     Lord, you have made all for your pleasure;
     you gave us food for all our days,
     giving in Christ the bread eternal;
     yours is the power, yours be the praise.

2   Watch over all your Church in mercy,
     save her from evil, guard her still.
     Perfect her in your love, unite her,
     cleanse and conform her to your will.
     As grain, once scattered on the hillsides,
     was in the bread we break made one,
     so may your world-wide Church be gathered
     into your kingdom by your Son.

             from prayer in the *Didache,* probably 2nd century,
                   translated Francis Bland Tucker (1895–1984)

Music Melody from *Genevan Psalter,* 1551
arranged Ralph Vaughan Williams (1872–1958)

LINSTEAD MARKET

LM and refrain

1   Let us talents and tongues employ,
reaching out with a shout of joy:
bread is broken, the wine is poured,
Christ is spoken and seen and heard.
Jesus lives again,
earth can breathe again,
pass the word around:
loaves abound!

2   Christ is able to make us one,
at his table he sets the tone,
teaching people to live to bless,
love in word and in deed express.

3   Jesus calls us in, sends us out
bearing fruit in a world of doubt,
gives us love to tell, bread to share:
God (Immanuel!) everywhere.

Fred Kaan (*b.* 1929)

Music Jamaican traditional melody
arranged Ethel Olive Doreen Potter (1925–1980)

HALLELUYA! PELOTSA RONA

Irregular

Hal - le - lu - ya! We sing your prai - ses, all our hearts are filled with glad - ness. Hal - le - lu - ya! We sing your prai - ses, all our hearts are filled with glad - ness. 1 Christ the Lord to us said: I am wine, I am bread; I am wine, I am bread, give to all who thirst and hun - ger.

Halleluya! Pelotsa rona

Halleluya! We sing your praises,
all our hearts are filled with gladness.
Halleluya! We sing your praises,
all our hearts are filled with gladness.

1   Christ the Lord to us said:
     I am wine, I am bread;
     I am wine, I am bread,
     give to all who thirst and hunger.

2   Now he sends us all out,
     strong in faith, free of doubt;
     strong in faith, free of doubt,
     tell to all the joyful Gospel.

          South African traditional song

Music South African traditional song
arranged Anders Nyberg (b. 1955)

KILLIBEGS   LM

1 Now let us from this table rise
   renewed in body, mind, and soul;
   with Christ we die and rise again,
   his selfless love has made us whole.

2 With minds alert, upheld by grace,
   to spread the Word in speech and deed
   we follow in the steps of Christ,
   at one with all in hope and need.

3 To fill each human house with love,
   it is the sacrament of care;
   the work that Christ began to do
   we humbly pledge ourselves to share.

4 Then grant us grace, Companion-God,
   to choose again the pilgrim way,
   and help us to accept with joy
   the challenge of tomorrow's day.

Fred Kaan (*b.* 1929)

Music William Davies (*b.* 1921)

LANSDOWNE

99 99

Briskly

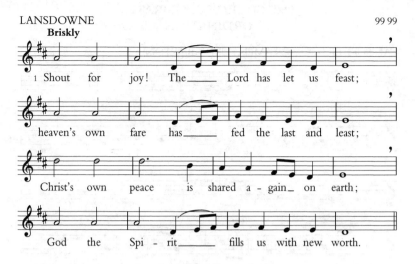

1 Shout for joy! The___ Lord has let us feast;
heaven's own fare has___ fed the last and least;
Christ's own peace is shared a-gain___ on earth;
God the Spi-rit___ fills us with new worth.

1   Shout for joy! The Lord has let us feast;
     heaven's own fare has fed the last and least;
     Christ's own peace is shared again on earth;
     God the Spirit fills us with new worth.

2   No more doubting, no more senseless dread:
     God's good self has graced our wine and bread;
     all the wonder heaven has kept in store
     now is ours to keep for evermore.

3   Celebrate with saints who dine on high;
     witnesses that love can never die.
     'Hallelujah!' — thus their voices ring:
     nothing less in gratitude we bring.

4   Praise the Maker, praise the Maker's Son,
     praise the Spirit — three yet ever one;
     praise the God whose food and friends avow
     heaven starts here! The kingdom beckons now!

John L. Bell *(b. 1949)*
and Graham Maule *(b. 1958)*

Music John L. Bell *(b. 1949)*

THE CHURCH CELEBRATES
ORDINATION

TANTUM ERGO SACRAMENTUM (GRAFTON)   87 87 87

Music French church melody from
Chants Ordinaires de l'Office Divin, Paris, 1881
harmonised Compilers of *Church Hymnary,* 3rd edition, 1973

1   In the name of Christ we gather,
    in the name of Christ we sing,
    as we celebrate the promise
    of your servant's offering,
    here ordained to lead God's people
    at the Gospel's beckoning.

2   Sons and daughters of the Spirit,
    we are called to teach and care,
    called as were the first disciples,
    Christ's own ministry to share,
    and in bread and wine and water
    sacraments of grace declare.

3   In our preaching, praying, caring
    may your word spring into life;
    in our time of doubt and challenge,
    may its truth affirm belief;
    and in days of pain and darkness,
    may it heal our guilt and grief.

4   Word of joy, enlivening Spirit,
    more than lover, parent, friend,
    born in Jesus, born in Mary,
    born in us, that love extend,
    grow within your chosen servant(s),
    life of God that has no end!

            *Shirley Erena Murray (b. 1931)

677 Words: © 1992, Hope Publishing Company. Administered by CopyCare Ltd,
PO Box 77, Hailsham, East Sussex, BN27 3EF, United Kingdom. <music@copycare.com> Used by permission.

SUANTRAI · 8 8 10 8

1   Here is the place, now is the time:
     an inner voice has bid me come;
     here, in the company where Christ is known,
     he claims my life, he speaks my name.

2   Here I declare a seed of faith,
     a will to learn, a gleam of truth,
     and ask for singleness of heart to speak
     what God has put into my mouth.

3   I seek the real and face the cost,
     I give away my lack of trust,
     in joyful hope I take the Spirit's lead;
     I go with all who follow Christ.

                    Shirley Erena Murray (*b.* 1931)

Music Irish traditional melody
arranged Thomas Henry Weaving (1881–1966)

PEACOCK   Irregular

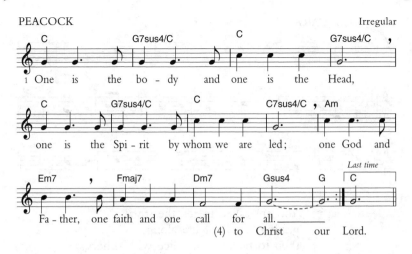

1 One is the bo-dy and one is the Head,

one is the Spi-rit by whom we are led; one God and

Fa-ther, one faith and one call for all.
(4) to Christ our Lord.

1   One is the body and one is the Head,
    one is the Spirit by whom we are led;
    one God and Father,
    one faith and one call for all.

2   Christ who ascended to heaven above
    is the same Jesus whose nature is love,
    who once descended
    to bring to this earth new birth.

3   Gifts have been given well suited to each;
    some to be prophets, to pastor, or preach,
    some, through the Gospel,
    to challenge, convert, and teach.

4   Called to his service are women and men,
    so that his body might ever again
    witness through worship,
    through deed and through word
    to Christ our Lord.

John L. Bell *(b.1949)*
based on *Ephesians 4: 11-16,*

Music John L. Bell *(b.1949)*

REGENT SQUARE   87 87 87

1   You are called to tell the story,
     passing words of life along,
     then to blend your voice with others,
     as you sing the sacred song.
     Christ be known in all our singing,
     filling all with songs of love.

2   You are called to teach the rhythm
     of the dance that never ends,
     then to move within the circle,
     hand in hand with strangers, friends.
     Christ be known in all our dancing,
     touching all with hands of love.

3   You are called to set the table,
     blessing bread as Jesus blessed,
     then to come with thirst and hunger,
     needing care like all the rest,
     Christ be known in all our sharing,
     feeding all with signs of love.

4   May the One whose love is broader
     than the measure of all space
     give us words to sing the story,
     move among us in this place.
     Christ be known in all our living,
     filling all with gifts of love.

                    Ruth C. Duck (b. 1947)

Music Henry Thomas Smart (1813–1879)

OLD CLARENDONIAN LM

A lower setting is found at 416.

1. Send out the gospel! Let it sound
   northward and southward, east and west;
   tell all the world Christ died and lives,
   he gives us pardon, life, and rest.

2. Send out your gospel, mighty Lord!
   Out of this chaos bring to birth
   your own creation's promised hope:
   the coming days of heaven on earth.

3. Send out your gospel, gracious Lord!
   Yours was the blood for sinners shed;
   your voice still pleads in human hearts —
   let all the world to you be led.

4. Send out your gospel, holy Lord!
   Kindle in us love's sacred flame;
   love giving all with heart and mind,
   for Jesus' sake, in Jesus' name.

5. Send out the gospel! Make it known!
   Christians, obey your Master's call;
   sing out his praise! He comes to reign,
   King of all kings and Lord of all.

Henry E. Fox (1841–1926)
adapted Hymns for Today's Church, 1982

Music Olwen Wonnacott (*b.* 1930)

ABBOT'S LEIGH   87 87 D irregular

Music Cyril Vincent Taylor (1907–1991)

1   Go in grace and make disciples,
    baptize in God's holy name;
    tell of death and resurrection,
    Easter's victory now proclaim.
    Christ's commission sends us forth
    to the nations of the earth.
    Go in grace and make disciples,
    midwives for the world's rebirth.

2   Go and follow Christ's example,
    not to vanquish, but to heal;
    mend the wounds of sin's divisions,
    servant love to all reveal.
    Roles and ranks shall be reversed,
    justice flow for all who thirst.
    Go and follow Christ's example,
    forge a world of last made first.

3   Go in Pentecostal spirit,
    many tongues and many gifts;
    feed the hearts of hungry people,
    spread the gospel that uplifts.
    As disciples, teach and learn,
    till the day of Christ's return.
    Go in Pentecostal spirit,
    let God's flame of witness burn.

Mary Louise Bringle (b. 1953)

ENGELBERG   10 10 10 4

1   Go to the world! Go into all the earth;
    go preach the cross where Christ renews life's worth,
    baptizing as the sign of our rebirth.
    Alleluia!

2   Go to the world! Go into every place;
    go live the word of God's redeeming grace;
    go seek God's presence in each time and space.
    Alleluia!

3   Go to the world! Go struggle, bless, and pray;
    the nights of tears give way to joyful day.
    As servant Church, you follow Christ's own way.
    Alleluia!

4   Go to the world! Go as the ones I send,
    for I am with you till the age shall end,
    when all the hosts of glory cry, 'Amen.'
    Alleluia!

Sylvia G. Dunstan (1955–1993)

Music Charles Villiers Stanford (1852–1924)
arranged Compilers of *BBC Hymn Book,* 1951

ELDEST SON   86 86 86

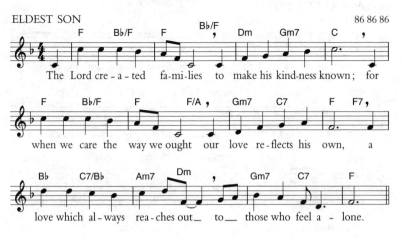

The Lord cre-a-ted fa-mi-lies to make his kind-ness known; for
when we care the way we ought our love re-flects his own, a
love which al-ways rea-ches out to those who feel a-lone.

1   The Lord created families
    to make his kindness known;
    for when we care the way we ought
    our love reflects his own,
    a love which always reaches out
    to those who feel alone.

2   The Lord has made a family
    with members everywhere;
    and Jesus is the eldest Son,
    the one whose name we bear,
    whose words and life show holiness,
    a likeness we can share.

3   We are your Church, your family,
    the children of your grace:
    inspire us, Lord, to show the world
    the warmth of your embrace,
    till all who long for wholeness find
    a welcome and a place.

Martin E. Leckebusch (b. 1962)

Music Source unknown
arranged Compilers

684   Words: © 2000 Kevin Mayhew Ltd, Buxhall, Stowmarket, Suffolk.   IP14 3BW,

A PLACE AT THE TABLE

11 10 11 10 and refrain

1 For ev-ery-one born, a place at the ta - ble, for ev-ery-one born, clean wa-ter and bread,___ a shel-ter, a space, a safe place for grow - ing, for ev-ery-one born, a star ov-er - head.___

Refrain

___ And God will de-light___ when we are cre-a - tors of jus - tice and joy,___ yes, God will de - light___ when we are cre-a - tors of jus - tice, ___

D.C. Last time

jus - tice and joy !___

Music Lori True (*b.* 1961)

1   For everyone born, a place at the table,
for everyone born, clean water and bread,
a shelter, a space, a safe place for growing,
for everyone born, a star overhead.
And God will delight
when we are creators of justice and joy,
yes, God will delight
when we are creators of justice,
justice and joy!

2   For woman and man, a place at the table,
revising the roles, deciding the share,
with wisdom and grace, dividing the power,
for woman and man, a system that's fair.

3   For young and for old, a place at the table,
a voice to be heard, a part in the song,
the hands of a child in hands kind and wrinkled,
for young and for old, the right to belong.

4   For just and unjust a place at the table,
abuser, abused, with need to forgive,
in anger, in hurt, a mind-set of mercy,
for just and unjust, a new way to live.

5   For everyone born, a place at the table,
to live without fear, and simply to be,
to work, to speak out, to witness and worship,
for everyone born, the right to be free.

Shirley Erena Murray (*b.* 1931)

685 Words: © 1998, Hope Publishing Company. Administered by CopyCare Ltd,
PO Box 77, Hailsham, East Sussex, BN27 3EF, United Kingdom. <music@copycare.com> Used by permission.

ST STEPHEN (NEWINGTON)   CM

PARAPHRASE 11

1   How happy are all they who hear
        true Wisdom's guiding voice;
        and who her understanding make
        their early, only choice.

2   For she has treasures greater far
        than east or west unfold;
        and her rewards more precious are
        than all their stores of gold.

3   In her right hand she holds to view
        a length of happy days;
        and riches with great honours joined
        are what her left displays.

4   She guides the young with innocence,
        in pleasure's paths to tread;
        a crown of glory she bestows
        upon the hoary head.

5   According as her labours rise,
        so her rewards increase;
        her ways are ways of pleasantness,
        and all her paths are peace.

Scottish Paraphrases, 1781
Proverbs 3: 13-17

Music William Jones (1726–1800)

LITTLE CORNARD   66 66 88

1   Lord of our growing years,
    with us from infancy,
    laughter and quick-dried tears,
    freshness and energy:
        your grace surrounds us all our days —
        for all your gifts we bring our praise.

2   Lord of our strongest years,
    stretching our youthful powers,
    lovers and pioneers
    when all the world seems ours:

3   Lord of our middle years,
    giver of steadfastness,
    courage that perseveres
    when there is small success:

4   Lord of our older years,
    steep though the road may be,
    rid us of foolish fears,
    bring us serenity:

5   Lord of our closing years,
    always your promise stands;
    hold us, when death appears,
    safely within your hands:

                        David Mowbray (*b.* 1938)

Music Martin Edward Fallas Shaw (1875–1958)

BELMONT   CM

A higher setting is found at 632.

1   By cool Siloam's shady rill
     how sweet the lily grows!
     How sweet the breath beneath the hill
     of Sharon's dewy rose!

2   Lo! such a child whose early feet
     the paths of peace have trod,
     whose secret heart with influence sweet
     is upward drawn to God.

3   By cool Siloam's shady rill
     the lily must decay,
     the rose that blooms beneath the hill
     must shortly fade away;

4   And soon, too soon, the wintry hour
     of life's maturer age
     will shake the soul with sorrow's power
     and stormy passion's rage.

5   O thou whose infant feet were found
     within thy Father's shrine,
     whose years, with changeless virtue crowned,
     were all alike divine,

6   Dependent on thy bounteous breath
     we seek thy grace alone,
     through every stage of life, and death,
     to keep us still thine own.

*Reginald Heber (1783–1826)

Music Melody by William Gardiner (1770–1853)
harmonised Compilers of *Revised Church Hymnary,* 1927

EVENTIDE   10 10 10 10

1   Just as the tide creeps over silver sand
    flooding the bay with slow and steady gain,
    like brightening dawn across the eastern land,
    certain and sure is love that comes again.

2   When empty eyes stare at the vacant chair
    and none can touch or fill the heart's deep pain,
    into our void of desolate despair,
    Jesus, pour out the love that comes again.

3   When every road ahead seems blocked and barred
    and doubt corrodes our will like acid rain,
    reveal your wounds to us whom life has scarred,
    and help us see the love that lives again.

4   When threat and fear conspire friends to betray,
    and bitter failure every hope has slain,
    when broken trust makes dark the dismal day,
    Jesus, speak of the love that comes again.

5   As sure as tide and dawn your love has come,
    come to redeem our failures and our pain;
    Jesus, come now, and find in us a home,
    revive us with the love that comes again.

                                    Leith Fisher (*b.* 1941)

Music William Henry Monk (1823–1889)

THOMAS

87 87 7

1. When the bonds of love are breaking,
   hands that linked withdraw and hide,
   eyes that once had met in candour
   now, distrustful, turn aside,
   God of healing, reconcile!

2. When our tongues are silent, sullen,
   closing doors through which love came,
   or, when words are fiery arrows
   wounding others with their flame,
   God of healing, reconcile!

3. When the bridges that we travelled
   have collapsed and left a void,
   when the chasm seems to widen,
   separating souls once joined,
   God of healing, reconcile!

4. God, in Christ you crossed the chasm
   when our hearts were far from you!
   Grant us grace to reach to others,
   broken bonds repair, renew!
   God of healing, reconcile!

Herman G. Stuempfle, Jr *(b. 1923)*

Music Marty Haugen *(b. 1950), harmonised* Compilers

691

FINLANDIA

10 10 10 10 10 10

Another version, with the composer's original harmonies, is at 701.

Stille, mein Wille; dein Jesus hilft siegen

1   Be still, my soul: the Lord is on your side;
    bear patiently the cross of grief or pain;
    leave to your God to order and provide;
    in every change he faithful will remain.
    Be still, my soul: your best, your heavenly Friend
    through thorny ways leads to a joyful end.

2   Be still, my soul: your God will undertake
    to guide the future as he has the past.
    Your hope, your confidence let nothing shake,
    all now mysterious shall be bright at last.
    Be still, my soul: the waves and winds still know
    his voice, who ruled them while he lived below.

3   Be still, my soul: when dearest friends depart
    and all is darkened in the vale of tears,
    then you shall better know his love, his heart,
    who comes to soothe your sorrow, calm your fears.
    Be still, my soul: for Jesus can repay
    from his own fullness all he takes away.

4   Be still, my soul: the hour is hastening on
    when we shall be for ever with the Lord,
    when disappointment, grief, and fear are gone,
    sorrow forgotten, love's pure joy restored.
    Be still, my soul: when change and tears are past,
    all safe and blessèd we shall meet at last.

Katharina Amalia Dorothea von Schlegel (b. 1697)
translated Jane Laurie Borthwick (1813–1897)

Music Adapted from the symphonic poem *Finlandia* by
Jean Sibelius (1865–1957)

SONG IN OUR HEARTS   Irregular

1 Je-sus puts this song in-to our hearts,_____

Je-sus puts this song in-to our hearts;_____

it's a song of joy no-one can take__ a-way._____

Je-sus puts this song_____ in-to our

hearts._____ *vv. 1 - 3* | *Last time* (Hey!)

1   Jesus puts this song into our hearts,
    Jesus puts this song into our hearts;
    it's a song of joy no one can take away.
    Jesus puts this song
    into our hearts.

2   Jesus teaches how to live in harmony,
    Jesus teaches how to live in harmony;
    different faces, different races, he makes us one.
    Jesus teaches how to live
    in harmony.

3   Jesus teaches how to be a family,
    Jesus teaches how to be a family,
    loving one another with the love that he gives.
    Jesus teaches how to be
    a family.

Music Graham Kendrick (*b.* 1950)
arranged David Christopher Peacock (*b.* 1949)

4 Jesus turns our sorrow into dancing,
   Jesus turns our sorrow into dancing;
   changes tears of sadness into rivers of joy.
   Jesus turns our sorrow
   into a dance. (*Hey!*)

Graham Kendrick (*b.* 1950)

93

WETHERBY   CM

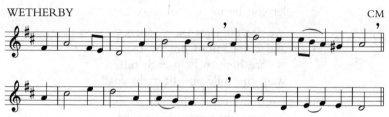

1 Help us forgive, forgiving Lord
   the wrong that others do,
   and, when our hearts are pierced by pain,
   to bring the hurt to you.

2 For on the cross you bore for us
   the curse, the scorn, the hate
   and gave your life to lift from us
   sin's cruel and crushing weight.

3 Let grace unlock each prisoned heart,
   uncoil each fisted hand
   until from hate our hearts are freed,
   our hands in love extend.

4 And then, the broken circle closed,
   the broken friendships healed,
   Lord, hold us fast within the bonds
   by your forgiveness sealed.

Herman G. Stuempfle, Jr (*b.* 1923)

Music Samuel Sebastian Wesley (1810–1876)

THE HOLY SPIRIT

87 87

1   Brother, sister, let me serve you,
        let me be as Christ to you;
        pray that I may have the grace to
        let you be my servant too.

2   We are pilgrims on a journey,
        and companions on the road;
        we are here to help each other
        walk the mile and bear the load.

3   I will hold the Christ-light for you
        in the night-time of your fear;
        I will hold my hand out to you,
        speak the peace you long to hear.

4   I will weep when you are weeping;
        when you laugh I'll laugh with you;
        I will share your joy and sorrow
        till we've seen this journey through.

5   When we sing to God in heaven
        we shall find such harmony,
        born of all we've known together
        of Christ's love and agony.

6   Brother, sister, let me serve you,
        let me be as Christ to you;
        pray that I may have the grace to
        let you be my servant too.

Richard A. M. Gillard (b. 1953)

Music Richard A. M. Gillard (b. 1953)
arranged Betty Jane Pulkingham (b. 1928)

O WALY WALY   LM

1   Your love, O God, has called us here,
     for all love finds its source in you,
     the perfect love that casts out fear,
     the love that Christ makes ever new.

2   O gracious God, you consecrate
     all that is lovely, good, and true.
     Bless those who in your presence wait,
     and every day their love renew.

3   O God of love, inspire our life,
     reveal your will in all we do;
     join every husband, every wife,
     in mutual love and love for you.

                        Russell Schulz-Widmar (b. 1944)

Music English traditional melody
arranged Compilers of *Church Hymnary,* 3rd edition, 1973

REPTON 86 88 66

Unison

1 We come, dear Lord, to celebrate
the love our friends have found;
and thank you, God, for their embrace,
the joy and promise in this place
which makes it holy ground,
which makes it holy ground.

2 Help them fulfil the vows made here;
let this new family share
a welcome home, a future blessed
by love and laughter, grace and guest,
with time enough to spare,
to listen, love, and care.

3 In seeking what the future holds,
in letting go the past,
we seek your grace to clear a way
through what must go and what should stay
if love is meant to last,
if love is meant to last.

John L. Bell (*b.* 1949)

Music Charles Hubert Hastings Parry (1848–1918)
from the oratorio *Judith*

THE ROAD AND THE MILES TO DUNDEE

12 11 12 11

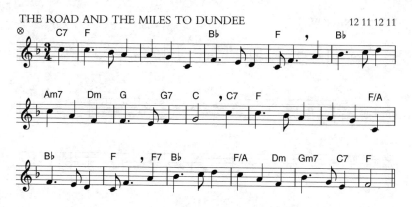

1   Let's praise the Creator who gave us each other
    in friendship and kinship to celebrate life;
    let's sing our delight in this man and this woman,
    the promise of joy as a husband and wife.

2   The love that we wish them, the love that we pray for
    is stronger than storms and more gentle than breath,
    endures every trouble, is selfless and faithful,
    more precious than life and more lasting than death.

3   In vows that are honoured, in kissing and blessing
    may happiness shine like the gold of a ring;
    in passionate joy and compassionate caring
    may theirs be the gifts that true loving can bring.

Shirley Erena Murray (b. 1931)

Music Scottish traditional melody
arranged Compilers

LOVE UNKNOWN   66 66 88

Unison

1   The grace of life is theirs
     who on this wedding day
     delight to make their vows
     and for each other pray.
     May they, O Lord, together prove
     the lasting joy of Christian love.

2   Where love is, God abides:
     and God shall surely bless
     a home where trust and care
     give birth to happiness.
     May they, O Lord, together prove
     the lasting joy of such a love.

3   How slow to take offence
     love is! How quick to heal!
     How ready in distress
     to know how others feel!
     May they, O Lord, together prove
     the lasting joy of such a love.

4   And when time lays its hand
     on all we hold most dear,
     and life, by life consumed,
     fulfils its purpose here:
     May they, O Lord, together prove
     the lasting joy of Christian love.

                    Frederick Pratt Green (1903–2000)

Music John Nicholson Ireland (1879–1962)

SCHÖNSTER HERR JESU (ST ELISABETH)   Irregular

1   God beyond glory,
         gracious and holy,
         in your own image each life is made.
         Love is the treasure,
         love is the measure
         of all your Son on earth displayed.

2   Here, in your presence,
         love is the essence
         sealing the vows shared by husband and wife.
         This love confessing,
         send them your blessing
         to guard and guide their chosen life.

3   When joys are deepest,
         where paths are steepest,
         whatever happens in years to come,
         let love in duty
         and love in beauty
         embrace their hearts, their hopes, their home.

John L. Bell (*b.*1949)
and Graham Maule (*b.*1958)

Music Silesian melody from *Schlesische Volkslieder,* Leipzig, 1842
harmonised Compilers of *Rejoice and Sing,* 1991

SUSSEX CAROL   88 88 88
Unison

1   As man and woman we were made,
     that love be found and life begun;
     the likeness of the living God,
     unique, yet called to live as one.
     Through joy or sadness, calm or strife,
     come praise the love that gives us life.

2   Now Jesus lived and gave his love
     to make our life and loving new;
     so celebrate with him today,
     and drink the joy he offers you
     that makes the simple moment shine
     and changes water into wine.

3   And Jesus died to live again,
     so praise the love that, come what may,
     can bring the dawn and clear the skies,
     and waits to wipe all tears away,
     and let us hope for what shall be,
     believing where we cannot see.

4   Then spread the table, clear the hall,
     and celebrate till day is done;
     let peace go deep between us all,
     and joy be shared by everyone:
     laugh and make merry with your friends,
     and praise the love that never ends!

                              Brian Wren *(b.* 1936)

Music English traditional melody
arranged Ralph Vaughan Williams (1872–1958)

FINLANDIA   10 11 10 11 11 10

Composer's original harmonies. Another arrangement is found at 691.

1   When memory fades and recognition falters,
    when eyes we love grow dim, and minds confused,
    speak to our souls of love that never alters,
    speak to our hearts by pain and fear abused.
    O God of life and healing peace, empower us
    with patient courage, by your grace infused.

2   As frailness grows, and youthful powers diminish
    and weary arms decline in strength and skill,
    your ageing servants faithfully shall finish
    their earthly tasks, obedient to your will.
    We grieve their fading, yet rejoice, believing
    your arms, unwearying, will uphold us still.

3   Within your Spirit, goodness lives unfading;
    the past and future mingle into one.
    All joys remain, with heavenly light pervading;
    no valued deed will ever be undone.
    Your mind enfolds all finite acts and offerings,
    held in your heart, our deathless life is won!

                                    Mary Louise Bringle (*b.* 1953)

Music Original arrangement
from the symphonic poem *Finlandia* by Jean Sibelius (1865–1957)

Also suitable
Womb of life and source of being   118
Praise to the Lord for the joys of the earth   165
For the beauty of the earth   181

THE CHURCH CELEBRATES
NATIONAL LIFE

BLAENWERN   87 87 D

A lower setting is found at 468.

1   Lord, in love and perfect wisdom
    times and seasons you arrange,
    working out your changeless purpose
    in a world of ceaseless change;
    you have formed our ancient nation,
    guiding it through all the days,
    to unfold in it your purpose
    to your glory and your praise.

2   To our shores remote, benighted,
    barrier of the western waves,
    tidings in your love you sent us,
    tidings of the cross that saves.
    Saints and heroes strove and suffered
    here your gospel to proclaim;
    we, the heirs of their endeavour,
    tell the honour of their name.

Music William Penfro Rowlands (1860–1937)

3   You maintain your ageless purpose
every change and chance above;
still your holy Church is bearing
witness to your changeless love.
Grant us vision, Lord, and courage
to fulfil your work begun;
in the Church and in the nation,
King of kings, your will be done.

*Timothy Rees (1874–1939)

03

GOD SAVE THE QUEEN   664 6664

1   God save our gracious Queen,
long live our noble Queen;
God save the Queen!
Send her victorious,
happy and glorious,
long to reign over us:
God save the Queen!

2   Thy choicest gifts in store
on her be pleased to pour;
long may she reign;
may she defend our laws,
and ever give us cause
to sing with heart and voice,
'God save the Queen!'

3   Not on this land alone,
but be God's mercies known
from shore to shore.
Lord, make the nations see
that all should kindred be,
and form one family
the wide world o'er.

Author unknown
Verses 1 & 2 from the version of 1745
verse 3 by W.E. Hickson (1803–1870)

Music Origin unknown, popularised in 1745

THAXTED   13 13 13 13 13 13

1 I vow to thee, my country, all earthly things above,
   entire and whole and perfect, the service of my love:
   the love that asks no question, the love that stands the test,
   that lays upon the altar the dearest and the best;
   the love that never falters, the love that pays the price,
   the love that makes undaunted the final sacrifice.

2 And there's another country I've heard of long ago,
   most dear to them that love her, most great to them that know;
   we may not count her armies, we may not see her King;
   her fortress is a faithful heart, her pride is suffering;
   and soul by soul and silently her shining bounds increase,
   and her ways are ways of gentleness and all her paths are peace.

                        Cecil Arthur Spring-Rice (1859–1918)

Music
from *The Planets,* by Gustav Theodore von Holst (1874–1934)
adapted Compilers of *Hymns Ancient & Modern Revised,* 1950

VISION   15 15 15 6

v.4 (God be praised!)

1   It is God who holds the nations in the hollow of his hand;
    it is God whose light is shining in the darkness of the land;
    it is God who builds the city on the rock and not on sand:
    may the living God be praised!

2   It is God whose purpose summons us to use the present hour;
    who recalls us to our senses when a nation's life turns sour;
    in the discipline of freedom we shall know his saving power:
    may the living God be praised!

3   When a thankful nation, looking back, has cause to celebrate
    those who win our admiration by their service to the state;
    when self-giving is a measure of the greatness of the great:
    may the living God be praised!

4   God reminds us every sunrise that the world is ours on lease —
    for the sake of life tomorrow may our love for it increase;
    may all peoples live together, share its riches, be at peace:
    may the living God be praised!

                                   Frederick Pratt Green (1903–2000)

Music Henry Walford Davies (1869–1941)
arranged John Whitridge Wilson (1905–1992)

TRIUMPH   87 87 87

1   For the healing of the nations,
    Lord, we pray with one accord;
    for a just and equal sharing
    of the things that earth affords.
    To a life of love in action
    help us rise and pledge our word.

2   Lead us forward into freedom,
    from despair your world release,
    that, redeemed from war and hatred,
    all may come and go in peace.
    Show us how through care and goodness
    fear will die and hope increase.

3   All that kills abundant living,
    let it from the earth be banned;
    pride of status, race, or schooling,
    dogmas that obscure your plan.
    In our common quest for justice
    may we hallow life's brief span.

4   You, Creator-God, have written
    your great name on humankind;
    for our growing in your likeness
    bring the life of Christ to mind;
    that by our response and service
    earth its destiny may find.

                                        Fred Kaan (b. 1929)

Music Henry John Gauntlett (1805–1876)

706 Words: © 1968, Stainer & Bell Ltd, PO Box 110, Victoria House, 23 Gruneisen Road, London N3 1DZ

JOEL   87 87 D

1   Healing river of the Spirit,
bathe the wounds that living brings.
Plunge our pain, our sin, our sadness
deep beneath your sacred springs.
Weary from the restless searching
that has lured us from your side,
we discover in your presence
peace the world cannot provide.

2   Wellspring of the healing Spirit,
stream that flows to bring release,
as we gain our selves, our senses,
may our lives reflect your peace.
Grateful for the flood that heals us,
may your Church live out your grace.
As we meet both friend and stranger,
may we see our Saviour's face.

3   Living stream that heals the nations,
make us channels of your power.
All the world is torn by conflict;
wars are raging at this hour.
Saving Spirit, move among us;
guide our winding human course,
till we find our way together,
flowing homeward to our Source.

Ruth C. Duck (*b.* 1947)

Music Sally Ann Morris (*b.* 1952)

708

O LORD THE CLOUDS (A NEVER-FAILING STREAM)   Irregular

1 O— Lord,— the clouds are ga-ther-ing, the fire of judge-ment burns.— How we have fal — len! O— Lord,— you stand ap-palled to see your laws of love so scorned.— and lives so bro — ken.

Refrain

Women: Have mer-cy, Lord,— for-give us, Lord. Re-store us, Lord; re-vive your church a-gain.—

Men: Have mer-cy, Lord,— for-give us, Lord.— Re-store us, Lord; re-vive your church a-gain.— Let

Let jus-tice flow,— like ri-vers, and jus-tice flow,— like ri-vers,— and right-eous-ness— like a ne-ver fail-ing stream.

vv. 1 - 3   *Last time*

2 O___   *A ne-ver fail-ing stream.* ___

1   O Lord, the clouds are gathering,
the fire of judgement burns.
How we have fallen!
O Lord, you stand appalled to see
your laws of love so scorned
and lives so broken.

> MEN: *Have mercy, Lord,*
> WOMEN: *Have mercy, Lord,*
> MEN: *forgive us, Lord.*
> WOMEN: *forgive us, Lord.*
> ALL: *Restore us, Lord;*
>   *revive your Church again.*

> MEN: *Let justice flow*
> WOMEN: *Let justice flow*
> MEN: *like rivers,*
> WOMEN: *like rivers,*
> ALL: *and righteousness*
>   *like a never-failing stream.*

2   O Lord, over the nations now
where is the dove of peace?
Her wings are broken.
O Lord, while precious children starve,
the tools of war increase,
their bread is stolen.

3   O Lord, dark powers are poised to flood
our streets with hate and fear.
We must awaken!
O Lord, let love reclaim the lives
that sin would sweep away,
and let your kingdom come!

4   O Lord, your glorious cross shall tower
triumphant in this land,
evil confounding;
through the fire, your suffering Church display
the glories of her Christ,
praises resounding.

Graham Kendrick (*b.* 1950)

Music Graham Kendrick (*b.* 1950)

RIGHT HAND

1 1 8 6 6 10

1 The right hand of God is writing in our land, writing with power and with love, our conflicts and our fears, our triumphs and our tears are recorded by the right hand of God.

Music Noel G. Dexter *(b. 1938)*
arranged Carlton (Sam) Raymond Young *(b. 1926)*

1   The right hand of God is writing in our land,
writing with power and with love,
our conflicts and our fears,
our triumphs and our tears
are recorded by the right hand of God.

2   The right hand of God is pointing in our land
pointing the way we must go,
so clouded is the way,
so easily we stray,
but we're guided by the right hand of God.

3   The right hand of God is striking in our land,
striking at envy, hate, and greed.
Our selfishness and lust,
our pride and deeds unjust
are exposed by the right hand of God.

4   The right hand of God is lifting in our land,
lifting the fallen one by one.
Each one is known by name,
and rescued now from shame
by the lifting of the right hand of God.

5   The right hand of God is healing in our land,
healing broken bodies, minds, and souls.
So wondrous is its touch
with love that means so much,
when we're healed by the right hand of God.

6   The right hand of God is planting in our land,
planting seeds of freedom, hope, and love.
In near and far-flung lands
let people all join hands,
and be one with the right hand of God.

*Patrick Prescod

REPTON   86 886 (6)

1   'I have a dream', a man once said,
     'where all is perfect peace;
     where men and women, black and white,
     stand hand in hand, and all unite
*   in freedom and in love.'

2   But in this world of bitter strife
     the dream can often fade;
     reality seems dark as night,
     we catch but glimpses of the light
     Christ sheds on humankind.

3   Fierce persecution, war, and hate
     are raging everywhere;
     God calls us now to pay the price
     through struggles and through sacrifice
     of standing for the right.

4   So dream the dreams and sing the songs,
     but never be content;
     for thoughts and words don't ease the pain:
     unless there's action, all is vain;
     faith proves itself in deeds.

5   Lord, give us vision, make us strong,
     help us to do your will;
     don't let us rest until we see
     your love throughout humanity
     uniting us in peace.

*   *The last line of each verse is repeated.*

Pamela J. Pettitt (*b.* 1954)

Music Charles Hubert Hastings Parry (1848–1918)
from the oratorio *Judith*

1   Loving God in heaven above,
     holy your name; we sing it with love.
     Help make our world a good place to be,
     happy and caring, peaceful and free.
     Help all your children to do as you say.
     Help us to listen to you every day.

2   Give to us all of the good things we need
     to help us grow strong, to go where you lead.
     Forgive us all of the wrong things we do.
     We will forgive each other too.
     Help all your children to do what is right.
     Hold us and keep us safe in your sight.

                                        Maria Millward

Music Damien Halloran

KINGSTON   88 84

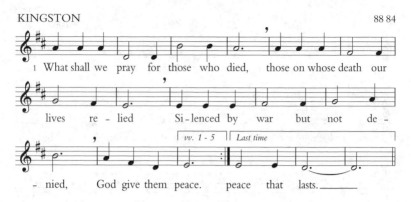

1 What shall we pray for those who died, those on whose death our lives re-lied Si-lenced by war but not de-nied, God give them peace. *vv. 1 - 5* | *Last time* peace that lasts._____

1   What shall we pray for those who died,
    those on whose death our lives relied?
    Silenced by war but not denied,
    God give them peace.

2   What shall we pray for those who mourn
    friendships and love, their fruit unborn?
    Though years have passed, hearts still are torn:
    God give them peace.

3   What shall we pray for those who live
    tied to the past they can't forgive,
    haunted by terrors they relive?
    God give them peace.

4   What shall we pray for those who know
    nothing of war, and cannot show
    grief or regret for friend or foe?
    God give them peace.

5   What shall we pray for those who fear
    war, in some guise, may re-appear
    looking attractive and sincere?
    God give them peace.

6   God give us peace and, more than this,
    show us the path where justice is;
    and let us never be remiss
    working for peace that lasts.

Carnwadric Parish Church (Glasgow)
Worship Group
and John L. Bell (*b.* 1949)

Music John L. Bell (*b.* 1949)

GONFALON ROYAL   LM

1   Come, all who look to God today,
        stretch out your hands, enlarge your mind,
        together share his living way
        where all who humbly seek will find.

2   Come, young and old of every faith,
        bring all your treasuries of prayer,
        and seek the living Spirit's breath
        to realise the truths we share.

3   Bring your traditions' richest store,
        your hymns and rites and cherished creeds;
        explore your visions, pray for more,
        since God delights to meet fresh needs.

4   Come, trust in God and live in peace,
        anticipate that final light
        when strife and bigotry shall cease,
        and faith be lost in praise and sight. Amen.

                       Richard G. Jones (*b.* 1926)

Music Percy Carter Buck (1871–1947)

Also suitable for this section

GATHER US IN   10 10 10 10 4

1 Ga - ther us   in,   thou Love that fill - est   all!

Ga - ther our   ri - val faiths with - in   thy fold!

Rend all our tem - ple veils and bid them fall,

that we may know that thou hast been of old; ga-ther us in.

1   Gather us in, thou Love that fillest all!
     Gather our rival faiths within thy fold!
     Rend all our temple veils and bid them fall,
     that we may know that thou hast been of old;
     gather us in.

2   Gather us in: we worship only thee;
     in varied names we stretch a common hand;
     in diverse forms a common soul we see;
     in many ships we seek one spirit-land;
     gather us in.

3   Each sees one colour of thy rainbow light;
     each looks upon one tint and calls it heaven;
     thou art the fullness of our partial sight;
     we are not perfect till we find the seven;
     gather us in.

4   Some seek a Father in the heavens above,
     some ask a human image to adore,
     some crave a spirit vast as life and love;
     within thy mansions we have all and more;
     gather us in.

George Matheson (1842–1906)

Music Composer unknown

GLASGOW

CM

PARAPHRASE 18

1   Behold! the mountain of the Lord
     in latter days shall rise
     on mountain tops above the hills,
     and draw the wondering eyes.

2   To this the joyful nations round,
     all tribes and tongues, shall flow;
     up to the hill of God, they'll say,
     and to his house we'll go.

3   The beam that shines from Zion hill
     shall lighten every land;
     the King who reigns in Salem's towers
     shall all the world command.

4   Among the nations he shall judge;
     his judgements truth shall guide;
     his sceptre shall protect the just,
     and quell the sinner's pride.

5   No strife shall rage, nor hostile feuds
     disturb those peaceful years;
     to ploughshares men shall beat their swords,
     to pruning-hooks their spears.

6   No longer hosts, encountering hosts,
     shall crowds of slain deplore:
     they hang the trumpet in the hall,
     and study war no more.

7   Come then, O house of Jacob! come
     to worship at his shrine;
     and, walking in the light of God,
     with holy beauties shine.

Scottish Paraphrases, 1781, *Isaiah 2: 2-5*

Music Melody from Moore's *Psalm-Singer's Pocket Companion*, 1756
harmonised The Psalter in Metre, 1899. Harmonies revised *RCH* and *CH3*

A list of items also suitable for this section is found after 713.

THE CHURCH CELEBRATES
WHOLENESS AND HEALING

LEWIS FOLK MELODY

87 87 D

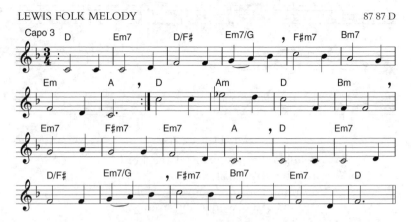

1   Come and find the quiet centre
    in the crowded life we lead,
    find the room for hope to enter,
    find the space where we are freed:
    clear the chaos and the clutter,
    clear our eyes, that we can see
    all the things that really matter,
    be at peace, and simply be.

2   Silence is a friend who claims us,
    cools the heat and slows the pace;
    God it is who speaks and names us,
    knows our being, touches base,
    making space within our thinking,
    lifting shades to show the sun,
    raising courage when we're shrinking,
    finding scope for faith begun.

3   In the Spirit let us travel,
    open to each other's pain;
    let our lives and fears unravel,
    celebrate the space we gain:
    there's a place for deepest dreaming,
    there's a time for hearts to care;
    in the Spirit's lively scheming
    there is always room to spare!

Shirley Erena Murray (*b.* 1931)

Music Lewis folk melody, *arranged* John L. Bell (*b.* 1949)

ANGELUS   LM

1   O Christ, the healer, we have come
    to pray for health, to plead for friends.
    How can we fail to be restored,
    when reached by love that never ends?

2   From every ailment flesh endures
    our bodies clamour to be freed;
    yet in our hearts we would confess
    that wholeness is our deepest need.

3   How strong, O Lord, are our desires,
    how weak our knowledge of ourselves!
    Release in us those healing truths
    unconscious pride resists or shelves.

4   In conflicts that destroy our health
    we diagnose the world's disease;
    our common life declares our ills:
    is there no cure, O Christ, for these?

5   Grant that we all, made one in faith,
    in your community may find
    the wholeness that, enriching us,
    shall reach the whole of humankind.

                Frederick Pratt Green (1903–2000)

Music Adapted from a melody contributed by Georg Joseph to
Heilige Seelenlust, Breslau, 1657
adapted Compilers of *Church Hymnary,* 3rd edition, 1973
from harmonies in *Revised Church Hymnary,* 1927

THE BANKS O' DOON (YE BANKS AND BRAES)   DLM

1 We can-not mea-sure how__ you heal__ or an-swer ev-ery suf-ferer's prayer, yet,__ we be-lieve__ your grace re-sponds where faith__ and doubt__ u-nite__ to care. Your hands, though blood-ied on the cross,__ sur-vive__ to hold__ and heal__ and__ warn, to__ car-ry all__ through death to life__ and cra-dle. chil-dren yet__ un-born.

Music Scottish folk melody
harmonised John L. Bell (*b.* 1949)

1   We cannot measure how you heal
or answer every sufferer's prayer,
yet we believe your grace responds
where faith and doubt unite to care.
Your hands, though bloodied on the cross,
survive to hold and heal and warn,
to carry all through death to life
and cradle children yet unborn.

2   The pain that will not go away,
the guilt that clings from things long past,
the fear of what the future holds,
are present as if meant to last.
But present too is love which tends
the hurt we never hoped to find,
the private agonies inside,
the memories that haunt the mind.

3   So some have come who need your help
and some have come to make amends
as hands which shaped and saved the world
are present in the touch of friends.
Lord, let your Spirit meet us here
to mend the body, mind, and soul,
to disentangle peace from pain
and make your broken people whole.

John L. Bell (*b.* 1949)
and Graham Maule (*b.* 1958)

THIRD MODE MELODY   DCM

1   The one who longs to make us whole
    is waiting to embrace
    our broken lives, so we can know
    the power of healing grace.
    God's love surrounds our suffering,
    and keeps us through the night;
    God helps us bear our deep despair
    till we see morning light.

2   The one who saves us from ourselves
    is waiting to release
    our hearts from chains of self-reproach
    and failure to find peace.
    When harmful habits leave us bruised,
    distraught by inner pain,
    God comes to us through trusted friends,
    and helps us hope again.

3   The one who understands our need
    accepts us as we are;
    and, like a loved one, welcomes us
    when we have wandered far.
    God never says we come too late
    to be forgiven, free,
    but promises we can become
    the self we're meant to be.

                    Edith Sinclair Downing (*b.* 1922)

Music Rhythmically simplified version of tune by
Thomas Tallis (*c.* 1505–1585)
adapted Compilers of *Church Hymnary*, 3rd edition, 1973

LONGING   Irregular

> *There is a longing in our hearts, O Lord,*
> *for you to reveal yourself to us.*
> *There is a longing in our hearts for love*
> *we only find in you, our God.*

1   For justice, for freedom, for mercy:
    hear our prayer.
    In sorrow, in grief:
    be near, hear our prayer, O God.

continued overleaf

Music Anne Quigley

THE HOLY SPIRIT

Steadily

There is a long-ing in our hearts, O Lord, for you to re-veal your-self to us.____ There is a long-ing in our hearts for love we on-ly find in you, our God.

(pause last time)

2   For wisdom, for courage, for comfort:
hear our prayer.
In weakness, in fear:
be near, hear our prayer, O God.

3   For healing, for wholeness, for new life:
hear our prayer.
In sickness, in death:
be near, hear our prayer, O God.

4   Lord save us, take pity, light in our
darkness.
We call you, we wait:
be near, hear our prayer, O God.

Anne Quigley

GARELOCHSIDE   SM

1   We lay our broken world
    in sorrow at your feet,
    haunted by hunger, war, and fear,
    oppressed by power and hate.

2   Here human life seems less
    than profit, might, and pride,
    though to unite us all in you,
    you lived and loved and died.

3   We bring our broken towns,
    our neighbours hurt and bruised;
    you show us how old pain and wounds
    for new life can be used.

4   We bring our broken loves,
    friends parted, families torn;
    then in your life and death we see
    that love must be reborn.

5   We bring our broken selves,
    confused and closed and tired;
    then through your gift of healing grace
    new purpose is inspired.

6   Come Spirit, on us breathe,
    with life and strength anew;
    find in us love, and hope, and trust,
    and lift us up to you.

                                        Anna Briggs (b. 1947)

Music Kenneth George Finlay (1882–1974)

721 Words: © Anna Briggs, from *This is the day,* Wild Goose Publications
721 Music: © Broomhill Church of Scotland, Glasgow G11.

LEAVING OF LISMORE   9998 and refrain

Unison

1 Spi - rit of God, come dwell with-in me. O - pen my heart, oh, come set me free, fill me with love for Je - sus, my Lord, come fill me with liv - ing wa - ter._____

Refrain, *Harmony*

Je - sus is liv - ing, Je - sus is here. Je - sus, my Lord, come clo - ser to me: Je - sus, our Sa - viour; dy - ing for me, and ris - ing to save his peo - ple._____

1   Spirit of God, come dwell within me.
     Open my heart, oh, come set me free.
     Fill me with love for Jesus, my Lord,
     come, fill me with living water.
          Jesus is living, Jesus is here.
          Jesus, my Lord, come closer to me:
          Jesus, our Saviour, dying for me,
          and rising to save his people.

2   Lord, how I thirst, my Lord, I am weak.
     Lord, come to me, you alone do I seek.
     Lord, you are life and love and hope,
     come, fill me with living water.

Music Scottish folk melody
harmonised Compilers of *Common Ground,* 1998

3   Lord, I am blind, my Lord, I can't see.
     Stretch out your hand, bring comfort to me.
     Lead me your way in light and in truth,
     come, fill me with living water.

Helen Kennedy

723

DOWNING   CM

Unison

How can we know how long you wait to see the set - ting

Harmony

sun,   or   how you yearn to__ hear God speak the

lov - ing words,___   'Well   done'?   song!

[vv. 1 - 3] [v. 4]

1   How can we know how long you wait
     to see the setting sun,
     or how you yearn to hear God speak
     the loving words, 'Well done'?

2   Your body cannot win the race
     your eager mind would run;
     yet God has seen your faithful course
     and counts the victory won.

3   Can we who walk with steady feet
     embrace you and extend
     the grace you need until you hear,
     'Come home now, faithful friend'?

4   All praise to God whose love abides
     in bodies weak or strong,
     and gives to us the strength to sing
     our own triumphant song!

Edith Sinclair Downing *(b.* 1922)

Music John L. Bell *(b.* 1949)

DREAM ANGUS   LM

1 Christ's is the world in which we move; Christ's are the folk we're sum-moned to love; Christ's is the voice that calls us to care, and Christ is the one who meets us here.

Refrain

To the lost Christ shows his face, to the un-loved he gives his em-brace, to those who cry in pain or dis-grace, Christ makes, with his friends, a touch-ing place.

Music Scottish folk melody
harmonised John L. Bell (*b.* 1949)

1   Christ's is the world in which we move;
    Christ's are the folk we're summoned to love;
    Christ's is the voice which calls us to care,
    and Christ is the one who meets us here.
        To the lost Christ shows his face,
        to the unloved he gives his embrace,
        to those who cry in pain or disgrace,
        Christ makes, with his friends, a touching place.

2   Feel for the people we most avoid —
    strange or bereaved or never employed.
    Feel for the women and feel for the men
    who fear that their living is all in vain.

3   Feel for the parents who've lost their child,
    feel for the women whom men have defiled,
    feel for the baby for whom there's no breast,
    and feel for the weary who find no rest.

4   Feel for the lives by life confused,
    riddled with doubt, in loving abused;
    feel for the lonely heart, conscious of sin,
    which longs to be pure but fears to begin.

John L. Bell (*b.* 1949)
and Graham Maule (*b.* 1958)

Also suitable
When Jesus the healer passed through Galilee   350
Jesus' hands were kind hands, doing good to all   351
Be still and know that I am God   755
Come to me, come to me   759
Lord of life, we come to you   782

725

THE CHURCH CELEBRATES
DEATH AND GRIEVING

ROBERT   10 11 10 11

Unison **Confidently**

1   Today I live, one day shall come my death;
    one day shall still my laughter and my crying,
    bring to a halt my heartbeat and my breath:
    Oh, give me faith for living and for dying.

2   How I shall die, or when, I do not know,
    nor where, for endless is the world's horizon;
    but save me, God, from thoughts that lay me low,
    from morbid fears that freeze my power of reason.

3   When earthly life shall close, as close it must,
    let Jesus be my brother and my merit.
    Let me without regret recall the past,
    and then, into your hands commit my spirit.

4   Meanwhile I live and move and I am glad,
    enjoy this life and all its interweavings
    each given day, as I take up the thread,
    let love suggest my mode, my mood of living.

Fred Kaan (*b.*1929)

Music Margaret R. Tucker (*b.*1936)

SOMOS DEL SEÑOR   10 10 10 10

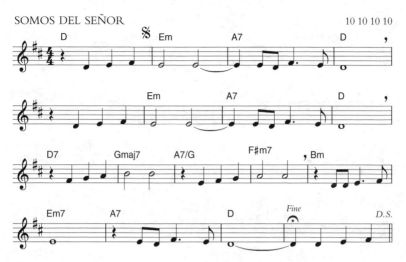

1   When we are living, we are in the Lord,
and when we're dying, we are in the Lord;
for in our living and in our dying
we belong to God, we belong to God.

2   Each day allows us to decide for good,
loving and serving as we know we should;
in thankful giving, in hopeful living,
we belong to God, we belong to God.

3   Sometimes we sorrow, other times embrace,
sometimes we question everything we face;
yet in our yearning is deeper learning:
we belong to God, we belong to God.

4   Till earth is over may we always know
love never fails us: God has made it so.
Hard times will prove us, never remove us;
we belong to God, we belong to God.

verse 1 Mexican traditional
verses 2-4 Roberto Escamilla
English version John L. Bell (*b.*1949)

Music Spanish traditional melody
arranged Compilers

HYMN OF PROMISE 87 87 D

1   In the bulb there is a flower;
     in the seed, an apple tree;
     in cocoons, a hidden promise:
     butterflies will soon be free!
     In the cold and snow of winter
     there's a spring that waits to be,
     unrevealed until its season,
     something God alone can see.

2   There's a song in every silence,
     seeking word and melody.
     There's a dawn in every darkness,
     bringing hope to you and me.
     From the past will come the future,
     what it holds, a mystery,
     unrevealed until its season,
     something God alone can see.

3   In our end is our beginning;
     in our time, infinity;
     in our doubt there is believing;
     in our life, eternity.
     In our death, a resurrection;
     at the last, a victory,
     unrevealed until its season,
     something God alone can see.

Natalie Allyn Wakeley Sleeth (1930–1992)

Music Natalie Allyn Wakeley Sleeth (1930–1992)

TYNEMOUTH (ST CATHERINE'S)   8888 88

1   God of the living, in whose eyes
     unveiled your whole creation lies,
     all souls are yours; we must not say
     that those are dead who pass away;
     for we believe and know it true,
     our dead are living, Lord, with you.

2   Released from earthly toil and strife,
     with you is hidden still their life;
     yours are their thoughts, their works, their powers,
     all yours, and yet most surely ours;
     for we believe and know it true,
     our dead are living, Lord, with you.

                              *John Ellerton (1826–1893)

Music Henri Friedrich Hémy (1818–1888)
Crown of Jesus Music, 1864
harmonised David Evans (1874–1948)

LONDONDERRY AIR   11 10 11 10 D

1   Hear me, dear Lord, in this my time of sorrow.
     For even if I turn from you today
     I need to know your love is there tomorrow
     and new hope still can lighten up my way.
     Forgive me, Lord, if in the tears of sadness
     my anger makes me take your name in vain,
     and life seems for a time to have no gladness,
     while I refuse to let you share my pain.

2   Help me, my God, in the surrounding darkness,
     to hold by faith the gospel I have read,
     that, even in death's unremitting starkness,
     the Son of Man has risen from the dead.
     So take my life that's left with its misgivings;
     from grief and pain create in me anew
     a faith that finds in you a way of living,
     a love that offers all it has to you.

Colin Ferguson (b. 1937)

Music Irish traditional melody
harmonised John L. Bell (b. 1949)

IONA BOAT SONG   669 D

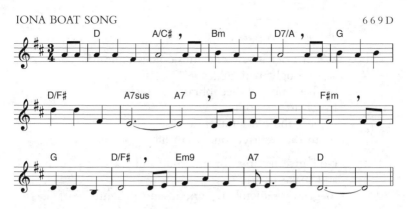

1   From the falter of breath,
     through the silence of death,
     to the wonder that's breaking beyond;
     God has woven a way,
     unapparent by day,
     for all those of whom heaven is fond.

2   From frustration and pain,
     through hope hard to sustain,
     to the wholeness here promised, there known;
     Christ has gone where we fear
     and has vowed to be near
     on the journey we make on our own.

3   From the dimming of light,
     through the darkness of night,
     to the glory of goodness above;
     God the Spirit is sent
     to ensure heaven's intent
     is embraced and completed in love.

4   From today till we die,
     through all questioning why,
     to the place from which time and tide flow;
     angels tread on our dreams,
     and magnificent themes
     of heaven's promise are echoed below.

                              John L. Bell (*b.* 1949)
                         and Graham Maule (*b.* 1958)

Music Scottish folk melody
arranged John L. Bell (*b.* 1949)

To be read by one voice.

1   When grief is raw and music goes unheard,
and thought is numb,
we have no polished phrases to recite.
In Christ we come
to hear the old familiar words:
'I am the resurrection. I am life'.

2   God, give us time for gratitude and tears,
and make us free
to grieve, remember, honour, and delight.
Let love be strong
to bear regrets and banish fears;
'I am the resurrection. I am life'.

3   The height and breadth of all that love prepares
soars out of time,
beyond our speculation and our sight.
The cross remains
to ground the promise that it bears:
'I am the resurrection. I am life'.

4   All shall be judged, the greatest and the least,
and all be loved,
till every hurt is healed, all wrong set right.
In bread and wine
we taste the great homecoming feast,
and in the midst of death we are in life.

Brian Wren *(b.* 1936)

732

GAELIC LULLABY   88 87

Music Scottish folk melody *arranged* John L. Bell (*b.* 1949)

731 Words: © 1983, Stainer & Bell Ltd, PO Box 110, Victoria House, 23 Gruneisen Road, London N3 1DZ

1 When Jesus longed for us to know
   how we should live and love and grow,
   he chose a child in whom to show
   some glimpses here of heaven.

2 Should children suffer pain and cry
   and lose their hold on life and die,
   while we must grieve and wonder why —
   Christ keeps them safe in heaven.

3 So we commend and give to God
   our child, now silent to the world,
   that hand in hand with Christ *her* Lord,
   she lives again in heaven.

4 Lord, tell *her* how we'll always care
   and miss the years we longed to share,
   until, in answer to our prayer,
   we meet again in heaven.

5 Alleluia.
   Alleluia.
   Alleluia.
   We'll meet again in heaven.

John L. Bell (*b.*1949)

JENNIFER   11 10 11

1. We cannot care for you the way we wanted,
   or cradle you or listen for your cry;
   but, separated as we are by silence,
   love will not die.

2. We cannot watch you growing into childhood,
   nor find a new uniqueness every day;
   but special as you would have been among us
   you still will stay.

3. We cannot know the pain or the potential
   which passing years would summon or reveal;
   but for that true fulfilment Jesus promised
   we hope and feel.

4. So through the mess of anger, grief, and tiredness,
   through tensions which are not yet reconciled,
   we give to God the worship of our sorrow
   and our dear child.

5. Lord, in your arms, which cradle all creation,
   we rest and place our baby beyond death,
   believing that *she* now, alive in heaven,
   breathes with your breath.

John L. Bell (*b.* 1949)

This hymn may be read aloud while the following sequence is played.

repeat ad lib.

Music John L. Bell (*b.* 1949)

ROCKINGHAM (COMMUNION) LM

1 O Christ, you wept when grief was raw
and felt for those who mourned their friend;
come close to where we would not be,
and hold us, numbed by this life's end.

2 The well-loved voice is silent now
and we have much we meant to say;
collect our lost and wandering words
and keep them till the endless day.

3 We try to hold what is not here
and fear for what we do not know;
O take our hands in yours, good Lord,
and free us now to let *him* go.

4 In all our loneliness and doubt,
through what we cannot realise,
address us from your empty tomb
and speak of life that never dies.

John L. Bell (*b.* 1949)
and Graham Maule (*b.* 1958)

Music Melody *Tunbridge* from
A Second Supplement to Psalmody in Miniature, c. 1780
arranged Edward Miller (1731–1807)
harmonised David Evans (1874–1948)

To be read by one voice.

1   Go, silent friend,
your life has found its ending;
to dust returns
your weary mortal frame.
God, who before birth
called you into being,
now calls you hence,
his accent still the same.

2   Go, silent friend,
your life in Christ is buried;
for you he lived
and died and rose again.
Close by his side
your promised place is waiting,
where, fully known,
you shall with God remain.

3   Go, silent friend,
forgive us if we grieved you;
safe now in heaven,
kindly say our name.
Your life has touched us,
that is why we mourn you;
our lives without you
cannot be the same.

4   Go, silent friend,
we do not grudge you glory;
sing, sing with joy
deep praises to your Lord.
You, who believed
that Christ would come back for you,
now celebrate
that Jesus keeps his word.

John L. Bell (*b.*1949)
and Graham Maule (*b.*1958)

SINE NOMINE

10 10 10 and Alleluias

Al - - le - lu - ia, Al - - le - lu - ia!

1 Give thanks for life, the measure of our days,
   mortal, we pass through beauty that decays,
   yet sing to God our hope, our love, our praise:
   Alleluia, Alleluia!

2 Give thanks for those whose lives shone with a light
   caught from the Christ-flame, gleaming through the night,
   who touched the truth, who burned for what is right:

3 Give thanks for all, our living and our dead,
   thanks for the love by which our life is fed,
   a love not changed by time or death or dread:

4 Give thanks for hope that, like the seed of grain
   lying in darkness, does its life retain
   to rise in glory, growing green again:

Shirley Erena Murray (*b.* 1931)

Music Ralph Vaughan Williams (1872–1958)

WILL YOUR ANCHOR HOLD

10 9 10 9 and refrain

Refrain

1   Will your anchor hold in the storms of life,
    when the clouds unfold their wings of strife?
    When the strong tides lift, and the cables strain,
    will your anchor drift, or firm remain?
        We have an anchor that keeps the soul
        steadfast and sure while the billows roll;
        fastened to the Rock which cannot move,
        grounded firm and deep in the Saviour's love!

2   Will your anchor hold in the straits of fear,
    when the breakers roar and the reef is near?
    While the surges rage, and the wild winds blow,
    shall the angry waves then your bark o'erflow?

3   Will your anchor hold in the floods of death,
    when the waters cold chill your latest breath?
    On the rising tide you can never fail,
    while your anchor holds within the veil.

4   Will your eyes behold through the morning light
    the city of gold and the harbour bright?
    Will you anchor safe by the heavenly shore,
    when life's storms are past for evermore?

                    Priscilla Jane Owens (1829–1907)

Music William James Kirkpatrick (1838–1921)

A list of items also suitable for this section is found on the previous two pages.

AUSTRIAN HYMN 87 87 D

1   Glorious things of thee are spoken,
    Zion, city of our God;
    he whose word cannot be broken
    formed thee for his own abode.
    On the Rock of Ages founded,
    what can shake thy sure repose?
    With salvation's walls surrounded,
    thou mayest smile at all thy foes.

2   See! the streams of living waters,
    springing from eternal love,
    well supply thy sons and daughters,
    and all fear of want remove.
    Who can faint while such a river
    ever will their thirst assuage —
    grace which, like the Lord the Giver,
    never fails from age to age?

3   Saviour, since of Zion's city
    I, through grace, a member am,
    let the world deride or pity,
    I will glory in thy Name.
    Fading is the worldling's pleasure,
    and all boasted pomp and show;
    solid joys and lasting treasure
    none but Zion's children know.

                        *John Newton (1725–1807)

Music Franz Joseph Haydn (1732–1809)
from a Croatian folk melody

739

AURELIA   76 76 D

1   The Church's one foundation
    is Jesus Christ her Lord:
    she is his new creation
    by water and the word;
    from heaven he came and sought her
    to be his holy bride;
    with his own blood he bought her,
    and for her life he died.

2   Called forth from every nation,
    yet one o'er all the earth,
    her charter of salvation:
    one Lord, one faith, one birth.
    One holy name she blesses,
    and shares one holy food,
    as to one hope she presses,
    with every grace endued.

3   In toil and tribulation,
    and tumult of her war,
    she waits the consummation
    of peace for evermore,
    till with the vision glorious
    her longing eyes are blest,
    and the great Church victorious
    shall be the Church at rest.

Music Samuel Sebastian Wesley (1810–1876)

4   Yet she on earth has union
with God the Three in One,
and mystical communion
with those whose rest is won.
O happy ones and holy!
Lord, give us grace that we,
like them, the meek and lowly,
on high may dwell with thee.

*Samuel John Stone (1839–1900)

740

SINE NOMINE   10 10 10 and Alleluias

Al - - le - lu - ia!   Al - - le - lu - ia!

1   For all the saints, who from their labours rest;
who thee by faith before the world confessed,
thy name, O Jesus, be for ever blest.
Alleluia! Alleluia!

2   Thou wast their rock, their fortress, and their might;
thou, Lord, their captain in the well-fought fight;
thou, in the darkness drear their one true light.
Alleluia! Alleluia!

3   Oh, may thy soldiers, faithful, true, and bold,
fight as the saints who nobly fought of old,
and win, with them, the victor's crown of gold.
Alleluia! Alleluia!

continued overleaf

Music Ralph Vaughan Williams (1872–1958)

740 Music: From *The English Hymnal*, 1906, Oxford University Press, Great Clarendon Street, Oxford. OX2 6DP.
Reproduced by permission.

Al - - le - lu - ia! Al - - le - lu - ia!

4   O blest communion, fellowship divine!
We feebly struggle, they in glory shine;
yet all are one in thee, for all are thine.
Alleluia! Alleluia!

5   And when the strife is fierce, the warfare long,
steals on the ear the distant triumph song,
and hearts are brave again, and arms are strong.
Alleluia! Alleluia!

6   The golden evening brightens in the west;
soon, soon to faithful warriors cometh rest;
sweet is the calm of paradise the blest.
Alleluia! Alleluia!

7   But, lo! there breaks a yet more glorious day;
the saints triumphant rise in bright array;
the King of Glory passes on his way.
Alleluia! Alleluia!

8   From earth's wide bounds, from ocean's farthest coast,
through gates of pearl streams in the countless host,
singing to Father, Son, and Holy Ghost,
Alleluia! Alleluia!

William Walsham How (1823–1897)

DARWALL'S 148th   66 66 44 44

1   Glory to you, O God,
     for all your saints in light,
     who nobly waged and won
     the fierce and well-fought fight.
     Their praises sing,
     who life outpoured
     by fire and sword
     for Christ their King.

2   Thanks be to you, O Lord,
     for saints your Spirit stirred
     in humble paths to live
     your life and speak your word.
     Unnumbered they
     whose shining light
     informs our sight
     from day to day.

3   Lord God of truth and love,
     'Your kingdom come', we pray;
     give us your grace to know
     your truth and walk your way.
     Your will be done
     here on this earth,
     till saints in earth
     and heaven are one.

                Howard Charles Adie Gaunt (1902–1983)

Music John Darwall (1731–1789)

LAUDATE DOMINUM   10 10 11 11

1   Rejoice in God's saints, today and all days!
       A world without saints forgets how to praise.
       Their faith in acquiring the habit of prayer,
       their depth of adoring, Lord, help us to share.

2   Some march with events to turn them God's way;
       some need to withdraw, the better to pray;
       some carry the gospel through fire and through flood:
       our world is their parish: their purpose is God.

3   Rejoice in those saints, unpraised and unknown,
       who bear someone's cross, or shoulder their own:
       they share our complaining, our comfort, our cares:
       what patience in caring, what courage, is theirs!

4   Rejoice in God's saints, today and all days!
       A world without saints forgets how to praise.
       In loving, in living, they prove it is true:
       their way of self-giving, Lord, leads us to you.

                           Frederick Pratt Green (1903–2000)

Music Charles Hubert Hastings Parry (1848–1918)

WETHERBY   CM

PARAPHRASE 59, verses 1–4, 13

1   Behold what witnesses unseen
encompass us around,
who, once like us, with suffering tried,
are now with glory crowned.

2   Let us, with zeal like theirs inspired,
begin the Christian race,
and, freed from each encumbering weight,
their holy footsteps trace.

3   Behold a witness nobler still,
who trod affliction's path,
Jesus, at once the finisher
and author of our faith.

4   He for the joy before him set,
so generous was his love,
endured the cross, despised the shame,
and now he reigns above.

5   Then let our hearts no more despond,
our hands be weak no more;
still let us trust our Father's love,
his wisdom still adore.

Scottish Paraphrases, 1781
Hebrews 12

Music Samuel Sebastian Wesley (1810–1876)

ST MAGNUS (NOTTINGHAM)   CM

An alternative tune DESERT (LYNGHAM) *is found at* 352 2.

PARAPHRASE 65, verses 5, 6, 8, 9, 11,

1   Hark how the adoring hosts above
    with songs surround the throne!
    Ten thousand, thousand are their tongues;
    but all their hearts are one.

2   Worthy the Lamb that died, they cry,
    to be exalted thus;
    worthy the Lamb, let us reply;
    for he was slain for us.

3   Thou hast redeemed us with thy blood,
    and set the prisoners free;
    thou mad'st us kings and priests to God,
    and we shall reign with thee.

4   From every kindred, every tongue,
    thou brought'st thy chosen race;
    and distant lands and isles have shared
    the riches of thy grace.

5   To him who sits upon the throne,
    the God whom we adore,
    and to the Lamb that once was slain,
    be glory evermore.

Scottish Paraphrases, 1781
Revelation 5: 11-14

Music Jeremiah Clarke (*c.* 1673–1707)

745

ST ASAPH   DCM

PARAPHRASE 66

1   How bright these glorious spirits shine!
    Whence all their bright array?
    How came they to the blissful seats
    of everlasting day?
    Lo! these are they, from sufferings great
    who came to realms of light,
    and in the blood of Christ have washed
    those robes which shine so bright.

2   Now, with triumphal palms they stand
    before the throne on high,
    and serve the God they love, amidst
    the glories of the sky.
    His presence fills each heart with joy,
    tunes every mouth to sing:
    by day, by night, the sacred courts
    with glad hosannas ring.

3   Hunger and thirst are felt no more,
    nor suns with scorching ray;
    God is their sun, whose cheering beams
    diffuse eternal day.
    The Lamb who dwells amidst the throne
    shall o'er them still preside,
    feed them with nourishment divine,
    and all their footsteps guide.

*4 'Mong pastures green he'll lead his flock,
    where living streams appear;
    and God the Lord from every eye
    shall wipe off every tear.

*   *Verse 4 is sung to the second half of the tune.*

                    Scottish Paraphrases, 1781
                    Revelation 7: 13—end

Music Possibly by Giovanni Marie Giornovichi (1745–1804)
published in Smith's *Sacred Music,* Edinburgh, 1825

DUNBLANE PRIMARY

11 10 11 4

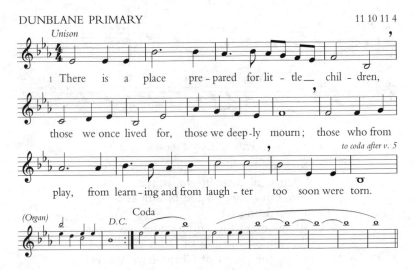

1 There is a place pre-pared for lit-tle chil-dren,
those we once lived for, those we deep-ly mourn; those who from
to coda after v. 5
play, from learn-ing and from laugh-ter too soon were torn.

(Organ)   Coda
D.C.

1   There is a place prepared for little children,
     those we once lived for, those we deeply mourn;
     those who from play, from learning and from laughter
     too soon were torn.

2   There is a place where hands which held ours tightly
     now are released beyond all hurt and fear,
     healed by that love which also feels our sorrow,
     tear after tear.

3   There is a place where all the lost potential
     yields its full promise, finds its true intent;
     silenced no more, young voices echo freely
     as they were meant.

4   There is a place where God will hear our questions,
     suffer our anger, share our speechless grief,
     gently repair the innocence of loving
     and of belief.

5   Jesus, who bids us be like little children,
     shields those our arms are yearning to embrace.
     God will ensure that all are reunited;
     there is a place.

John L. Bell (*b.* 1949)

Music John L. Bell (*b.* 1949)

EWING   76 76 D

1   Jerusalem the golden,
      with milk and honey blessed,
      beneath your contemplation
      sink heart and voice oppressed:
      I know not, oh, I know not
      what joys await us there,
      what radiancy of glory,
      what bliss beyond compare.

2   They stand, those halls of Zion
      all jubilant with song,
      and radiant with the angels
      and all the martyr throng;
      the Prince is ever in them,
      the daylight is serene,
      the pastures of the blessèd
      are decked in glorious sheen.

3   There is the throne of David;
      and there, from care released,
      the shout of those who triumph,
      the song of those who feast;
      and they who, with their Leader,
      have conquered in the fight,
      for ever and for ever
      are clothed in robes of white.

continued overleaf

Music Alexander Ewing (1830–1895)

4   O sweet and blessèd country,
     the home of God's elect!
     O sweet and blessèd country
     that eager hearts expect!
     Jesus in mercy bring us
     to that dear land above,
     where you, with God the Father
     and Spirit, reign in love.

                    Bernard of Cluny (12th century)
          translated *John Mason Neale (1818–1866)

WAREHAM   LM

1.   As stars adorn the night-veiled sky,
     arrayed like jewels rare and bright,
     so shine God's saints in every age
     to give the world new hope, new light.

2.   The light saints bear is not their own
     but shines through them as gift and sign:
     to show how God can use and bless
     frail human means for ends divine.

3.   Through saints we glimpse the light of Christ,
     the Morning Star that crowns the night,
     whose rising heralds God's new day,
     the promised dawn of life and light.

4.   That light is ours to claim and share,
     not merely praise or gaze upon:
     for all who are baptized become
     light-bearers through the Risen One.

5.   The saints inspire and challenge us
     our holy calling to embrace:
     to bear Christ's light in our own day,
     to be the vessels of God's grace.

Carl P. Daw, Jr (b. 1944)

Music Melody by William Knapp (1698–1768)
harmonised David Evans (1874–1948)

SOON AND VERY SOON 57 57 57 and refrain

Rhythmically

1 Soon and very soon,
   we are going to see the King!
   Soon and very soon,
   we are going to see the King!
   Soon and very soon,
   we are going to see the King!
   Hallelujah! Hallelujah!
   We're going to see the King!

2 No more crying there —
   we are going to see the King!
   No more crying there —
   we are going to see the King!
   No more crying there —
   we are going to see the King!

3 No more dying there —
   we are going to see the King!
   No more dying there —
   we are going to see the King!
   No more dying there —
   we are going to see the King!

Andrae Crouch (*b.*1945)

Music Andrae Crouch (*b.*1945)
arranged David Christopher Peacock (*b.*1949)

A list of items also suitable for this section is found on the previous page.

SHORT SONGS

750

ADORAMUS TE   Irregular

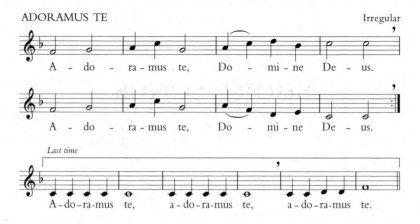

A - do - ra - mus te, Do - mi - ne De - us.

A - do - ra - mus te, Do - mi - ne De - us.

Last time

A - do - ra - mus te, a - do - ra - mus te, a - do - ra - mus te.

Adoramus te, Domine Deus.
Adoramus te, Domine Deus.
Adoramus te, adoramus te,
adoramus te.

(We adore you, O Lord God.)

Liturgical text

Music Margaret Rizza (b. 1929)

751

Brightly

Al - le - lu - ia! Al - le - lu - ia!

Al - le - lu - ia! Al - le - lu - ia!

Alleluia!   Alleluia!
Alleluia!   Alleluia!

Music Norah Duncan, IV

752

Al - le - lu - ia,   al - le - lu - ia.   Al - le - lu -
- ia,   al - le - lu - ia.   Al - le - lu - ia,   al -
- le - lu - ia.   Al - le - lu - ia,   al - le - lu - ia.

Alleluia, alleluia.
Alleluia, alleluia.
Alleluia, alleluia.
Alleluia, alleluia.

Music South African traditional

753

Al - le - lu - ia,   al - le - lu - ia.   Al - le - lu - ia,   al - le -
- lu - ia.   Al - le - lu - ia, al - le - lu - ia. El Se - ñor re - su - ci - to.
(1) Christ the Lord is risen in - deed.
(2) Glo - ry, love, and praise to God.

Alleluia, alleluia.
Alleluia, alleluia.
Alleluia, alleluia.
El Señor resucito.

1   Alleluia, alleluia.   2   Alleluia, alleluia.
    Alleluia, alleluia.   Alleluia, alleluia.
    Alleluia, alleluia.   Alleluia, alleluia.
    Christ the Lord   Glory, love,
        is risen indeed.   and praise to God.

Music Honduran traditional melody
arranged John L. Bell (*b.*1949)

MORTON   87 87

Be still and know that I am God,
and there is none beside me.
Be still and know that I am God,
and there is none beside me.

Psalm 46: 10

Music John L. Bell (*b.* 1949)

755

888

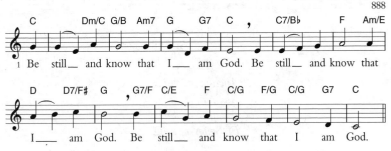

1   Be still and know that I am God.
     Be still and know that I am God.
     Be still and know that I am God.

2   I am the Lord who saves and heals.
     I am the Lord who saves and heals.
     I am the Lord who saves and heals.

3 In you, Lord God, I put my trust.
  In you, Lord God, I put my trust.
  In you, Lord God, I put my trust.

Author unknown
based on *Psalm 46: 10*

Music Source unknown
arranged Compilers

756

Cantor

My sis - ters, my sis - ters, my sis - ters,

All:

Bless the Lord, bless the Lord;

My bro - thers,

bless the Lord, there is no o - ther God.

Bless the Lord,
bless the Lord;
bless the Lord, there is no other God.

(ad lib call by cantor between verses)
  My sisters …
  My brothers …
  You children …
  You elders …
  Together …

Text derived from Psalms

Music Kenyan traditional song

Music Alexander Gondo
arranged John L. Bell (*b.* 1949)

Original Shona text:
Uyai mose,
tinamate Mwari,
uyai mose,
tinamate Mwari,
uyai mose,
tinamate Mwari,
uyai mose zvino.

Come all you people,
come and praise your Maker,
come all you people,
come and praise your Maker,
come all you people,
come and praise your Maker,
come now and worship the Lord.

Alexander Gondo

757 Words: © Alexander Gondo, World Council of Churches

Come, Ho - ly Spi - rit, gra - cious heaven - ly

dove; come, fire of love. *Last time* love.

Come, Holy Spirit,
gracious heavenly dove;
come, fire of love.

John L. Bell (*b.* 1949)
and Graham Maule (*b.* 1958)

Music John L. Bell (*b.* 1949)

759

Gently

Come to me, come to me, weak and

hea - vy la - den; trust in me,

lean on me. I will give you rest.

Come to me, come to me,
weak and heavy laden;
trust in me, lean on me.
I will give you rest.

John L. Bell (*b.* 1949)

Music John L. Bell (*b.* 1949)

760

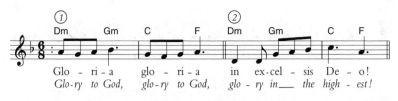

Glo - ri - a,   glo - ri - a,   in ex-cel - sis De - o!
Glo-ry to God,   glo-ry to God,   glo - ry in___ the high - est!

Glo - ri - a,   glo - ri - a,   al - le - lu - ia,   al - le - lu - ia!
Glo-ry to God,   glo-ry to God,   al - le - lu - ia,   al - le - lu - ia!

Gloria, gloria
in excelsis Deo!
Gloria, gloria,
alleluia, alleluia!

Glory to God, glory to God,
glory in the highest!
Glory to God, glory to God,
alleluia, alleluia!

This may be sung in canon.

Taizé Community

Music and words Taizé Community

761

Glo - ri - a,   glo - ri - a,   glo - ri - a,

in   ex - cel - sis   De - - o.

Gloria, gloria, gloria,
in excelsis Deo.

(Glory to God in the highest.)

Liturgical text

Music Iona Gloria

Cantor

Glo-ry to God, glo-ry to God, glo-ry in the high-est! Glo-ry to God,

Glo-ry to God, glo-ry in the high-est! To God be glo-ry for-ev-er!

To God be glo-ry for-ev-er! Al-le-lu-ia! A-men! Al-le-lu-ia! A-men!

Al-le-lu-ia! A-men! Al-le-lu-ia! A-men!

Al-le-lu-ia! A-men! Al-le-lu-ia! A-men! Al-le-lu-ia! A-men!

Al-le-lu-ia! A-men! Al-le-lu-ia! A-men! Al-le-lu-ia! A-men!

CANTOR:	Glory to God, glory to God, glory in the highest!
ALL:	Glory to God, glory to God, glory in the highest!
CANTOR:	To God be glory forever!
ALL:	To God be glory forever!
CANTOR:	Alleluia! Amen!
GROUP 1:	Alleluia! Amen!
CANTOR:	Alleluia! Amen!
GROUPS 1, 2:	Alleluia! Amen!
CANTOR:	Alleluia! Amen!
GROUPS 1, 2, 3:	Alleluia! Amen!
ALL:	Alleluia! Amen! Alleluia! Amen!

Peru

Music Peruvian traditional chant

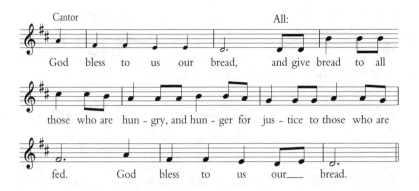

CANTOR: God bless to us our bread,
ALL: and give bread to all those who are hungry,
    and hunger for justice to those who are fed.
    God bless to us our bread.

Argentinian text, collected by Federico Pagura
English text John L. Bell (*b.*1949)

Music Argentinian melody, collected by Federico Pagura
arranged John L. Bell (*b.*1949)

LAUGHTER

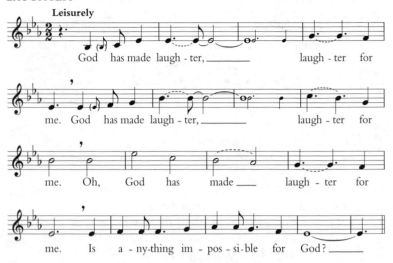

God has made laugh-ter, _____ laugh-ter for me. God has made laugh-ter, _____ laugh-ter for me. Oh, God has made _____ laugh-ter for me. Is a-ny-thing im-pos-si-ble for God? _____

1   God has made laughter, laughter for me.
    God has made laughter, laughter for me.
    Oh, God has made laughter for me!
    Is anything impossible for God?

2   Everyone who hears will laugh with me.
    Everyone who hears will laugh with me.
    Oh, everyone will laugh with me!
    Is anything impossible for God?

Kathy Wonson Eddy (b.1951)
based on Genesis 21: 6

Music Kathy Wonson Eddy (b.1951)

765

God's love is for ev-ery-bo-dy, ev-ery-one a-round the world; you and me and all ___ God's child-ren from a-cross the street to a-round the world, a-cross the street to a-round the world.

God's love is for everybody,
everyone around the world;
you and me and all God's children
from across the street to around the world,
across the street to around the world.

Bryan Moyer Suderman

Music Bryan Moyer Suderman

766

Hal - le - lu - jah, hal - le - lu - jah,
hal - - - - - le - lu - jah!

Hallelujah,
hallelujah,
hallelujah!

Music Ukrainian liturgical chant

767

Hal - le - lu - jah,_____ hal - le - lu - jah,
hal - le - lu - jah,_____ hal - le - lu - jah!

Hallelujah, hallelujah,
hallelujah, hallelujah!

Music Abraham Maraire

767 Music: © United Methodist Music Service, Mutambara, PO Box 61, Cashel, Zimbabwe

SANCTUS and BENEDICTUS (Columba)

Sanctus and *Benedictus qui venit*

1   Holy, holy, holy,
     God of power and might,
     heaven and earth are full,
     are full of your glory.
     Glory to your name!
     Glory to your name!
     Glory to your name, O Lord most high!

2   Blessèd, blessèd, blessèd,
     blessèd is the one,
     is the one who comes
     in the name of the Lord.
     Hosanna!
     Hosanna!
     Hosanna in the highest!

                              Sanctus and Benedictus

Music John L. Bell (*b.*1949)

769

SANTO   67 85

Ho - ly ho - ly ho - ly, my heart, my heart a - dores you! My
San - to, san - to, san - to, mi co - ra - zon te a - do - ra! Mi

heart is glad to say the words: you are ho - ly, Lord.
co - ra - zon te sa - be de - cir: san - to e - res Se - ñor

Holy, holy, holy,
my heart, my heart adores you!
My heart is glad to say the words,
'You are holy, Lord.'

Original Hispanic text:
Santo, santo, santo,
mi corazon te adora!
mi corazon te sabe decir:
santo eres Señor.

Variation on liturgical text (Argentina)

Music Argentinian chant

770

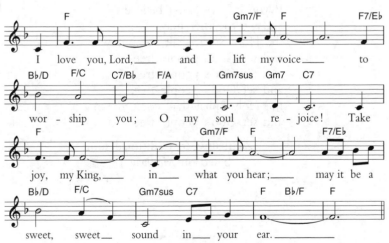

I love you, Lord,___ and I lift my voice___ to

wor - ship you; O my soul re - joice! Take

joy, my King,___ in___ what you hear;___ may it be a

sweet, sweet___ sound in___ your ear.___

I love you, Lord, and I lift my voice
to worship you; O my soul rejoice!
Take joy, my King, in what you hear;
may it be a sweet, sweet sound in your ear.

Laurie Klein (*b.*1950)

Music Laurie Klein (*b.*1950)

If you believe and I believe
and we together pray,
the Holy Spirit shall come down
and set God's people free,
and set God's people free,
and set God's people free,
the Holy Spirit shall come down
and set God's people free.

Zimbabwean traditional song
based on *Matthew 18: 19*

Music Zimbabwean variant of English folk melody
arranged John L. Bell (*b.* 1949)

772

In the Lord I'll be ev-er thank-ful, in the Lord I will rejoice! Look to God, do not be a-fraid. Lift up your
voi-ces, the Lord is near. Lift up your voi-ces, the Lord is near.

In the Lord I'll be ever thankful,
in the Lord I will rejoice!
Look to God, do not be afraid.
Lift your voices, the Lord is near.
Lift your voices, the Lord is near.

Taizé Community

Music Jacques Berthier (1923–1994)

773

JESU TAWA PANO   66 69

Version for Shona text

Version for English text

Original Shona text: Jesus, we are here,
Jesu, tawa pano;   Jesus, we are here,
Jesu, tawa pano;   Jesus, we are here,
Jesu, tawa pano;   we are here for you.
tawa pano, mu zita renyu.
                                Patrick Matsikenyiri (*b.*1937)

Music Patrick Matsikenyiri (*b.*1937)

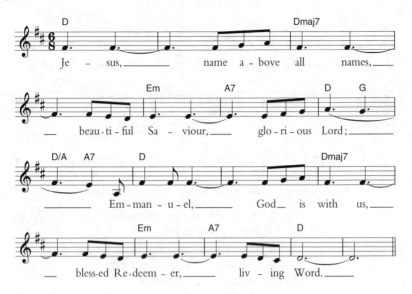

Je - sus,_____ name a - bove all names,_____ beau - ti - ful Sa - viour,_____ glo - ri - ous Lord;_____ Em - man - u - el,_____ God_ is with us, _____ bless-ed Re-deem - er,_____ liv - ing Word._____

Jesus, name above all names,
beautiful Saviour, glorious Lord;
Emmanuel, God is with us,
blessèd Redeemer, living Word.

Naida Hearn (*b.* 1944)

Music Naida Hearn (*b.* 1944)
arranged Roland T. Fudge (*b.* 1947)

775

Je - sus re - mem-ber me when you come in - to your king - dom.

Je - sus re - mem-ber me when you come in - to your king-dom.

Jesus, remember me
when you come into your kingdom.
Jesus, remember me
when you come into your kingdom.

Taizé Community

Music Jacques Berthier (1923–1994)

776

Ky - ri - e e - lei - son. Ky - ri - e e - lei - son.

Ky - ri - e e - lei - - - - son.

Kyrie eleison.
Kyrie eleison.
Kyrie eleison.

(Lord, have mercy.)

Ukraine

Music Ukrainian traditional chant

777

KYRIE (Bridget)

Ky - ri - e e - lei - son. Ky - ri - e e - lei - son.

Chris - te e - lei - son. Chris - te e - lei - son.

Ky - ri - e e - lei - - son.

All: Ky - ri - e e - lei - - son.

Kyrie eleison.
Christe eleison.
Kyrie eleison.

Each line is sung first by cantor,
then repeated by the congregation.

Music John L. Bell (*b.* 1949)

777 Music: © WGRG, The Iona Community

AGNUS DEI   Irregular

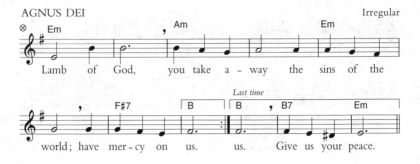

Lamb of God,
you take away the sins of the world;
have mercy on us.

Last time only:
Give us your peace.

Music Celebration Hymnal
arranged Fride Gustafsson

779

Music Zimbabwean traditional

CANTOR: Listen now for the Gospel!
ALL:　　Alleluia!
CANTOR: It is God's word that changes us!
ALL:　　Alleluia!

1　Come, Holy Spirit, melt and break our hearts of stone,
　until we give our lives to God, and God alone.

2　Come, Holy Spirit, root in us God's living word,
　that we may show the faithfulness of Christ our Lord.

3　Come, Holy Spirit, bind the broken, find the lost,
　confirm in us the fire and love of Pentecost.

Each verse is sung first by a cantor, then repeated by the congregation.

Zimbabwean liturgical acclamation

780

Lis-ten to the word which God has spo-ken, lis-ten to the One who is close at hand, lis-ten to the voice which be-gan cre-a-tion, lis-ten ev-en if you don't un-der-stand.

Listen to the word which God has spoken,
listen to the One who is close at hand,
listen to the voice which began creation,
listen even if you don't understand.

This may be sung as a round, successive voices entering ad lib.

Canadian original, adapted

Music Canadian original
adapted Compilers

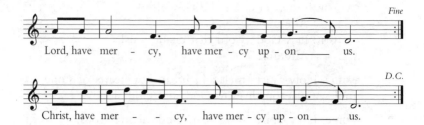

Lord, have mer - cy, have mer - cy up - on____ us.

Christ, have mer - - cy, have mer - cy up - on____ us.

Lord, have mercy, have mercy upon us.
Christ, have mercy, have mercy upon us.

Each line is sung first by a cantor or choir,
then repeated by the congregation.

Nkasi Nkosi (South Africa)

Music G. M. Kolisi

782

ERISKAY LOVE LILT   77 66

1 Lord of life, we come to you. Lord of all, our Sa-viour be,

come to bless and to heal with the light of your love.

1   Lord of life, we come to you.
     Lord of all, our Saviour be,
     come to bless and to heal
     with the light of your love.

2   Through the days of doubt and toil,
     in our joy and in our pain,
     guide our steps in your way,
     make us one in your love.

Catherine Walker (*b.* 1958)

Music Scottish folk melody
arranged Compilers of *Common Ground,* 1998

783

88 44 6

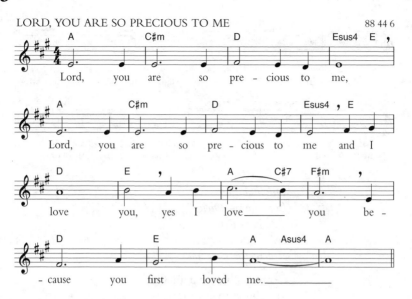

1   Lord, you are so precious to me,
     Lord, you are so precious to me
     and I love you,
     yes, I love you
     because you first loved me.

2   Lord, you are so gracious to me,
     Lord, you are so gracious to me
     and I love you,
     yes, I love you
     because you first loved me.

                        Graham Kendrick (*b.* 1950)

Music Graham Kendrick (*b.* 1950)

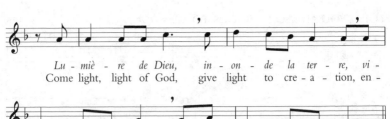

Lu - miè - re de Dieu,   in - on - de la ter - re,   vi -
Come light, light of God,   give light   to cre - a - tion, en -

- si - - te   nos   cœurs   et   de - meure   a - vec   nous.
- light - en   our hearts   and   re - main   with your world.

Original French text:
Lumière de Dieu,
inonde la terre,
visite nos cœurs
et demeure avec nous.

Come light, light of God,
give light to creation,
enlighten our hearts
and remain with your world.

Sisters of the Grandchamp
Community, Switzerland

Music Sisters of the Grandchamp Community, Switzerland

785

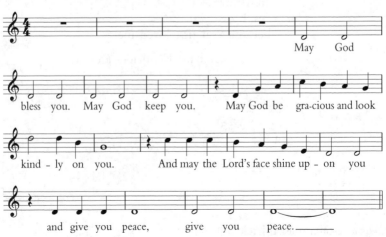

May   God

bless you. May God keep you.   May God be gra-cious and look

kind - ly on you.   And may the Lord's face shine up - on you

and give you peace,   give   you   peace._____

May God bless you.
May God keep you.
May God be gracious and look kindly on you.
And may the Lord's face shine upon you
and give you peace, give you peace.

Aaronic Blessing, from Numbers 6: 24
adapted Compilers

Music Source unknown
arranged Compilers

786

AE FOND KISS   87 87

May the God of peace go with us
as we travel from this place;
may the love of Jesus keep us
firm in hope and full of grace.

Ian Jamieson (*b.* 1939)

Music Scottish traditional melody
arranged Compilers

786   Words: © Ian Jamieson, 2 Whinfield Avenue, Prestwick. KA9 2BH

WEN-TI

1 May the Lord, mighty God, bless and keep you for ev - - er; grant you peace, per - fect peace, cou - rage in ev - ery en - dea - - vour.

Descant
Lift up and see his face, his

2 Lift up your eyes and see his face and his

grace for ev - - er; may the Lord, migh - ty

grace for ev - - er; may the lord, migh - ty

God, bless and keep you for ev - - er.

God, bless and keep you for ev - - er.

1   May the Lord, mighty God,
    bless and keep you for ever;
    grant you peace, perfect peace,
    courage in every endeavour.

Music Chinese origin *adapted* I-to-Loh

2 Lift up your eyes and see his face
and his grace for ever;
may the Lord, mighty God,
bless and keep you for ever.

Descant for verse 2:
Lift up and see his face,
his grace for ever;
may the Lord, mighty God,
bless and keep you for ever.

Aaronic Blessing
from *Numbers 6: 24*

788

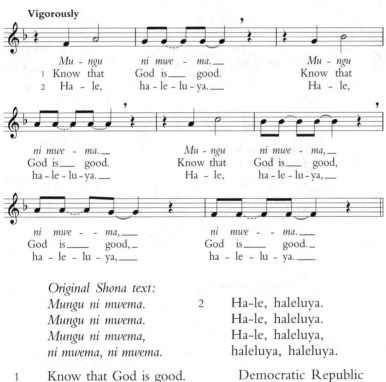

Vigorously

Mu - ngu   ni mwe - ma.__   Mu - ngu
1 Know that God is__ good.   Know that
2 Ha - le,   ha - le - lu - ya.__ Ha - le,

ni mwe - ma.__   Mu - ngu   ni mwe - ma,__
God is__ good.   Know that   God is__ good,
ha - le - lu - ya.__ Ha - le, ha - le - lu - ya,__

ni mwe - - ma,__   ni mwe - - ma.__
God is__ good,_   God is__ good._
ha - le - lu - ya,__ ha - le - lu - ya.__

Original Shona text:
Mungu ni mwema.
Mungu ni mwema.
Mungu ni mwema,
ni mwema, ni mwema.

2 Ha-le, haleluya.
   Ha-le, haleluya.
   Ha-le, haleluya,
   haleluya, haleluya.

1 Know that God is good.
   Know that God is good.
   Know that God is good,
   God is good, God is good.

Democratic Republic
of Congo

Music arranged Edo Bumba

788 Music: © Edo Bumba, 423139 Västra Frölunda, Sweden. Permission applied for.

JUNKANOO   Irregular

Now go in peace,
now go in love,
from the Father above.
Jesus Christ the Son
stay with you till the day is done.
Holy Spirit encircle you
in all you think and do.
Once again God's blessing be with you.
Amen.

This may be sung in canon.

Michael Mair (*b.* 1942)

Music Caribbean folk melody
arranged Michael Mair (*b.* 1942)

AGNUS DEI (St Bride)

O Lamb of God, you take a - way the sin___ of the world; O Lamb of God, you take a - way the sin___ of the world; have mer - - cy, have

(Last time) grant __ us,___

mer - - cy, have mer - - cy on us.
grant___ us,___ grant___ us your peace.

Repeat ad lib.

O Lamb of God,
you take away the sin of the world;
O Lamb of God,
you take away the sin of the world;
  have mercy on us, have mercy,
  have mercy on us.

Last time only:
  Grant us, grant us,
  grant us your peace.

Music John L. Bell (*b.* 1949)

Open your eyes, see the glory of the King;
lift up your voice, and his praises sing!
I love you, Lord. I will proclaim,
Alleluia! I bless your name.

Carl Tuttle (*b.* 1953)

Music Carl Tuttle (*b.* 1953)
arranged Christopher Norton (*b.* 1953)

1   Our God is a God who makes friends,
    our God is a God who makes friends,
    our God is a God who is faithful to the end;
    our God is a God who makes friends.

2   Our God calls us all to make friends,
    our God calls us all to make friends.
    Yes, you as well as I, we're the very ones God sends.
    Our God calls us all to make friends.

Bryan Moyer Suderman

Music Bryan Moyer Suderman

793

Stay with me, re - main here with me, watch____ and pray,____ watch and pray.____

Stay with me,
remain here with me,
watch and pray,
watch and pray.

Taizé Community

Music Jacques Berthier (1923–1994)

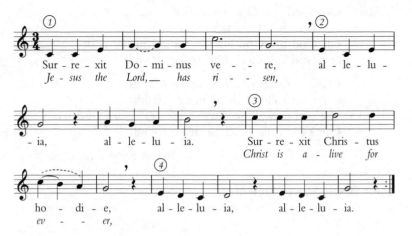

This may be sung in canon.

Surrexit Dominus vere,
alleluia, alleluia.
Surrexit Christus hodie,
alleluia, alleluia.

Alternative English words:
Jesus the Lord has risen,
alleluia, alleluia.
Christ is alive for ever,
alleluia, alleluia.

Taizé Community

Music Jacques Berthier (1923–1994)

795

Take, oh, take me as I am; sum-mon out what I shall be; set your seal up-on my heart and live in me.

> Take, oh, take me as I am;
> summon out what I shall be;
> set your seal upon my heart
> and live in me.

John L. Bell (b. 1949)

Music John L. Bell (b. 1949)

796

Irregular

The Lord bless you and keep you; the Lord make his face to shine up-on you, and be gra-cious un-to you: the Lord lift up his coun-te-nance up-on you and give you peace.

> The Lord bless you and keep you;
> the Lord make his face to shine upon you,
> and be gracious unto you:
> the Lord lift up his countenance upon you
> and give you peace.

Numbers 6: 24

Music Lowell Mason (1792–1872)

HE'S ALIVE

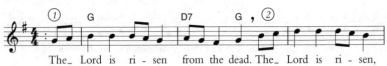

The_ Lord is ri - sen from the dead. The_ Lord is ri - sen,

as __ he said. He's a - live! He's a - live! He's a - live!

The Lord is risen from the dead.
The Lord is risen, as he said.
He's alive!   He's alive!

Liturgical text
Dimi Halleyi

Music Dimi Halleyi

798

LA PAZ DE LA TIERRE

Gently

1 The peace of the earth   be with you, the peace of the hea-vens too; the

peace of the riv - ers   be with you, the peace of the o - ceans too.

Deep   peace   fall - ing ov - er   you.
God's   peace   grow - ing in   you.

The peace of the earth be with you,
the peace of the heavens too;
the peace of the rivers be with you,
the peace of the oceans too.
Deep peace falling over you;
God's peace growing in you.

Guatemalan text
translated Christine Carson

Music Guatemalan folk melody
arranged John L. Bell (*b.*1949)

799

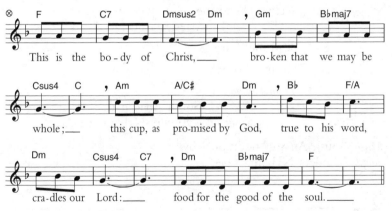

This is the body of Christ,
broken that we may be whole;
this cup, as promised by God,
true to his word, cradles our Lord:
food for the good of the soul.

John L. Bell (*b.*1949)

Music John L. Bell (*b.*1949)

Original Xhosa text:
CANTOR: *Thuma mina.*
ALL: *Thuma mina, thuma mina,*
thuma mina, Somandla

1 CANTOR: Send me, Lord.
ALL: Send me, Jesus, send me, Jesus,
send me, Jesus, send me, Lord.

2 Lead me, Lord …

3 Fill me, Lord …

Thuma mina …

South African traditional
adapted Anders Nyberg (*b.* 1955)

Music South African traditional hymn
adapted Anders Nyberg (*b.* 1955)

801

Ubi caritas et amor,   (Where there is charity
ubi caritas,   and love, God is there.)
Deus ibi est.

Taizé Community

Music Jacques Berthier (1923–1994)

WE ARE HERE TO PRAISE YOU   Irregular

We are here to praise you,
lift our hearts and sing.
We are here to give you
the best that we can bring.
And it is our love
rising from our hearts:
everything within us cries,
'Abba, Father'.
Help us now to give you
pleasure and delight,
heart and mind and will that say,
'I love you, Lord'.

Graham Kendrick (b. 1950)

Music Graham Kendrick (b. 1950)
arranged David Christopher Peacock (b. 1949)

SIZOHAMBA NAYE

Brightly

We will walk — with God, my bro-thers, we will walk — with God.

We will walk — with God, my sis-ters, we will walk — with God.

we will go re - joic-ing — till the king - dom has come.

we will go re - joic-ing — till the king - dom has come.

Sizohamba Naye

We will walk with God, my brothers,
we will walk with God.
We will walk with God, my sisters,
we will walk with God.
We will go rejoicing
till the kingdom has come.
We will go rejoicing
till the kingdom has come.

Swaziland traditional hymn

Music Swaziland traditional hymn

804

You shall go out with joy and be led forth with peace,
and the mountains and the hills shall break forth before you.
There'll be shouts of joy, and the trees of the field
shall clap, shall clap their hands,
and the trees of the field shall clap their hands,
and the trees of the field shall clap their hands,
and the trees of the field shall clap their hands,
and you'll go out with joy.

Stuart Dauermann (*b.* 1944)

Music Stuart Dauermann (*b.* 1944)
arranged Roland T. Fudge (*b.* 1947)

Original Xhosa text:
Mayenziwe 'ntando yakho.

Your will be done on earth, O Lord.

Music South African traditional

DOXOLOGIES
and AMENS

ST MAGNUS (NOTTINGHAM) CM

To Father, Son and Holy Ghost,
the God whom we adore,
be glory, as it was, and is,
and shall be evermore.

Music Jeremiah Clarke (*c.* 1673–1707)

807

OLD 100TH LM

Praise God, from whom all blessings flow;
praise him, all creatures here below;
praise him above, ye heavenly host;
praise Father, Son, and Holy Ghost.

Thomas Ken (1637–1711)

Music Melody from *Genevan Psalter,* 1551

TALLIS'S CANON   LM

> Praise God from whom all blessings flow;
> praise God all creatures here below;
> praise God, the Trinity of love,
> before, beneath, around, above.

Music Melody and most of the harmony by
Thomas Tallis (*c.* 1505–1585) from Ravenscroft's *Psalmes*, 1621

809

> Praise God, the Source of life and birth;
> praise God, the Word, who came to earth;
> praise God the Spirit, holy flame:
> all glory, honour to God's name.

Ruth C. Duck (*b.* 1947)

810

GONFALON ROYAL   LM

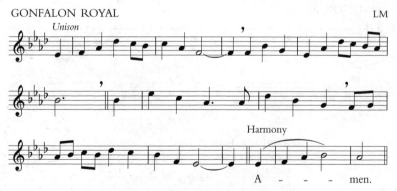

> Sing to the Lord of heaven and earth,
> whom angels serve and saints adore,
> the Father, Son, and Spirit blest
> to whom be praise for evermore. Amen.

John Samuel Bewley Monsell (1811–1875)

Music Percy Carter Buck (1871–1947)

GONFALON ROYAL   LM

A – – men.

To God the Father, God the Son,
and God the Spirit, praise be done;
may Christ the Lord upon us pour
the Spirit's gift for evermore. Amen.

Based on *Acts 2: 1-4,* c. 4th century
translated Richard Ellis Roberts (1879–1953)

Music Percy Carter Buck (1871–1947)

812

CONDITOR ALME   LM

A - men.__

To God the Father, God the Son,
and God the Spirit, three in one,
praise, honour, might and glory be
from age to age eternally. Amen

Latin hymn, 9th century
translated John Mason Neale (1818–1866)
as in *The Hymnal* 1940

Music Mode iv
harmonised Compilers

NUN DANKET

67 67 66 66

Lob, Ehr' und Preis sei Gott

All praise and thanks to God
who reigns in highest heaven,
the Father and the Son
and Spirit, now be given:
the one, eternal God,
whom earth and heaven adore;
for thus it was, is now,
and shall be evermore.

Martin Rinkart (1586–1649)
translated *Catherine Winkworth (1827–1878)

Music Johann Crüger. Later form of a melody in Crüger's *Praxis
Pietatis Melica* c. 1647, harmony chiefly from *Lobgesang* 1840
harmonised Felix Mendelssohn (1809–1847)

MOVILLE   76 76 D

Unison

Capo 3

Glory to God the Father,
the unbegotten One;
all honour be to Jesus,
his sole-begotten Son;
and to the Holy Spirit -
the perfect Trinity.
Let all the worlds give answer,
'Amen, so let it be'.

St Columba (521–597)
translated Duncan Macgregor (1854–1923)

Music Irish traditional melody *arranged* John L. Bell (b. 1949)

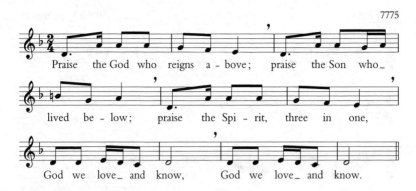

7775

Praise the God who reigns above;
praise the Son who lived below;
praise the Spirit, three in one,
God we love and know,
God we love and know.

Daniel Manastireanu

Music Daniel Manastireanu

TRIUMPH

87 87 87

Now to him who loved us, gave us
every pledge that love could give,
freely shed his blood to save us,
gave his life that we might live,
be the kingdom,
power and glory
and thanksgiving evermore.

*Samuel Miller Waring (1792–1827)

Music Henry John Gauntlett (1805–1876)

STU MO RUN   10 9 8 11 and refrain

Sing to God the Father, all creation,
sing to God his dear and only Son,
sing to God the loving Spirit,
sing with joy to God, one God, for evermore.
Sing to the Lord, sing Alleluia,
sing to the Lord, sing with joy!

James Quinn (*b.*1919)

Music Gaelic folk melody *arranged* John L. Bell (*b.*1949)

OLD 124th   11 10 11 10 and refrain

1   Praise ye the Lord, ye servants of the Lord:
praise ye his name; his lordly honour sing:
thee we adore; to thee glad homage bring;
thee we acknowledge; God to be adored
for thy great glory, Sovereign, Lord, and King.

2   Father of Christ — of him whose work was done,
when by his death he took our sins away —
to thee belongeth worship, day by day,
yea, Holy Father, everlasting Son,
and Holy Ghost, all praise be thine for aye!

from *Apostolic Constitutions* 3rd century
translated George Ratcliffe Woodward (1848–1934)
and Compilers of *BBC Hymn Book,* 1940

Music Melody from *Genevan Psalter,* 1551, rhythm adapted
harmonised Compilers of *Church Hymnary,* 3rd edition, 1973

Also suitable as Doxologies are the last verses of the following hymns
110, 147, 200, 209, 319, 324, 410, 427, 498, 612, 667, 676

THREEFOLD AMEN

A – men.   A – men.   A – – – men.

* *The notes of this bar may be doubled in value.*

Music Danish

820

DRESDEN AMEN

A – – – – – – men.

Music Johann Naumann (1741–1801)

821

A – – – men, A – – men. ——

Music from the verse anthem *Blessed are all they that fear the Lord*
Orlando Gibbons (1583–1625)

822

Unison Canon

A – men, a – – men, al – le – lu – ia, a – – men.

Harmony version

A – men, a – – men, al – le – lu – ia, a – – men..

Music John L. Bell (*b.* 1949)

A — — — — — — men.

Music William Smith (*d*. 1645)

824

Ma - si - thi._____ Ma - si - thi, ___

A - men si - a - ku - du - mi - sa.

Ma - si - thi, ___

A - men si - a - ku - du - mi - sa. A - men ba - wo,

(except last time)

Ma - si - thi, ___

Fine

A - men Ba - wo, A - men si - a - ku - du - mi - sa.

Xhosa text
Amen siakudumisa.
Amen siakudumisa.
Amen bawo, amen bawo,
amen siakudumisa

Amen, we praise your name, O Lord.
Amen! Amen!

South African Traditional

Music South African Traditional attributed to S. C. Molefe

A - - - men. A - - - men.

A - - - men, a - - men, a - men.

Music and words South African Traditional

INDEXES

TOPICAL INDEX

The Table of Contents at the beginning of the book is part of this Topical Index and should be consulted along with it. There are four entries for Holy Baptism, for instance, in this index, and a further ten items in the section 'The Church celebrates – Holy Baptism' in the Table of Contents.

BIBLICAL INDEX

BIBLICAL

ALPHABETICAL INDEX of TUNES

An asterisk indicates an alternative name for a tune: this name is in parenthesis above the music at the specified hymn numbers. Where the same name is used for different tunes, in this index the composer's name or the source appears in italics in parenthesis.

TUNES (ALPHABETICAL)

TUNES (ALPHABETICAL)

INDEXES

TUNES (ALPHABETICAL)

METRICAL INDEX of TUNES

SM

Calabria 464
Carlisle 202
Garelochside 21.i, 721
Rossleigh 227
St Michael (Old 134th) 643
Sandys 45
Serenity 21.ii
Southwell 491, 492
Veni Spiritus 596

DSM

Diademata 459, 594
From Strength To Strength 515
Ich Halte Treulich Still 270
Leominster 534

CM

Abbey 18.ii
Amazing Grace
  (New Britain) 555.i, 555.ii
Ballerma 30, 668
Belmont 632, 688
Billing 183
Bishopthorpe 22, 424
Bon Accord 59.ii
Brother James's Air 16
Caithness 50, 630
Chorus Angelorum
  (Somervell) 378.ii
Coleshill 68, 546
Crediton 277
Crimond 14.i, 14.ii
Desert (Lyngham) 352.ii
Detroit 486
Diadem 457.ii
Downing 723
Dunfermline 70
Dunlap's Creek 308
Edgbaston 545
Effingham 48
French (Dundee) 81.i, 81.ii
Gerontius 378.i
Glasgow 715
Harington (Retirement) 52
Horsley 380
Howard (Dublin) 42
I Waited Patiently For God 31
Irish 59.i, 473
Jackson (Byzantium) 76, 645
Kedron 482.ii
Khandallah 488

Kilmarnock 69, 482.i
Land Of Rest 333, 343
London New 28, 158
Martyrdom (Fenwick) 32, 87, 552.i
Martyrs 34.i, 34.ii, 583
Mckee 624
Miles Lane 457.i
Orlington 15
Richmond 352.i
St Agnes (Dykes) 560
St Andrew (Tans'ur) 425
St Anne 161, 520
St Botolph (Slater) 1
St Columba (Erin) 598
St Flavian (Old 132nd) 75
St Fulbert 56
St Magnus (Nottingham)
  61, 290.i, 438, 744, 806
St Paul (Aberdeen) 82, 272
St Peter 461
St Stephen (Abridge) 44, 190
St Stephen (Newington)
  53, 478, 686
Salzburg (Haydn) 268
Sheffield 46
Southwark 78
Stracathro 548, 637
Stroudwater 6, 36, 37, 57
Tiverton 290.ii
Wetherby 9, 693, 743
Wigtown 41.i, 41.ii
Wiltshire 14.iii
Winchester Old 4.i, 4.ii, 296
York (Stilt) 79.i, 79.ii

CM and refrain

Pulling Bracken 386

DCM

Coe Fen 128
Ellacombe 247
Forest Green 304
Invocation 35
Kingsfold 291.i, 291.ii
Macpherson's Rant 88
Noel 303
Resignation 43
St Asaph 745
St George's, Edinburgh 19
St Matthew 18.i
Seven Joys Of Mary 340
The Flower O' The Quern 552.ii

TUNES (METRICAL)

TUNES (METRICAL)

INDEXES

TUNES (METRICAL)

TUNES (METRICAL)

INDEXES

TUNES (METRICAL)

INDEX of COMPOSERS, ARRANGERS and SOURCES

INDEXES

INDEXES

COMPOSERS

INDEX of AUTHORS, TRANSLATORS and SOURCES

INDEXES

AUTHORS

AUTHORS

AUTHORS

INDEX of PSALMS

PSALMS

*The following hymns are either metricisations of, or based
substantially on, psalms or portions of psalms.*

INDEX of items suitable for
CHILDREN and YOUNG PEOPLE

CHILDREN and YOUNG PEOPLE

INDEX of FIRST LINES and TUNES

INDEXES

FIRST LINES

INDEXES

FIRST LINES

INDEXES

INDEXES

INDEXES

FIRST LINES

INDEXES

INDEXES

INDEXES

FIRST LINES

INDEXES

FIRST LINES

INDEXES

Addresses of principal Scottish copyright holders

Church Hymnary Trust (CH Trust)
c/o Balfour and Manson, 54–66 Frederick Street, Edinburgh EH2 1LS

Church of Scotland Panel on Worship
121 George Street, Edinburgh EH2 4YN

Wild Goose Resource Group (WGRG)
4th Floor, Savoy Centre, 140 Sauchiehall Street, Glasgow G2 3DH

Addresses of other major copyright holders

Boosey & Hawkes Music Publishers Ltd
295 Regent Street, London W1B 2JH

Continuum International Publishing Group Ltd
The Tower Building, 11 York Road, London SE1 7NX

CopyCare Ltd
PO Box 77, Hailsham, East Sussex, BN27 3EF
<music@copycare.com>

CRC Publications
2850 Kalamazoo Avenue, Grand Rapids, MI 49560, USA

Timothy Dudley-Smith
7 Ashlands, Ford, Salisbury, Wiltshire SP4 6DY *(Europe and Africa)*
Permissions for the rest of the world administered by
Hope Publishing Company *(see below)*

Gregorian Institute of America
GIA Publications Inc., 7404 S. Mason Avenue, Chicago, IL 60638, USA

Hope Publishing Company
Administered in the UK by CopyCare Ltd *(see above)*

Jubilate Hymns
4 Thorne Park Road, Chelston, Torquay TQ2 6RX
<enquiries@jubilate.co.uk>

Kingsway Music
26-28 Lottbridge Drove, Eastbourne, East Sussex BN23 6NT

Music Sales Ltd
8/9 Frith Street, London W1D 3JB

continued overleaf

OCP Publications
5536 NE Hassalo, Portland, OR 97213, USA

Oxford University Press
Great Clarendon Street, Oxford OX2 6DP

Royal School of Church Music
Cleveland Lodge, Westhumble, Dorking, Surrey RH5 6BW

Selah Publishing Co. Inc.
4143 Brownsville Road, Suite 2, Pittsburgh, PA 15227-3306, USA
<www.selahpub.com>

Stainer & Bell Ltd
PO Box 110, Victoria House, 23 Gruneisen Road, London N3 1DZ

Ateliers et Presses de Taizé
71250 Taizé-Community, France

Thankyou Music
Administered (UK and Europe) by Kingsway Music *(see above)*
<tym@kingsway.co.uk>